Sung-Hee Yoon

# The Question of the Beginning and the Ending of the So-Called History of David's Rise

# Beihefte zur Zeitschrift für die alttestamentliche Wissenschaft

---

Edited by
John Barton, Ronald Hendel,
Reinhard G. Kratz and Markus Witte

## Volume 462

Sung-Hee Yoon

# The Question of the Beginning and the Ending of the So-Called History of David's Rise

A Methodological Reflection and Its Implications

DE GRUYTER

G

ISBN 978-3-11-034980-1
e-ISBN 978-3-11-035292-4
ISSN 0934-2575

**Library of Congress Cataloging-in-Publication Data**
A CIP catalog record for this book has been applied for at the Library of Congress.

**Bibliographic Information published by the Deutsche Nationalbibliothek**
The Deutsche Nationalbibliothek lists this publication in the Deutsche Nationalbibliografie;
detailed bibliographic data are available on the Internet at http://dnb.dnb.de.

© 2014 Walter de Gruyter GmbH, Berlin/Boston
Printing and binding: CPI books GmbH, Leck
♾ Printed on acid-free paper
Printed in Germany

www.degruyter.com

MIX
Papier aus verantwor-
tungsvollen Quellen
FSC
www.fsc.org   FSC® C003147

# Acknowledgments

This monograph is a slightly revised version of my doctoral thesis, completed and examined in 2011. Without many people's help, the completion of this work would have been impossible, and I am pleased to have a chance to express my gratitude to them. Above all, I express my sincere gratitude to my *Doktorvater* Prof. John Barton for his unfailing support and continuous inspiration. His support never ceased even after my doctoral years, and indeed, without his encouragement, I could not have pulled myself together to get this work published. I am also grateful to my doctoral examiners, Dr. John Jarick and Prof. Francesca Stavrakopoulou for their constructive critique and helpful advice. For failing to follow their suggestions, I have nobody to blame but myself.

I thank those who have helped me greatly at various stages of this project. Prof. Kevin Cathcart has always been kind to offer me wise advice and priceless friendship. It was always a great pleasure to have a chat with him about all sorts of topic. Dr. Gerry J. Hughes also helped me a great deal, especially by challenging my position with pleasantly provocative questions. Prof. Reinhard Kratz kindly invited me to work in the University of Göttingen for a term, so that I could engage more intensively with German scholarship. Jesuits in Britain and in Korea provided me with financial and spiritual support, so that I could concentrate on my work without much distraction. I also would like to thank my former teachers, Prof. Bong-mo Song, SJ, Drs. Ann Jeffers and Jennifer Dines, for their inspiration and encouragement. And my special thanks are extended to Sabina Dabrowski, Sophie Wagenhofer and Katrin Mittman for helping me to prepare the manuscript for publication.

Finally, I would like to thank my family and my friends. I offer my affectionate thanks to my mother for her love and care, and to my wife So Young and my son Sang-Hyeon for being my source of joy. And to Peter Gallagher, Alan Harrison, John Montoya, Jonah Suh, and Ji-Won Jung, I owe a debt of gratitude—for their priceless friendship. This book is dedicated to the late Fr. Matthias Chae whose friendship and wise advice I miss so much.

# Contents

# Abbreviations and Sigla

AB      Anchor Bible
*ABD*     *Anchor Bible Dictionary*
*ANET*    J. B. Pritchard, ed., *The Ancient Near Eastern Texts Relating to the Old Testament,* 3rd edn (Princeton: Princeton University Press, 1969).
*BAR*     *Biblical Archaeology Review*
*BASOR*  *Bulletin of the American Schools of Oriental Research*
BDB     Brown, F., S. R. Driver, and C. A. Briggs, *A Hebrew and English Lexicon of the Old Testament with an Appendix Containing the Biblical Aramaic* (Oxford: Clarendon Press, 1907).
*BHS*     *Biblia Hebraica Stuttgartensia*
*Bib*      *Biblica*
*BuK*     *Bibel und Kirche*
BZAW   Beihefte zur *Zeitschrift für die alttestamentliche Wissenschaft*
*CBQ*     *Catholic Biblical Quarterly*
*COS*     William W. Hallo, ed., *The Context of Scripture: canonical compositions, monumental inscriptions, and archival documents from the biblical world,* 3 vols (Leiden: Brill, 2003).
*ET*       *Expository Times*
*ETL*     *Ephemerides Theologicae Lovanienses*
FOTL    Forms of the Old Testament Literature
G-K      Wilhelm Gesenius, *Hebrew Grammar*, ed. by Emil Kautzsch, trans. by A. E. Cowley, Dover edn (Mineola, N.Y.: Dover Publications, 2006).
ICC      International Critical Commentary
*JBL*     *Journal of Biblical Literature*
*JCS*     *Journal of Cuneiform Studies*
*JETS*    *Journal of the Evangelical Theological Society*
*JHS*     *The Journal of Hebrew Scripture*
*JJS*      *Journal of Jewish Studies*
*JNSL*   *Journal of Northwest Semitic Languages*
JQR      Jewish Quarterly Review
*JSOT*    *Journal for the Study of the Old Testament*
JSOTSup Journal for the Study of the Old Testament, Supplement Series
*JSS*      *Journal of Semitic Studies*
Lambdin Thomas O. Lambdin, *Introduction to Biblical Hebrew* (New Jersey: Prentice Hall, 1971).
LXX      Septuagint
MT       Masoretic Text
NCBC    New Century Bible Commentary
*OLZ*     *Orientalistische Literaturzeitung*
OTL      Old Testament Library
OTS      Oudtestamentische Studiën
*RB*       *Revue Biblique*
RSV      Revised Standard Version
*SJOT*    *Scandinavian Journal of the Old Testament*

| | |
|---|---|
| *TDOT* | Botterweck, G. Johannes, and Helmer Ringgren, eds, *Theological Dictionary of the Old Testament*, 15 vols (Grand Rapids: Eerdmans, 1974–2006). |
| *TLZ* | *Theologische Literaturzeitung* |
| *TynB* | *Tyndale Bulletin* |
| *UF* | *Ugarit-Forschungen* |
| *ÜS* | Martin Noth, *Überlieferungsgeschichtliche Studien,* 3rd edn (Tübingen: Max Niemeyer, 1967). |
| *VT* | *Vetus Testamentum* |
| VTSup | Supplements to *Vetus Testamentum* |
| WBC | Word Biblical Commentary |
| *ZAW* | *Zeitschrift für die Alttestamentliche Wissenschaft* |
| *ZWT* | *Zeitschrift für wissenschaftliche Theologie* |

# Introduction

Until Leonhard Rost published his seminal work *Die Überlieferung von der Thronnachfolge Davids*,[1] the composition history of the books of Samuel was understood mainly in the light of the documentary hypothesis which had been dominant in biblical scholarship since Julius Wellhausen. Karl Budde, for instance, argued that there were two parallel strands in Samuel, J and E, and the combination of two sources was done with a substantial deuteronomistic redaction.[2] Similarly Carl Steuernagel, although he was reluctant to accept the theory of two sources, recognized in 1Sam two strands running in parallel and mutually exclusive. He called them $S^a$ and $S^b$ respectively, and thought that $S^a$ was an older and more trustworthy account of David, and $S^b$ was a more religious one.[3] Although Hugo Gressmann challenged the mainstream view by proposing a kind of fragmentary hypothesis that sees the books as a collection of single narratives,[4] it was only when Rost published his work that there was a major breakthrough in the understanding of the books of Samuel.

In a sense, Rost's view was not totally different from the two source theory, because he also acknowledged that there were two main sources in Samuel. Rost differed from his predecessors, however, in not seeing the books as consisting of narrative strands parallel to one another, but as two narratives running consecutively, each having its own structure and purpose. In reminiscence of Gressmann, Rost even acknowledged the existence of smaller narratives in the books of Samuel such as the Ark Narrative, the Prophecy of Nathan, and the Account of the Ammonite War. However, the composer of the second part of the David story used them with modifications to serve his own purpose, and produced the "Succession Narrative" which deserves to be praised as the most outstanding piece of Hebrew narrative art.[5] As to the first part, Rost did not explore it very much. Nonetheless, he affirmed that there was an account of the early days of David in the books of Samuel, and concluded that it provides "without a gap, a continuous depiction of David's condition while on the run from Saul

---

1 Leonhard Rost, *Die Überlieferung von der Thronnachfolge Davids* (Stuttgart: W.Kohlhammer, 1926). ET, *The Succession to the Throne of David* (Sheffield: Almond, 1982). References are to the English translation.
2 Karl Budde, *Die Bücher Samuel* (Tübingen: J.C.B. Mohr, 1902), xii-xxi.
3 Carl Steuernagel, *Lehrbuch der Einleitung in das Alte Testament* (Tübingen: J.C.B. Mohr, 1912), 331–334.
4 Hugo Gressmann, *Die älteste Geschichtsschreibung und Prophetie Israels: von Samuel bis Amos und Hosea* (Göttingen: Vandenhoeck & Ruprecht, 1921).
5 Rost, *Succession*, 102.

and of the events which led to his ruling over Judah and Israel and to the conquest of Jerusalem".[6]

Since then, it has been generally accepted that there was an independent source describing the early days of David in 1Sam 15 (16)–2Sam 5 (8), and scholars have commonly called the narrative "History of David's Rise (HDR)" (*Aufstieg Davids* in German). Despite the wide agreement on its existence, however, commentators have been puzzled by the uncertainty about the precise extent of the source. There are such diverse views about the beginning and the ending of the HDR, that one of the most recent commentaries concluded, "it is probably right to speak of a Story of David's Rise. It would not be right to be dogmatic about its beginning, its ending, or about details of its content."[7] More and more people, however, are uneasy at the uncertainty about the beginning and the end of the HDR, and question the existence of the HDR as an independent source. Indeed, the point of Rost's initial argument was not that the HDR existed independently before its incorporation into the books of Samuel, but that the Succession Narrative was not a part of a larger literary tradition which also included the HDR. The HDR as such was not his concern, and that was why he did not explore the precise extent and nature of the HDR in more detail. In order to speak of the HDR at all, we need to give more information about the HDR, and above all, its beginning and ending.[8] Otherwise, it would be better to give up the hypothesis, and find an alternative way to explain the composition history of the books of Samuel. The purpose of this monograph is therefore to identify the beginning and the ending of the so-called History of David's Rise, with a view to clarifying the issues around the source. If we successfully demarcate the extent of the source, we will be able to make reasonable assumptions about the composition of the books of Samuel as well as about the origin and redaction of the HDR. If it turns out to be impossible to identify the extent, however, we will raise more fundamental questions about Rost's view about the composition of the books of Samuel.

---

**6** Rost, *Succession*, 109.

**7** Antony Campbell, *1 Samuel* (Grand Rapids: Eerdmans, 2003), 11.

**8** The necessity of identifying the beginning and end for source division is emphasized in Wilhelm Caspari, "Der Stil des Eingangs der israelitischen Novelle," *ZWTh* 53 (1911): 218–253 (218).

# Chapter 1
# The Beginning and the Ending of the So-Called History of David's Rise

In order to proceed in our investigation with regard to the beginning and the ending of the HDR, we need to ask first what is the most appropriate method for such a task. Scholars interested in source-critical questions tend to believe that the beginning and the ending of a literary source should be discovered by "objective" and "scientific" methods, because we are dealing with questions about objective facts. They do not deny that the literary aspect of the investigation is indispensable, because even in dealing with source-critical questions, the literary meaning of a text plays a certain role. However, the emphasis is certainly on the "scientific" and "diachronic" aspect, and the discussion has been conducted as if there were no concern for the larger picture, and has concentrated on infinitesimal details. Two things, in my view, might explain such an unbalanced emphasis on the "scientific/diachronic" aspect in discussing source-critical questions. First, it has been assumed that the literary meaning should be also discovered by an objective and scientific method, because otherwise, statements about source-critical issues, which cannot be free from the literary meaning of the text, cannot be established objectively. Second, it is also assumed that the overall meaning of a text is not different to the extent that it can affect our investigation. Every educated person knows what a text means! These two assumptions have prompted scholars to separate "scientific" and "diachronic" aspects from "literary" and "synchronic" ones, and place more emphasis on the former. One might say that it was an old habit, now outgrown. However, we discover such a tendency in Walter Dietrich's recent remark on methodology, "it is methodologically sensible to begin by carefully distinguishing the respective stages – diachronically – from each other, to describe each by itself, and then to observe – synchronically – their biblical juxtaposition and interpenetration and to reflect on the whole."[1]

A part of the aim of this monograph is to challenge such a long held view, and to show that the role of literary interpretation is more important, and the meaning of a text is more flexible, than has been thought. However, for heuristic

---

1 Walter Dietrich & Thomas Naumann, *Samuelbücher* (Darmstadt: Wissenschaftliche Buchgesellschaft, 1995), 66 [Eng. 293]. The English translation of Part C "Die David-Saul-Geschichte" is in Gary N. Knoppers and J. Gordon McConville, eds., *Reconsidering Israel and Judah: Recent Studies on the Deuteronomistic History* (Winona Lake: Eisenbrauns, 2000), 276–318.

purposes, I will follow the conventional assumption, and apply various traditional criteria to the text, and try to identify the beginning and the ending of the HDR. The different criteria will be applied, as if they are separate from literary understanding of the text. The outcome of the investigation will be, however, to show that the process of diachronic and scientific investigation such as "carefully distinguishing the respective stages" is possible only with the help of literary interpretation, i. e. "reflection of the whole".

# 1 The Ending of the HDR

Between the two tasks given, we first ask where the HDR ends. The reason we begin with the ending rather than the beginning is because we have a clearer idea about the source following the HDR than the source preceding it. In comparison to the rather loosely connected materials about Saul, the tradition about David's later life and Solomon's rise has long been recognized as a self-contained tradition, and given the name "the Succession Narrative".[2] And it is widely believed among scholars that from 2Sam 9 at the latest, a new literary source starts.[3] Therefore, if we start from the question of the ending, we can base our discussion on the relatively safe ground that the HDR cannot go beyond 2Sam 9.

## 1.1 Criteria for the Identification: Textual Evidence

There have been several methods to differentiate various sources in the Bible, and we will apply them to the question of the ending of the HDR. We start from "lower" methods and go on to the "higher" ones, and the most obvious evidence enabling us to identify the ending of the HDR would be textual. If any ancient Version or Masoretic manuscript were to provide us with a witness to a major break somewhere between 2Sam 2–9, this would be an extremely valuable clue to our question. The difference among the Hebrew manuscripts and the Versions would be the best indication for major breaks. Although it may not be able to tell us the precise boundary of the sources, it may well tell us how ancient people understood the flow of the narrative, and this is important because the

---

2 The title is disputed. For convenience's sake, hereafter we use the most widely known term "Succession Narrative". But to express its disputability, we place it and its abbreviation SN in inverted commas.

3 This is not immune from debate. In Chapter 5 of this dissertation, we will look at different views about the source in more detail.

literary custom of the ancient Israelites such as how one ends a narrative might well have been quite different from ours. Unfortunately for our investigation, however, 2Sam 2–8 in the Versions is almost identical with MT, and the manuscripts of the MT do not hint at any obvious trace of a major break. This prompts us to an alternative way to find out how the ancient scribes understood the narrative flow, and we are drawn to the paragraph divisions in the ancient manuscripts.

The Masoretes, while they copied and edited the Hebrew text available to them, indicated the divisions of larger sense units *parash(iyy)ot*, either by leaving a section open or closed. In other words, they indicated a larger unit delimitation by leaving the space empty and beginning the next verse in the next line. This "open" section is called *petuḥah*, and the *BHS* indicates it by the Hebrew letter פ. The Masoretes indicated also a smaller unit delimitation by leaving a shorter space empty but beginning the next verse in the same line. This "closed" section is called *setumah*, and the *BHS* indicates it by the Hebrew letter ס. Apparently, *petuḥah* indicates the beginning of a larger section, and *setumah* marks the beginning of a smaller section.[4] Therefore, we might expect that the source division should be found in one of the *petuḥot*. Some people are doubtful about it, because they think that these markers were introduced by the Masoretes, and do not tell us much about the original demarcation. However, since the discoveries in the Judaean Desert, some scholars have claimed that the divisions of larger sections in the MT were not the invention of the Masoretes, but much earlier practice. In particular, Josef Oesch claims that text division seems to have belonged to the tradition of the writing down of a text,[5] and the "Pericope group" led by Marjo C. A. Korpel launched a project of investigating the unit delimitation in various manuscripts, to find out what the original demarcations of the biblical texts were.[6] Of course, paragraph divisions appear very frequently, and therefore it is pointless to identify the beginning of a source on this basis alone. Nonetheless, it shows where the ancient scribes saw major breaks, and this might give us important clues to our question. Ideally, we should look at as many textual witnesses as possible, but space allows us to examine only the most important ones. We begin with the two oldest Masoretic manuscripts:

---

**4** Ernst Würthwein, *The Text of the Old Testament: An Introduction to the Biblia Hebraica*, 2nd edition (Grand Rapids: Eerdmans, 1995), 20.
**5** Josef M. Oesch, *Petucha und Setuma: Untersuchungen zu eine überlieferten Gliederung im hebräischen Text des Alten Testaments* (Göttingen: Vandenhoeck & Ruprecht, 1979), 335–339.
**6** The first of the series is Marjo C. A. Korpel and Josef M. Oesch, eds., *Delimitation Criticism: A New Tool in Biblical Scholarship* (Assen: Van Gorcum, 2000).

the Aleppo Codex from early 10th century CE, and the Leningrad Codex from early 11th century CE.

According to the Aleppo Codex, the larger units in 2Sam 2:1–10:19 are 2:1–7 / 2:8–9 / 2:10–3:5 / 3:6–39 / 4:1–12 / 5:1–10 / 5:11–16 / 5:17–19a / 5:19b–21 / 5:22–25 / 6:1–23 / 7:1–17 / 7:18–29 / 8:1–10:19.[7] It is interesting that between 8:18 and 9:1, we find *petuḥah* and *ziaḥ*, the combination of which is believed to equal the marker for the smaller unit, *setumah*.[8] This means that the ancient scribes or even the final redactor thought the narrative in 8:1–10:19 to be continuous, and this weakens the generally agreed view that we have a totally different source from chapter 9 onwards. It was not unanimously agreed among the ancient scribes that there was a major break between chapters 8 and 9. In the Leningrad Codex, however, the larger units of 2Sam 2:1–10:19 are 2:1–7 / 2:8–9 / 2:10–3:5 / 3:6–30 / 3:31–32 / 3:33–37/ 3:38–39 / 4:1–12 / 5:1–3 /5:4–10 / 5:11–16 / 5:17–21 / 5:22–25 / 6:1–23 / 7:1–29 / 8:1–18 / 9:1–13 /10:1–19.[9] There are 18 open sections in 2Sam 2:1–10:19, and the number is larger than that of the Aleppo Codex which has 15. More importantly, it divides 9:1–10:19 into two sections, whereas it takes chapter 7 as one unit.

The earliest Hebrew manuscripts now available to us are not these Masoretic manuscripts, however. In the 20th century, the Dead Sea Scrolls were discovered, and we now have manuscripts dated as early as mid-3rd century BCE, and for the books of Samuel, three manuscripts are available: 4QSam[A], 4QSam[B], and 4QSam[C]. 4QSam[B] is dated mid-3rd century BCE, but there are only fragments. It has 16:1–11, which might help us to establish the beginning of the HDR, but without the immediately preceding passages, it cannot tell us about the unit delimitation. Similarly, 4QSam[C] is very fragmentary, and does not have the passages which we are discussing. Most useful for textual studies of Samuel is 4QSam[A] which is dated 50–25 BCE. This is not complete either, but there is a space deliberately made between 5:10–11.[10] This might support the widely held view that the HDR finishes with 5:10. However, an even longer space is found after 4:12, and the space is also found after 5:16; 6:8. Furthermore, 2Sam 7–8 are too fragmentary to show whether the ancient scribe saw a major break between chapters 7 and 8, and chapters 8 and 9.

---

**7** The full text in facsimile is now available online in www.aleppocodex.org.

**8** C. A. Korpel, "Introduction to the Series Pericope", in Korpel and Oesch, eds., *Delimitation Criticism*, 1–50 (4).

**9** David Noel Freedman, ed., *The Leningrad Codex: A Facsimile Edition* (Grand Rapids: Eerdmans, 1998), 364–366.

**10** The relevant texts are found in Eugene Ulrich, ed., *The Biblical Qumran Scrolls. Transcriptions and Textual Variants* (Leiden/Boston: Brill, 2010), 259–322 (295–300).

Apart from the Hebrew manuscripts, we should consult the Septuagint manuscripts that might reflect the 2nd century BCE original. Korpel suggests that we could see how they delimited the units by examining spaces and other delimiting markers such as "a large capital at the beginning of a new unit – often this capital is protruding in the left margin; small capital (equal to the other letters to the text) but also protruding into the left margin; a paragraph marker in the margin (without doubt by a later hand); a wide inline space (comparable to the *setumah* in Hebrew manuscripts); an open space to the right (comparable to the *petuḥah* in Hebrew manuscripts)".[11] Among the Septuagint manuscripts, the three earliest containing all or most are Codex Vaticanus, Codex Sinaiticus, and Codex Alexandrinus. Codex Sinaiticus from the 4th century CE, however, lacks most of the Pentateuch and the historical books. Codex Vaticanus from the 4th century CE, which is regarded as a prime textual witness to the original LXX, has no *Kais* in larger character as Codex Alexandrinus has, but there are some indications for breaks. For instance, 2Sam 1 is preceded by an inline paragraph marker, and has another paragraph marker in the left margin. 2Sam 6:1; 7:1; 8:1 have a short inline space before the verse, and a paragraph marker in the left margin. 2Sam 9:1 has no inline space before the verse, but it has two paragraph markers, one precedes the verse within the line, and the other is in the left margin. In 5:10, which is seen by many as marking the end of the HDR, there is neither a protrusion to the left margin nor a paragraph marker in the margin. A divisional marker is found, but nothing else to indicate a major break between 5:10 and 5:11, unless one sees a short horizontal line marked above the verse as a significant indication. After all, according to Codex Vaticanus, one might suspect that there were the beginnings of new units in 2:1; 6:1; 7:1; 8:1; 9:1, but not in 5:11.

Another major uncial from the 5th century CE, Codex Alexandrinus, gives clearer indications for delimitation. Scholars have valued it less in comparison to Codex Vaticanus, because it seems that there was systematic revision toward the developing tradition of the MT.[12] But it is sometimes an important witness to very early readings.[13] The most evident marker in the Codex Alexandrinus is the larger character of *Kai* at the beginning of a section, and the divisions more or less correspond to the MT's division. It has the *Kais* in larger character at the beginning of 2Sam 2:1... 5:9; 5:13b; 6:1; 8:1; 9:1. Interestingly, however, as in Codex Vaticanus, there is no unit division between 5:10 and 5:11. In fact, 5:11 is found

---

11 Korpel, "Introduction", 14.
12 P. Kyle McCarter, *I Samuel* (Garden City, N.Y.: Doubleday, 1980), 9.
13 Jennifer M. Dines, *The Septuagint* (London: T & T Clark, 2004), 7.

in the middle of the paragraph, and it seems that the ancient scribe thought the narrative to be continuous there. This may weaken one of the major views concerning the ending of the HDR that the source ends in 5:10. The scribes of the earliest manuscripts of LXX did not see any major break after 5:10.

## 1.2 Formal Markers

The paragraph division, although it gives us a hint that a certain view (the ending in 5:10, for instance) may not be as convincing as we have believed, cannot answer our question on its own. Moreover, despite Oesch's claim, it is more likely that they were added later, say, for a liturgical reason. This means that we do not have sufficient "scientific" evidence on the textual level, and need to consult other evidence. So in addition to the textual evidence, we ask whether there are formal markers which might indicate a conclusion or an end of a section or a unit. In the biblical narratives, especially in the books of Kings, we often see more or less continuous narratives finish with informative reports or accounts, and it is argued that certain verses "repeated unnecessarily, especially if they are cumbersome and seem misplaced chronologically" can demarcate the boundaries of a unit.[14] Therefore, if we can find similar markers in 2Sam 5–8, we might think of them as possible candidates for the joint of different sources, and one of them will be the ending of the HDR.

### 1.2.1 The List of the Officials in 2Sam 8:16–18

Moving backwards from chapter 9, which is regarded by many as the beginning of the "Succession Narrative", the first formal marker which we can notice is the list of the officials in 2Sam 8:16–18. Wellhausen already recognized its concluding character, and argued that just as the Saul cycle finishes with the list of Saul's sons and officials in 1Sam 14:46–51, David's early history ends with the list of David's officials in 2Sam 8:16–18. The very similar layouts of the two also support the view. Both traditions describe first how – whether ideally and rapidly, or humanly and gradually – the hero ascends to the throne. This is followed by the military achievements that place the kings in high ranks, and then by short surveys of the reigns. Wellhausen finally strengthens his view by proposing as a possibility that before 8:16, there were more elaborate re-

---

**14** Marc Zvi Brettler, *The Creation of History in Ancient Israel* (London: Routledge, 1995), 98. See also his article, "The Structure of 1 Kings 1–11," *JSOT* 49 (1991): 87–97.

ports about David's family, some bits of which are now scattered in 2Sam 3:2–5 and 5:13–16. The list was even more similar to that in 1Sam 14:46–51, and both lists were clearly intended to indicate the end of each tradition.[15] This view was generally accepted before the emergence of the hypothesis of the HDR, but has not been popular since then.[16] More recently, however, Hans J. Stoebe acknowledges the possibility that the HDR may extend to 2Sam 8:15–18.[17] Similarly, Marc Zvi Brettler recognizes the structure of "victory plus cabinet" and the similarity of the countries conquered in both 14:47–52 and 2Sam 8:16–18, and argues that the redactor used those verses as demarcating devices, and the HDR finishes with 2Sam 8: 15.[18]

To confirm such a conclusion, however, we need to show that the author of the HDR was responsible for the list. Or, we should be able to prove that the later hands who inserted the list did not artificially divide the originally continuous material. However, neither of these things can be shown, and this makes it difficult for us to conclude that 2Sam 8:15 is the end of the HDR. In fact, not a few scholars think that the list we have in 8:16–18 – even if one admits that it was from an ancient source – was inserted by the Deuteronomist. Budde already suspected it to be from a deuteronomistic hand,[19] and more recently, Timo Veijola claimed that 8:16–18 was inserted by the Deuteronomist (DtrG). According to Veijola, the list in 2Sam 8:16–18 was inserted after 8:15 which had been written by the Deuteronomist, and this is known from the following: (1) the formulation of David being king over all Israel in 8:15a shows a similarity with that of Solomon in 1Kings 4:1 which introduces the list of Solomon's high officials in 4:2–6. But 1Kings 4:1 seems to be from the Deuteronomist; (2) the expression "David was doing justice and righteousness" in 8:15b is mentioned by the queen of Sheba as the goal of the Solomonic rule in 1Kings 10:9. This verse is a deuteronomistic expansion of the queen's speech, and therefore, it is likely that the expression in 8:15b is also from the Deuteronomist. Thus, he concludes that the list in 8:16–18 was introduced to the David tradition by the DtrG.[20] In fact, if the list of David's officials here is inserted by the same hand responsible for 1Sam 14:47–52 as Well-

---

**15** Julius Wellhausen, *Die Composition des Hexateuchs und der historischen Bücher des Alten Testaments*, 3rd edition (Berlin: Georg Reimer, 1899), 255.

**16** Cf. Budde, *Samuel*, 237–238; Steuernagel, *Einleitung*, 323.

**17** Hans Joachim Stoebe, *Das zweite Buch Samuelis* (Gütersloh: Gütersloher Verlagshaus, 1994), 254–255.

**18** Brettler, *Creation*, 100.

**19** Budde, *Samuel*, 237.

**20** Timo Veijola, *Die ewige Dynastie: David und die Entstehung seiner Dynastie nach der deuteronomistischen Darstellung* (Helsinki: Suomalainen Tiedeakatemia, 1975), 95–97 (97).

hausen and Brettler believe, there is an even higher possibility that 2Sam 8:16–18 was not in the original HDR, because, as we shall see later, the list of Saul's officials in 1Sam 14 also shows several deuteronomistic features.[21]

Of course, even if we admit that the list was inserted by a later editor, we can still maintain that the list indicates the ending of the HDR, because the editor could have carefully joined the different sources without making any artificial breaks. For instance, the Deuteronomist might have added the list just after the original ending of the source. This raises questions about how ancient redactors dealt with the materials they had inherited. How much freedom did they enjoy, when they compiled the different sources? What was the general attitude of the Deuteronomist in dealing with the traditions? Martin Noth was of the opinion that the Deuteronomist was rather loyal to the traditions available to him,[22] and indeed, it seems that ancient redactors in general were very cautious in their treatment of whatever material they inherited, and did their best to preserve the already semi-sacrosanct sources as fully as possible, losing as little as possible.[23]

Nevertheless, this cannot prove that the redactor never made some artificial breaks in order to make his redactional point clearer. For instance, we can imagine that the Deuteronomist made the pattern of sin-punishment-repentance clearer by inserting a demarcating marker before 2Sam 9 where David's decline starts.[24] David's too soft attitude toward his possible enemies begins in 2Sam 9 with his treatment of Mepibosheth, and the Deuteronomist, who identified the compromising – cultic, in particular – attitude of Israel's leaders as the source of Israel's sins, may well have wanted 2Sam 9 to be the beginning of the same old pattern. Indeed, a similar demarcation seems to be working in 1Sam 14–15. It may well be argued that the Deuteronomist made a break before 1Sam 15 by inserting 14:47–52, in order to make the same pattern more evident. The sin is committed by Israel's king (Saul) in 1Sam 15, and the punishment is described through the internal conflicts that result in the death of the king and the loss of territories (1Sam 17–31). And finally, the emergence of a new king (David) who makes up for Saul's shortcomings is narrated in 2Sam 2–8.

---

**21** Timo Veijola, *Das Königtum in der Beurteilung der deuteronomistischen Historiographie: eine redaktionsgeschichtliche Untersuchung* (Helsinki: Suomalainen Tiedeakatemia, 1977), 79–82.

**22** Martin Noth, *Überlieferungsgeschichtliche Studien*, 3rd edition (Tübingen: Max Niemeyer Verlag, 1967), 95–100.

**23** Herbert Donner, "Der Redaktor. Überlegungen zum vorkritischen Umgang mit der Heiligen Schrift," *Henoch* 2 (1980): 1–30 (27–28).

**24** Hans W. Wolff, "The Kerygma of the Deuteronomistic Historical Work," in *The Vitality of Old Testament Traditions*, eds. Walter Brueggemann and Hans W. Wolff (Atlanta: John Knox Press, 1975): 83–100.

The division in 8:15–18 seems to fit very well with the deuteronomistic scheme of sin-punishment-repentance/restoration, and one may well argue that the Deuteronomist made an artificial break where the narrative in fact continues. After all, there is no decisive evidence that the formal marker in 8:15–18 is from the original compiler of the HDR, and therefore, we are unable to conclude that the HDR finishes with 8:18.

### 1.2.2 The List of the Sons in 2Sam 5:13–16

The next consideration as a possible formal marker indicating the end of the HDR is the list of David's sons in 2Sam 5:13–16. Whether the list of sons alone can have the demarcating character is not certain, and the list may well have been with the list of the officials, and possibly, also with the list of David's sons from Hebron in 2Sam 3:2–5.[25] For the moment, however, we set aside the question of the relationship between those lists, and since the list in 2Sam 5:13–16 certainly makes a break in the flow of the narrative, we ask whether it marks the end of the HDR.

The first question to be asked is of course whether the list is from the original author of the HDR, but it is generally agreed among scholars that such was not the case. Veijola thinks that it was inserted by the DtrG, together with the information about the official in 2Sam 8,[26] and Grønbaek is of a similar opinion, that the list, which reminds us of the annalistic summary in 5:4–5, was a later insertion by the Deuteronomist.[27] Noth objected to the idea of the Deuteronomist's insertion, but he agrees that they were post-HDR.[28] After all, the list seems to be later than the original HDR, and therefore, the question comes down again to whether the later editor made an artificial insertion or not. It is impossible to be absolutely certain about it, but if we cannot find out the rationale for rather a violent insertion, there is a higher probability that the original source had a break before 5:13–16. If we can guess a reason for the insertion, however, the list will not be able to tell us about the original demarcation.

To explain the insertion, the following suggestions have been made. First, Hertzberg argues that the list was inserted where it is now, because it could

---

**25** 1Chr 3:1–9 has the combined list of David's sons. For the difference between the lists, see Jakob H. Grønbaek, *Die Geschichte vom Aufstieg Davids (1. Sam. 15 – 2. Sam. 5); Tradition und Komposition* (Copenhagen: Prostant Apud Munksgaard, 1971), 255 (#117); Stoebe, *Das zweite Buch Samuelis*, 121, 175.

**26** Veijola, *Dynastie*, 98.

**27** Grønbaek, *Aufstieg*, 255 (#117).

**28** Noth, *ÜS*, 63 (#3).

be connected with the capture of Jerusalem. The compiler wanted to provide the information about David's sons at some point, and he thought after the conquest of Jerusalem to be the best location, because without the conquest, David would not have been able to beget so many sons. Besides, this emphasizes how blessed David was by God, and how great the king was.[29] Second, Grønbaek, who thinks the same hand is responsible both for the insertion of 5:4–5 and that of 5:13–15, speculates that the Deuteronomist wanted to frame the conquest of Jerusalem with statistical materials in these two places. Apparently, the Deuteronomist wanted to make some notes after the two most important events in David's early days, i.e., the ascension to the throne over both Northern Israel and Judah, and the king's and the ark's settlement in Jerusalem. [30] Finally, Noth suggests the possible connection between 5:13–16 and the "Succession Narrative" – more specifically, Absalom's revolt, as it mentions David's "concubines (פְלַגְשִׁים)" and "wives (נָשִׁים)" (2Sam 15:16; 20:3).[31] Perhaps, the compiler wanted to connect the two traditions by revealing in advance the important characters in the following tradition, and thought it best to do so immediately after David's settlement in Jerusalem which is the main stage for the "Succession Narrative". It is difficult to tell which among these was the original purpose of the redactor. But it is sufficiently clear that the redactor may well have had some reason to make rather an artificial break in the originally continuing narrative. Therefore, the existence of the list of David's sons in 2Sam 5:13–16 cannot tell us decisively that the ending of the HDR is found in 2Sam 5:10–12.

### 1.2.3 The annalistic note in 2Sam 5:4–5

The next candidate would be the chronological data found in 2Sam 5:4–5, "David was thirty years old, when he became the king, (and)[32] for forty years, he reigned. In Hebron, he reigned over Judah for seven years and six months, and in Jerusalem, he reigned for thirty-three years over all Israel and Judah." The triple construction – the king's age at the time of the beginning of the reign, the length of his reign, and his ruling area – is formulaic in the books

---

29 Hans Wilhelm Hertzberg, *I & II Samuel: a Commentary* (London: SCM Press, 1964), 272.
30 Grønbaek, *Aufstieg*, 255, #117.
31 Noth, *ÜS*, 63 (#3).
32 MT has אַרְבָּעִים, but we should read וארבעים. This is supported by 14 Masoretic manuscripts, the Versions (LXX, Syr., Vulg.), and parallel passages such as 1Kings 14:21. See S. R. Driver, *Notes on the Hebrew Text and the Topography of the Books of Samuel* (Oxford: Clarendon Press, 1913), 258; McCarter, *II Samuel*, 131.

of Kings for marking the beginning of a king's reign,[33] and 5:4–5 seems to show the stereotyped pattern of the deuteronomistic notices on the accessions of the kings of Israel and Judah. Therefore, we might well conclude with Noth that these verses function as "the formulaic introduction to the reign of David",[34] and that the story of his rise finishes with 5:3. Indeed, if the HDR is purely about the "rise" of David, it is reasonable that the HDR finishes where the elders of Israel anoint him as king of Israel, and his "rise" is complete.

However, there is still a possibility that 5:4–5 was an artificial break inserted by the Deuteronomist or a later editor. The Deuteronomist, for whom the bringing of the Ark to Jerusalem was exceedingly important, might have changed the order of the materials at this point, in order to show that the conquest of Jerusalem was the first thing David did after the official beginning of his reign.[35] The Deuteronomist could have a good reason to make the narrative pause at this point, and this keeps us from making any conclusion on the basis of the formal marker. In fact, it is also possible that the chronological data was inserted even later than the Deuteronomist's work. The verses are missing in 4QSam^A, the Old Latin, and Josephus, and probably, in the Old Greek,[36] and accordingly, McCarter thinks that they might be "very late additions to the text in the spirit of the authentically deuteronomistic notices that pertain to the reigns of the kings of the divided monarchy."[37] To confirm the argument, further research may be required, but this makes it more difficult to use these verses as a demarcating indicator.

### 1.2.4 The List of the Sons in 2Sam 3:2–5

In addition to the list of David's sons born in Jerusalem, we have one more list of his sons in 2Sam 3:2–5. It seems obvious that this list does not mark the end of the HDR, because David has not accomplished the goal of his rise yet. However, this is something we know from our literary judgement that the narrative should finish with David's rise to the throne over all Israel. From the formal perspective – as for the moment we attempt to reach the conclusion without any synchronic aspect – we have no reason to exclude this list from the candidates. Indeed, if we accept the view that 2Sam 3:6–4:12 could have come from the same author as the

---

**33** Cf. 1Kings 14:21; 22:42; etc.
**34** Noth, *ÜS*, 63.
**35** Noth, *ÜS*, 63–64.
**36** Eugene Charles Ulrich, Jr., *The Qumran Text of Samuel and Josephus* (Ann Arbor, MI: Scholar Press, 1978), 60–62.
**37** McCarter, *II Samuel*, 88,130–133 (133).

"Succession Narrative",[38] there is a fairly high possibility that 3:2–5 marks the formal ending of the tradition that comes before the "Succession Narrative". The question is whether the person responsible for the insertion[39] made an artificial break here, and the answer is again that it is possible that the redactor made a violent insertion, because there are a couple of plausible reasons. The later redactor might have wanted "to show that in this sphere, too, David constantly increased, and slowly but surely prepared for himself the dynasty that God willed."[40] Or, the list could have been "attracted to this position by the reference to the waxing of the house of David in 3:1."[41] It is not impossible to imagine that there was a particular reason for the insertion or the creation of the list here, and therefore, we cannot conclude that the HDR ends in 3:1, on the basis of the formal marker.

### 1.2.5 The annalistic note in 2Sam 2:10–11

We have one more chronological datum about Ishbosheth's reign and David's reign in 2Sam 2:10–11, and without thematic consideration, we cannot exclude the possibility that it indicates a source division. Like the similar note in 5:4–5, it is characteristic of the biblical materials about the kings of Israel and Judah, and indicates the beginning of a new era, i.e. the era of the conflict between the house of Saul and the house of David. Then, does the source dealing with David's rise against Saul's fall finish in 2:9, and from 2:10 do we have a new source dealing with the tension between David and Saul's followers? The answer cannot be conclusive, because if the editor was eager to make David the legiti-

---

**38** Rolf Rendtorff, "Beobachtungen zur altisraelitischen Geschichtsschreibung anhand der Geschichte vom Aufstieg Davids," in *Probleme biblischer Theologie*, ed. Hans Walter Wolff (München: Chr. Kaiser, 1971): 428–439 (432). A similar view is found in David Gunn, *The Story of King David: Genre and Interpretation* (Sheffield: JSOT Press, 1976), 75–81. Similar views are expressed in Henry P. Smith, *A Critical and Exegetical Commentary on the Books of Samuel* (Edinburgh: T&T Clark, 1899); Hannelis Schulte, *Die Entstehung der Geschichtsschreibung im alten Israel* (Berlin: de Gruyter, 1972); Rudolf Ficker, "Komposition und Erzählung: Untersuchungen zur Ladeerzählung (1 S 4–6; 2 S 6) und zur Geschichte vom Aufstieg Davids (1 S 15–2 S 5)" (unpublished doctoral thesis, University of Heidelberg, 1977); John Van Seters, *In Search of History* (New Haven: Yale University Press, 1983), 280–286. Noth already suggested the connection in *ÜS*, 63 (#3).
**39** Grønbaek denies that the list was a later insertion. However, the repetition of v. 1 in v. 6, and the interruption of continuity caused by the list make it more likely that the list was inserted. See Grønbaek, *Aufstieg*, 234–5; McCarter, *II Samuel*, 101; Stoebe, *Das zweite Buch Samuelis*,120–121.
**40** Hertzberg, *Samuel*, 254.
**41** McCarter, *II Samuel*, 102.

mate successor to the northern kingdom, it is quite understandable that by inserting the formulaic introduction of both reigns, he made his point clearer. In other words, the compiler might have wanted to make a point that Ishbosheth was a legitimate king before he was killed, and therefore, the power handed over to David after his death entails the rule of the Northern kingdom. Moreover, there is a possibility that 2:10–11 was added later than the Deuteronomist's work.[42] The chronological data here cannot tell us where the HDR ends.

### 1.2.6 The formulaic expression וַיְהִי אַחֲרֵי־כֵן in 2Sam 2:1

Finally, one might ask whether the formulaic expression וַיְהִי אַחֲרֵי־כֵן in 2Sam 2:1; 8:1; 10:1; 13:1; (15:1); 21:18 can be seen as some kind of a formal marker. It is certainly a less common way of demarcation, but it seems plausible that the compiler used it as a link, and the joint seems to indicate a new section although it does not tell us about the chronological sequence.[43] This makes it possible that there were about 5 groups of tradition in 2Sam (chapters 2–7; 8–9; 10–12; 13–20; 21), and these were combined by a formulaic expression וַיְהִי אַחֲרֵי־כֵן. The question is then who was responsible for the expression. At first glance, the strongest candidate is the author of the "Succession Narrative", because the expression occurs at least twice in the source (10:1; 13:1). The possibility goes even higher, if we accept the view that the author of the "Succession Narrative" affixed chapters 10–12 to the account of Absalom's rebellion (chapters 13–20) as "a kind of theological preface".[44] While joining those two, the author seems to have used the expression וַיְהִי אַחֲרֵי־כֵן, and it is plausible that he used the same to join other traditions. (Indeed, Stoebe thinks that the HDR ends in 2Sam 1.[45]) However, the same expression occurs elsewhere in the Hebrew Bible in Judges 16:4; 2Sam 24:6; 2Kings 6:24, and this raises the question whether the same person is responsible for connecting all these traditions. This prompts us to consider a significantly different – but by no means, new – view about the composition history of Judges–2Kings. In other words, the expression in fact might reflect a particular style of an author who is responsible for narratives scattered in Judges–2Kings. We do not have space to examine the possibility, but at this stage, it is sufficient to conclude that the formulaic expression וַיְהִי אַחֲרֵי־כֵן cannot tell us about the trace of source division.

---

42 McCarter, *II Samuel*, 88.
43 Stoebe, *Das zweite Buch Samuelis*, 97.
44 McCarter, *II Samuel*, 275–276.
45 Stoebe, *Das erste Buch Samuelis* (Gütersloh: Gütersloher Verlagshaus, 1973), 296 ff.

## 1.3 Linguistic Features and Phraseology

Since we could not get a decisive answer to our question from the evidence of the formal markers, we now turn to investigate the linguistic features and phraseology. Whether there are words or phrases that are peculiar to the HDR in 2Sam 5–8 will be our main interest. Of course, this will not be able to tell us the precise source division. Nonetheless, it may help us to identify which passages belong to the HDR, and bring us nearer to the most plausible conclusion.

### 1.3.1 YHWH's being with David

The first candidate for our inspection is the phrase "YHWH was with him [David] (יהוה עמו)", which occurs in 2Sam 16:18; [17:37]; 18:12,14,28; [20:13]; 2Sam 5:10; 7:3,9. The motif of YHWH being with a person or Israel might have originally come from the nomadic idea of God shepherding His people,[46] and possibly it also had some connection with coronation ritual.[47] In any case, it has been argued that the phraseology was of great importance to the HDR as its theological leitmotiv,[48] and from a literary perspective, it has been held that it enables us to distinguish the HDR from other materials. In particular, Mettinger believes that the way in which the motif is formulated enables us to separate the HDR from the "Succession Narrative". Although the formula appears twice in the "Succession Narrative" (2Sam 14:17; 2Kings 1:37), the assertive use of it only occurs in the HDR.[49] Therefore, it might be possible that if the phrase occurs somewhere in 2Sam 5–9, we can extend the ending at least to the passage which contains it.

The last occurrence of the motif before 2Sam 9 is in 7:9 where YHWH says through Nathan to David "And I have been with you wherever you go (וָאֶהְיֶה עִמְּךָ בְּכֹל אֲשֶׁר הָלָכְתָּ)." We have a similar expression in 2Sam 14:17 where the wise woman from Tekoa talks to David while asking for Absalom's amnesty.

---

46 Horst Dietrich Preuß, "… ich will mit dir sein!" *ZAW* 80 (1968): 139–173 (171–173).

47 Stoebe, *Das erste Buch Samuelis*, 172.

48 Artur Weiser, "Die Legitimation des Königs David: Zur Eigenart und Entstehung der sogen. Geschichte von Davids Aufstieg," *VT* 16 (1966): 325–354 (334–335); P. Kyle McCarter, "Apology of David," *JBL* 99 (1980): 489–504 (503).

49 Preuß divides the so-called *Beistand* formula into three groups according to its usage: (i) promise and assurance through God; (ii) promise, assurance, request or wish by a man (never by a woman); (iii) assurance by a man (again, never by a woman), not promisingly, but assertively. The assertive usage (iii) is not found in 2Sam 8–2Kings 18. Preuß, "… ich will mit dir sein!", pp. 140–152; Tryggve N. D. Mettinger, *King and Messiah: the Civil and Sacral Legitimation of the Israelite Kings* (Lund: Gleerup, 1976), 43.

However, the usage in this verse is rather promissory, and different from the way it is used in the HDR. Then, could we conclude that the HDR at least reaches to chapter 7, and since the verse is a part of Nathan's oracle (7:1–17), the end of the HDR is found in 7:17? Indeed, whatever the original conclusion might have been, it is difficult to deny that chapter 7 in its final form provides a "culminating retrospective and conclusion".[50] It summarizes all the events that took place in the HDR, and forms the climax of the narrative. Despite the great emphasis on the significance of the phrase, however, whether the so-called *Beistand* formula is really characteristic for the HDR is uncertain. For example, F. M. Cross holds that the phrase refers to YHWH's presence with or support of a leader, and is spread widely in the deuteronomistic work.[51] McCarter believes that the expressions occurring within the HDR might well have been in the original composition, but the phrase in 7:10, together with 1Sam 3:19, is likely to be from a prophetic writer.[52] Furthermore, although it is true that the assertive use in the HDR is different from the promissory use in the "Succession Narrative", the assertive use in the HDR, if we set aside 2Sam 7, occurs only three times in the HDR (1Sam 16:18; 18:12; 2Sam 5:10) out of 28 occurrences, and the promissory use is also found twice in the HDR (1Sam 17:37; 20:13). The expression seems too common to suggest any specific literary authorship, and in fact, we must bear in mind that the assertive use of the motif occurs three times in the Joseph story (Genesis 39:2,21,23),[53] while the phrase never occurs in the passages which Rost regarded as "the most important part" of the HDR, i.e., 1Sam 23:1–13; 27:1–28:2; 29:1–30:26; 2Sam 1:1; 2:4a,20–29; 3:31–37; 4:1a,5–12; 5:3; 5:17–25 (ch. 8?).[54] The phrase might well have been a key for the author of the HDR when different materials were compiled. However, the phraseology itself cannot tell us about the origin of certain passages. It is too common.

### 1.3.2 The title נָגִיד

In his book *King and Messiah*, Mettinger proposed three linguistic features that can help us to separate the HDR from the "Succession Narrative", so let us examine whether his proposal helps. First, he suggested that the use of the title

**50** McCarter, *II Samuel*, 201.
**51** Frank M. Cross, *Canaanite Myth and Hebrew Epic* (Cambridge, MA: Harvard University Press, 1973), 252.
**52** McCarter, *II Samuel*, 202.
**53** The difference of the preposition – ta in the Joseph story and Mo in the HDR – seems insignificant. See Preuß, "… ich will mit dir sein!", 144.
**54** Rost, *Succession*,109.

נָגִיד can be evidence that a certain passage belongs to the HDR. Believing that the term mostly refers to the king designate or the crown prince in the historical books, Mettinger argues that the title used in 2Sam 7:8 shows the particularity of the HDR (2Sam 5:2; 6:21; cf. 1Sam 25:30), because unlike its use in the "Succession Narrative" (1Kings 1:35), the one who designates נָגִיד here and elsewhere in the HDR is God, not David.[55] Therefore, the different usage enables us to separate those passages from the "Succession Narrative", and prompts us to include chapter 7, or at least Nathan's oracle, in the HDR.

The difficulty however is that neither 2Sam 5:2 nor 6:21, which Mettinger thinks show the same feature with 2Sam 7:8, can be safely assigned to the original HDR. For example, Veijola, followed by McCarter, thinks that the word-for-word repetition of vv. 1a and 3a, and the expression "your bone and your flesh" for the whole Israelites rather than for kinsmen (Gen 29:14; Judges 9:2) or a tribal association (2Sam 19:13,14) indicate that 5:1–2 is a later insertion by the Deuteronomist.[56] As to 6:21, although the awkward relative sentence which separates שׂחַקְתִּי from לִפְנֵי יְהֹוָה can be explained as a case of *homoioteleuton*,[57] it is also possible that the repetition of לִפְנֵי יְהֹוָה indicates that the relative sentence, which includes the title נָגִיד, was a later insertion.[58] Indeed, McCarter, who acknowledges the textual problem in the verse pointed out by Crüsemann, concludes that "[t]his pious exclamation, though *textually* primitive as here restored, is probably *literarily* secondary, a contribution of the deuteronomistic hand responsible for the final arrangement of 5:11–8:18".[59]

Furthermore, with the exception of 1Kings 1:35 and 2Chr 11:22, the title is always given by YHWH: to Saul (1Sam 9:16; 10:1); to David (1Sam 13:14; 25:30; 2Sam 5:2; 6:21; 7:8; 1Chr 11:2; 17:7; 2Chr 6:5); to Jeroboam (1Kings 14:7); to Baasha (1Kings 16:2). Thus the designation as נָגִיד by David in 1Kings 1:35 is more likely to be an exception. Indeed, from the very beginning, the theological usage of the term

---

55 Mettinger, *King and Messiah*, 43.

56 Veijola, *Dynastie* pp. 63–66; McCarter, *II Samuel*, 131.

57 LXX[B] has ὀρχήσομαι εὐλογητὸς κύριος "... I will dance! Blessed be YHWH..." between יְהֹוָה and אֲשֶׁר, probably reflecting ארקד ברוך יהוה. Some commentators hold that the phrase was omitted, because the eye of the scribe jumped from the first יהוה to the second. Julius Wellhausen, *Der Text der Bücher Samuelis* (Göttingen: Vandenhoeck und Ruprecht, 1871), 169; Driver, *Notes*, 273; McCarter, *II Samuel*, 184; Stoebe, *Das zweite Buch Samuelis*, 203.

58 The relative sentence was inserted after יהוה, and this made the repetition of לפני יהוה necessary. As to the question why the redactor did not insert it before hwhy ynpl, Veijola thinks that it was because the following זאת in זאת מזאת עוד ונקלתי in v. 22a requiresשחקתי as the antecedent. See Veijola, *Dynastie*, 66–67.

59 McCarter, *II Samuel*, 187; Frank Crüsemann, "Zwei alttestamentliche Witze. I Sam 21:11–15 und II Sam 6:16,20–23," *ZAW* 92 (1980): 215–227 (223).

seems to have reflected YHWH's initiative,[60] and therefore, it is unlikely that the seemingly different usage can serve as a criterion to distinguish the "Succession Narrative" from the HDR. This is confirmed by the fact that Grønbaek distinguishes the usage on a different ground. According to his observation, the title in 1Sam 25:30 and 2Sam 5:2 refers to the future event, whereas in 2Sam 6:21 and 7:9 David's designation as נָגִיד is presupposed.[61] Whether 7:8 is from a prophetic circle[62] or from the Deuteronomist,[63] it seems evident that the use of the title נָגִיד does not tell us about the origin of the passage.

### 1.3.3 The divine name יְהוָה צְבָאוֹת

Mettinger also draws attention to the divine title יְהוָה צְבָאוֹת that appears in 2Sam 7:8,26,27; cf. 6:2,18. The title does not occur even once in the "Succession Narrative" but is found three times in the HDR (1Sam 15:2; 17:45; 2Sam 5:10). Therefore, Mettinger claims, the title can be evidence for the hand of the HDR throughout chapter 7. The difficulty of this view is, however, that not a few scholars exclude 1Sam 15 from the HDR, and the divine name in 2Sam 5:10 may be just a case of amplification making the verse an "emphatic statement". The uncertainty about the origin of some verses also deters us from accepting Mettinger's view as conclusive. The messenger form "thus says YHWH of Hosts" as uttered by Samuel (1Sam 15:2) and Nathan (2Sam 7:8) may well have derived from a prophetic influence,[64] and 7:22–26 might be a deuteronomistic expansion.[65] Indeed, when the title is deemed to be "the most frequently used divine epithet in the Old Testament",[66] it is precarious to make an argument on the basis of its occurrence.

### 1.3.4 The phrase גלה אזן

Mettinger also suggests that the phrase גלה אזן "to uncover an ear", found in 2Sam 7:27 (= 1Chr 17:25), is found in texts clearly belonging to the HDR (1Sam 20:2; 22:8 twice; 22:17). According to the evidence from this linguistic feature, he argues, the end of the HDR should be found at the end of chapter 7, since

---

**60** G. F. Hasel, "נָגִיד," *TDOT*, IX, 187–202 (199).
**61** Grønbaek, *Aufstieg*, 176.
**62** McCarter, *II Samuel*, 201.
**63** Veijola, *Dynastie*, 76–77.
**64** McCarter, *II Samuel*, 228; Hans-Jürgen Zobel, "צְבָאוֹת," *TDOT*, XII, 227; Stoebe, 279.
**65** McCarter, *II Samuel*, 237.
**66** Zobel, "צְבָאוֹת," *TDOT*, XII, 215–232 (p. 227).

verse 27 is a part of "David's prayer". However, the phrase in the above passages within the HDR has the sense of "proclaiming something to someone", used in the secular realm, whereas in 2Sam 7:27, as in 1Sam 9:15; Job 33:16; 36:10,15, it is used rather as "a technical term for revelation".[67] If we rule out the semantic difference and consider only the occurrence of the phrase, we may have to accept that 1Sam 9:15 also belongs to the HDR, or even more unlikely, Ruth 4:4 where Boaz announces to his kinsmen his wish to redeem Ruth. In fact, from the linguistic point of view, the parallel with Ruth 4:4 is much closer than with any other passage in the HDR, because both in 2Sam 7:27 and Ruth 4:4, the phrase is followed by לֵאמֹר, but not in the passages within the HDR.

## 1.4 Stylistic Features

Since it turned out that textual, formal, and linguistic evidence is not sufficient to provide us with a satisfactory answer, we now turn to the possibility of finding the end of the HDR on the basis of stylistic features.[68] This can be done by asking (i) where the last trace of the stylistic features peculiar to the HDR is found, and (ii) where the first trace of the stylistic features peculiar to the "Succession Narrative" is found. Again, this will not tell us about the precise ending of the HDR. Yet, it might help us to identify the origin of a certain passage, and to recognize the ending.

### 1.4.1 The stylistic features of the HDR

What are the possible stylistic features of the HDR and where do they occur for the last time? Scholars have proposed several features which clearly separate the HDR from other traditions, and some of them are as follows. First, a religious or cultic element is conspicuous in the HDR. In particular, whenever David has to make an important decision, he inquires of YHWH (1Sam 23:2,4,9ff; 30:7ff; etc.). This was already recognized by Rost who regarded the consultation of YHWH as an important element that separates the HDR from the "Succession Narrative" in which any cultic element recedes into the background.[69] Second, quasi-prophetic utterances about or allusions to David's future kingship are made by unexpected characters. For instance, Saul, who is unexpected in the sense that he is the last

---

**67** Hans-Jürgen Zobel, "גָּלָה," *TDOT*, II, 476–488 (483).
**68** "Stylistics, in short, is an attempt to put criticism on a scientific basis." Stanley Fish, *Is There a Text in this Class* (Cambridge, MA: Harvard University Press, 1980), 70.
**69** Rost, *Succession*, 110–111.

person to acknowledge David's future kingship, says in 1Sam 24:21 (ET 24. 20), "Now I know that you shall surely be king, and the kingdom of Israel will rise in your hand." Similarly, Jonathan speaks out of context, "You shall be king over Israel [...] and my father Saul also knows that this is so" (1Sam 23:17). Third, there is a trace of chronological and purposeful arrangement of the materials, which gives a history-like flavour to the narrative and makes all the sections organically interconnected. Weiser points out particularly that the way the composer inserted a reminder about Samuel's death before the En-dor episode indicates the composer's intentional structuring of the materials.[70] Rendtorff goes further to argue that the most peculiar features of the HDR are what he calls "short reports (*kurze Mitteilungen*)" that complete the narrative by bridging the larger narratives with comments of the author's reflection, purpose, and feelings.[71] Now let us ask where we find these features for the last time before 2Sam 9.

When it comes to the religious or cultic element, we have a similar consultation of YHWH in 2Sam 5:19,23 where David asks YHWH whether he should attack the Philistines and how. Then, according to this criterion, one might conclude that the last passage of the HDR is 2Samuel 5:17–25, and the HDR ends probably in 5:25. However, the religious and cultic interest is most evident in 2Sam 6–7 where the very focus of the event is the Ark and the temple. Therefore, if we want to distinguish the HDR from other sources on the basis of the cultic element, we cannot exclude 2Sam 6–7. One might object to this view, saying that we should limit ourselves only to the consultation motif. But the consultation motif first appears in 1Sam 23, and between 1Sam 15 and 2Sam 8, it occurs only thrice (the Keilah incident, the Ziklag incident, the movement to Hebron). With further specification, the evidence is too little to suggest any significant information about the author's stylistic features, and even less about the source division.

Even if we accept the consultation motif as a distinguishing feature, it is difficult to settle for 2Sam 5:25 as the ending, because a different conclusion is reached if another stylistic feature is considered. According to the criterion of the quasi-prophetic utterances of unexpected characters about David's future kingship, the ending should be found much earlier than 2Sam 5. As mentioned above, it is quite peculiar to the HDR that unexpected characters rather than the narrator or pro-Davidic Samuel reveal David's future in the narrative, and we find the last example in 1Sam 26:25 where Saul foretells David's success. Possi-

---

70 Weiser, "Legitimation," 330.
71 Rendtorff, "Beobachtung," 436.

bly, we can stretch the stylistic feature a little bit more, and include those remarks of minor characters referring to the divine predestination of David's ascension.[72] Then, the last example is found in 2Sam 3:17–18 where Abner persuades the elders of Israel to subject themselves to David, and quotes the alleged promise to David, "In the hand of David my servant, I[73] will deliver my people Israel from the hand of the Philistines and from the hand of all their enemies." Whether it is 1Sam 26 or 2Sam 3, however, one might well feel that it is too early to talk of the ending of the HDR, because David will not be enthroned over the whole of Israel until 2Sam 5. Furthermore, we do not know exactly why such prophetic remarks are missing in 2Sam 4–5. Is it because the enthronement is so imminent that such remarks are unnecessary? Is it because chapter 4 is not a part of the HDR? The former seem more likely, but the latter is also possible because Ishbosheth's death in the chapter may well be seen as contradicting 1Sam 31:2 that reports the deaths of Saul's three sons.[74] After all, it is too simplistic to identify the ending of the HDR according to the use of minor characters as quasi-prophets or indicators of David's future enthronement. The evidence is too ambiguous.

The contradictory results or the insufficiency of the evidence so far lead us to consider the last stylistic feature in the HDR, namely, to what extent each unit shows a trace of intentional structuring. This is probably the most important evidence for the existence of an independent source HDR. Indeed, confronted with uncertainty about the existence of the HDR, Campbell and O'Brien conclude, "[t] he likely narrative organization around areas such as 1Sam 17–18, 23–26, and 28–31 points to the probability of such a text having existed."[75] That a narrative has been structured not by accident but on purpose can be known mainly from two indications: (i) it has been chronologically arranged, or (ii) a passage is organically connected with the other parts of the HDR. When it comes to the chronological arrangement, not only 2Sam 2–8, but also the whole of Sam–Kings seem to show a smooth progression. Therefore, it does not help us to distinguish the HDR from other materials, and whether the passages in these chapters are organically interconnected with each other, and with earlier parts of the HDR in 1Sam remains a crucial question.

---

72 Weiser, "Legitimation," 336–338.

73 MT has יהושיע "he saved". But several manuscripts have אושיע, and LXX (σώσω) seems to read the same. Thus I read אושיע, following Wellhausen, *Der Text der Bücher Samuelis*, 159; Driver, *Notes*, 249.

74 Van Seters, *In Search of History*, 281.

75 Antony Campbell and Mark O'Brien, *Unfolding the Deuteronomistic History: Origins, Upgrades, Present Text* (Minneapolis: Fortress Press, 2000), 219.

Obviously, the last passage which shows the least connection with other parts of the HDR will be able to tell us where the HDR ends. Let us start with the sections that scholars have held to be more likely a part of the HDR. First, David's anointment as king of Judah in 2:1–7. Here, after the consultation of YHWH, David goes up to Judah, and is anointed by the people of Judah in Hebron. In describing David's household, the author refers to Abigail as the "wife" of Nabal from Carmel, [76] and this seems to presuppose the reader's knowledge of the event in 1Sam 25, because otherwise, the author would not have reminded the reader of the fact which might give a false impression that David took someone else's wife. The section certainly seems to belong to the HDR.

The next section, i.e. the battle between Ishbosheth and David, however, seems not to be well connected with earlier parts of the HDR. Van Seters lists several points that suggest the independence of 2:8–4:12 from the HDR. First, the name of Ishbosheth, Saul's son and the heir to the throne, never appears before 2:8, especially not in 1Sam 31:2, where Jonathan, Abinadab, and Malchishua are mentioned as Saul's sons. Second, David's invitation to the people of Jabesh-Gilead in 2:4b–7 does not fit very well with the following context. They are the people most faithful to Saul (1Sam 31:11–13), and the invitation should be sent out after David becomes king over both Israel and Judah. Third, in 2:9 Ishbosheth is said to rule over Jezreel, but this contradicts 1Sam 31:7 which reports that the people of Israel abandoned it, and the Philistines occupied it.[77] Furthermore, the characterization of the key figures is different. In the HDR, David is depicted as "a man of transparent principles who does not strive in any way for the crown and who always leads his men personally into battle against the enemy".[78] By contrast, in the war with Ishbosheth, David sits at home in Hebron while his men do all the fighting, a pattern that is consistent in the "Court History" (This continues to be the case in the series of reports in 2Sam 5 and 8 as well.) Similarly, the figure of Joab is different in each. In the HDR, Joab is mentioned merely as the brother of Abishai (1Sam 26:6), but in the war with Ishbosheth, he is a well-known figure who plays the key role in the course of the event.[79]

So, does this tell us that the HDR finishes in 2Sam 2:7? David is not anointed as king of all Israel until 5:3, and 5:1–5 seems well connected with the HDR. The passage recalls David's military leadership in the Saulide court by using the

**76** Several English translations including RSV and NRSV translate the word as "widow". However, the Hebrew word used is אֵשֶׁת, the construct of אִשָּׁה, the normal term for wife.
**77** Van Seters, *In Search of History*, 281–282. However, Hertzberg thinks that Asher and Jezreel might have been ceded by the Philistines to Ishbosheth to hold. Hertzberg, *Samuel*, 249–250.
**78** Van Seters, *In Search of History*, 283.
**79** Van Seters, *In Search of History*, 283–284.

words from יצא and בוא (1Sam 18:13,16; 2Sam 5:2), and David's previous occupation as shepherd by using the verb רעה (2Sam 5:2). Besides, the location of David is said to be Hebron, which presupposes 2Sam 2:1–4. Then, is the ending of the HDR found in 2Sam 5:3 with 2:8–4:12 an interpolation? This is plausible, since the section that immediately follows is the conquest of Jerusalem, and the city has no role in other parts of the HDR, and is never mentioned before. Yet, we cannot be sure that the trace of the HDR is last found in 2Sam 5:1–5, because unsolved business with the Philistines is dealt with in 2Sam 5:17–25.[80] Israel's struggle against the Philistines was a major issue during Saul's reign, and David's victories over the Philistines may well mark the end of David's successful succession to Saul. The story of the bringing up of the Ark to Jerusalem is not connected with the HDR either, and if the conquest of Jerusalem is not a part of the HDR, 6:1–23 is more likely to be independent from the HDR because here the city is another focus in the story.[81] To summarize what we have seen so far, 2:1–7; 5:1–5; 5:17–25 are closely interconnected with earlier parts of the HDR, whereas 2:8–4:12; 5:6–13; 6:1–23 seem quite isolated from the HDR. Then the end of the HDR is 5:25, or if we accept the view that 5:17–25 was displaced from somewhere earlier,[82] it should be found in 5:3. Can we be content with such a conclusion?

The inconclusiveness of the conclusion, however, becomes evident if we apply the same question to 2Sam 7. Apparently, chapter 7 is very well connected with other parts of the HDR. It speaks of David's rise from shepherd to the throne in v. 8, reminiscent of the HDR's earlier reports (2Sam 16:19; 17:12ff), and the motif of YHWH's being with David in vv. 3 and 9 echoes the same motif in the HDR. Furthermore, it makes clear that David's present situation is the fulfilment of the promises made in the HDR. Using the same word נָגִיד, v. 8 confirms that David's kingship was the fulfilment of the divine promise mentioned in 1Sam 25:30 and 2Sam 5:2. And the promise of "cutting off (כרת)" David's enemies, repeatedly mentioned in the HDR, especially in 1Sam 20:15 and 25:16, is said to be fulfilled in vv. 9 and 11.[83] It seems obvious that the other parts of the HDR are well connected with this chapter, and the ending should be found at least at the end of Nathan's oracle in 7:17.

However, the provenance of verses 8–11a is not clear, and some think that they are from the Deuteronomist. For instance, Dennis McCarthy notes that the

---

**80** Albrecht Alt, "Zu II Samuel 8:1," *ZAW* 13 (1936): 149–152 (150–151).
**81** Mettinger's argument that 2Sam 5:17–25 and 6:1–23 were transmitted together seems feeble. Mettinger, *King and Messiah*, 42.
**82** Driver, *Notes*, 263; Grønbaek, *Aufstieg*, 250–254.
**83** Weiser, "Legitimation," 347–349; Mettinger, *King and Messiah*, 42–45.

phrase "my servant David" in v. 8 shows a particularly deuteronomistic feature, and the hiphil of נוח used in vv. 1,11a is practically a technical term in the deuteronomistic work.[84] This is more or less followed by Cross who maintains that vv. 8–10a is a deuteronomistic link connecting the two pre-deuteronomistic oracles in vv. 1–7 and vv. 11b–16.[85] Others are more careful about the deuteronomistic origin of the verses. Veijola admits that the so-called *Ruheformel* in v. 11a clearly shows the deuteronomistic character, but thinks that vv. 8a,9,10 belongs to one of the two older oracles which the Deuteronomist put together in chapter 7.[86] McCarter sees three layers in the oracle. Verses 1a,2–3,11b–12, and 13b-15a were from a primitive document, and vv. 4–9a and 15b were from a prophetic circle. The Deuteronomist added verses 9b–11a and 13b to this prophetic edition of the oracle.[87] Mettinger holds that 10–11a is deuteronomistic, but vv. 8–9 are from the Solomonic prophecy of Nathan.[88] Although it is a minority view now, there is also a group of scholars who believe that chapter 7 as a unity is from an older tradition that is similar to the Egyptian *Königsnovelle*, maintaining that the verses are pre-deuteronomistic.[89] The extraordinary diversity of views on these verses tells us that we cannot be absolutely sure about where verses 8–10a are from. And consequently, whether chapter 7 is well connected to the rest of the HDR and whether the HDR extends to chapter 7 are far from clear.

Now we move to chapter 8 where David secures his kingdom by defeating all the surrounding enemies. In a sense, chapter 8 seems well connected to the other parts of the HDR. In particular, the bridging character of 8:1 might indicate that chapter 8 belonged to the same literary tradition with 5:6–25. Several points were suggested by Albrecht Alt, to support the idea: (1) 5:25 and 8:1 are read together very smoothly; (2) in terms of content, the loss of the Philistine hegemony and the rise of the Davidic power in the area in chapter 8 is the necessary consequence of David's military success against the Philistines in 5:17–25; (3) the siege of Jerusalem in 5:6–10 and the fate of neighbouring states in 8:2ff may well be seen as the same tradition. [90] Indeed, one may well wonder why the HDR had to run on after David becomes king over Israel in 5:3, because David's

---

**84** Dennis McCarthy, "II Sam 7 and the Structure of the Deuteronomistic History," *JBL* 84 (1980): 131–138 (132).

**85** Cross, *Canaanite Myth and Hebrew Epic*, 253–254.

**86** Veijola, *Dynastie*, 72–79.

**87** McCarter, *II Samuel*, 224–231.

**88** Mettinger, *King and Messiah*, 48–63.

**89** The idea was first proposed by Siegfried Herrmann in, "The Royal Novella in Egypt and Israel. A Contribution to the History of Genre in the Historical Books of the Old Testament", in *Reconsidering Israel and Judah*, eds. Knoppers and McConville, 493–515.

**90** Alt, "Zu II Samuel 8:1," 150–151.

rise is completed there. Normally, it is explained as an attempt to include the siege of Jerusalem, and this has been the argument for the origin of the tradition in the city. However, why Jerusalem suddenly becomes important at the end of the HDR is not clear. If the author wanted to present the conquest of Jerusalem as the completion of David's rise, one might expect more occurrences of the theme in the course of the narrative. By contrast, if we admit that 5:6–10 and chapter 8 as a subunit are intended to round off David's rise by making it not only the rise to the throne, but also to the hegemony of Israel in the region, the inclusion of the conquest of Jerusalem to the HDR is easily explained. It is a part of the description of how David gradually takes over the hegemony of the area.

Then, could we conclude that chapter 8 – more precisely, 8:15 – is the end of the HDR? We might be able to do so, but this asks us whether the conclusion is eventually reached not on the basis of the stylistic feature of how the chapter is closely connected with other parts, but on the basis of the interpretation of the whole. Whether the HDR should carry on till David's kingship is secured both internally and externally is not something we can decide "objectively" from detailed investigations of certain passages. It is a decision that can be made only after the consideration of the entire work, even if, since the precise extent is uncertain, this is provisional. Only when we understand what the whole of the HDR is about, and what the author's purpose is, can we decide whether the HDR should finish with David's takeover of the hegemony of the area or not. This indeed pushes us further to ask whether the concluding part of the HDR should necessarily show clear connections with the other parts. The HDR is a composite work, and this opens up the possibility that the author used frames at the beginning and at the end to hold different materials together. Granted, the frame does not need to betray total integration into the other materials or to demonstrate a direct connection with the other parts in detail. Rather, it just needs to reiterate the most important elements of the work, and reveal the intention of the composer. As long as it includes in a nutshell the motive and the purpose of the entire composition, and gives the grandeur of the finale, say, any part of 2Sam 2–8 can be the ending of the HDR. After all, whether a passage can be the ending of the HDR depends largely on the understanding of the motive and the purpose of the whole. This is a literary and semantic operation which has been regarded as not that important for historio-traditional issues. But if we set aside such a semantic element of the investigation, it is difficult to know whether the chapter is closely connected with other parts or not, and consequently, where the HDR ends.

### 1.4.2 The stylistic features of the "Succession Narrative"

Since we cannot find where the HDR ends, on the basis of the stylistic features of the HDR, we now ask whether the style of the "Succession Narrative" can help us to do so. It has been long argued that the HDR is an independent source from the "Succession Narrative", because the stylistic features peculiar to the "Succession Narrative" are not found in the HDR. Some of such features are listed as follows: (i) the speeches constructed as inclusios with the round-off scenes; (ii) frequent use of simile; (iii) the dominating and creative power of direct speech; (iv) the brevity and power of the speeches, (v) the recession of the cultic element, especially the consultation of YHWH; (vi) more sophisticated and psychologically insightful characterisation.

Despite the conviction of Rost and his followers, whether these features can distinguish the HDR from the "Succession Narrative" seems less clear than Rost first imagined. David Gunn, inspired by Schulte's earlier work, already recognized the prevalence of the stylistic features of the "Succession Narrative" in 2Sam 2–4. Inclusios, similes, chiasmus, the use of repetition, irony, foreshadowing – all the features that have been regarded as the distinctive mark of the "Succession Narrative" – are found in those chapters,[91] and this led Gunn to conclude that 2Sam 2–4 belong to the "Succession Narrative" or "The Story of King David" as he calls it. Indeed, we may well wonder whether such stylistic differences can be criteria to distinguish between them, because it is not only in these chapters in 2Sam that we come across the stylistic features that are comparable to those of the "Succession Narrative". Let us take 1Sam 16:13–24, one of the earliest parts of the HDR, as an example.

The scene, which is taken by several scholars as the beginning of the HDR, describes how David is summoned to the court, and relieves Saul from the tormenting influence of the evil spirit. The scene is generally regarded as a unit, and we can easily discover artistic skills comparable to those shown in the "Succession Narrative." For example, the scene begins with YHWH's spirit (רוּחַ)'s turning away (סָרָה) from Saul, and ends with the turning away (סָרָה) of the evil spirit (רוּחַ). Structurally, the scene is composed of an a-b-a' pattern, with the last verse rounding off the scene by relieving the tension raised in the first verse. Moreover, the author's creative usage of language is evident. In addition to the obvious word play between רוּחַ and רוּחַ in v. 23, the author foreshadows – another stylistic feature of the "Succession Narrative" – what is ahead in the narrative through the use of particular verbs. For instance, Saul orders his servants to "see (רָאה)" for himself a lyre-player or a musical therapist (v. 17),

---

91 Gunn, *King David*, 76–81.

and an anonymous servant says that he "saw (ראה)" a suitable man (v. 18). The reciprocal use of the verb ראה functions to foreshadow what follows, because in the following chapters, Saul will be unable to "see" that David is virtuous and loyal, whereas all the others "see" – as Saul ironically ordered them to do so – the true identity of David, the anointed of God.[92] The use of the verbs בקש and מצא has a similar function. Saul is advised to "seek (בקש)" (v. 16), but it is David who "finds (מצא)" (v. 22). This defines the future of Saul and of David in the following chapters. Saul continues to "seek" in his last days (1Sam 19:2,10; 20:1; 22:23; 23:10,14,15,25; 24:3; 26:2,20; 27:1,4; 28:7), but it is not Saul but David who always "finds" (20:3,29; 24:20; 27:5; 30:11). When Saul is "found", the results are tragic: he is caught by David in 24:20, and killed by the Philistines in 31:3,8. Finally, the unit is purely secular, similar to the court history. All the actors are human beings, and there is no mention of God's work in Saul's bringing David in. All these certainly show that the author of the passage was as creative and artistic as that of the "Succession Narrative", and make us wonder whether the style in 1Sam 16:14–23 is drastically different from other scenes in the "Succession Narrative".

Finally, we need to consider the view that sees the peculiarity of the HDR in comparison with the "Succession Narrative" in its fragmentariness. Among those who hold such a view, Rendtorff in particular thinks that the moderate fragmentariness of the HDR is what makes it distinct from other traditions: the HDR is not as fragmentary as the Samuel-Saul tradition, but not as unified as the "Succession Narrative".[93] Larger materials were linked together through the short reports (*kurze Mitteilungen)*, and these short reports reflect the genuine characteristic of the author of the HDR.[94] True, it has been argued that 2Sam 9–20 + 1Kings 1–2 is a self-contained unified work with a great artistic quality, whereas 1Sam 15–2Sam 8 are more fragmentary. However, even as to the "Succession Narrative", no one claims that the work was written by a single author from cover to cover. The author used some older traditions, and the joint is sometimes not perfect as Whybray admits in the case of 2Sam 9–12. He writes, "[t]he first chapters (2Sam 9–12) are somewhat less perfect from the literary point of view, partly because the author has here used an older source and partly because the beginning of the work

---

**92** Polzin thinks that the verb ראה is one of the two key words in 1Sam 16, which provides a guide to the reader as the chapter plays between appearance and reality. Robert Polzin, *Samuel and the Deuteronomist: a Literary Study of the Deuteronomistic History*, part. 2: *1 Samuel* (Bloomington: Indiana University Press, 1993), 152.
**93** Rendtorff, "Beobachtungen," 430.
**94** Rendtorff, "Beobachtungen," 436

is lost."[95] If we admit this, however, it is difficult to maintain that the more fragmentary character of the HDR is a sign of different authorship, because it could have been due to the different degree of availability of the materials at the author's disposal. For instance, we can easily imagine an author who was gathering all the materials about David, in order to write a single story about him. A lot of materials were available to him, but the materials about David's earlier life were relatively rare in comparison with those about the latter part of his life which were more or less a continuous story. And this is not surprising, because David was rather an unknown figure in his early life. In writing the earlier part, the author had to fill up the gaps with "short reports", while he did not need to do so for the narration of David's later days. Consequently, the early part looked more fragmentary and less continuous than the latter part.[96] This shows that there is no reason to exclude the possibility that the same author is responsible for the HDR and the "Succession Narrative." The greater fragmentariness of the HDR might have been due to the relative scantiness of the traditions, which caused the author to create *kurze Mitteilungen*.

### 1.4.3 The stylistic feature as a criterion for source division

To summarize what we have seen so far, the stylistic features of the HDR are so sporadic that we cannot identify the ending from them alone. The stylistic features of the "Succession Narrative" can also be found earlier than in 2Sam 9 – possibly even in the very beginning of the HDR, and it is impossible to distinguish them on the basis of such a criterion. In fact, we need to ask whether style can be a reliable criterion for authorship attribution, especially in the case of the biblical narratives. In the study of literature, the problem of stylistic analysis and the authorship attribution has long been recognized, and most radically, Stanley Fish rejects stylistics entirely, believing that its procedures are an illegitimate leap from description to interpretation.[97] I do not think that stylistic analysis is a totally futile operation, because if we can reach the unconscious level of linguistic usage, it is not impossible to recognize different stylistics and consequently, authorship attribution with reasonable certainty. Besides,

**95** R. N. Whybray, *The Succession Narrative: A Study of II Samuel 9 – 20; I Kings 1 and 2* (London: SCM Press, 1968), 28.

**96** Indeed, not a few scholars now maintain that the HDR was composed to connect the Succession Narrative with the Samuel-Saul narrative. For the most influential representative, see Reinhard Kratz, *Die Komposition der erzählenden Bücher des Alten Testament* (Göttingen: Vandenhoeck & Ruprecht, 2000), 182–188.

**97** Stanley Fish, *Is There a Text*, 70 – 96 (94).

the recent development of computational stylistic analysis seems to throw an optimistic light on the future of such researches. However, even if stylistic analysis is done in its best sense, it is less likely that it alone can do much to identify different sources of the biblical narratives. This can be best shown if we look at the conditions which the computation stylisticians regard as ideal for an authorship attribution on stylistic grounds: (i) The doubtful text is long; (ii) There is a small number of candidates; (iii) There is no significant involvement in the doubtful text by other writers as collaborators or revisers, and very few changes have been made by third parties such as printers and editors between composition and the surviving texts; (iv) There is a lot of securely attributed text by the candidates, in a genre and from a period similar to the doubtful text.[98] It is evident that neither the HDR nor the "Succession Narrative" satisfies any of these conditions. The length of both narratives is extremely short for reliable stylistic analysis, and above all, nobody takes them to be a work by a single author. Almost everybody agrees that the HDR – to a certain extent, even the "Succession Narrative" – is a composite work holding various materials together. In this situation, the attempt to identify different sources on the basis of the stylistic features alone seems totally unpromising.[99]

## 2 The Beginning of the HDR

### 2.1 Criteria for the Identification: Textual Evidence

We have investigated whether we can identify the ending of the HDR on the basis of textual evidence, or formal characteristics, or linguistic features, or style, and the conclusion so far is negative. Now we ask whether we can identify the beginning of the HDR on the basis of the same criteria. Here again, we apply the criteria rather mechanically, and try to consider the literary aspect or the understanding of the whole as little as possible. Among the traditional criteria that might help us to identify the beginning of the HDR, we start again with probably the strongest criterion, the textual evidence. Like 2Sam 5–8, 1Sam 15–16 in the Versions is almost identical with MT, and the MT manuscripts do not hint at

---

**98** Hugh Craig, "Stylistic Analysis and Authorship Studies," in *A Companion to Digital Humanities*, ed. Susan Schreibman, Ray Siemens, and John Unsworth (Oxford: Blackwell, 2004): 273–288 (287).

**99** Eissfeldt already raised a problem in differentiating literary sources on the basis of stylistics in his "Text-, Stil-, und Literarkritik in den Samuelbüchern," *OLZ* 30 (1927): 657–664; "Noch einmal: Text-, Stil-, und Literarkritik in den Samuelbüchern," *OLZ* 31 (1928): 801–812.

any trace of a major break. Thus, we need to investigate how the ancient scribes used special structuring markers while transmitting the text, and find out whether there are such markers in the manuscripts. The Dead Sea scrolls are not very useful here, because they are very fragmentary.[100] The unit delimitation according to the two major Masoretic manuscripts is as follows. The Aleppo Codex has unit divisions in 14:36–48 / 14:49–52 / 15:1–9 / 15:10–15 / 15:16–35 / 16:1–12a /16:12b–16 /16:17–23, and the Leningrad Codex in 14:36–15:9 / 15:10–35 / 16:1–12a / 16:12b–16 / 16:17–23. Both manuscripts support that the HDR may well begin with 16:1, but neither of them sees a major break between 16:1–13 and 16:14–23. This is also confirmed by Codex Vaticanus, according to which one might find the beginning of new units in 15:1 or 16:1 or 17:1, but not in 16:14.[101] It is interesting that these ancient textual witnesses – except Codex Alexandrinus that has larger *Kai*s at the beginning of 15:1; 16:1; 16:14 – contradict the most common view held by modern commentators that there is a major break between 16:1–13 and 16:14–23. As we mentioned earlier, however, this does not tell us definitively where the beginning is found, and we cannot be sure that the unit divisions in the manuscripts correspond to the source divisions. Thus we have to turn to other evidence.

## 2.2 Formal Markers

### 2.2.1 The summary in 14:46–51

As with the question of the ending, we ask whether there is any formal marker that might point to a beginning or an end of a section in 1Sam 14–16. The most obvious candidate for such an indicator is 14:46–51, and indeed, many scholars have regarded these verses as clearly demarcating the end of a section. Wellhausen, for example, sees here the conclusion of the "History of Saul" with the summary of his achievements,[102] and Otto Eissfeldt holds that the pattern of a short survey of the king's wars followed by the list of the cabinet members clearly marks the conclusion of the narrative of the king's reign.[103] If this observation is correct, 14:52 or 15:1 will be the strongest candidate for the beginning, since the next summary appears only in 2Sam 8:16–18. However, the formal indicator

---

**100** 4QSam[A] has only 15:20–21,24–32; 17:3–8, with a demarcating space after 15:31, while 4QSam[B] has 1Sam 15:16–18; 16:1–11, with demarcating spaces after 15:16 and 16:10–11.

**101** 16:14 appears in the middle of the line with no paragraph marker. There is a divisional marker in the left margin, but this is most likely to be a late addition.

**102** Wellhausen, *Composition*, 244.

**103** Otto Eissfeldt, *The Old Testament: An Introduction* (Oxford: Basil Blackwell, 1965), 275–6.

does not give us a decisive clue, because it is not all that clear whether 14:46–51 is pre-deuteronomistic. In fact, several commentators believe that these verses are from a later hand. Budde already recognized the deuteronomistic hand in these verses,[104] and more recently, Timo Veijola assigned them to the first edition of the Deuteronomistic History (DtrG), because the expression סָבִיב בְּכָל־אֹיְבָיו is a term exclusively found in the deuteronomistic literature in the context of the "saviour deliverance",[105] and the use of the participle of the root שׁסה for a designation of Israel's enemy (v. 48) is also deuteronomistic.[106] Of course, this does not necessarily mean that 14:47–51 does not have a concluding character, and certainly, the Deuteronomist wanted to end the Saul cycle there. However, if these verses do not belong to a pre-deuteronomistic layer, we cannot safely exclude what precedes chapter 15 from the HDR on the basis of formal features, because it is possible that the deuteronomistic redactor artificially divided the originally single source with a demarcating formula.

### 2.2.2 The Bridge in 15:35b

Another candidate for the formal marker indicating the beginning of a new section might be found in 16:1 on the basis of the repetition of Samuel's mourning motif in 15:35 and 16:1. Artur Weiser is convinced that 15:35 shows an evidently bridging character, which indicates that 16:1 starts a totally new tradition about David.[107] This seems to fit very well with the most natural view that the HDR begins with the section where David first appears, i. e. 16:1. However, this cannot be argued simply from a formal characteristic, because it is also possible that 16:1 was inserted, picking up the vocabulary used in chapter 15 such as "mourning (אבל)" and "rejected (מאס)", with a view to linking the two chapters. Even if one admits that chapter 15 is linked with 16:1–13 through 15:35b, 16:1 does not show sufficiently clear formal characteristics that can be taken as a marker indicating a new beginning.[108]

### 2.2.3 The Folkloristic Introduction in 17:12

The last and rather surprising candidate for the formal marker which might indicate the beginning of a new section is found in 17:12. Some might find it a bit

---

**104** Budde, *Samuel*, 104–105.
**105** Cf. Deut 12:10; 25:19; Josh 21:44; 23:1; 2Sam 7:1b; 1Kings 5:18.
**106** Veijola, *Königtum*, 79–82.
**107** Weiser, "Legitimation," 326.
**108** Grønbaek, *Aufstieg*, 29,69.

odd to take this verse as the beginning of a source, because it appears in the middle of the David and Goliath narrative. However, considering the discrepancy between MT and LXX[B], it is likely that 17:1–11 and 17:12ff belonged to different traditions, and they were put together in the present order later.[109] And the similarity with 1Sam 1:1 and 9:1 suggests that the verse may well mark the beginning of a David tradition, just as 1Sam 1:1 and 9:1 mark the beginning of the Samuel tradition and the Saul tradition respectively.[110] The question is whether this tradition belonged to the HDR or not, and theoretically, it is not impossible to conclude that the beginning of the HDR is found in 17:12, and 1Sam 16:1–17:11 was a later addition. Scholars have thought this unlikely, because 17:12ff seriously contradicts 16:14–23 which no one excludes from the HDR. Nonetheless, from a formal perspective, 17:12 may well be the beginning of the HDR, and even if it is not, it is certainly the beginning of a certain David tradition. There must have been at least two different traditions about David: one beginning with 16:14–23, and the other with 17:12.[111] We will discuss the implication of the existence of different David traditions later in this monograph.

## 2.3 Phraseology and Style

We have seen so far that there is no tangible evidence such as textual witnesses to help us to identify different sources, and neither can the formal signs give us a decisive clue to the question where the HDR begins. This prompts us to use slightly "higher" tools such as the comparison of phraseology and style. If we

---

**109** Quite a number of scholars, however, maintain that LXX[B] is an abridgement of MT. There is a more detailed discussion in Chapter 4.

**110** 1Sam 17:12 is different from 1Sam 1:1 and 9:1 in that the former begins with the introduction of David, not with the father of the hero. However, this seems to be due to a later modification. Very recently, David Tsumura has suggested that the problematic הזה is not the definite article + demonstrative pronoun, but the demonstrative pronoun used as the relative pronoun like Ugaritic *hnd* ("this"), and argues that 17:12 as it is, nicely follows the previous section. This is an interesting idea explaining the text as we have it, but such a use is unusual both in Hebrew and in Ugaritic. See Wellhausen, *Der Text der Bücher Samuelis*, 105; Driver, *Notes*, 140; McCarter, *I Samuel*, 301; David Toshio Tsumura, *The First Book of Samuel*, (Grand Rapids: Eerdmans, 2007), 446; Cyrus. H. Gordon, *Ugaritic Textbook* (Rome: Pontifical Biblical Institute, 1965), §§6.22, 19.786; Josef Tropper, *Ugaritische Grammatik* (Münster: Ugarit-Verlag, 2000), 229–230.

**111** Cf. Erik Aurelius, "Wie David ursprünglich zu Saul kam (1Sam 17)," in *Vergegenwärtigung des Alten Testaments: Beiträge zur biblischen Hermeneutik; Festschrift für Rudolf Smend zum 70. Geburtstag*, eds. Christopher Bultmann, Walter Dietrich, and Christoph Levin (Göttingen: Vandenhoeck & Ruprecht, 2002): 44–68 (60–64). Aurelius, however, believes that the older tradition begins with 1Sam 17:1. More discussion will follow in chapter 5.

find phraseology or style particular to the HDR somewhere in the early parts of the David tradition, it may help us to identify the beginning of the HDR. Of course, this cannot tell us precisely which verse is the beginning. However, since there is general agreement about the division of chapters 15–16 into three units (15:1–35; 16:1–13; 16:14–23), the investigation of phraseology and style may tell us which units are likely to belong to the HDR, and perhaps which unit is the beginning of the HDR.

As for phraseology, we again ask whether there is any expression peculiar to the HDR, and whether it appears in any of these three passages. The only consideration in chapters 15–16 is the expression "YHWH is with him [David] (יהוה עמו)," and we find its first occurrence in 16:18, with none in chapter 15 and 16:1–13. Therefore, according to the criterion of phraseology, we might conclude that 16:14–23 belongs to the HDR, and 16:14 is its beginning. Such a conclusion is too simplistic, however, because we cannot expect typically HDR phraseology to appear in every unit within the whole HDR. Furthermore, as we saw above, whether the phrase is really peculiar to the HDR is uncertain.

With regard to style, the features which have been mentioned above are considered again. Among those, we first ask whether there is any religious or cultic element in chapters 15–16. 16:14–23 reveals no interest in cultic or religious elements, but is purely a secular story. 16:1–13 seems more concerned with cultic matters, as the initial setting of the anointing appears to be a cultic sacrifice. However, the cultic element in the passage soon evaporates, and as the story unfolds, the atmosphere becomes more like that of the Joseph story. Some see a cultic element in the use of the word נסב in v. 11, as the verb סבב was used of going about the altar as a part of the sacrificial worship.[112] However, whether it has a cultic sense in the present context is far from clear. LXX[B] translated it as "sit down" (κατακλιθῶμεν), and S. R. Driver, followed by many others, maintains that we should take a post-biblical meaning of the word here, or read נשׁב for נסב, and understand it as having the ordinary sense of "sitting at table".[113] Grønbaek, on the other hand, draws attention to the use of the verb סבב in 16:11 and in Gen 37:7, and notes that the setting of the anointing is comparable to Joseph's dream in Gen 37 where the sheaves of Joseph's brothers gather around (תְּסֻבֶּינָה) Joseph's sheaf and bow down to it.[114] In any case, the term does not have a cultic sense, and the cultic element of 16:1–13 is indeed very thin. By contrast, chapter 15 shows the clearest religious or cultic interest, and

---

**112** Smith, *Samuel*, 146.
**113** Driver, *Notes*, 134; McCarter, *I Samuel*, 275; Robert P. Gordon, *I & II Samuel* (Exeter: Paternoster, 1986), 151.
**114** Grønbaek, *Aufstieg*, 70.

the setting is cultic throughout.[115] Therefore, if we make a decision on the basis of the religious and cultic element, 15:1 should be the beginning.

Yet another conclusion is reached, if a different stylistic feature is considered, namely, the quasi-prophetic utterances of unexpected characters about David's future kingship. We find the first example in 16:18 where an unnamed servant in Saul's court summarizes David's personality as if he were predicting the whole of David's career; "I saw a son of Jesse, a Bethlehemite, a player (of the lyre), a valiant man, a man of battle, prudent in speech, a man of good appearance, and YHWH is with him." Neither in chapter 15 nor in 16:1–13, however, have we such a quasi-prophetic utterance. In chapter 15, the (presumably) crucial message of the HDR is declared by Samuel, the main character of the passage; "Since you rejected the word of YHWH, He rejected you from [being] king (v. 23)" and "YHWH has torn the kingdom of Israel away from you, and He will give it to your companion who is better than you (v. 28)". In 16:1–13, it is the narrator who utters a message anticipatorily summarizing what is going to happen later in the HDR; "the spirit of YHWH rushed upon David *from that day forward* (v. 13)". Since the narrator occasionally utters important messages elsewhere in the HDR, 16:1–13 may not be unusual. Yet Samuel's prophecy in chapter 15 is quite different from the usual style of the HDR, for it is the only place where Samuel functions as a prophet in the HDR, with the exception of 28:17 which is often regarded as a later addition.[116] Chapter 15 does seem to be alien to the HDR on the basis of this stylistic feature.

The contradictory results obtained so far lead us to consider the last stylistic feature in the HDR, namely, to what extent each unit shows a trace of intentional structuring. That a narrative has been structured not by accident but deliberately can be known mainly from two indications: (i) it has been chronologically arranged, or (ii) a passage is organically connected with the other parts of the HDR. When it comes to the chronological arrangement, there is a fairly smooth movement in 1Sam 15–16. The visits are arranged chronologically, and all of them seem to fit very well with the flow of the narrative. However, if we ask whether these units are well connected with the rest of the HDR, we get a different answer. Among the three units, 16:14–23 seems best connected with other materials in the HDR. In 18:10 and 19:9, David is described as playing the lyre in Saul's court, and the fact that David is expected to be at the royal table

---

115 But how much was later addition in chapter 15 is arguable. See Artur Weiser, "1 Samuel 15," *ZAW* 13 (1936): 1–28.
116 McCarter, *I Samuel*, 423.

every day (20:25–28) seems to show that David was indeed Saul's armour-bearer as depicted in 16:14–23.

Chapter 15 is less clear in its connection with other materials. One might point to Samuel's last message to Saul in 28:17 which makes a clear allusion to 15:28. However, the relationship between the two verses is elusive. 15:25–29 might be a secondary addition,[117] or 28:17 is a post-HDR addition.[118] Others may see the connection between 15:27 and 24:5, as both verses seem to use the image of tearing the robe as a symbolic act for Saul's loss of kingship. Again, however, the provenance of these two verses is not certain, and moreover, whether the tearing of the robe is deliberately symbolic is another question. Grønbaek argues that chapter 15 is well connected to the rest of the HDR, because it first mentions Judah in 1Sam and designates the Amalekites as the arch-enemy. According to his view, Judah and the Amalekites play very important roles in the later part of the HDR, as it is Judah which provides David with the foothold for his rise to the kingship, and the Amalekites are those whom David utterly destroys just before his rise to the throne.[119] Yet, as we shall see later, whether we can put great emphasis on Judah and the Amalekites depends upon how we understand the overall theme of the HDR. And if they are not that important, the mention of Judah and of the Amalekites may not be particularly significant here.

Finally, 16:1–13 is even less connected to other parts of the HDR. The anointing of David is mentioned only in the later texts such as 1Sam 24:7; 26:9; and 2Sam 1:14; 3:39,[120] and neither 2Sam 2:4 nor 5:3 seem to be conscious of the previous anointing. Weiser thinks that it was due to the compiler's literary strategy and faithfulness to the traditions inherited.[121] However, the composer often uncovers David's future kingship either through minor characters or through his own comment, and it is very unlikely that he keeps silent about the anointing as if he had no interest in it. From the perspective of intentional structuring, therefore, 16:1–13 has to be excluded from the HDR, and chapter 15 is also suspicious.

But such a conclusion is again too simplistic, because even if these units were not written together with other parts of the HDR and thus are not directly connected with them, it is possible that the composer of the HDR could have

---

117 Weiser, "1 Samuel 15," 4–5.
118 McCarter, *I Samuel*, 423.
119 Grønbaek, *Aufstieg*, 26–27.
120 Walter Dietrich, *The Early Monarchy in Israel: The Tenth Century B.C.E.* (Atlanta: Society of Biblical Literature, 2007), 285.
121 Weiser, "Legitimation," 336.

used chapter 15 or 16:1–13 in order to frame the HDR. In other words, while collecting and arranging the already available traditions, the composer could have framed the HDR with a newly created or edited passage. Indeed, both Weiser and Grønbaek think that chapter 15 and 16:1–13 are separate traditions both from the preceding and the following chapters. The point of the argument that the beginning is 15:1 or 16:1 is that the composer of the HDR used an independent tradition to frame the main parts of his work. The frame does not need to be completely integrated into the other materials or to demonstrate a direct connection with the other parts in detail. Rather, the function of the frame would be to introduce the most important elements of the HDR, and the more important question is whether any of these units (15:1–35; 16:1–13; 16:14–23) functions as an introduction by anticipating the essential elements of the HDR, or by revealing the intention of the composer. Now, this implies that whether we can include chapter 15 or 16:1–13 as a part of the HDR, regardless of their connections with other parts, depends heavily upon the understanding of the whole of the HDR and its overall purpose. In fact, this confirms our reluctance to depend too much on style for the decision of the extent of the HDR. Even if a passage does not exactly correspond to the general stylistic feature of the HDR, it could have been used as an imported frame for the main materials.

## 3 How is the Decision Made?

We have investigated so far whether we can identify both the ending and the beginning of the HDR on the basis of textual evidence, or formal characteristics, or linguistic features, or style, and the conclusion so far is negative. Nonetheless, not a few scholars make a decision on the matter, and claim that such and such is the ending and the beginning of the HDR. What leads them to make such a decision even when the evidence is conflicting? In my view, their understanding of the whole plays a crucial role here. In other words, how they understood the whole of the HDR and what they thought the purpose of the composer was is fundamental to their interpretation of the conflicting evidence, or equally convincing evidence. This tells us that we do not make traditio-historical statements only by applying strictly scientific methods to the text,[122] but there is al-

---

[122] For instance, Wolfgang Richter and his school advocate a more rigorous methodical approach to biblical texts. They stress that different methods should be applied in a very orderly manner, without mixing them up. See Wolfgang Richter, *Exegese als Literaturwissenschaft. Entwurf einer alttestamentlichen Literaturtheorie und Methodologie* (Göttingen: Vandenhoeck &

ways a certain interaction between the understanding of the parts and the whole, and textual, linguistic, and redactional criticism is inevitably in conversation with literary criticism. We have already glimpsed how it is so, while we were trying to find the extent of the HDR on the basis of the traditional criteria. But let me elaborate the point by looking at how scholars reach conclusions about the extent of the HDR when there is a range of different evidence. We first look at how decisions about the ending have been made. Three groups of scholars will be discussed for our purpose.

## 3.1 The Decision about the Ending

### 3.1.1 Wellhausen, Steuernagel, Brettler for 8:15–18

Before the hypothesis of the HDR was widely accepted, the majority of scholars held that there was a clear break between 2Sam 8 and 9. Of course, whether there was a division in the source level was debated, and Budde, although he acknowledged a certain level of break between 2Sam 8 and 9, did not recognize a source division.[123] For him, 2Sam 8 was a deuteronomistic insertion, and 2Sam 9 continued the narrative in 2Sam 2–7. However, Wellhausen thought that "the second part of the history of David" is found in 2Sam 9–20 (+ 1Kings 1–2), and these chapters, which constitute a court history located in Jerusalem, are separated from the previous chapters through chapter 8, although the way in which they are joined is similar to that in which 1Sam 15 is joined to 1Sam 9–14.[124] Similarly, Steuernagel held that there was a source division between 2Sam 2–8 and 2Sam 9ff, because the latter's difference in narrative character (*Erzählungscharakter*) and its greater unity make it difficult to assign it to the same source as the former.

Since the hypothesis of the HDR was proposed, however, the view that sees the end of a source in 2Sam 8 has not been widely held. Those who acknowledge the existence of the source about David's early days tended to see the ending of the source much earlier. Recently, however, Brettler revived the view, and argued that the ending of the HDR should be found in 2Sam 8:15. His argument is based on most of the traditional criteria which have been listed above. Formally, the repetition of 2Sam 8:16–18 in 20:23–26 indicates that they were used to demarcate the intervening material as an editorial unit. Linguistically, the syntax of

---

Ruprecht, 1971); Walter Gross, Hubert Irsigler, and Theodor Seidl, eds., *Text, Methode und Grammatik: Wolfgang Richter zum 65. Geburtstag* (St. Ottilien: EOS Verlag, 1991).

**123** Budde, *Samuel*, xvi-xvii.

**124** Wellhausen, *Composition*, 255–256,263.

"noun first followed by unconverted verb" in 2Sam 8:15 is a sign of late biblical Hebrew, and may be from a later redactional layer of the book. Stylistically, 2Sam 8:15 sounds like a concluding formula.[125] As shown above, however, the argument based on these evidences is unsteady. The formal indicator seems to have been inserted by the Deuteronomist, and there is no certainty that the Deuteronomist inserted an additional demarcation where there was already a break in the original source. As to the linguistic evidence, as Brettler himself admits in the endnotes,[126] dating a verse on the basis of a single linguistic feature is precarious, and the statement that the verse "sounds like" a concluding formula seems to have no supporting evidence.

It is not difficult therefore to see that Brettler's decision about the ending largely depends on his understanding of the whole narrative. Indeed, while his argument based on the traditional criteria is presented rather briefly, the discussion about the literary aspect of the HDR and the argument on the basis of it is much more detailed. He separates 2Sam 9ff from the previous material, because the former is a theological unit, whereas the latter is interested in secular, political ideology.[127] This is certainly a question about the genre and the purpose of the HDR, which can be only discussed when one understands the whole. Furthermore, he makes clear that the two materials are distinct thematically, because the material preceding the HDR is favourable to Saul, while that which follows points to David's sins and (the resulting) military weakness.[128] In brief, although there is evidence which can support his view that the HDR finishes in 2Sam 8:15, the factor controlling the insufficient evidence is his interpretation of the whole HDR.

### 3.1.2 Weiser, Mettinger for 7:29

Weiser did not accept the then dominant view that the HDR finishes in 2Sam 5:10 – 12, because in form and content, they are "too lean to be the literary finale of the work". Furthermore, he thinks that the interest of the author was not to describe the historical facts, in which case the ending should be found in 2Sam 5:1–3, but to make clear that David was from the very beginning chosen by God to be the successor to Saul as king over Israel.[129] Then he argues that 2Sam 6 was also a part of the HDR, used by the compiler to serve his purpose,

---

**125** Brettler, *Creation*, 98.
**126** Brettler, *Creation*, 201.
**127** Brettler, *Creation*, 99.
**128** Brettler, *Creation*, 100.
**129** Weiser, "Legitimation," 343.

especially to make David's legitimation more religious and theological. With chapter 6 included, Weiser asks whether the HDR extends to chapter 7, and concludes that the chapter indeed marks the ending of the HDR, as it echoes several leitmotifs of the HDR, whereas chapter 8 is excluded for its interest in historical facts. Of course, he is aware that chapter 7 is different from the other parts of the HDR in form and content. However, as long as the HDR is a composite work, the possibility cannot be excluded that the author used the chapter as the frame.[130] And since he thinks that the chapter serves the *Grundanliegen* of the work very well, it is included in the HDR.

Again, it is not difficult to see that Weiser's argument is very much based on his understanding of the genre and of the *Tendenz* of the HDR. His impression that 5:10–12 lacks the grandeur of a finale prompts him to find the ending somewhere else. His identification of the genre as ideological literature rather than a historical record allows him to go beyond 5:10–12, and to exclude chapter 8. His understanding of the *Tendenz* as the "theological" legitimation of David as successor to Saul prompts him to include chapters 6 and 7 in the HDR. Above all, his judgment that the HDR is a composite work permits him to include slightly different kinds of materials, and to focus the question of the *Grundanliegen* of the work. All these conclusions, however, can be reached only through the understanding of the whole HDR, and it is clear that for Weiser as well as for Brettler, the controlling factor in interpreting the equally plausible evidence is what he thinks is the nature and the purpose of the HDR.

Weiser's view was not accepted by many scholars, but Mettinger expressed a similar view saying, 'Also 5:17–25; 6:1–23, and, in particular, a pre-Dtr form of the prophecy of Nathan made up the conclusion of the work."[131] Apparently, Mettinger attempts to support the view with linguistic evidence which he believes to be more objective. However, as we saw above, his linguistic argument is based on only a couple of lexical occurrences, and it is risky to connect the question of literary authorship with that meagre evidence. By contrast, his judgement that the pre-Deuteronomistic portion in Nathan's prophecy was included in the HDR owes much more to his understanding of the purpose of the HDR as the legitimation of David's succession to Saul as king over "both Israel and Judah". Mettinger basically follows Grønbaek in understanding the purpose of the HDR, and thinks that the continuity between Saul and David is a "theme of infinite importance to the author of the HDR". However, unlike Grønbaek, he allows the narrative to go further than the completion of David's succession in

---

**130** Weiser, "Legitimation," 346.
**131** Mettinger, *King and Messiah*, 46.

chapter 5, because he believes that the theme of the rejection of Saul and the election of David, which is a theological justification of the succession, reappears in a more extended version in the rejection of Saulide descendants in 6:20–23 and the promise of the Davidic dynasty in 7:9 ff.[132] This is certainly a semantic and literary judgment about the perspective of the HDR. In the end, Mettinger too evaluates the ambiguous evidence against the background of his understanding of the whole HDR.

### 3.1.3 Grønbaek, Veijola, McCarter for 5:10

A large group of scholars hold that the ending is found in chapter 5, probably in 5:10. Grønbaek, for instance, objects that the HDR finishes in chapter 7, because the perspective of chapter 7 is too "*umfassend*" for the HDR.[133] He thinks that the dynastic promise and the building of the temple is at the centre of chapter 7, while neither of them – the latter in particular – is important in the HDR. His identification of the genre of the HDR as a "historical work" also prompts him to exclude chapters 6–7.[134] This of course raises questions about 5:17–25 which records an important historical achievement of David for his completion of the succession. The battle against the Philistines was the major historical issue for Saul, and his legitimate successor has to solve the problem better than the unsuccessful predecessor. Grønbaek thus includes 2Sam 5:17–25. However, he is convinced that the concluding character is evident in 5:10–12, and holds that 5:17–25 was transposed from its original position after 5:3 to its present place by a redactor.[135] Now we can notice that when Grønbaek sets the boundary of the HDR, his understanding of the whole HDR plays a key role. His judgment about the perspective of the HDR – including what is important in the HDR – and its main interest is the key to the decision about where the HDR ends.

Veijola is also of the view that the HDR ends with 2Sam 5:10. 2Sam 7 cannot be the ending, because David's prayer has a concluding character that should be attributed to the Deuteronomist, and it has a wider perspective of dynastic theology.[136] Yet, we have already seen how varied are the scholarly views about how much in chapter 7 is deuteronomistic. Most scholars – including Veijola himself – admit that there are pre-deuteronomistic layers in the chapter, and the exclusion of the whole chapter from the HDR should be explained in another

---

**132** Mettinger, *King and Messiah*, 43.
**133** Grønbaek, *Aufstieg*, 33.
**134** Grønbaek, *Aufstieg*, 33.
**135** Grønbaek, *Aufstieg*, 250–254.
**136** Veijola, *Dynastie*, 100.

way. After all, what makes Veijola exclude chapter 7 is also his understanding about the scope or the nature of the HDR: that it focuses on the legitimation of David, and does not go further to dynastic ideology. Veijola's understanding of the whole has preconditioned to a large extent his interpretation of the evidence. In addition to chapter 7, Veijola claims that 2Sam 5:11–8:14 are mainly from DtrG, and tries to support his view by referring to only a couple of the deuteronomistic phrases found in the passages.[137] As mentioned above, however, the claim for deuteronomistic authorship on the basis of only one or two linguistic features is very shaky. It is more like a juggling with uncertain evidences, not acknowledging the actual force behind his decisions.

Veijola's view is followed more recently by McCarter, who argues, "[t]he end of the HDR is found in 2Sam 5:10, where a conclusion is reached with a final reiteration of what we have just described as the theological leitmotiv of the entire story."[138] As to the passages from 5:13–8:18, like Veijola, he suspects that they are the work of the Deuteronomist. McCarter acknowledges that some of those passages betray some connections or contact with the HDR, but he thinks that they were added later to the original HDR, or dislocated from the original position. However, the crucial factor for McCarter's conclusion seems based on his understanding of the whole, and this is most evident when he excludes chapter 7 from the HDR, and says:

> It is true that from the perspective of the text in its present, deuteronomistically edited form chapter 7 can be considered the conclusion, indeed the capstone, of the story of David's rise. But the original, much older narrative said nothing of an eternal kingship or a dynastic promise, the central themes of Nathan's oracle; it attempted nothing more than to demonstrate the legitimacy of David's succession of Saul and, more especially, David's innocence of any wrongdoing in the course of his ascent to the throne.[139]

In other words, his judgement about the purpose and the theme of the HDR (the legitimation of David's succession, and more specifically, the apology for David) makes it unnecessary to include chapter 7 which has a much broader perspective.

**137** Veijola, *Dynastie*, 94–102.
**138** McCarter, *I Samuel*, 30.
**139** McCarter, *II Samuel*, 142.

## 3.2 The Decision about the Beginning

The situation is not all that different for the question of the beginning of the HDR. Here again, scholars make traditio-historical statements, not by applying strictly scientific methods to the text, but by considering various aspects, the most fundamental one of which is how one understands the whole. Three major scholarly views on the matter will be discussed to make this point more evident: Artur Weiser for 16:1, Jakob Grønbaek for 15:1, and Kyle McCarter for 16:14.

### 3.2.1 Weiser for 16. 1

Weiser argues that the beginning of the HDR is found in 16:1. There are several elements that made him reach the conclusion. Some of them are as follows: (i) the finale of the HDR, which he believes is found in 2Sam 7, recalls the event of David's anointing in 16:1–13. "Thus says YHWH of hosts: I took you from the pasture, from following the sheep to be prince over my people Israel..." (7:8); (ii) 15:35 is clearly a redactional bridge to 16:1; (iii) 16:1–13 points to the aim of the HDR whose *Tendenz* is the legitimation of David "through YHWH"; (iv) 16:1–13 fits very well with the intention of the composer, as it makes a good parallel with Saul in 10:1ff; (v) the motif of *"Geistbegabung Davids"* in 16:13 has a clearly thematic importance in the HDR; (vi) 16:1–13 also creates a contrast with 16:14–23, and justifies the spirit-endowed David's replacement of the spirit-lost Saul.[140]

It is not difficult to see that his argument relies very much on his understanding of the whole, namely that the main theme of the HDR is the theological legitimation of David as king over Judah and Israel. The appeal to the finale obviously depends on how we interpret the whole, and as we saw above, the ending of the HDR is a debatable issue. The redactional bridge can also be interpreted differently. It could be 16:1 rather than 15:35 that was reworked to make a link with the rejection of Saul. The other criteria are certainly based on the understanding of the theme or the purpose of the HDR, and the most important factor leading Weiser to decide on 16. 1 is his particular emphasis on the *theological* aspect of the legitimation of *David*. 16:1– 13 makes a good beginning, he seems to believe, because it highlights the point that David's legitimation is fundamentally theological. David's succession is legitimate, because it was first initiated by the anointing of David by God's prophet. One might then ask why he excluded

---

140 Weiser, "Legitimation," 325–328.

15:1–35 where theological de-legitimation of Saul is concerned. The answer might be that, for Weiser, only David was of importance, and Saul was just one of the minor characters through whose mouth the narrator confirms David's future kingship.

### 3.2.2 Grønbaek for 15:1

Grønbaek holds that the HDR begins with 15:1. He agrees with the majority of scholars that chapter 15 is an independent tradition, but argues that the compiler used the already existing tradition to frame the whole HDR. In particular, he thinks that we can see the intention of the composer most clearly in vv. 25–29, which Weiser excludes from the original tradition as secondary, because v. 28 points to the following chapters which Grønbaek characterises not merely as the "David Story" (as Weiser does), but more precisely as "the History of David's Rise to the Kingship over Israel (as a successor to King Saul)."[141] He admits that these verses were influenced by the Ahijah episode in 1Kings 14, but holds that the symbolic act of the tearing of the robe was transformed by the compiler of the HDR to serve the overall purpose.[142]

Again, we can see that the tool which Grønbaek uses in order to control ambivalent evidence is his interpretation of the whole. We already saw one such case when he argued that chapter 15 is well connected with other parts of the HDR, because it introduces Judah and the Amalekites. His view that Judah and the Amalekites are of great importance in the HDR is based on his particular reading of the whole which stresses David's kingship as a successor to Saul. Of course, Weiser also held that the theme of the HDR is the legitimation of David's kingship over Judah and Israel. But for him, the figure of David was so important that he was not so particularly bothered about characterising the narrative as "*Davidsgeschichte*". Grønbaek, however, seized upon this, and put more emphasis on the fact that David was a legitimate *successor to Saul*. For him, in the HDR, "David does not play the only role, but David [plays the role] in relation to King Saul,"[143] and the HDR is about how David rose to the kingship out of the relationship between Saul and David with Samuel's intercessory role. This explains why Grønbaek was keen to include chapter 15 in the HDR. The point that the relationship between David and Saul is at the centre of the HDR is made clearest if the story starts with the rejection of Saul followed by the election of David. If the nar-

---

141 Grønbaek, *Aufstieg*, 26.
142 Grønbaek, *Aufstieg*, 44.
143 Grønbaek, *Aufstieg*, 26.

rative begins with 16:1, the focus moves mainly to David as the one chosen by God, whereas if it starts in 15:1, the spectrum is broadened, and Saul's role as the flawed predecessor or counter-type of David is made evident. His interpretation that Saul is depicted totally positively in the chapters up to 14:51, while he is exclusively the negative opponent of David from chapter 15, is another reason he thinks that the HDR begins with 15:1.[144] This is obviously a thematic observation, which is only possible after understanding the whole.

### 3.2.3 McCarter for 16:14

McCarter, by contrast, claims that the HDR begins with 16. 14. He does not say much to justify this view, probably because it was the view that has been widely accepted by scholars since Wellhausen. The only reason he mentions to explain why he does not include chapter 15 and 16. 1–13 is that they are "secondary with respect to the earliest sources."[145] Apparently, the decision is solely traditio-historical, and quite detached from his reading of the whole. However, both Weiser and Grønbaek thought chapter 15 and 16:1–13 "secondary", but they still included those passages, because they believed that the composer had used either chapter 15 or 16:1–13 as a frame of the HDR. The question is then why McCarter excluded the possibility of seeing those passages as a frame for the HDR used by the compiler of the HDR. One might answer that it is because he is interested in the earliest source. However, if he is really interested in the earliest source, he should have gone further behind the HDR, because the HDR is also a collection of small narratives. The main concern for him is the major sources in the books of Samuel, and there is no reason to exclude chapter 15 or 16:1–13.

In McCarter's case as well, the interpretation of the whole of the HDR was the main force behind his decision. For him, the HDR is above all an apology for David, and how he understood the whole HDR is most clearly revealed when he dates the HDR: "it was written in the atmosphere illustrated by the accounts of the Shimei incident in 2Sam 16:5–14 and Sheba's revolt in 2Sam 20:1–22."[146] This shows that McCarter understands the HDR as a document which was occasioned by a specific political crisis. His comparison of the HDR with the so-called "Apology of Hattušiliš" makes this even more evident. For McCarter, the HDR is closer to political propaganda designed to defend the hero against particular accusations such as David's involvement with a series

---

144 Grønbaek, *Aufstieg*, 29.
145 McCarter, *I Samuel*, 30.
146 McCarter, *I Samuel*, 29.

of murders. Obviously, such a document shows less interest in the divine rejection and election. It would be sufficient for it simply to introduce the main characters (Saul and David) and the main stage (Saulide court). Why, McCarter would ask, does it need to include later secondary passages?

To summarize, as far as textual, linguistic, and stylistic features are concerned, we have evidence too ambiguous to tell us where the HDR begins and ends. However, with the help of a literary reading of the whole, scholars have interpreted ambiguous evidence, and arrived at certain conclusions. And as their readings of the whole HDR were different, they made different decisions on the issue. Of course, when I speak of their "different readings", I do not mean that they understood the matter completely differently from each other. All of them are competent readers, and they rightly understood that the HDR is a pro-Davidic document which aims at legitimating David's succession to Saul. Nevertheless, there is a difference in where the emphasis is laid, and this affects how they decide about the genre, purpose, theme, and eventually the extent of the HDR. For instance, if the emphasis is on the theological aspect of the legitimation of David, one might well follow Weiser's view, whereas if one wants to stress how the legitimation is worked out in the relationship between Saul and David, Grønbaek's view will be more persuasive. If one reads the HDR more like a political document, McCarter's option looks attractive. And this shows that the way in which we understand the whole is crucial to our investigation, and leads us to ask what the appropriate or acceptable method for it is. Without reaching an agreement on the interpretation of the whole HDR, one will have a different view of the extent of the HDR, depending on the different interpretations of the whole. The next chapter will discuss this issue in more detail.

# Chapter 2
# Towards Understanding the Whole HDR

## 1 How We Understand the Whole HDR

In the previous chapter, we saw that the question of the beginning and the ending of the HDR cannot be adequately tackled without understanding clearly what the entire HDR is all about. In other words, unless there is a consensus about its theme, its purpose, and so on, any attempt to identify the beginning and the ending of the source is on shaky ground. Such a literary investigation is like a thread that connects all the pearls of hard evidence to make a necklace, and provides us with a background against which the ambiguities of the evidence can dissolve. Some might say that this point is too obvious to make. Any serious commentator is aware of the fact that we are dealing with a literary text; as with any such text a grasp of its meaning as a whole is already presupposed even if it is not explicitly mentioned. The necessary literary understanding is presupposed, and all the discussions in the previous chapter presuppose that basic operation. But this assumes that the literary understanding is straightforward, and that we have a unanimous interpretation of the HDR. Unfortunately, this is the very source of confusion in our historical-critical discussion, because, as we saw above, the current situation exposes diversity in interpretation, especially when it comes to the question of where the emphasis is laid. This makes it necessary to find out where such differences come from, and if possible, how to assess them, so that we can reach a consensus about the interpretation of the whole HDR. Only when we have reached a reliable agreement about the theme of the HDR and its purpose without error or difference, will we be in a position to compare the various evidences and reach a conclusion about the beginning and the ending of the HDR.

How then can we achieve a convincing, or widely acceptable interpretation of a literary work? It has long been believed that we could interpret a text as objectively as possible by following a series of fairly mechanical rules. Misinterpretation or difference in understanding is caused by inaccurate reasoning of the interpreter, or by insufficient knowledge about the language and historical background. Therefore, what is needed for the correct interpretation is to lay down the rules that will prevent the errors of the interpreter, and to gather objectively as much information as possible. Of course, the evidence or data needed for the perfect decoding of a text may not be sufficient at the moment, or even permanently. Nonetheless, the principle of interpretation is to follow objective rules that are free from subjective and psychological interferences, and produce the result accordingly. The diversity of interpretation in our present case is due to inappropriate reading and insufficient knowledge of the historical background of the text.

This is obviously an extension of the Enlightenment world-view that the only reliable method in science is that of natural science, and if human science is to be a science at all, it should follow as closely as possible the same methodology used in natural science. In the late 19th century, Wilhelm Dilthey saw the problem in making the assumption that human science is an inferior cousin of proper science, and emphasised the importance of the life-world in human sciences, most clearly in history.[1] However, his endeavour to justify the methodological independence of human sciences was not successful, and the dominant position of natural science is not challenged even now.[2] Indeed, Wolfgang Richter's view that the meaning of a text is to be found by following rules most rigorously seems to return again to the assumption which Dilthey wanted to abandon.[3] And when Dietrich and Naumann wrote, "it is methodologically sensible to begin by carefully distinguishing the respective stages – diachronically – from each other, to describe each by itself, and then to observe – synchronically – their biblical juxtaposition and interpenetration and to reflect on the whole,"[4] we can see that they were still following more or less the same assumption. Only after the careful application of presumably already established methods to the text, is it possible to reflect on the text as a whole. Scientific and critical investigation comes first, and interpretation of the whole, which is less pure in its scientific rigour, comes second.

However, understanding any written work involves a more complex process. In particular, the inevitability of circularity in understanding suggests that the interpretation of the whole literary work cannot be done in the same way in which we solve mathematical problems. It is not the result of the application of certain mechanical rules, but something that arises out of a circular move-

---

1 Richard E. Palmer, *Hermeneutics: Interpretative Theory in Schleiermacher, Dilthey, Heidegger, and Gadamer* (Evanston: Northwestern University Press, 1969), 103–105.

2 Hans-Georg Gadamer, *Truth and Method*, 2nd edition (London/New York: Continuum, 2004), 6–7, 278.

3 Wolfgang Richter, *Exegese als Literaturwissenschaft. Entwurf einer alttestamentlichen Literaturtheorie und Methodologie* (Göttingen: Vandenhoeck & Ruprecht, 1971). See also the essays inspired by Richter's methodology in Walter Gross, Hubert Irsigler, and Theodor Seidl, eds., *Text, Methode und Grammatik: Wolfgang Richter zum 65. Geburtstag* (St. Ottilien: EOS Verlag, 1991). This book, however, includes an essay that stresses the necessity of the hermeneutical aspect. See in the volume, Christof Hardmeier, "Hermeneutik und Grammatik. Zum Zusammenhang von Sprachbeschreibung und Textwahrnehmung," 119–140.

4 Dietrich & Naumann, *Samuelbücher*, 66 [Eng. 293].

ment between various elements necessary for the process of understanding. Such a fundamental process of understanding has been called the "hermeneutic circle", and it seems essential to figure out what it is and what it implies, so that we can have a clearer idea about the task we are taking on when we talk about the interpretation of the whole HDR.

## 1.1 The Hermeneutic Circle as Fundamental Structure of Under-standing

### 1.1.1 Friedrich Schleiermacher

Although several people had anticipated the point,[5] it was Friedrich Schleiermacher who first recognized the hermeneutic circle as a fundamental principle of understanding. Immediately before Schleiermacher, Friedrich Ast already observed that there is an element of circularity in interpretation. From the conception of the spiritual unity of the humanities, he argued that the imprint of the spirit of the whole is found in the individual part, and consequently, the whole is understood from the parts, and the parts can be understood only from the whole.[6] Schleiermacher took this up, but extended the principle much further, and argued that it is "of such consequence for hermeneutics and so incontestable that one cannot even begin to interpret without using it".[7] For him, it is rather a general principle of human understanding, and concerns various relationships within the process of understanding. Among them, the following are particularly relevant for our discussion.

First, in addition to the relationship between the parts and the whole, the hermeneutic circle is the basis for understanding the interaction between grammatical and psychological hermeneutics. For Schleiermacher, understanding is possible "only in the coinherence of these two moments",[8] i.e., the grammatical aspect and psychological aspect of understanding. The former reflects the essential linguisticality of communication, and the latter is concerned with how the grammatical utterance reflects the author's individuality. Since Schleiermacher said that the goal of the interpreter is to reproduce the whole internal process

---

**5** Dilthey traces it as early as in the work of Matthias Flacius, a Lutheran theologian in 16th century. See Wilhelm Dilthey, "The Development of Hermeneutics," in *Wilhelm Dilthey: Selected Writings*, ed. and trans. Hans Peter Rickman (Cambridge: Cambridge University Press, 1976), 246–263 (253–254).

**6** Palmer, *Hermeneutics*, 77–78.

**7** Friedrich Schleiermacher, *Hermeneutics: The Handwritten Manuscripts*, ed. by Heinz Kimmerle, trans. by James Duke and Jack Forstman (Missoula: Scholars Press, 1977), 195–196.

**8** Schleiermacher, *Hermeneutics*, 98–99.

of an author's way of combining thoughts,[9] it was once believed that the psychological aspect of understanding had the upper hand in Schleiermacher's hermeneutics.[10] However, Schleiermacher insisted that the tasks of psychological interpretation and grammatical interpretation were "completely equal", and it is necessary to move back and forth between them, without any rule to stipulate exactly how it works.[11] For him, "just as both methods are necessary to obtain complete understanding, so every combination of the two must proceed in such a way that the initial result of the one method will be supplemented by further applications of the other."[12]

Secondly, in terms of more concrete methods used in understanding, there is also a circular movement in the interaction between what he calls "divination" and "comparison". According to Schleiermacher, both grammatical and psychological interpretations involve those two methods: "divination", a mental process similar to intuitive thinking, and "comparison", a method close to critical inquiries. He admits that in psychological interpretation, the greater emphasis is given to divination, but he also made it clear that the two methods are complementary, and work out in a circular movement.[13] Intuitive thinking should be checked by critical enquiries, and at the same time, linguistic and philological study ought to be accompanied and directed by intuitive perception. Only out of this continuous circular movement, is appropriate understanding possible.

Thirdly, there is also a circular movement between the content of a text and its range of effects. "The idea of the work, as the will which leads to the actual composition, can be understood only by the joint consideration of two factors: the content of the text and its range of effects."[14] Those who want to distinguish the meaning of a text and its significance might well be surprised to see that already in Schleiermacher, the possibility of reader-effect theory is to be found. Yet it seems clear that Schleiermacher thought that the relationship between the author and the reader is much more dynamic.

To summarize, Schleiermacher recognized various bipolar dimensions in understanding, and the actual process is conducted on the basis of the fundamental principle that there is a hermeneutic circle between the parts and the whole, grammatical and psychological, divinatory and comparative, content of a text and its range of effects. The implication of the recognition of this principle is

---

9 Schleiermacher, *Hermeneutics*, 188.
10 See in particular Dilthey, "The Development of Hermeneutics," 258–259.
11 Schleiermacher, *Hermeneutics*, 100–101.
12 Schleiermachei, *Hermeneutics*, 191.
13 Schleiermacher, *Hermeneutics*, 151,205–208.
14 Schleiermacher, *Hermeneutics*, 151.

that the interpretation is an ongoing interaction between equally important but very different aspects, and therefore it is impossible to follow some mechanical rules to produce interpretation. Furthermore, since understanding on the basis of such a principle is "an unending task",[15] it is in principle not possible to arrive at a definitive interpretation.

### 1.1.2. Martin Heidegger

The hermeneutic circularity in understanding, which was first set up as the fundamental structure of understanding by Schleiermacher, is brought to an even deeper level by Martin Heidegger. In his *Being and Time*, he shows that the hermeneutic circle is not just a fundamental structure for interpreting individual texts, but an existential structure of Dasein's being or human understanding.[16] Heidegger's immediate concern was of course not hermeneutical, but ontological. However, the pursuit of Being led Heidegger to the insight that his philosophical task was essentially a hermeneutical one. From the awareness that in inquiring about Being, "the meaning of Being must already be available to us in some way",[17] Heidegger concludes that the meaning of Being can be approached only by the analytic of human existence or Dasein. "Therefore *fundamental ontology,* from which alone all other ontologies can take their rise, must be sought in the *existential analytic of Dasein.*"[18] And "the existential analytic of Dasein" is essentially hermeneutical, because the "State-of-mind (*Befindlichkeit*)", a basic mode of Dasein's Being, entails understanding.

Among the insights from Heidegger's analysis of Dasein, his conception of Dasein's basic mode as "Being-in-the world" has made the greatest impact on hermeneutics. Against the traditional view that sees the subject as a separate entity from the object, and sets "I" against "the world", Heidegger sees the essential and inseparable connection between Dasein and the world.

> Dasein is an entity which, in its very Being, comports itself understandingly towards that Being [...] Dasein is an entity which in each case I myself am [...] In each case Dasein exists in one or the other of these two modes, or else it is modally undifferentiated. But these are both ways in which Dasein's Being takes on a definite character, and they must be seen and understood *a priori* as grounded upon that state of Being which we have called "*Being-in-the-world*".[19]

---

15 Schleiermacher, *Hermeneutics*, 41.
16 Martin Heidegger, *Being and Time* (Oxford: Blackwell, 1962).
17 Heidegger, *Being and Time*, 19.
18 Heidegger, *Being and Time*, 34.
19 Heidegger, *Being and Time*, 78.

Here, we can see that Heidegger extended the principle of the hermeneutic circle, so that it now becomes a feature of human existence in general. It is not just a principle between interpreter and text, but one operating at the most fundamental level of human existence.[20] The implication of this for hermeneutics is that the subject is now not the knower standing over against what is to be known, or the objective world. Dasein and world are coterminous in understanding, and accordingly, "the Romantic notion of the sovereignty of the author as the subjective creator of his work, as well as that of the reader who, through the work, 'understands' the author" is denied.[21] Understanding is not the knower's grasping something from what is out there, but an ever-corrigible result of continuous interaction between Dasein and the world.

Another relevant point for our discussion in Heidegger is that interpretation, which he thinks is the "working out of possibilities projected in understanding",[22] has what he calls the "as-structure". This means that we always see something as something, not as a collection of pure perceptions. For example, we hear a noise from a motorcycle as motorcycle noise, not as a conglomeration of pure sounds. In fact, "when we merely stare at something, our just-having-it-before-us lies before us *as a failure to understand it any more.*"[23] Heidegger also claims that interpretation is grounded in a fore-structure the elements of which he calls *fore-having (Vorhabe), fore-sight (Vorsicht),* and *fore-conception (Vorgriff).* In other words, interpretation is always based in something we have in advance (*fore-having*), and in something we see in advance (*fore-sight*), in something we grasp in advance (*fore-conception*). The implication of the fore-structure of understanding and the as-structure of interpretation is that there is no presuppositionless interpretation, and this confirms the fundamental structure of the hermeneutic circle in interpretation. It reveals that "any interpretation which is to contribute understanding must already have understood what is to be interpreted".[24]

In short, with his conception of Dasein as inseparably intermingled with the world and the analysis of the interpretative process as "as-structure" and "fore-structure", Heidegger extends the significance of the hermeneutic circle even further than Schleiermacher, and turns it into something that is going on even be-

---

**20** David Couzens Hoy, "Heidegger and the hermeneutic turn," in *The Cambridge Companion to Heidegger,* ed. Charles B. Guignon (Cambridge: Cambridge University Press, 1993): 170–194 (172).
**21** Kurt Mueller-Vollmer, "Introduction," in *The Hermeneutics Reader* (Oxford: Basil Blackwell, 1986), 1–53 (33).
**22** Heidegger, *Being and Time,* 189.
**23** Heidegger, *Being and Time,* 190.
**24** Heidegger, *Being and Time,* 194.

fore any attempt of interpretation – indeed something that operates in human existence itself. Of course, Heidegger is aware that the traditional view has seen it as *circulus vitiosus*, which is to be avoided and overcome in science by all means. However, his ingenious turn of thought is most evident in his response to such a view. He writes, "*If we see this circle as a vicious one and look out for ways of avoiding it* [...] *then the act of understanding has been misunderstood from the ground up.*"[25] The circle is an essential condition for understanding, and what we need is "not to get out of the circle but to come into it in the right way [...] It is not to be reduced to the level of a vicious circle, or even of a circle which is merely tolerated. In the circle is hidden a positive possibility of the most primordial kind of knowing [...] The 'circle' in understanding belongs to the structure of meaning."[26]

### 1.1.3 Hans-Georg Gadamer

After Heidegger, the positive, or indeed essential nature of the hermeneutic circle in understanding finds a clearer and more developed expression in Gadamer's writings, especially in his *Truth and Method*. As the first step to articulate his version of the hermeneutic circle, Gadamer follows Heidegger's insight that the basic condition of Dasein is "thrownness (*Geworfenheit*)" and temporality, and revives the positive value of "prejudice (*Vorurteil*)" in understanding. Just as metaphysics before Heidegger tried to take away "time" from the discussion about Being, hermeneutics before Gadamer attempted to get rid of "prejudice" of the interpreter, in order to approach the object of interpretation in the purest condition. Consequently, the most important hermeneutical task left to the interpreter was to leave one's immediate situation in the present, and to apply "scientific" method to the text which is presumably kept bio-clean. This seems to have been still at work in Schleiermacher. Although he extended the scope of hermeneutics as a general science, Schleiermacher defined hermeneutics mainly as "the art of avoiding misunderstanding",[27] and basically saw the interpreter as an obstacle to get over. By contrast, Gadamer diagnoses that "the fundamental prejudice of the Enlightenment is the prejudice against prejudice itself, which denies tradition its power",[28] and argues that the idea of overcoming all prejudices is

---

25 Heidegger, *Being and Time*, 194.
26 Heidegger, *Being and Time*, 195.
27 Hans Georg Gadamer, "The Universality of the Hermeneutical Problem," in *Philosophical Hermeneutics*, ed. and trans. David E. Linge (Berkeley: University of California Press, 1976): 3–17 (7).
28 Gadamer, *Truth and Method*, 273.

"naïve openness".[29] We need to recognize the value of "true prejudices", or "a deep accord (*tiefes Einverständnis*)"[30] that is presupposed in every understanding. Indeed, without any prejudice, understanding is an impossible task. For Gadamer, "the historicity of our existence entails that prejudices, in the literal sense of the word, constitute the initial directedness of our whole ability to experience. Prejudices are biases of our openness to the world. They are simply conditions whereby we experience something – whereby what we encounter says something to us."[31]

The reconfiguration of prejudice as conditions of understanding leads Gadamer to his next task – the rehabilitation of authority and tradition. Against the Enlightenment project which sets reason against authority, and freedom against knowledge, Gadamer points out that "authority has to do not with obedience but rather with knowledge".[32] Similarly, there is no need of unconditional antithesis between tradition and reason. Tradition is something that needs "to be affirmed, embraced, cultivated. It is, essentially, preservation".[33] The Enlightenment has persuaded people to believe that accepting authority or tradition is forfeiting reason. But preservation is not an uncritical acceptance or subservient laziness of mind, but a rational and deliberate choice. It is "as much a freely chosen action as are revolution and renewal".[34] To a large extent, this is a development of Heidegger's point already made in his analysis of Dasein. The interpreters are not free-floating subjects which can and must separate themselves from the situation surrounding them. Just as Dasein is always thrown into the world and surrounded by the worldhood, the interpreter is "always situated within traditions".[35] Therefore, "*[u]nderstanding is to be thought of less as a subjective act than as participating in an event of tradition*, a process of transmission in which past and present are constantly mediated."[36]

This finally leads to Gadamer's version of the hermeneutic circle. Gadamer follows Heidegger in holding that "the circle of understanding is not a 'methodological' circle, but describes an element of the ontological structure of understanding".[37] And yet he introduces the term "horizon" to explain the circle

---

**29** Gadamer, *Truth and Method*, 283.

**30** Gadamer, "The Universality of the Hermeneutical Problem," 7.

**31** Gadamer, "The Universality of the Hermeneutical Problem," 9.

**32** Gadamer, *Truth and Method*, 281.

**33** Gadamer, *Truth and Method*, 282.

**34** Gadamer, *Truth and Method*, 283.

**35** Gadamer, *Truth and Method*, 283.

**36** Gadamer, *Truth and Method*, 291.

**37** Gadamer, *Truth and Method*, 294.

more appropriately. The term was already used since Nietzsche and Husserl to stress both the finite determinacy and the possibility of expansion. Both the interpreter and the text exist in their own horizons, and only by transposing oneself into the other's horizon, does the event of understanding come to pass. This however is not a static movement on either side, because horizons "change for a person who is moving. Thus the horizon of the past, out of which all human life lives and which exists in the form of tradition, is always in motion."[38] Therefore, *"understanding is always the fusion of these horizons supposedly existing by themselves"*,[39] and the circle "describes understanding as the interplay of the movement of tradition and the movement of the interpreter".[40]

To summarize, every attempt at understanding involves an inevitable circularity between various dimensions. Indeed, this circle is a fundamental structure of human existence, because we exist by understanding where we are existentially. If we want to launch the task of understanding the whole HDR, therefore, we ought to take this fundamental structure of understanding into account. The hermeneutic circle is inevitably involved in our task, and we need to humbly admit that all our interpretations are provisional, and open to further improvement. We are all conditioned in our understanding by our history and our temporality, and what we can do is to find the best possible interpretation in the given moment of the continuous hermeneutic circle.

## 1.2 Indeterminacy of Meaning?

Although now everybody agrees that there is an element of circularity in the process of interpretation, quite a number of scholars are concerned that too much emphasis on it can endanger the possibility of objective interpretation. They wonder whether the acknowledgement of the circle makes it impossible to decide which is the better of a number of interpretations. To put it more simply, they suspect that the promotion of the hermeneutic circle can end up with rejecting the very notion of an objective and valid meaning of a text, and force us to accept the fundamental indeterminacy of meaning. Indeed, if we accept the hermeneutic circle as fundamental in all understanding, it is not difficult to go further and agree that the meaning of a text goes beyond its author, "not just occasionally but always".[41] And if the meaning of a text is disconnected

---

**38** Gadamer, *Truth and Method*, 303.
**39** Gadamer, *Truth and Method*, 305.
**40** Gadamer, *Truth and Method*, 293.
**41** Gadamer, *Truth and Method*, 296.

from the authority of the author, it might well seem that there is no control over the interpretation, and no one can tell us which interpretation is valid, or at least better.

This has prompted the emergence of a group of critics who opposed such "phenomenological" hermeneutics. Of course, these do not deny the role of the interpreter in understanding. However, they insist on an essential distinction between what is in the text and the application of it. Schleiermacher already held to the distinction, and among more recent scholars, Emilio Betti stresses that there is an essential distinction between *Auslegung* (interpretation) and *Sinngebung* (the interpreter's function of conferring meaning on the object), and criticizes Gadamer for lumping them together.[42] Similarly, E. D. Hirsch laments the situation that "verbal meaning" and "significance" are confused in a certain branch of hermeneutics.[43] "Meaning" is what the text says, while "significance" is what the interpreter makes of it, and the objective of hermeneutics is "not to find the 'significance' of a passage for us today but to make clear its verbal meaning".[44] He admits that the interpretation of the significance is also meaningful – or even "more valuable"[45], but such a task is left to literary criticism not to hermeneutics. Hermeneutics is rather "the modest, and in the old-fashioned sense, philological effort to find out what the author meant",[46] whereas Heideggerian hermeneutics, by blurring the borderline between meaning and significance, mixes all up, threatening the objectivity of interpretation. As the object of scientific understanding, the meaning of a text should be fixed and immutable, and can be discovered by carefully applying scientific methods, and the validity of interpretation should be measured by the author's historical intention.

Although the concern for securing the objectivity of interpretation is understandable, at least a certain degree of indeterminacy of meaning cannot be denied, since the idea of an absolutely clear distinction between meaning and significance is not very convincing. Indeed, Hirsch modifies his view later, and admits that it is impossible to make a cut-and-dried distinction between meaning and significance. The author's intention, as Hirsch's own example of Shake-

---

**42** Emilio Betti, "Hermeneutics as the general methodology of the Geisteswissenschaften," in *Contemporary Hermeneutics: Hermeneutics as Method, Philosophy, and Critique*, ed. Josef Bleicher (London: Routledge & Kegan Paul, 1980): 51–94.
**43** E. D. Hirsch, *Validity in Interpretation* (New Haven: Yale University Press, 1967), 255.
**44** Hirsch, *Validity*, 252–254; Palmer, *Hermeneutics*, 61.
**45** E. D. Hirsch, "Meaning and Significance Reinterpreted," *Critical Inquiry* 11 (1984): 202–25 (202).
**46** Hirsch, *Validity*, 57.

speare's sonnet 55 shows, might well be an open-ended one, and future applications of meaning could be a part of the author's intention. Besides, since the writing inevitably presupposes more spatial and temporal distance of the interpreter than speaking, the intention of the writer is more likely to be future-oriented, and takes a certain freedom of the reader for granted.[47] Above all, when it comes to biblical narrative, which is undeniably religious in its essence, we cannot rule out the possibility that "an essential aim of the innovative technique of fiction worked out by the ancient Hebrew writers was to produce a certain indeterminacy of meaning, especially in regard to motive, moral character, and psychology".[48]

Despite the acknowledgement that "certain present applications of a text may belong to its meaning rather than to its significance", Hirsch still tries to keep his distance from hermeneutics along the lines of Gadamer, and writes, "[t]he chief divergence is that Gadamer argues for the necessity of differences of meaning, and I for the possibility of sameness of meaning, in different applications of a text."[49] Probably, Hirsch here makes a fair point, because it is absurd to believe that the meaning of a text is limitlessly expandable, changing every time it is read. However, it seems unlikely that Gadamer really meant the indeterminacy of meaning in the same sense that Hirsch does. Gadamer regards Paul Valéry's objection to Goethe's romanticised view of authors that stresses the reader's right to create meaning as "an untenable hermeneutic nihilism", and makes clear that we should not transfer "the authority of absolute creation" to reader and interpreter.[50]

As to Betti's similar criticism, Gadamer says that his purpose is "not to offer a general theory of interpretation and a differential account of methods (which Emilio Betti has done so well) but to discover what is common to all modes of understanding and to show that understanding is never a subjective relation to a given 'object' but the history of its effect".[51] What concerns Gadamer is to deny the too neat distinction between the subject and the object, reader and text, and consequently, to free us from the guilt of being temporal and limited, or from the inferiority complex of doing "humanities" rather than natural sci-

---

**47** Hirsch, "Meaning and Significance Reinterpreted"; For criticism of Hirsch's intentionalism, see David Hoy, *The Critical Circle: Literature, History, and Philosophical Hermeneutics* (Berkeley: University of California Press, 1978), 28ff; Georgia Warnke, *Gadamer: Hermeneutics, Tradition and Reason* (Oxford: Polity Press, 1987), 43–48.
**48** Robert Alter, *The Art of Biblical Narrative* (New York: Basic Books, 1981), 12.
**49** Hirsch, "Meaning and Significance Reinterpreted," 212–215 (214).
**50** Gadamer, *Truth and Method*, 82.
**51** Gadamer, *Truth and Method*, "Foreword," xxviii.

ence. Indeed, we might well be reminded of Gadamer's remark that he did "not remotely intend to deny the necessity of methodical work within the human sciences".[52] Besides, considering Gadamer's talk of "superior understanding" and "higher universality",[53] it seems unlikely that Gadamer had in mind the fundamental indeterminacy of meaning in the relativist sense, when he claims that the meaning of a text is open. Rather, as Richard Palmer observes, their difference partly comes from the different views about the purpose of hermeneutics,[54] and the recognition of circularity in understanding should not be interpreted as promoting the view that the meaning of a text is essentially indeterminate. It only reminds us that we are on the journey toward the meaning of a text, so we should not claim an unchallengeable authority over the meaning of a text.

### 1.3 Nothing New Under the Sun?

If Betti and Hirsch were concerned that the emphasis on the hermeneutic circle inculcates too liberal a view of meaning and interpretation, Habermas and Apel are critical of its implied conservatism. It is undeniable that we are inevitably affected by what we have already received from the past, and in this sense, our understanding is, to use Gadamer's terminology, "a historically effected event",[55] or "the interplay of the movement of tradition and the movement of the interpreter."[56] Habermas therefore acknowledges the value of such recognition, as it helps to pull down the false objectivism claimed by natural science and aspired to by the human sciences. He also celebrates the retrieval of the value of application in understanding, and writes of Gadamer's work, "I find Gadamer's real achievement in the demonstration that hermeneutic understanding is linked with transcendental necessity to the articulation of an action-orienting self-understanding."[57] Nevertheless, Habermas sees a potential danger in the view that the hermeneutic circle is a fundamental structure of every understanding, particularly because he thinks that such a view leads to uncritical accept-

---

52 Gadamer, *Truth and Method*, "Foreword," xxvi; "On the Scope and Function of Hermeneutical Reflection," in *Philosophical Hermeneutics*, ed. and trans. Linge, 26.
53 Gadamer, *Truth and Method*, 304.
54 Palmer, *Hermeneutics*, 59.
55 Gadamer, *Truth and Method*, 299.
56 Gadamer, *Truth and Method*, 293.
57 Jürgen Habermas, "A Review of Gadamer's *Truth and Method*," in *The Hermeneutic Tradition. From Ast to Ricoeur*, eds. Gayle L. Ormiston and Alan D. Schrift (New York: SUNY, 1990), 213–244 (230).

ance of authority and to underestimation of the reflective power of reason, which will make radical social renewal impossible. This is made explicit in the course of his debate with Gadamer.

First of all, Habermas is against Gadamer's identification of authority with knowledge. For Habermas, "[i]f the framework of tradition as a whole is no longer regarded as a production of reason apprehending itself, then the further development of tradition fostered by hermeneutic understanding cannot eo ipso count as rational".[58] Contrary to Gadamer's enclosed structure of human reflection according to which the subject cannot be free from the effect of history, Habermas believes, "[a] controlled distanciation (*Verfremdung*) can raise understanding from a prescientific experience to the rank of a reflected procedure. In this way hermeneutic procedures enter into the social sciences."[59] Moreover, Habermas thinks that Gadamer's critique of a false objectivistic self-understanding does not necessarily lead to "a suspension of the methodological distanciation of the object, which distinguishes a self-reflective understanding from everyday communicative experience".[60] On the basis of this rests Habermas's faith in the capacity of the reflected appropriation of tradition which "breaks up the nature-like (*naturwüchsige*) substance of tradition and alters the position of the subject in it".[61] "Gadamer fails to appreciate the power of reflection that is developed in understanding", and his "prejudice for the rights of prejudices certified by tradition denies the power of reflection".[62] Consequently, Habermas argues that a hermeneutic approach should restrict itself, and calls for "a reference system that goes beyond the framework of tradition as such."[63] Of course, Habermas acknowledges the limitation of the reflective power, but he is fiercely against any implication that "reason remain[s] stuck on the path of a relative idealism",[64] because he is convinced, "[s]uch a reference system can no longer leave tradition undetermined as the all-encompassing; instead it comprehends tradition as such and in its relation to other aspects of the complex of social life, thereby enabling us to designate the conditions outside of tradition under which transcendental rules of world-comprehension and of action empirically change."[65] And psychoanalysis can be the model for such a reference system or the regulative principle.

---

58 Habermas, "A Review," 233–234.
59 Habermas, "A Review," 234.
60 Habermas, "A Review," 235.
61 Habermas, "A Review," 236.
62 Habermas, "A Review," 237.
63 Habermas, "A Review," 238.
64 Habermas, "A Review," 239.
65 Habermas, "A Review," 241.

Just as psychoanalysis helps patients to overcome their symptomatic behaviours "through the combined use of causal explanation and deepened self-understanding", critical hermeneutics can help the interpreters to break the bonds of false tradition.[66]

Gadamer responded to Habermas's criticism mainly by appealing to the universality of hermeneutic experience. Although he acknowledges the value of methodical sciences and the importance of the renewal, he thinks that such a development cannot be done outside the framework of tradition. What we can achieve is not something totally new, but "a new and distinct familiarity".[67] To believe that it is possible to achieve something absolutely new which would do without the power of tradition is, according to Gadamer, merely a "naïve and unreflective historicism".[68] As to Habermas's stress on the power of reflective reason, Gadamer insists that we should be aware of our limitation and finitude, and criticises Habermas for granting "a false power" in the spirit of the Enlightenment.[69] Social renewal on the basis of such a powerful reflection can become another dogmatism, and we may have to suffer from such a misinterpretation of reflection.[70] Gadamer then claims that we should be more moderate in hoping for what is new. Human beings are ceaselessly forming a new preunderstanding in the process of learning the "untiring power of experience", and this can guarantee that we will not be stuck in the inescapable circle. Strictly speaking, it is not a circle, but a spiral movement that is happening in understanding. Finally, regarding the "reference system" the model of which for Habermas is psychoanalysis, Gadamer returns to the model of "play" in understanding. "A game partner who is always 'seeing through' his game partner, who does not take seriously what they are standing for, is a spoil sport whom one shuns."[71]

The so-called Gadamer-Habermas debate went on for some time, and the detailed discussion goes beyond the limits of this monograph. The view that, even if it is true that all understanding presupposes previous knowledge of some sort, reason is able to break off the tradition, and is genuinely capable of initiating something new is quite convincing. If our hermeneutic reflection prescribes that we cannot go beyond the already existing border of tradition, such herme-

---

66 A similar view is expressed in Karl-Otto Apel, "Scientistics, Hermeneutics, Critique of Ideology: An Outline of a Theory of Science from an Epistemological-Anthropological Point of View," in *The Hermeneutical Reader*, ed. Mueller-Vollmer, 321–345 (341).
67 Gadamer, "On the Scope and Function," 25.
68 Gadamer, "On the Scope and Function," 29.
69 Gadamer, "On the Scope and Function," 33.
70 Gadamer, "On the Scope and Function," 34–35.
71 Gadamer, "On the Scope and Function," 41.

neutics will be relegated to merely a device for defending the status quo of the society. The possibility of something utterly new should be open, and in this sense Habermas's concern is perfectly justifiable. Nevertheless, the absence of a fixed criterion such as Habermas's "reference system that goes beyond the framework of tradition as such" does not necessarily lead to the denial of our capacity to evaluate the plausibility of competing interpretations, and to distinguish the better interpretation from the worse. Rather, as Richard Bernstein claims, "Gadamer's analysis of understanding and the hermeneutical circle shows us that we can and do make comparative judgments in concrete cases and that we can support them with the appeal to reasons and argumentation."[72] Habermas thinks that this is not objective enough. But we know from our experience that the innocent and often admirable desire to reach the ideal often ends up with a terrible disaster, precisely because we aspired to something more certain, and forgot the limitation of our reflective power. Habermas's criticism is certainly valuable, and the critique of the framework in which we find ourselves should be open to a new perspective. However, it seems too optimistic and potentially dangerous to believe that we can find a reference system as Habermas envisages. Here Gadamer seems to have more to say: "What man needs is not just the persistent posing of ultimate questions, but the sense of what is feasible, what is possible, what is correct, here and now."[73]

## 1.4 Relevance of Hermeneutical Reflection to Our Question

The discussion so far tells us that we cannot maintain that the appropriate understanding of the whole HDR can be done by simply decoding the signs, or by using some methodical techniques. It involves a much more complicated interpretative process, maybe so complicated that we may well be discouraged from getting involved in any discussion of this sort. The whole discussion of philosophical hermeneutics may sound totally irrelevant to our task of identifying the beginning and the ending of the HDR. However, as repeatedly argued above, the understanding of the HDR as a whole is essential to our historical-traditional investigation, and without appropriate hermeneutical reflection, a particular interpretation of the whole can be hastily presupposed and be granted an unchallengeable status. Then, without being aware of it, we may find our-

---

72 Richard Bernstein, *Beyond Objectivism and Relativism* (Philadelphia: University of Pennsylvania Press, 1983), 196.
73 Gadamer, *Truth and Method*, xxxiv.

selves justifying what we already take for granted with "scientific" methods and "hard" evidence. The reflection on the inevitability of the hermeneutic circle in this sense helps us to be aware of what we are doing, and keeps us from hoping for the impossible and from a false pretence of being objective.

Furthermore, our hermeneutical reflection – the structure of the hermeneutic circle in particular – can provide a productive impetus for clearing out unnecessary antitheses within recent biblical scholarship. It makes us realize that there is no one correct way to penetrate a text, and thus no need to proclaim one preferred approach to the exclusion of all others. Elements of all the newer approaches such as new criticism, intertextual reading, and reader-response criticism inevitably happen when we attempt to understand a text, and we do not select one of them for a particular reason. Hermeneutical reflection on the interpretative process also helps us to see that the so-called synchronic approaches and the diachronic approaches are not contradictory, but a simultaneous operation, both elements of which are essential for a better understanding of the biblical text. One might well think that understanding the whole is purely a synchronic operation. However, as we shall see below, even the genre, theme, and purpose of a piece of literature cannot be figured out appropriately without diachronic information. All these indicate that the hermeneutical reflection has direct relevance to the question of the beginning and the ending of the HDR, because they tell us that the demarcation cannot be discovered by any particular method, whether it is historical-critical or literary. Rather, it will be the result of various operations, and we will not hesitate to call the results of our research scientific. Now let us look more concretely at how different insights work together in a circular or spiral movement, giving an impetus for a fresh understanding of the HDR.

## 2 Synchronic Approaches[74]

Only when we consider various aspects and approaches to the text, can the HDR be appropriately understood, and it is almost impossible therefore to pinpoint the starting point – not only in its importance, but also in its order. Nonetheless, we need at least a heuristic point to start with, and I propose that we should

---

**74** The term "synchronic approach" can have a wider meaning, and does not exclude historical aspects. However, it is now exclusively reserved for an interpretation of the "Endgestalt". See Erhard Blum, "Von Sinn und Nutzen der Kategorie 'Synchronie' in der Exegese," in *David und Saul im Widerstreit – Diachronie und Synchronie im Wettstreit*, ed. Walter Dietrich (Göttingen: Vandenhoeck & Ruprecht, 2004), 16–30 (16–19).

begin with the reading of the text as we have it. This sounds so obvious that one might well laugh at its lack of novelty. However, recent developments in biblical scholarship have made the issue more complicated than it first sounds, and there is a need of further clarification. I want to make clear first that I am not suggesting here that the so-called literary criticism comes first; and the doctrine of "reading the text as it is" should be the obvious starting point in understanding. Since the emergence of New Criticism in the early 20th century and that of Structuralism soon afterwards, reading the final form has been influential in biblical studies. In particular, Robert Alter's and Robert Polzin's readings of the narratives in Samuel have made a considerable impact, turning the tide against the "excavative" work of biblical scholarship of the time.[75] Thus when I say that the understanding of the HDR begins with reading the text in its final form, one might think that I am in the league of those "new" literary critics or of the structuralists. However, my decision about the starting point is based on a different reason. I suggest reading the final form, not because I am against the traditional "excavative" approach, nor because I have already seen the aesthetic beauty and seamless integrity of the HDR or the unconscious working-out of universal human mentality in the text, but because the final form is the only available source for us. Nobody has seen the HDR except in its final form, and thus nobody gets the sense of it from anything other than the final form. Whether the HDR or the books of Samuel taken as a whole have a "beautiful integrity" is secondary to the question what the HDR is about, because "only when we understand it, when it is 'clear' to us, does it exist as an artistic creation for us".[76] Only after we have a general idea of a work, will we be able to see whether it is a seamlessly integrated piece of literature or rather a collection of diverse traditions. As John Barton points out, the semantic operation is prior to the historical inquiries, and the argument for a "seamless unity" among the literary critics assumes already a certain historical concern.[77]

Of course, even the most basic semantic operation should be based on certain diachronic information, most importantly, about the language used in a particular time period and the socio-political background of the text. Without considering such historically influenced aspects, reading is impossible and thus there can be no understanding. Therefore, Sternberg's point should be generally

---

**75** Alter, *The Art of Biblical Narrative*; Robert Polzin, *Samuel and the Deuteronomist. A Literary Study of the Deuteronomistic History*, Part Two, *1 Samuel* (Bloomington & Indianapolis: Indiana University Press, 1989).

**76** Gadamer, *Truth and Method*, 79.

**77** John Barton, "Historical Criticism and Literary Interpretation," in *Crossing the Boundaries*, eds. Stanley E. Porter, Paul Joyce, David E. Orton (Leiden: Brill, 1994): 3–15 (8–9).

maintained that just as "the operations of reading must intervene between the encounter with the extant text and its approval, reshaping, or decomposition", so does the intervening "literary treatment" rest on "a variety of assumptions about the source: the acceptability of the text, the underlying language system, the implied world picture, the operative codes of form and meaning".[78] It is impossible to tell which comes first among the two, and maybe it is unnecessary to do so in whatever way. Nonetheless, if we push the question further to its foundation, we can affirm that the understanding of the whole comes prior to that of the parts. Here Heidegger's existential analysis of Dasein can be helpful. The existential mode of being of Dasein is to understand *Befindlichkeit*, and the understanding of *Befindlichkeit* belongs to the understanding of the whole, because we perceive something always *as* something, rather than the conglomeration of the parts recognized separately.[79] As Gadamer mentioned, "[p]ure seeing and pure hearing are dogmatic abstractions that artificially reduce phenomena. Perception always includes meaning."[80] This is true even when we want to figure out what a certain word means, because the knowledge of a word presupposes some level of understanding of the whole. *Qui non intelligit res, non potest ex verbis sensum elicere*, and the attempt to grasp the whole – even if it is merely provisional – precedes any attempt to know the details. In this sense, it is not just heuristically, but phenomenologically more appropriate to approach the text first in its final form. In understanding the HDR as a whole, what actually happens first is that we read the whole as we have it.

## 2.1 In the Text: Literary Artistry of the Narrative

Reading the text as it is, although it sounds most simple and basic, is far from uncomplicated, however. One reads a text not just by decoding the signs printed on the paper, but reading requires a high degree of literary sensitivity, and the contribution of the New Critics and of Structuralism – Alter and Polzin in particular – is the first to be appreciated. Whether it is completely interfused with theological, moral, or historiosophical vision,[81] or it is a part of the biblical poetics together with ideological and historical principles,[82] the literary art and the aes-

---

**78** Meir Sternberg, *The Poetics of Biblical Narrative. Ideological Literature and the Drama of Reading* (Bloomington: Indiana University Press, 1987), 18.
**79** See above, 74–77.
**80** Gadamer, *Truth and Method*, 80.
**81** Alter, *The Art of Biblical Narrative*, 19.
**82** Sternberg, *The Poetics of Biblical Narrative*, 41–46.

thetic element of the biblical narratives affect how we understand them. "[T]he minute choice of words and reported details, the pace of narration, the small movements of dialogue, and a whole network of ramified interconnections in the text"[83] directly influence on how we understand the genre, theme, and purpose of a narrative, so that we cannot do without the close reading of the text and the sense of how it is. A concrete example of how it is so can be found in the Jonathan narratives in the HDR. Although it is widely agreed that the Jonathan narratives function to legitimate David's succession to Saul, a closer look at the text and attention to its literary artistry can suggest that the purpose of the narratives is not as straightforward as has been widely believed.

From the very first reading, it is not difficult to notice that Jonathan in 1Sam does not look very real. Despite his important position as the crown prince, his role in the story of Saul's fall and David's rise is merely subsidiary, and his unrealistically noble character makes a stark contrast with the highly sophisticated and thus very realistic protagonists Saul and David. Moreover, the Jonathan passages (1Sam 18:1–5; 19:1–7; 20:1–42; 23:15b–18) seem very much independent of their context, and the other parts of chapters 18–23, with the single exception of 22:8, do not seem to be aware of Jonathan's existence.[84] By contrast, Jonathan as a character in 1Sam 18–23 works so well for the legitimation of David's succession to Saul: He loves David from the first moment of their encounter, and remains faithful to the end. Although he is the most legitimate successor of troubled Saul, he gives up everything for his friend David. Indeed, even a close reading of the narratives confirms that Jonathan exists in the HDR only for David. He communicates to the reader how lovable and valuable David is by begging for David's friendship (1Sam 20:14–17), how unfit Saul is as king by becoming the target of his own father's spear (1Samuel 20:27–33),[85] and how David's succession is divinely sanctioned, by announcing his future kingship in a prophetic manner, replacing the failed prophet Samuel (1Sam 23:17).

However, if we pay more attention to the delicate nuances of the narrative, a different reading of the Jonathan passages is possible, according to which Jonathan's function in the narrative is at least ambiguous, and possibly anti-Davidic, revealing David's darker side. For instance, the recognition of "the technique of

---

**83** Alter, *The Art of Biblical Narrative*, 3.

**84** David Jobling, *1 Samuel* (Berit Olam; Collegeville: The Liturgical Press, 1998), 95.

**85** According to the vocalization of MT, Saul actually cast (וַיָּטֶל) the spear at Jonathan. However, LXX has καὶ ἐπῆρεν, the Vulgate *et arripuit*, and Targum has וזקף. All these witnesses seem to read וַיִּטֹּל for MT's וַיָּטֶל, and suggest that Saul did not actually cast the spear, but just lifted it up. In any case, the intention is clearly expressed by the following לְהַכֹּתוֹ "to strike him", and Saul is depicted as mad enough to deserve dethronement.

contrastive dialogue", which functions to differentiate characters in the biblical narratives,[86] helps us to see the hidden aspects of David. More concretely, the evident contrast between ever-communicating Jonathan and puzzlingly silent David discloses the calculating and unloving character of David. In the Jonathan passages, more than one third of the verbs used of Jonathan as the subject (approximately 18 verbs out of 48 verbs) are related to Jonathan's communicating either with David or with Saul, and saying (אמר), reporting (הגיד), and answering (ענה) are his main activities. The transparency of Jonathan in dialogues makes a stark contrast with the secretiveness of David who only speaks once to Jonathan in the relevant passages, only for his own security (1Sam 20:1–10). As a persecuted person, this is perfectly understandable, but the way in which the dialogues are constructed makes David's secretively calculating character stand out. Moreover, in contrast with Jonathan – and indeed all other characters in the HDR – who is reported repeatedly to "love (אהב)" David throughout the narrative, David never uses the same verb.[87] And if we follow Alter's observation that the exclusion of a particular lexical item is quite important,[88] we can discern another montage of David here: in the narrative, David is not a loving person. And if this is the way the narrative depicts David, we might wonder whether the purpose of the HDR to which the Jonathan passages belong was just apologetic, as many think.

Besides, the attention to the repetition of a particular word prompts us to reconsider the genre of the Jonathan narrative and the HDR. For example, in 1Sam 18:4, we come across a rather detailed description of how Jonathan takes off (וַיִּתְפַּשֵּׁט) his robe and gives everything to David, and similarly in 19:24, the situation is clearly explained how Saul takes off (יִפְשַׁט) his garment and lies down naked under the influence of the spirit. At a first glance, these verses are unconnected, and simply mean that Jonathan loved David extremely, and Saul was mad. But if we draw attention to the "network of ramified interconnections in the text"[89] through the repeated word "taking off" using the same root פשט, we may wonder whether the verb was used to turn the two apparently different events into a pair, and raises an important question to the reader. "Will you willingly give up like Jonathan what you have for David, and be an eternal friend of David's? Or, like Saul, will you be forced to give up what you have, and go

---

**86** Alter, *The Art of Biblical Narrative*, 72.
**87** More precisely, the narrator does not make David the subject of the verb. See John Jarick, *2 Chronicles* (Sheffield: Phoenix, 2007), 84–86.
**88** Alter, *The Art of Biblical Narrative*, 180.
**89** Alter, *The Art of Biblical Narrative*, 3.

mad?"[90] If this is what the verses actually mean, then the text is not just about Jonathan's love of David and Saul's madness. It may be more about the reader and their political positions. Then, the genre of the narrative might not be folklore or a story, but a piece of political writing.

Finally, attention to the technique of repetition can prompt the reader to question whether Jonathan was really naïve[91] and accords with the picture of "the *anima candida*... a real noble man"[92] without ambiguity. According to Alter, the biblical narratives express a particular message by repeating previous dialogues with a sophisticated change.[93] For instance, while repeating verbatim the lines which Nathan gave before the meeting with the old king David, Bathsheba adds two words בַּיהוָה אֱלֹהֶיךָ (1Kings 1:17). This small addition reveals however quite a lot about Bathsheba, especially the picture of "the distressed mother and suppliant wife" who does not hesitate to appeal to – possibly to "make wrongful use of" – God's name, in order to protect her son and herself.[94] A similar case is found also in the HDR, in the scene where Jonathan repeats David's words to Saul, but with some small changes (in 1Sam 20:6,28–29). Seeing that Jonathan additionally appeals to the family pressure for David's absence, Alter thinks that Jonathan's expansion was designed to defend David from Saul, but only to produce an opposite effect. However, it is equally possible that the small changes tell us about a certain aspect of Jonathan's character, especially when Jonathan uses the verb מלט (get away) for David's רוץ (run). Alter supposes that Jonathan used the verb inadvertently,[95] but if, as Alter himself argues, a small change in repetition is a well-established technique in the biblical narratives to convey a certain message, Jonathan's choice of the verb, which is used almost exclusively to refer to David's escape from Saul (1Sam 19:10–12,17–18; 22:1; 23:13; 27:1), might reveal something less innocent in Jonathan's character. That is, we could glimpse some sort of "passive aggression" in Jonathan's rather exaggerated naivety and goodwill, which in fact aggravates the relationship between David and Saul. In fact, it is plausible that Saul's obsession with David

---

**90** Possibly, Jonathan's willingness to give up is sensed from the force of the hithpael form of the verb, in contrast with Saul's taking off in the qal form. When used with an accusative (here, מְעִיל), the hithpael verb can have a connotation of performing an act for "one's own special interest" (G-K, § 54 f). Then, the use of the verb already indicates that the giving up serves the interest for those who give up. It is as if saying, "Give in to David! It is for your own interest!"
**91** Robert Alter, *The David Story. A Translation with Commentary of 1 and 2 Samuel* (New York: W.W. Norton, 1999), 123.
**92** Hertzberg, *Samuel*, 172.
**93** Alter, *The Art of Biblical Narrative*, 97–98.
**94** Alter, *The Art of Biblical Narrative*, 98–99.
**95** Alter, *David Story*, 128.

created jealousy and resentment in Jonathan who is never called "my son" by his father,[96] and the unconscious sentiment was expressed by the "slip of the tongue" – if Jonathan used the verb inadvertently – or by the deliberate choice of the word. This will certainly prompt us to reconsider the widely held view that Jonathan is "the extreme case of character being emptied into plot"[97] with a view to legitimate David's succession to Saul. The character of Jonathan looks much more real, and we will ask whether the Jonathan passages are univocally pro-Davidic.

## 2.2 Between Texts: Inevitable Influences from Other Texts

We have seen so far that attention to various literary techniques makes us see the Jonathan passages as implicitly but most effectively exposing David's cunning and unloving character. Probably, it is far-fetched to interpret the Jonathan passages as straightforwardly anti-Davidic. Yet it certainly makes us reconsider our assumptions about the genre and the theme of the HDR: the HDR may not be straightforward pro-Davidic literature as has been widely believed. Attention to the literary artistry in the biblical narrative, however, raises a question about the origin of such aesthetic beauty. Those who urge us to appreciate the literary dimension of the biblical narrative seem to believe that the techniques were deliberately used by the authors of the narratives. Thus Alter speaks of "innovative technique [...] worked out by the ancient Hebrew writers"[98], and Sternberg declares that the biblical writer "is determined to operate as an artist".[99] However, it is far from clear whether the aesthetic beauty of the biblical narrative is to be credited to the author's artistic talent, or to the reader who has learned how a piece of literature "works" by reading other texts. To put it bluntly, is it the author, or the reader who is ingenious?

We already looked at Gadamer's insight that every understanding is affected by the essential historicity of the interpreter, i.e., a historically effected event. This has relevance for us as we interpret the HDR, because it implies that contrary to the claims of the New Criticism and Structuralism, our interpretation of the HDR will be inevitably under the influence of things external to the text of the HDR. A text is not an enclosed system, but inevitably invites the experience of other texts to come into play. This sounds very similar to the theory of

**96** Robert B. Lawton, "Saul, Jonathan, and the 'Son of Jesse'," *JSOT* 58 (1993): 35–46.
**97** Jobling, *1 Samuel*, 95.
**98** Alter, *The Art of Biblical Narrative*, 12.
**99** Sternberg, *The Poetics of Biblical Narrative*, 42.

intertextuality, which "insists that a text [...] cannot exist as a hermetic or self-sufficient whole, and so does not function as a closed system".[100] But when I say that the interpretation of the HDR is not free from the experience of other texts, I am not committed to the theory of intertexuality, but describing what is actually happening in more transparent interpretation. Let me clarify this a little bit more.

The term "intertextuality" was first used by Julia Kristeva in her essay "Word, Dialogue and Novel",[101] where she, on the basis of Bakhtin's claim that any text is constructed as a mosaic of quotations – any text is the absorption and transformation of another – argued that "the notion of intertextuality replaces that of intersubjectivity".[102] Although the term was introduced by Kristeva, a similar insight had been around in the sixties and the seventies. Derrida's "iterability",[103] and Barthes's discussion about textuality[104] in particular are in the same line, as they all subscribe to the view that "a text [...] cannot exist as a hermetic or self-sufficient whole, and so does not function as a closed system". The concept is now used in different circles with slightly different connotations, but in most cases, it is aligned with the post-modern theories which hold that the meaning of a text is not determinate. As long as the meaning of a text exists in continuous interaction with other factors, it cannot be fixed. In practice, however, the theory has more political dimensions. Worton and Still therefore observe that the practice of intertextual interpretation now is generally "an attempt to struggle against both complicity and exclusion – perhaps something, some shifting of barriers, can thus be achieved even if, in general, none of our thinking can escape constructing identity against differences".[105] The theory of intertextuality in practice is not so much theoretical as ideological, and Thiselton is convinced that "[t]o replace inter-subjectivity by intertextuality is a philosophical, not a semiotic or linguistic move".[106]

---

**100** Michael Worton and Judith Still, "Introduction," in *Intertextuality: Theories and Practices*, eds. Michael Worton and Judith Still (Manchester: Manchester University Press, 1990): 1–44 (1).
**101** Julia Kristeva, *The Kristeva Reader*, ed. Toril Moi (Oxford: Basil Blackwell, 1986), 34–61; idem, *Revolution in Poetic Language* (New York: Columbia University Press, 1984), pp. 69–70.
**102** Kristeva, *The Kristeva Reader*, 37.
**103** Jacques Derrida, "Signature Event Context," in *A Derrida Reader*, ed. Peggie Kamuf (New York: Columbia University Press, 1991): 80–111.
**104** Roland Barthes, "From Work to Text," *Textual Strategies. Perspectives in Post-Structuralist Criticism*, ed. (London: Methuen, 1980): 73–81.
**105** Worton and Still, "Introduction," 33.
**106** Anthony C. Thiselton, *New Horizons in Hermeneutics. The Theory and Practice of Transforming Biblical Reading* (Grand Rapids, Michigan: Zondervan, 1992), 97.

Setting aside the question about whether I agree with such a political move, or how much I agree with it, let us focus on our immediate question about how the intertextual element in interpretation affects our understanding of the HDR. And I submit here that regardless of our political view, a certain degree of intertextual interpretation is unavoidable, because the interpretation of the HDR is always influenced by our understanding of the larger body of literature. In this sense, I am not endorsing the recent theory of intertextuality as such, but reaffirming that every interpretation is essentially an "effected event". This is particularly true in the interpretation of the HDR, because we do not know yet where the HDR begins and ends, and it is inevitable that we read the HDR together with the surrounding materials, i. e. under the influence of the Saul cycle and the so-called Succession Narrative. No one has had the experience – at least, so far – of reading the HDR as a separate entity. We always read it as a part of the books of Samuel, or as a part of the Hebrew Bible. Thus whatever conclusion we may draw with regard to the theme or the *Tendenz* of the HDR, it is understood against other parts of the Old Testament, especially against the background of the Saul story, and of the not-so-glorious days of David. This implies that the interpretation of the HDR is affected by our judgement of how positively Saul is described in the Saul cycle, and how negative the depiction of David is in the so-called Succession Narrative. If we interpret the Saul cycle as a straightforward pro-Saulide narrative and the so-called Succession Narrative as clear-cut anti-Davidic,[107] we are likely to see the HDR as anti-Saulide and pro-Davidic, because the depictions of Saul and David are distinct from those in the previous and the following narratives. But if we read the Saul cycle and the so-called Succession Narrative more as the story of Saul's and Solomon's rise respectively, the HDR may not be too different from those narratives. It might be neither anti-Saulide nor pro-Davidic, but just the "story" of David's rise.

Let me elaborate this with a more specific example that is found in the interpretation of the Abigail episode. As it stands, the episode is located between David's twice-sparing of Saul in chapters 24 and 26, and may look rather disruptive. However, the narrative has the character of "narrative analogy", and the foolish husband Nabal is described in such a way that we may easily identify him with Saul.[108] This creates an even greater contrast between virtuous David and wicked Saul, and makes the pro-Davidic tendency clearer. However, if we read this episode "intertextually" or *wirkungsgeschichtlich* with the Bathsheba episode in the so-called Succession Narrative, we can have a different sense of

---

107 Brettler, *Creation*, 99.
108 Robert P. Gordon, "David's Rise and Saul's Demise," *Tyndale Bulletin* 31 (1980): 37–64.

the narrative. As Jon D. Levinson observed, there is a striking similarity between the Bathsheba narrative and the Abigail narrative. "[I]n both cases and them alone, David moves to kill a man and to marry his wife."[109] Read with the knowledge of the Bathsheba episode, then, the Abigail episode is not as pro-Davidic as it first looks. Rather, we may well see it as "a proleptic glimpse, within David's ascent, of his fall from grace".[110] Between the pictures of virtuous David in chapters 24 and 26, we glimpse David's murderous nature which is indeed actualized later in his life. Of course, this may not be *the correct* interpretation, and Robert Gordon believes that chapter 25 contributes to the character development of David. David was on the verge of rebellion by "cutting the robe" – a symbolic act of rebellion – of his master in chapter 24, but does not do so in chapter 26, because in chapter 25, he "is given a preview of what will happen if he commits his case to God and leaves Saul unharmed".[111] Moreover, one might well argue that we should not allow the Bathsheba episode, which comes much later in the books of Samuel, to confuse our interpretation. However, as mentioned earlier, it is almost impossible to read the Abigail episode without preknowledge of the Bathsheba story. Here I am not making the case that the author deliberately inserted chapter 25 so that the pictures of virtuous David in chapters 24 and 26 are levelled down. The point I am making is that when we interpret a text (the Abigail narrative), it is almost impossible not to be affected by what we already know about the larger body (the Bathsheba story), and if we allow our understanding of other texts to engage in the interpretation of the immediate text, we can get a different sense of the text.

## 2.3 Between the Text and the Reader

To make the issue even more complicated, the reader's role in interpretation should also be recognized, and since the HDR – indeed, most biblical narratives – has a "mosaic" character with lots of what Wolfgang Iser would call "blanks",[112] it seems particularly necessary for the reader to fill them to make the narrative sensible. One might claim that we should avoid mixing up the meaning of the text and its effect, and following Hirsch's distinction between meaning and significance, maintain that the interpreter's job is to find the meaning, and the reader's role is only to do with the significance. Indeed, even among

---

109 Jon D. Levenson, "1 Samuel 25 as Literature and as History," *CBQ* 40 (1978): 11–28 (24).
110 Levenson, "1 Samuel 25," 24.
111 Gordon, "David's Rise and Saul's Demise", 57.
112 Wolfgang Iser, *The Act of Reading* (London: Routledge & Kegan Paul, 1978), 194–5.

the so-called literary critics, such a distinction is presumed. "What text the author made and what sense a reader or public made of it are always distinct in principle."[113] However, as we saw above, it seems almost impossible to distinguish unambiguously the difference between the meaning and the significance. What people think belongs to "meaning" is expandable, and the border between meaning and significance is not always clear. Indeed, the fact that the understanding of the phrase "the meaning of the text" can vary from one culture to another helps to crack the widely held belief about meaning. For example, the common Chinese word for "meaning" is a combination of two words, 意 (yì; meaning, thought), and 味 (wèi; taste). This shows that at least for those under the influence of the classical Chinese such as China, Japan, and Korea, "meaning" cannot be separate from its aesthetic element and its connectedness to the interpreter. In other words, more than one fifth of the world's population take it for granted that what a text means and how it affects the reader are not separable. This of course does not mean that the Chinese definition of "meaning" is better than the common Western one. But it urges us to rethink how our concept of "meaning" can be better understood. Or in Gadamer's terminology, it gets us to see our "blind prejudice" when we talk about "meaning", and reveals that the strict separation of significance from meaning is not universal, but historical-local. This circumstance also nullifies the view of some people who argue that even if we acknowledge the reader's role, interpretation need not be problematic, because the common experience of reading enables a competent reader to identify the correct meaning of the text. However, the readers of the Bible are now not limited to the European/Occidental population, but extend much farther to the whole globe, and consequently, the reading experience of students of the Bible today is astonishingly different from those in the 19th and the early 20th century.

This seems to make diverse interpretations inevitable and the very talk of misunderstanding or misinterpretation anachronistic. In fact, not a few people nowadays believe that there is no need of *correct* interpretation, because the reader's activity is a part of the text – or even more radically, the text *is* a creation of the reader.[114] I do not agree with the view allowing the reader's role to expand limitlessly, because if a text is to be authoritative at all, there should be some-

---

113 Sternberg, *The Poetics of Biblical Narrative*, 10.
114 For different degrees of the reader-response theory, see Anthony Thiselton, *New Horizons in Hermeneutics*, 516–555.

thing *in the text* which is out of the reader's hands.[115] Moreover, it should not be overlooked that even if one wants to get away from all the constraints of the text, the common language itself remains as the fundamental constraint. Finally, even the advocates of the most radical reader-response theory do not promote absolutely limitless interpretations, i.e. totally subjective interpretations, but take the interpreting community as the criterion for interpretation. But if the interpreting community is brought into play, a certain degree of objectivity is already postulated. This is because the social dimension of interpretation, unless we see *sensus communis* as merely a subjective principle, restrains us from "anything goes". More fundamentally, however, "if textual meaning cannot be located in the author's intentions, neither can it be identified with a reader's – even an informed or ideal reader's – experience. Rather, when a text is understood its meaning cannot be attributed to either writer or reader. The meaning of the text is a shared language, shared in the sense that it is no one person's possession but is rather a common view of a subject-matter."[116]

In any case, there is certainly a role left to the reader in interpretation, because "all reading involves application, so that a person reading a text is himself part of the meaning he apprehends. He belongs to the text that he is reading".[117] This is even more true in biblical writing, because it was produced in a culture where the author was less venerated, and the application by the reader was taken for granted.[118] This certainly opens the door to different interpretations of the same text, and let me illustrate this with a concrete example from the HDR. In 1Sam 24:10–16 (ET 24:9–15), we hear David's speech to Saul, claiming his innocence and protesting Saul's persecution. David begins his speech with the following question, "Why do you listen to the words of the people who say that David is seeking to do you harm?" This is a surprising comment, because there was nothing mentioned in the narrative about the "people (אדם)" telling Saul that David is trying to do something evil to Saul. In fact, the opposite is true. Everybody loves David, and it is only Saul in whom "evil is complete" and who wants to kill David. This certainly creates a space for readers to think, and obliges them to fill the gap on their own. The invitation to the reader's response

---

115 For further discussion, see Fish, "Introduction, or How I Stopped Worrying and Learned To Love Interpretation," in *Is There a Text in this Class?*, 1–17; Kevin J. Vanhoozer, *Is There a Meaning in this Text?* (Leicester: Apollos, 1998).
116 Warnke, *Gadamer*, 48.
117 Gadamer, *Truth and Method*, 335.
118 John Barton, "Reading the Bible as Literature: Two Questions for Biblical Critics," *Journal of Theology and Literature* 1 (1987): 135–153; idem, *The Nature of Biblical Criticism* (Louisville/London: Westminster John Knox Press, 2007), 78–79.

is strengthened by David's thrice-repeated use of the imperative רְאֵה in the next verse (v. 12). Although they are primarily directed toward Saul, stimulated by the "blank" created by v. 11, David's urge might well encourage the reader to put the question to themselves, "Is it right to listen to what other people say about David?" And this certainly affects what to make of the HDR, especially in understanding its genre.

To summarize, when we interpret a biblical narrative, the interpretative process at a synchronic level includes various elements such as the recognition of the delicate literary techniques of the text, the inevitable interdependence with other parts of the Bible, and the gap-filling role of the reader. Interpretation of a biblical narrative is not just a simple decipherment of linguistic signs printed on the scrolls or the manuscripts, but a much more multi-faceted operation which includes lots of other factors which themselves are open to various possibilities. This confirms the general point made above in our hermeneutical reflection in general. Every interpretation is a historically effected event, and the fusion of different horizons. No one can claim to have acquired one correct interpretation that never changes, because one interprets a text in a constant interplay with those diverse factors.

# 3 Diachronic Approaches

The hermeneutical reflection and the recognition of the text's richness have in recent decades produced a certain antipathy toward the historical-critical approach to the Bible, on the grounds that this approach minimizes the importance of theology in biblical studies.[119] In some circles, a political dimension fuelled the resistance to the idea that we should spend so much effort on the diachronic dimension in the interpretative process. For them, reading and understanding a biblical text is open to everyone, whereas historical-critical understanding seems to be a privilege given to a small group of intellectual elites in the West. Every-

---

**119** Perhaps, the most significant one of such movements was Childs's canonical approach. See Brevard S. Childs, *Biblical Theology in Crisis* (Philadelphia: Fortress Press, 1970); "Interpretation in Faith: The Theological Responsibility of an Old Testament Commentary," *Interpretation* 18 (1964): 432–49; *Introduction to the Old Testament as Scripture* (Philadelphia: Fortress Press, 1979). For more recent advocates of a similar view, see *Reclaiming the Bible for the Church*, ed. by Carl E. Braaten and Robert W. Jenson (Edinburgh: T. & T. Clark, 1996); Christopher R. Seitz, *Word without End: The Old Testament as Abiding Theological Witness* (Grand Rapids: Eerdmans, 1998); R. W. L. Moberly, *The Bible, Theology, and Faith: A Study of Abraham and Jesus* (Cambridge: Cambridge University Press, 2000).

body can read or listen to the Bible, and understand what it is about, and the so-called "Introduction" is rather a barrier to the interpretation, designed by those elitists with a view to monopolizing the Bible and thus to manipulating the ordinary reader. Indeed, as we are asking now how one figures out the genre, theme, and purpose of the HDR, with a view to dealing with a historical-critical issue, diachronic elements at this stage appear to be totally irrelevant. However, even in understanding the whole, consideration of diachronic aspects is essential. This can be demonstrated by the following examples.

First, we saw above that the interpretation of a biblical narrative is based on the text in its final form. To be more precise, however, one needs to ask which version of the Bible we refer to when we talk of the "final form". Is it the text as it stands in the King James Version? Or that in the New English Bible? In most cases, which translation of the Bible we read will not affect our understanding of what the HDR is about. But when there is an uncertainty about the meaning, we will have to ask which text we should turn to. Normally, the Masoretic Text is regarded as the standard textual evidence, and when scholars talk of the "final form", they refer to that of the Masoretic Text (MT), or more precisely, that as represented in the *BHS*. However, MT was established by a group of scholars in Tiberias between the 7-10th century C.E., and the oldest but incomplete manuscript available, the "Allepo Codex", dates from about the 10th century C.E., and the best complete manuscript known as the Leningrad Codex is from 1009 C.E.[120] This means that MT is neither an original nor an infallible textual witness, but an edited version of the original consonantal text by a particular group in a particular time. Therefore, the final form as preserved in MT cannot be free from historical concerns, and it is a product of historical development which invites historical investigations. Furthermore, where MT is evidently corrupt, we have to rely on other textual witnesses,[121] and when there is a serious discrepancy between the textual witnesses, we need to ask which one reflects the better reading. One might argue that the differences are minuscule, and do not affect our overall understanding of a biblical narrative. However, the notoriously enigmatic verses in 20:14–16, or the serious discrepancy between MT and LXX[B] in chapters 17–18 show that the textual issues do affect our overall understanding of the HDR. The faith-filled David in the LXX version of chapters 17–18 certainly looks different from the ambitious David in the MT version, and one

---

**120** E. J. Revell, "Masoretic Text," *ABD*, IV, 597–599.
**121** For the books of Samuel, the following textual witnesses other than MT need to be consulted: LXX[B], LXX[A], LXX[L], the Old Latin, the Targum Jonathan, the Syriac, the Vulgate, 4QSam[b], 4QSam[a], and Josephus' *Jewish Antiquities*. See Stoebe, *Das erste Buch Samuelis*, 25–32; McCarter, *I Samuel*, 8–11; Klein, *1 Samuel*, xxvi-xxviii; Tsumura, *The First Book of Samuel*, 2–4.

might well wonder whether the pro-Davidic writer who wanted to present David's rise as the work of God included the picture of success-oriented David in the narrative. In short, even in understanding the "final form" of the biblical text, a diachronic dimension is inevitable.

Secondly, as Sternberg observed, language exposes the Achilles' heel of the opponents of historical-critical investigations,[122] because linguistic understanding is not possible without appropriate knowledge of its historical development. The meaning of a word is not changeless, and sometimes it can have a totally different connotation depending on where or when it is used. For example, the verb "love (אהב)" is extensively used in the Jonathan narratives in the HDR. Saul loves David when he first meets David in 1Sam 16:18, and later, Jonathan loves David also at first sight in 1Sam 18:2. Then, all Israel and Judah love David (1Sam 18:6), and Michal, Saul's daughter also loves David (1Sam 18:20). If "love" is understood as what it means nowadays, the report that everybody loves David would reveal David's personal attractiveness or merit, and Saul's hatred of David will be seen as just a paranoiac jealousy of a man with an inferiority complex. However, it has been shown that the verb "love" in Akkadian texts often has political overtones, and the same applies to the word in the HDR.[123] The meaning of "love" discovered by the comparison with contemporary literature then certainly makes a difference to the overall understanding of the HDR, because the Jonathan passages are seen now not just as a "psychodrama",[124] or a story of two gay heroes,[125] but as a record of the political battle at the time. Saul was not suffering from his paranoiac temperament, but was actually struggling to establish the monarchy against the threat of usurpation. Here we have a clear case that confirms Alter's more recent comment, "narrative interpretation

---

**122** Sternberg, *The Poetics of Biblical Narrative*, 11.

**123** J. A. Thompson, "The Significance of the Verb Love in the David-Jonathan Narratives in 1 Samuel," *Vetus Testamentum* 24 (1974): 334–338; William L. Moran, "Ancient Near Eastern Background of the Love of God in Deuteronomy," *CBQ* 25 (1963): 77–87; Jacquline E. Lapsley, "Feeling Our Way: Love for God in Deuteronomy," *CBQ* 65 (2003): 350–69; Susan Ackerman, "The Personal is Political: Covenantal and Affectionate Love ('ĀHĒB, AHĂBÂ) in the Hebrew Bible," *VT* 52 (2002): 437–58.

**124** J. P. Fokkelman, *Narrative Art and Poetry in the Books of Samuel: a full interpretation based on stylistic and structural analyses*, 4 vols (Assen: Van Gorcum, 1986), II, 394.

**125** David M. Gunn, *The Fate of King Saul* (Sheffield: JSOT Press, 1980), 93; Silvia Schroer & Thomas Staubli, "Saul, David und Jonatan – eine Dreiecksgeschichte? Ein Beitrag zum Thema 'Homosexualität im Ersten Testament'," *BK* 51 (1996): 15–22, (15). For objection, see Marcus Zehnder, "Exegetische Beobachtungen zu den David-Jonathan Geschichten," *Biblica* 79 (1998), 153–79; Martti Nissinen, "Die Liebe von David und Jonatan also Frage der moderne Exegese," *Biblica* 80 (1999): 250–263.

and philological analysis are not competing activities but mutually instructing moments in a single dynamic process of understanding."[126]

Thirdly, certain socio-political knowledge of the ancient Near East is also essential to understanding a text better. For instance, in 1Sam 22, we read one of the most terrible accounts about Saul's wickedness – perhaps the "darkest passage in the story of David's rise to power".[127] After a tip from a foreigner, Doeg, the king orders the entire priestly family in Nob to be killed, and the Edomite kills "eighty five" priests and destroys the priestly town Nob (22:18–19). Saul comes off particularly badly in this event, because – we might think – he does not separate religious and humanitarian concerns from political alliances. What was wrong with the priest who gave food to and prayed for the one in need? Moreover, what was the point of killing not only Ahimelech but also all members of his house? Indeed, Josephus, who generally minimizes Saul's fault, writes that the massacre was the main reason for Saul's rejection along with the Amalekite incident.[128] The comparison with ancient Near Eastern documents, however, places the episode in the context of its historical background, and enables us to understand what it really describes. In particular, "Instructions for Temple Personnel" from the Hittite texts of *išhiul* shows us that in the ancient world, a priest's loyalty towards the gods was actually loyalty towards the king, and being a priest was not just a religious commitment but a political one. Certainly, this explains why Saul condemned Ahimelech for inquiring of God on behalf of David: for Saul, Ahimelech thereby expressed his political support for David. Furthermore, the same literature helps us to understand why Saul destroyed all his family and the town, because the instruction decrees concerning the punishment of the disloyal servant were as follows, "whenever he dies, he will not die alone, his family is together with him."[129] Indeed, the fact that the punishment of the entire priestly house in Nob was according to the legal custom of the day also explains why David stays calm, and admits his partial responsibility when he is told of the annihilation of the priestly family, "I knew that day that Doeg the Edomite was there, and that he would surely

**126** Alter, *The David Story*, xxxii.
**127** McCarter, *I Samuel*, 365.
**128** Josephus, *Jewish Antiquities*, 6.378.
**129** Ada Taggar-Cohen, "Political Loyalty in the Biblical Account of 1 Samuel XX-XXII in the Light of Hittite Texts," *VT* 40 (2005): 251–268 (263–6). The Hittite texts are in E.-H. Sturtevant and G. Bechtel, eds., *A Hittite Chrestomathy* (Philadelphia: Linguistic Society of America, 1935), 127–174. Earlier, Jim Roberts saw the legal basis for Saul's slaughter in a text from Mari, "The Protocol of the diviner." See his article, "Legal Basis for Saul's Slaughter of the Priests of Nob (1 Samuel 21–22)," *JNSL* 25 (1999): 21–29.

tell Saul. It is I who am responsible[130] for all the lives of your father's household (22:22)." David here is not just showing incredible humility, but admitting his partial, but actual, guilt. Whether the historical background of the Ahimelech incident makes us see Saul more negatively or not is a question further to be asked. Yet it certainly helps us to understand what is described in the narrative.

Fourthly, information from archaeological evidence also affects how we understand the whole of the narrative. This is demonstrated by the way in which the archaeological discovery of the Tel Dan Inscription affects the understanding of the HDR. Although David is the most prominent figure in the Hebrew Bible, his historical existence had no extrabiblical evidence until about the 1990 s. David existed only in biblical literature, and therefore, apart from a religious or political reason, there was no objective support for denying the view that the story of David was a complete fiction. And indeed, the so-called historical minimalists such as Philip Davies and Thomas L. Thompson have argued that the Bible was a late literary creation purely for religious and ideological purposes. The discovery of the Tel Dan inscription in 1993, however, certainly challenged such a view. The inscription included the Aramaic letters *bytdwd*, and the first decipherers read it to mean "the house of David". Since the inscription is broken and damaged, no one can be certain whether the letters really refer to the "house of David". Indeed, immediately after the publication about the discovery, several scholars objected to reading too much from it, and argued that the letters were more likely to refer to the temple of the local deity Dod.[131] The second discovery in 1994, however, heightened the possibility that the letters do refer to the house of David, because the fragments additionally discovered suggested that the name of the Judean king Ahaziahu son of Jehoram is mentioned just before the *bytdwd*, just as the name of the Israelite king Jehoram son of Ahab is mentioned with "Israel". The Aramaic letters seem to make a parallel with "Israel", and thus are likely to be "the House of David". Of course, this involves quite an extensive reconstruction, and there are lot of other possible objections to such a reading. Moreover, even if the letters refer to the House of David, it does not mean that David existed as an individual, and certainly not

---

**130** The use of the word סַבֹּתִי here is perplexing. Most commentators read חבתי for סַבֹּתִי on the basis of LXX's εἰμι αἴτιος, and translate, "I am guilty of...". By contrast, Gordon, followed by Tsumura, maintains that the verb echoes the key verb סבב, and implies David's indirect responsibility. In any case, the meaning is clear that David acknowledges some degree of his responsibility. Driver, *Notes*, 182; McCarter, *1 Samuel*, 363–365; Gordon, *I & II Samuel*, 175; Tsumura, *The First Book of Samuel*, 548–9.

**131** Frederick H. Cryer, "On the Recently-Discovered 'House of David' Inscription," *SJOT* 8 (1994): 3–19.

with any proximity to the picture depicted in the Bible.[132] Nonetheless, the discovery of this archaeological evidence keeps us from too rashly concluding that the David narrative was a pure fiction. In other words, the archaeological information affects how we understand the David narrative in terms of its genre.

All these examples show that the knowledge of historical background does help to clarify the meaning of biblical texts, and the deeper understanding of the textual history, the language used, the socio-political background, and the archaeological data affect how we understand the genre, the theme, and the purpose of the HDR. This may lead some people to argue that the reason we have different interpretations is because we have not yet reached the completion of the necessary historical knowledge. The interpretative process is linear, they would say, in the sense that the meaning of a text is the goal, and it can be achieved by continual advances through historical investigation. The current "crisis" of the historical-critical approach is not because it was too excavative, but because it has not been sufficiently excavative. Such a view, however, is not sustainable any more, not only because "complete" historical knowledge seems impossible, but also because it does not recognize the fundamental structure of understanding. In any attempt to understand a literary work, parts are understood in the light of the whole, and the whole is understood through the parts. This fundamental principle is also applied to the question of synchronic and diachronic aspects in any interpretation of a literary work. To understand the meaning of the whole, it is necessary to know the linguistic and historical background of the work, but at the same time, the linguistic and historical background is made available only through the help of the literary interpretation of the whole work. Thus it is highly unlikely that the relevant historical knowledge alone can remove all possibility of diverse interpretations. In fact, as we saw above, historical questions are dealt with very much on the basis of literary interpretation, and interpretation of historical data itself involves a process of interpretation. Even the archaeology, which is often believed to produce only "hard" and objective evidence, is not free from interpretation.[133] "Historical crit-

---

**132** The second objections were raised by Cryer and Thompson in Frederick H. Cryer, "King Hadad," *SJOT* 9 (1995): 223–35; Thomas L. Thompson, "'House of David': An Eponymic Referent to Yahweh as Godfather," *SJOT* 9 (1995): 59–74; "Dissonance and Disconnections: Notes on the Bytdwd and Hmlk.hdd Fragments from Tel Dan," *SJOT* 9 (1995): 236–240. For more recent discussion around the discovery of the Tel Dan inscription, see George Athas, *The Tel Dan Inscription: a reappraisal and a new interpretation* (London: T. & T. Clark, 2005); Hallvard Hagelia, *The Dan Debate: the Tel Dan Inscription in recent research* (Sheffield: Sheffield Phoenix, 2009).
**133** Shlomo Bunimovitz, "How Mute Stones Speak: Interpreting What We Dig Up," *BAR* 21 (1995), 58–67, 96–100.

ics who speak of the 'assured results' are still clinging to the myth of objectivity, namely to the idea that their historical reconstructions are value-neutral and their observations theory-free."[134]

To conclude, the fundamental principle of the hermeneutic circle tells us that the understanding of the whole HDR, which we believe is foundational to more specific historical-critical discussions, is an ever-corrigible outcome of the interpretative process that involves diverse approaches to the text. Not only the text itself, but also other biblical texts and the reader will affect how the whole is understood, and even historical information will be required for this apparently literary and semantic operation. We shall read a biblical text and interpret it, and then the interpretation will shed light on what is behind the text. The historical knowledge in turn will give us further insights in our interpretation of the text, which will open the possibility of deeper understanding. And although we submitted above that the semantic and literary operation comes first in principle, in practice, the whole process of interpretation is more a unified operation than the back-and-forth movement between two separate operations.[135] All this implies that the interpretative process is an ongoing one, which will have no end. It involves diverse elements open to change, and therefore, no one can claim the last word about the meaning of the text. We are on a journey to the meaning, and the journey is an ongoing one, always open to revision. Understanding the whole HDR will change over time, and no one is able to pin down *the* correct meaning of the HDR. This circular movement in understanding, however, is not a meaningless repetition, but a spiral leading to the truth of the text. What we are trying to achieve in biblical criticism is to find out the best possible answer to a question, and this has been what biblical critics have actually been doing. In the next chapter, therefore, we will discuss not *the* correct understanding of the whole HDR, but what is the most appropriate understanding at this moment of interpretative history. We hope that this will provide us with a foundation stone for building up hypotheses about the extent of the HDR and its composition history in the last two chapters. Of course, since the understanding of the whole is provisional, the answer to such historical-critical questions will be hypothetical.

---

**134** Vanhoozer, *Is There a Meaning in this Text?*, 298.

**135** Barton holds that understanding a text is a two-stage operation which cannot be collapsed into a single process. I agree with this view in as much the first stage, i. e. perception of the text's meaning, is the subject for biblical criticism. However, I want to highlight that the first stage is already an outcome of a complex interpretative operation that cannot be easily dissected. See Barton, *The Nature of Biblical Criticism*, 158–164.

# Chapter 3
# The Nature of the HDR as a Whole

I have stressed so far the importance of understanding the whole in discussing the question of the beginning and the ending of the HDR. In this chapter, I attempt to reach the most appropriate understanding of the HDR as a whole. For this, two questions have to be answered initially. First, what does the "whole" refer to here? Without knowing the exact extent of the HDR, we cannot know what it means, and this requires us to posit a heuristic starting point in order to avoid falling into hopeless circularity. And I suggest that we should take the whole HDR to extend from 1Sam 16:14–2Sam 5:3, because among those who believe in the existence of the HDR, no one denies that it begins after David's introduction to the Saulide court and that it ends before David's enthronement. Second, what do we mean by "understanding of the whole"? Obviously, it can include a wide range of questions, and defies a simple equation with any one particular issue. Nonetheless, we should make the issue more explicit, and I believe that the understanding of the whole is first and foremost to do with the understanding of its genre, and then, with its theme and function. To put it more bluntly, the most essential questions for the understanding of the whole are: what kind of text is it? What is it all about? What is it trying to do?[1] Of course, it has been long believed that the HDR is historiography, and

---

1 The use of the term "genre" and the emphasis on it could be seen as a signal that I am actually advocating some sort of form criticism here. But this is true only insomuch as both recent form critics and I emphasise the importance of the understanding of the whole. Indeed, Antony F. Campbell maintains that the core of form-critical insight is the focus on the whole, and the nature of form criticism is "to name the whole". My approach warms to such a modified version of form criticism that endorses "generic nominalism" rather than "generic realism", i.e., the type of form criticism which sees form or *Gattung* not so much a fixed type developed in a particular time as a more flexible image or *Gestalt*. However, in that case, we might want to ask whether we can still call it "form criticism", because the modified version of form criticism has so many convergences with other approaches that it loses its distinctiveness. One might suggest then that I am doing a kind of genre criticism. Again, this is only partially true, because the discussion about the genre of the HDR is not the final aim, but a necessary step to find out the beginning and the ending of the HDR, which will lead further to deepen the understanding of the text. The ultimate destination of the investigation is nothing but to facilitate the deeper understanding of the text, and to contribute to the clarification of the "plain sense" of the text, which I believe with John Barton is the core of biblical criticism. In this sense, I personally prefer to call the approach adopted here simply "biblical criticism" such as defined by Barton in his recent book *The Nature of Biblical Criticism*. The source critical question of the extent of the HDR is discussed here, in conjunction with a form critical question (genre), a literary question (theme), and a

is mainly about David's legitimate succession to Saul under the guidance of YHWH. However, the concept of "historiography" in the ancient world is so difficult to pin down, that without further clarification and specification, it does not tell us much about the text. Similarly, too general an understanding of the theme and function can blind us to the richness of the text, and hinder adequate appreciation of it. In this chapter, we discuss these issues more intensively, so that we may grasp the nature of the HDR, and be ready for dealing with the source critical question of its extent.

# 1 The Genre of the HDR

## 1.1 What is Genre? How do we know it?

"The processes of generic recognition are in fact fundamental to the reading process,"[2] and "[i]t is impossible to understand any text without at least an implicit recognition of the genre to which it belongs."[3] Both literary critics and biblical scholars agree that the understanding of genre is crucial in the interpretation of a text, and it does seem that disagreement about genre is one of the main reasons for disagreement about interpretation.[4] And yet, the definition of genre and the method of its recognition have long perplexed scholars, to the extent that some critics dismiss it as chimerical, or take it to imply merely a certain similarity between certain literary works.[5] Several reasons for the difficulty can be mentioned, but the most challenging of them would be the instability of genre. Contrary to the ancient view represented by Plato and Aristotle, it is now accepted that a genre is continuously changing, and has "haziness" or *Unschärfe* as one of its essential features.[6] There are many ways to cause the modification of a genre, but generic assimilation and generic extension are the most obvious ones. Generic assimilation happens when one combines an existing

---

redactional question (collection and edition of diverse materials). See Antony F. Campbell, "Form Criticism's Future," in *The Changing Face of Form Criticism for the Twenty-First Century*, eds. Marvin A. Sweeny and Ehud Ben Zvi (Grand Rapids: Eerdmans, 2003): 15–31 (23–24); Kenton Sparks, *Ancient Texts for the Study of the Hebrew Bible. A Guide to the Background Literature* (Peabody: Hendrickson, 2005), 5–7; Barton, *The Nature of Biblical Criticism*, 101–116.
**2** Alastair Fowler, *Kinds of Literature: an Introduction to the Theory of Genres and Modes* (Oxford: Clarendon, 1985), 259.
**3** Barton, *Reading the Old Testament*, 16.
**4** Hirsch, *Validity in Interpretation*, 98.
**5** Fowler, 40.
**6** Richter, 132.

genre – often a smaller one – with a new one, and generic extension arises when an existing genre is used in a new context for a different purpose. One can subdivide these into more diverse ways of modification such as topical invention, combination, aggregation, mixture, and so on.[7] In any case, the recent development in genre theory has shown that genre is now not to be seen as something fixed and ready-made, which provides the author with a format to follow and the reader with a means of classification. Genres are rather initial frameworks through which the reader can journey through the text, and are better compared to what Hirsch calls "corrigible schemata", i. e., the frameworks for reading that can yet be corrected in the light of further investigation of the text being read.[8] We need to figure out what kind of questions we can raise, when we come across a text, and such initial guesses about the nature of a text or "to name the whole" is what we mean by "genre recognition" in our discussion.

Then, how can we recognize genre?[9] Wolfgang Richter observes that the traditional ways of genre-recognition with regard to the biblical narratives have been to examine the content and the historicity, and to compare them with other (mostly, ancient Near Eastern) literature. But he objects to such content oriented methods, and contends that genre should be recognized and named mainly on the basis of formal character – the structure in particular.[10] True as this may be, genre-recognition on the basis of structure is not possible in our case, because while the beginning and the ending of a narrative are crucial to understand the structure of a work, we do not know exactly where the HDR begins and ends. This urges us to rely on other ways of genre recognition, and we turn to contemporary genre theory that regards authorial statement, contemporary practice, early readers' comments, and indirect constructive inference as most useful.[11] The clearest and most reliable among them would be the direction given by the text itself. In the Bible as well as in ancient Near Eastern docu-

---

7 Sparks, "Introduction", 8; Fowler, 170–190.

8 E. D. Hirsch, *The Aims of Interpretation* (Chicago: University of Chicago Press, 1976), 32.

9 Of course, as mentioned above, genre recognition is a result of interpretation, and thus, it is possible only when one understands the meaning of every bit in the work. This seems to contradict our initial stance that every understanding starts from genre-recognition, and we find ourselves again in the hermeneutic circle. But neither the genre of a work nor the meaning of each part is a fixed entity. As Barton observed, "[o]ur initial judgement about genre and our initial attempt at exegesis play back and forth on each other and are mutually corrective." Therefore, if we bear this in mind, we can say with reasonable confidence what kind of literature the work we are dealing with is, without denying the necessary structure of circularity involved. Cf. Barton, *Reading the Old Testament*, 18.

10 Richter, 125–152 (137).

11 Fowler, 52.

ments, we often find some authorial statements or signals within the text that can tell us what kind of literature we are dealing with. For instance, a phrase like "The vision (חֲזוֹן) of Isaiah (Isa 1:1)" tells us that we are reading a prophecy, and "Proverbs (מִשְׁלֵי) of Solomon (Prov 1:1)" indicates that the following text is a proverb. Even in the level of sub-genres, there can be some indications such as "the list of the descendants (סֵפֶר תּוֹלְדֹת) of humans (Gen 5:1)", or "a copy of the letter (פַּרְשֶׁגֶן אִגַּרְתָּא) (Ezra 4:10)". All these are clear indications of what kind of text they are, and probably most reliable ones, although it is possible that the author deliberately attempted to deceive the reader. The HDR, however, has no such statement or signal, with the exception of 1Sam 24:14, where David's quotation is designated as a "מָשָׁל". Therefore, we have to rely on other evidence to find out the genre of the HDR.

The early readers' comment can also provide us with some clue to understand the genre. As to the HDR, one could, inferring from the fact that Josephus used it as a source for his own history writing, conclude that the early readers understood the HDR as a historical record about the early days of David. However, we do not know exactly what it was to write a history for the ancient people. There were already different types of historical writing in the first millennium B.C.E., as exemplified by the different types in Greek historiography,[12] and in particular, Herodotus, while writing "history", used a lot of myths and legends which, for us, would not be taken seriously as a reliable historical source. This tells us that the fact that the early readers used the HDR as a source for their history writing is not a guarantee that we can also read the HDR as historiography. Indeed, it is interesting that in Chronicles, David's early days are mostly omitted. This is normally explained by the fact that the Chronicler had very specific interests, like kings and priests, which led him to omit those materials not directly relevant. Yet, it is also possible that the Chronicler understood the genre of the HDR differently, and did not see much historical value in it. The Chronicler might have regarded the HDR as heroic sagas just like those found in the Judges, and that was why he did not include them in what he – perhaps under the Greek influence – might have thought would be a proper history.[13] In other words, the

---

12 Donald Lateiner, "Historiography: Greco-Roman," in *ABD*, III, 212–219.

13 This sounds a bit speculative, but as Williamson pointed out, one should beware of attempts simplistically to reduce the Chronicler's use of sources to a single category. In fact, if the Chronicler's use of genealogies manifests traces of Greek influence as Knoppers argued, one cannot exclude the possibility that the Chronicler's selection of biblical narratives was also influenced by a Greek historiography that was closer to Thucydides's than Herodotus's. H.G.M. Williamson, *1 and 2 Chronicles* (NCBC; London: Marshall & Scott, 1982) p. 23; Gary N. Knoppers, "Greek Historiography and the Chronicler's History: A Reexamination," *JBL* 122 (2003): 627–650.

absence of the account of David's early years in Chronicles may testify that some ancient readers did not see the genre of the HDR as proper historiography.

Apart from the "indirect constructive inference" which will be discussed later, this leaves us only with the contemporary practice to help us to figure out what kind of text the HDR is. In other words, we may be able to guess the genre of the HDR on the basis of similar literature found in the ancient Near East. In the last 30 years there has been a great advance in discovering ancient Near Eastern texts and deciphering them, and this has led to the common view that the HDR is best compared with the ancient Near Eastern apologies or propaganda. This can be the starting point for our discussion about the genre of the HDR, and the discussion about whether such a framework is still valid for understanding the text will follow.

## 1.2 The HDR as Propaganda/Apology

### 1.2.1 Reading the HDR as Propaganda/Apology

The Oxford English Dictionary defines propaganda as "the systematic dissemination of information, esp. in a biased or misleading way, in order to promote a political cause or point of view", and apology as "the pleading off from a charge or imputation, whether expressed, implied, or only conceived as possible; defence of a person, or vindication of an institution, etc., from accusation or aspersion". Among biblical scholars or orientalists, Kenton Sparks most recently gives the following definition: "propaganda is a systematic effort to conform social opinion to the ideologies or viewpoints of those who hold or seek power."[14] There is a lot more to discuss, with regard to the definition of the term, and we will come back to the issue later. But whatever it means precisely, in biblical scholarship, "propaganda/apology'" is widely used as the most convenient label for the HDR, and this was initiated by the comparative study of ancient Near Eastern literature. From the 1970 s, Mesopotamian royal apologies such as the Inscription of Idrimi of Alalakh,[15] Esarhaddon's Apology,[16] the Tale of Two

---

14 Kenton Sparks, "Propaganda," in *Dictionary of the Old Testament: Historical Books*, eds. Bill T. Arnold and H. G. M. Williamson (Leicester: Inter-Varsity, 2005): 819–825 (819).
15 The translation of the original text is found in *ANET*, 557–558; *COS* 1.148: 479–480. For discussion about the date and the theme, see Na'aman, "A Royal Scribe and his Scribal Products in the Alalakh IV Court," *Oriens Antiquus* 19 (1980): 107–116; Jack M. Sassoon, "On Idrimi and šarruwa the Scribe," in *Studies on the Civilization and Culture of Nuzi and the Hurrians in Honor of Ernest R. Lacheman on His Seventy-fifth Birthday*, eds. M. A. Morrison and D. I. Owen (Winona Lake: Eisenbrauns, 1981): 188–191; W. Mayer, "Die historische Einordnung der 'Autobiographie'

Brothers,[17] the Adad-guppi Inscription[18] and the so-called "Nabonidus and His God",[19] and the Hittite apologies such as the Telipinu edict and the so-called Apology of Hattušili III[20] were discovered and analyzed, and compared to the narrative which we find in the books of Samuel. This was followed by a great number of biblical scholars who became enthusiastic to label the David narratives as apology or propaganda. And consequently, from about 1980, it became

---

des Idrimi von Alalah," *UF* 27 (1995): 333–350; Gary H. Oller, "The Inscription of Idrimi: A Pseudo-autobiography?" in *DUMU-E²-DUB-BA-A*, eds. Hermann Behrens, Darlene Londing, and Martha T. Roth (Philadelphia: Samuel Noah Kramer Fund, University Museum, 1989): 411–417. For comparison with the HDR, see Klaus-Peter Adam, *Saul und David in der judäischen Geschichtsschreibung. Studien zu 1 Samuel 16–2 Samuel 5* (Tübingen: Mohr Siebeck, 2007), 163; Niels Peter Lemche, *Prelude to Israel's Past: Background and Beginnings of Israelite History and Identity* (Peabody: Hendrickson, 1998), 157–159.

**16** The English translation is in *ANET*, 289–290; *COS* 2.113–119: 261–306. For the comparison with the David narrative, see Hayim Tadmor, "Autobiographical Apology in the Royal Assyrian Literature," in *History, Historiography, and Interpretation*, eds. Hayim Tadmor and Moshe Weinfeld (Jerusalem: Magnes, 1983), 36–57 (56); Sparks, "Propaganda", 822; Tomoo Ishida, "The Succession Narrative and Esarhaddon's Apology: A Comparison," in *Ah, Assyria: Studies in Assyrian History and Ancient Near Eastern Historiography Presented to Hayim Tadmor*, eds. Mordechai Cogan and Israel Eph'al (Jerusalem: Magnes, 1991), 166–173. In his earlier study, following H. M. Wolf, Ishida calls the HDR "the defence of David". Tomoo Ishida, *The Royal Dynasties in Ancient Israel: A Study on the Formation and Development of Royal Dynastic Ideology* (Berlin/New York: W. de Gruyter, 1977), 55–63.

**17** The English translation is in *COS* 1.99: 309–327. For discussion, see R. C. Steiner and C. F. Nims, "Ashurbanipal and Shamash-shum-ukin: A Tale of Two Brothers form the Aramaic Text in Demotic Script," *RB* 92 (1985): 60–81; W. L. Moran, "Assurbanipal's Message to the Babylonians (*ABL 301*), with an Excursus on Figurative *Biltu*," in *Ah, Assyria*, eds. Cogan and Eph'al, 305–336 (320); R. C. Steiner, "Papyrus Amherst 63: A New Source for the Language, Literature, Religion, and History of the Arameans," in *Studia Aramaica*, eds. M. J. Geeler, J. C. Greenfield, and M. P. Weitzman (New York: Oxford University Press, 1995): 204–205; Sparks, *Ancient Texts*, 292; "Propaganda", 821.

**18** The English translation is in *ANET* 560–62; *COS* 1.147: 477–78. For further discussion, see C. J. Gadd, "The Harran Inscriptions of Nabonidus," *Anatolian Studies* 8 (1958): 35–92; Tremper Longman III, *Fictional Akkadian Autobiography* (Winona Lake: Eisenbrauns, 1991), 102–103; Sparks, *Ancient Texts*, 292–293.

**19** Dick also mentions the use of clothes for legitimation both in David and in Nabonidus. However, Nabonidus's case is based on not the text, but iconography. See Michael B. Dick, "The 'History of David's Rise to Power' and the Neo-Babylonian Succession Apologies," in *David and Zion: Biblical Studies in Honour of J.J.M. Roberts*, eds. Bernard F. Batto and Kathryn L. Roberts (Winona Lake: Eisenbrauns, 2004), 12–19.

**20** Herbert M. Wolf, "The Apology of Hattushilish Compared with Other Political Self-Justifications of the Ancient Near East" (unpublished doctoral thesis, Brandeis University, 1967); Harry Hoffner, Jr., "Propaganda and Political Justification," in *Unity and Diversity*, eds. Goedicke and Roberts, 49–62; Sparks, *Ancient Texts*, 393.

fashionable to discount the historical value of the figure of David described in the books of Samuel on the basis of such understanding of the genre of the HDR.[21] For example, Lemche declared that David "obtained the highest position in his country, but he used every means to get so far [...] was a tough practitioner of *Realpolitik* who was not too particular about his means".[22] More specifically, Whitelam expressed the suspicion that David was involved with the deaths of prominent members of the Saulide court,[23] and VanderKam, from the "overkill" in denying David's involvement with the deaths of Abner and Ishbaal, speculated that David was indeed behind the murders.[24] David's ethnic background was also suspected, and G. W. Ahlström suggested that David was in fact a Jebusite subject, and such a non-Israelite origin pushed him to legitimate his kingship even more vigorously, producing an "apologia davidica".[25]

The most influential among all was probably P. Kyle McCarter, Jr., who, in his 1980 article and the Anchor Bible commentary, consistently argued that the HDR is royal propaganda, written in the manner of the Apology of Hattušili III. According to his observation, there were at least seven charges against David: (i) David advanced to the throne at Saul's expense; (ii) he was a deserter; (iii) an outlaw; (iv) a Philistine mercenary; (v) he was involved with Saul's death; (vi) with Abner's death; (vii) with Ishbaal's death, and the HDR was written to clear David of those charges.[26] As the Hittite apology purported to legitimate Hattušili III's accession to the throne as being achieved by the will of the god Ištar without his acting against his brother Muršili, the HDR tried to convey the message that David rose to the throne by the will of YHWH without harming anybody from the previous royal house. McCarter of course tries to avoid making the comparison too absolute, and hesitates to present "royal propaganda" as a fixed literary genre of the time. However, he believes, "the apology of Hattushilish demonstrates the potential for an elaborate development of this genre in the general cultural milieu in which the history of David's rise was composed."[27]

---

**21** But already in 1967, G. Buccellati, *Cities and Nations of Ancient Syria: An Essay on Political Institutions with Special Reference to Israelite Kingdoms* (Rome, University of Rome, 1967), 195–212.

**22** Niels Peter Lemche, "David's Rise," *JSOT* 10 (1978): 2–25 (18).

**23** Keith Whitelam, *The Just King: Monarchical Judicial Authority in Ancient Israel* (Sheffield: JSOT, 1979), 91–166.

**24** James C. VanderKam, "Davidic Complicity in the Deaths of Abner and Eshbaal: A Historical and Redactional Study," *JBL* 99/4 (1980): 521–539.

**25** G. W. Ahlström, "Was David a Jebusite Subject?" *ZAW* 92 (1980): 285–287 (287).

**26** Kyle McCarter, "The Apology of David," *JBL* 99/4 (1980): 489–504 (499–502).

**27** McCarter, "The Apology of David", 498.

Since McCarter's observation, reading the HDR as propaganda or apology has been a common practice in biblical scholarship. Keith Whitelam, reaffirming his previous view, identified the target audience as a privileged elite group, and concluded that the HDR is "the highly subjective *self-perception* of the Davidic monarchy as portrayed by the royal bureaucracy".[28] Robert Gordon thinks that it is fair to read the HDR as "an apologetic work composed to defend David against slanderous charges of complicity in the deaths of key members of the Saulide family during the early part of his career".[29] Though he is more nuanced, Brettler similarly observes that the HDR is "very serious propaganda; its aim is to help create a people Judah centred upon the royal Davidic dynasty".[30] And most recently, Baruch Halpern, thinking that the profile of David given in 1Sam and 2Sam provides only the sides of him that "an apologist was interested in our seeing"[31] did not only follow McCarter, but also went further to increase the allegations, suggesting that David was actually involved (or accused of being involved) not only with the deaths of Saul, Abner, and Ishbaal, but also with Nabal, Saul's other descendants, Amnon, Absalom, Amasa, and Uriah.

Probably, no one will deny that there are apologetic elements in the HDR, and it is certainly pro-Davidic. Therefore, it is not totally wrong to read the HDR as propaganda. Indeed, reading the HDR as propaganda or apology for David solves the apparent problem of the discrepancy in the descriptions of David in the first part of the David story and the latter part. Apparently, David in the first part looks entirely virtuous. He relieves Saul from the influence of the evil spirit, fights for Saul and Israel even in the most hostile situations, and remains loyal to the persecuting master Saul to the end. He is indeed "a valiant warrior, a man of war, prudent in words, handsome man, and YHWH is with him (1Sam 16:18)". By contrast, in the latter part, the figure of David is extremely ambiguous, contradicting his image in the first part. He does not go to war, but gets his men to fight on his behalf. He is adulterous and murderous, unable to deal with the infamous behaviours of his sons, imprudent in weeping over Absalom while humiliating those who fought for him, old and impotent, and is manipulated by a particular faction in the court. These discrepancies certainly raise a narratological problem, if we want to read the David narratives as one unified story. How can one and the same person be so different? Reading the HDR as Davidic propaganda and separating it from the later description can certainly

---

**28** Keith Whitelamn, "The Defence of David," *JSOT* 29 (1984): 61–87 (79).
**29** Robert Gordon, *I & II Samuel* (Exeter: Paternoster, 1986), 149.
**30** Brettler, *Creation*, 108.
**31** Baruch Halpern, *David's Secret Demons: Messiah, Murderer, Traitor, King* (Grand Rapids: W.B. Eerdmans, 2001), 14.

solve such an apparent thematic disunity. In fact, this appears to solve another problem of the inconsistent description of Saul in the first part and in the latter part. One could now say that Saul is described totally negatively in the latter part of 1Sam, because this was absorbed into the Davidic propaganda. In short, there was a problem, and reading the HDR as propaganda for David seems to have solved it. But does the solution still work? Or, more fundamentally, does the problem still exist?

### 1.2.2 Resistance to the Framework

In my opinion, reading the HDR as propaganda, or labelling it as such does not seem appropriate any longer. This is difficult to prove however, because there is no clear method to identify the genre of a work. As Fowler pointed out, genre recognition requires a certain competence, just as one needs a linguistic competence to communicate at all, and such generic competence seems to be acquired not by learning some rules, but by a complicated and lengthy process that is never complete.[32] Consequently, among the evidence for genre that we mentioned earlier, "indirect constructive inference" provides the most information for genre-recognition.[33] This implies that the objection to naming the HDR as propaganda/apology is difficult to demonstrate as well, and explains why many scholars, even when they oppose such a label for the HDR, do not articulate their position more clearly. Since I have stressed the importance of genre-recognition so much, however, I will deal with this issue more extensively. And for this, since there is no easy way to establish my view beyond any doubt in a methodical way, I will take rather a long and indirect route to "convert" readers and scholars from the view that has been widely accepted as persuasive. The following questions will lead us through. First, is the HDR straightforwardly anti-Saulide and pro-Davidic? Second, is the HDR really similar or comparable to the royal apologies from the Mesopotamian or the Hittite literature? Third, is the reading context at this point of the interpretative history congenial to reading the HDR as propaganda?

### 1.2.2.1 Is the HDR unambiguously Anti-Saulide?

Whether a certain work is propaganda or not depends on various elements such as the tone, the context, and the historical background. But the first thing to be

---

32 Fowler, 45.
33 Fowler, 52.

asked is whether the work in question shows a clear tendentious slant toward one side over against another. All propaganda has the same goal of propagating the view of a certain party by vilifying the opponent, or by putting them in a negative light. Therefore, to evaluate whether the HDR is propaganda or not, we may well first ask whether the HDR shows a clearly tendentious slant as most instances of propagandas do. In other words, we should ask whether the HDR is clearly anti-Saulide and pro-Davidic. If it is, the possibility is high that the work is propaganda that legitimates David's enthronement against the Saulide house. Indeed, those who support the framework of reading the HDR as propaganda have seen the black and white view about Israel's first two kings, Saul and David. According to their reading, in the HDR Saul is the villain, and David is the hero.

A close reading of the text however makes us resist such understanding, and the contribution of recent literary criticism is most evident here. First of all, an interpretation sensitive to the details of the text shows that Saul in the HDR is predominantly described as a tragic hero, and arouses the sympathy of the reader toward the rejected. This has been pointed out by many scholars, and von Rad already saw in the story "close affinity with the spirit of Greek tragedy", while Northrop Frye identified Saul as "the one great tragic hero of the Bible".[34] But it was David M. Gunn who made the point most explicitly in his monograph *The Fate of King Saul*. In his literary analysis of 1Sam 8–2Sam 2 in its final form, Gunn points out that the narrative does not tell us clearly what Saul's sin was,[35] but shows how he was trapped between conflicting interests and am-

---

34 Gerhard von Rad, *Old Testament Theology*, 2 vols (London: SCM Press, 1975), I, 325; Northrop Frye, *The Great Code: the Bible and Literature* (London: Routlegde & Kegan Paul, 1982), 181. See also, W. Lee Humphreys, "The Tragedy of King Saul: A Study of the Structure of 1 Samuel 9–31," *JSOT* 6 (1978): 18–27; idem, "From Tragic Hero to Villain: A Study of the Figure of Saul and the Development of 1 Samuel," *JSOT* 22 (1982): 95–117; Georg Hentschel, *Saul: Schuld, Reue und Tragik eines 'Gesalbten'* (Leipzig: Evangelische Verlagsanstalt, 2003), 11, 27–9.

35 There have been many discussions about Saul's sins. In chapter 13, Saul's performing the ceremony is not itself a sin, because it was acceptable for a king to assume a priestly role. David (2Sam 6:17–18; 24:25), Solomon (1Kings 3:15), and Ahaz (2Kings 16:1–20) offer sacrifices, and none of them are criticised for that. Saul's sin was probably due to a misinterpretation of Samuel's instruction. Saul might have interpreted Samuel's instruction literally, and waited for exactly seven days, although what Samuel meant was that he had to wait until he came. Saul's sin in chapter 15 is more complicated. The narrator and Samuel suggest that Saul's sin is basically disobedience. However, whether Saul was deliberately disobedient is doubtful, because Saul intended to sacrifice the spared ones later at Gilgal. He might have not noticed the difference between ritual ban (חֵרֶם) and sacrifice (זֶבַח). If so, his sin lies in the lack of knowledge about cultic matters. However, precisely what Saul's sin was is not clear, and invites various interpretations. See Weiser, "1 Samuel 15", 1–28; David Gunn, *The Fate of King Saul* (Sheffield: JSOT

biguous demands. Saul was "subject to forces beyond his control",[36] and his sin was not a "sin of devastating consequences, warranting God's rejection".[37] He is described more like a "plaything of fate",[38] and therefore, essentially "an innocent victim of God" rather than a villain.[39] J. Cheryl Exum is of a similar view, but in contrast with Gunn who emphasizes the tragic element in Saul's life by playing down Saul's guilt, she points out that guilt and fate are not clearly distinguished in tragedy. Saul is a tragic hero not because of his innocent suffering, but because of the disproportion of his guilt and his punishment. His misfortune is far greater than what his deeds have provoked, and this crystallizes the "tragic vision" of the whole story in which the unfathomable divine hostility lurks in its depth.[40] Saul's tragedy is deepened even further, by his struggle against fate and by his isolation from YHWH and his people, and this brings the narrative nearer to other tragedies. Therefore, the description of Saul in 1Sam is properly called a picture of a tragic hero.[41]

Indeed, there are many others who see Saul as a tragic hero in the Saul-David narrative, and only a few would deny such an element. The objection comes, however, from the reading that the positive or heroic picture of Saul in the HDR is intermittent, and the dominant depiction is negative. There are undeniably horrible pictures of the rejected king at the centre of the narrative. He throws his spear at his son-in-law David and at his own son Jonathan, and attempts to entrap his rival using his own daughter. He even massacres Ahimelech and the priests in Nob who seem to be innocent. Can these be the pictures of a tragic hero, and not rather of a mad and vicious oppressor? However, even in these horrendous events, we are led to see him more as a victim than as a villain because of the way in which the narrative is structured. In particular, the positioning of the account about the "evil spirit" at the very beginning of the Saul-David conflict protects the rejected king from unsympathetic criticism.

The "evil spirit from YHWH/Elohim"[42] first appears in 1Sam 16:14, and introduces David into the Saulide court. Despite the auspicious beginning, this brings

Press, 1980), 33–56; Diana V. Edelman, *King Saul in the Historiography of Judah* (Sheffield: Sheffield Academic Press, 1991), 76–82, 99–111.

**36** Gunn, *The Fate of King Saul*, 18–19.

**37** Gunn, *The Fate of King Saul*, 54.

**38** Gunn, *The Fate of King Saul*, 66.

**39** Gunn, *The Fate of King Saul*, 123.

**40** J. Cheryl Exum, *Tragedy and Biblical Narrative: Arrows of the Almighty* (Cambridge: Cambridge University Press, 1992), 5–10.

**41** Exum, *Tragedy and Biblical Narrative*, 36–41.

**42** The phrase "evil spirit" occurs only seven times in the whole Hebrew Bible, and six of them occur in 1Sam 16–19 that constitutes the beginning of David's rise and Saul's decline. It occurs

the whole series of unfortunate events into motion: Saul's hatred and persecution of David, Saul's estrangement from his son, his daughter, and his servants, and the deaths of the Saulides and the unfortunate endings of those who loved David (Jonathan, Michal). One might think that the narrative fairly clearly suggests that the reason for all the tragic events was because Saul was jealous, paranoid, and terrified. However, the concentrated occurrences of the evil spirit tormenting Saul at the very beginning of the whole story gives the reader the impression that everything happens under a force that goes well beyond Saul's control. In particular, if we remember that the verb צלח points to a total and permanent transformation of a person,[43] we cannot certainly say that the influence of the evil spirit is limited only to Saul's first two murder attempts. In the Hebrew Bible, the verb in Qal normally means "succeed", but there is one textual group in which the verb appears with רוח as its subject and means "take over" or "come upon". This usage of the verb occurs only eight times in the Hebrew Bible, and before 1Sam 18:10, it is used when the spirit turns the possessed into a completely different person. For example, the spirit "takes over" the person of Samson, and endows him with superhuman power, so that he tears apart a lion, kills thirty Ashkelonites, and breaks himself free from the ropes binding him for the Philistines (Judg 14:6,19; 15:14). Similarly, when the spirit "takes over" the person of Saul, it kindles his military zeal against the Ammonites, and leads him to proclaim a national war (1Sam 11:6). Thinking of Saul who used to hide himself among the baggage to avoid discovery (I Sam 10:22), this picture of mustering people for war shows that "take-over" by the spirit has made Saul a different person. The verb, however, can also add the sense that such an activity of the divine spirit is definitive to the character of the possessed, unless it is undone as in the case of Saul. For instance, the person of Saul is "taken over" by the spirit soon after he is anointed, and acquires the "enduring charisma of the king" (1Sam 10:6,10).[44] More evidently, when the spirit "took over" the person of David,

---

elsewhere only in Judges 9:23, and the evil spirit there functions to create enmity between the proto-monarch Abimelech and the lords of Shechem. In I Samuel, the phrase shows some variations: "evil spirit from YHWH (רוּחַ־רָעָה מֵאֵת יְהוָה)" (16:14), "evil spirit of Elohim (רוּחַ־אֱלֹהִים רָעָה)" (16:15,16; 18:10), "spirit of Elohim... evil spirit" (16:23), and "evil spirit of YHWH (רוּחַ יְהוָה רָעָה)" (19:9). In the first and the last, the evil spirit is explicitly ascribed to YHWH, whereas in the middle, evil spirit is linked with Elohim. Some argue that the evil spirit from YHWH and that of Elohim can be or should be distinguished, but it is better to take them to mean the same, because the servants of Saul's court identify the spirit tormenting Saul as "the evil spirit of Elohim", although the narrator called it "the evil spirit from YHWH" in the previous verses (16:14–16).

**43** J. Hausmann, "צלח," in *TDOT*, XII (2003), 382–385.
**44** S. Tengström, "רוח," in *TDOT*, XIII (2004), 365–402 (392).

the narrator reports that it never left him (I Samuel 16. 13). In brief, "take-over" by the spirit in the Hebrew narrative means that the person taken over is made into a totally different person, and this is more or less a permanent transformation. Therefore, the work of the evil spirit at the beginning defines the whole picture of what is going on in the following Saul-David narrative, and this provides the background against which the reader evaluates the rejected king.[45] Consequently, when we see Saul who, knowing what God has already decided about him (1Sam 24:21), weeps (24:17) and asks his successor for mercy (24:22), and yet pursues David soon again (ch. 26), the image left in our mind is a poor human being haunted by the evil spirit from God. He is indeed a victim of God's unfathomable hostility, and we have this impression precisely because the narrative informs us at the very beginning that the evil spirit tormented Saul. Ironically, the evil spirit that tormented Saul in his lifetime saved him from outright condemnation after his death.[46]

Further evidence that the *Tendenz* of the HDR is not to vilify Saul can be found in the fact that the narrative does include positive but unnecessary reports about Saul. From the earliest parts to the end, we come across those who remain faithful to Saul. In chapter 16, we see Saul's servants caring for their tormented king, and volunteering to help him (1Sam 16:16). Even after Saul's unstable behaviour, people in the narrative show loyalty to the king. The Ziphites volunteer to help Saul by informing him of David's hiding place twice (1Sam 23 & 26), and after Saul's death, presumably to honour the dead king's body,[47] the people of Jabesh-Gilead are reported to have "run all night, and taken the corpse of

---

45 Actions frequently repeated can be introduced by the use of וְהָיָה at the beginning (G-K, §122ee), and therefore, the syntax in 1Sam 16:23 that begins with וְהָיָה might suggest that being possessed was not his constant state. However, even if Saul was not always under the influence of the evil spirit, both attempts to kill David, which initiate the whole series of unfortunate events, are explicitly related to the spirit, and this indicates that the attack was, albeit intermittent, crucial in how Saul behaved. Cf. Fredrik Lindström, *God and the Origin of Evil: A Contextual Analysis of Alleged Monistic Evidence in the Old Testament* (Lund: CWK Gleerup, 1983), 78–84.

46 It is often argued that the evil spirit was sent to Saul, because Saul was sinful and deserved it. However, as I mentioned earlier in the footnote (#34), the text does not make clear that Saul deserved YHWH's rejection and the evil spirit.

47 Whether the cremation of the royal bodies was considered acceptable practice for a royal Judahite burial is not certain. It was the preferred method for Hittite royalty and an accepted form of honourable burial for the Greeks. But there is some evidence that it was not the case for the Judahites. The context here, however, suggests that the cremation of Saul's body was to honour the king. Otherwise, the Jabesh-Gileadites would not have run all night to save the body. Cf. Edelman, *King Saul in the Historiography of Judah*, 292–4.

Saul and the corpses of his sons (1Sam 31:12)".[48] Considering that Saul complained to his servants for not showing compassion[49] to him (1Sam 22:8), and that he praised the Ziphites for having shown "compassion (חמל)" to him (1Sam 23:21), the pictures of these loyal to Saul urge the reader to show compassion on Saul, and "be blessed". Finally, the narrator includes another unnecessary verse in 24:10, where David says to Saul, "Why do you listen to the words of people (אדם) who say that David is now seeking to do you harm?" To a large extent, this clears Saul of the charge of unfounded persecution, because David's words indicate that Saul's suspicion of David's disloyalty was not from Saul's madness or paranoia, but from ill advice from the unknown "people".

One might argue that the sympathetic view about Saul is not from the text, but from the ingenious reading strategy of the modern literary critics. Brettler in particular thinks that such a sympathetic reading is anachronistic, because the time of the composition was an "era of competing royal ideologies in ancient Israel, and it was necessary for them to combat propaganda with counter-propaganda".[50] However, even if we set aside the fact that interpretation cannot be immune from the reader, it is unlikely that the sympathetic reading is merely a clever interpretation of trendy criticism, because some early readers' comments testify that there were similar interpretations in the very early days. For instance, Josephus in the 1st century C.E. already evaluated Saul as a "uniquely just, courageous, and prudent man",[51] and dedicated an encomium to the tragic king, which is three times longer than that of David, urging "kings of nations and rulers of cities" to learn from his courage,

---

**48** Edelman thinks that the Jabesh-Gileadites had lost trust in Saul, because they did not respond to Saul's muster of "all Israel" in 1Sam 29:4, even though they are depicted as corporate members of Israel in 11:1–4. In my view, however, David's persuasion or threat (?) in 2Sam 2:5–7 demonstrates the ongoing loyalty of the Jabesh-Gileadites to Saul. Their failure to respond might have been due to the geographical distance. See Edelman, *King Saul in the Historiography of Judah*, 291–2.

**49** The exact meaning of the Hebrew word חֹלֶה in the verse is disputed. LXX has πονῶν, and Vulgate has *doleat*. Stoebe links them to the verb כאב (be sick). Driver and McCarter follow the Greek word, but think that it reflects חמל, and translate "have compassion". By contrast, James Barr, followed by Tsumura, defends the MT, and believes that the word derives from the root which has the meaning "be sorry, think". Whatever the original reading was, it is clear that the point of Saul's complaint is that they are not sympathetic to Saul. See Stoebe, *Das erste Buch Samuelis*, 408–9; James Barr, *Comparative Philology and the Text of the Old Testament* (Oxford: Clarendon, 1968), 326; Tsumura, *The First Book of Samuel*, 541.

**50** Brettler, *Creation*, 109.

**51** Flavius Josephus, *Judean Antiquities*, Books 5–7. *Translation and Commentary by Christopher Begg* (Leiden: Brill, 2001), 6.346.

for he, though he knew what was to happen and the death awaiting him – the prophet having foretold [this] – gave no thought to flight, nor was he so attached to life as to hand over his people to the enemy and thus dishonour the dignity of his kingship. Instead, he thought it noble to expose himself, his house, and his sons to these dangers, to fall with them, fighting on behalf of those ruled by him.[52]

It is possible that Josephus' sympathetic description of Saul was due to his desire to identify himself with biblical heroes. He made Jeremiah, Esther, Daniel, and Mordecai some kind of prototype of his own destiny, and he might have seen Saul's tragic end as another prototype of his fate as a "martyred general".[53] However, thinking that Josephus followed closely the books of Samuel when he wrote *Judean Antiquities*, his depiction of Saul cannot be a total invention or a product of over-interpretation. Rather, it indicates that he did not interpret the narrative in Samuel as anti-Saulide.

Several rabbinic and midrashic interpretations are other examples of early readers who interpret Saul in 1Sam more positively. The examples are introduced by Hanna Liss in her essay "The Innocent King. Saul in Rabbinic Exegesis", and only a few are cited here. Midrash Tanḥuma 2b:4 and t. Ber 4:18 for example emphasize Saul's modesty by making his sense of unworthiness and reluctance to be king explicit in the narrative, and Midrash Sam 7:2 praises Saul's halakhic obedience on the basis of 1Sam 14:32ff where Saul instructs people to follow meticulously the sacrificial laws. Sometimes Saul's mistakes are defended or ex-

---

52 Josephus, *Judean Antiquities*, 6.344–345; James Montgomery however thinks that it is not praise at all, and writes, "I doubt if there in any better example in all literature of absurd homiletics... than his moral reflections on Saul and the witch of Endor in *Antiquities* 6.340–350." However, if we understand how much the heroic deaths in the Greek tragedies appealed to the audience in the Greco-Roman world, we could see that Josephus used the best way possible in order to make Saul seen as a great hero of the Jews. For example, the portrait of Homer's Achilles, who knew that he would die prematurely if he continued to fight against the Trojans, but chose to gain glory by fighting, was regarded as the classical example of heroism (*Iliad* 9.410–16). Similarly, Hector, who did not cease fighting even if he lost his spear in the final combat against Achilles, was another example which showed how a hero should accept their last moment (*Iliad* 22.304–305). Indeed, as Josephus knew the Homeric heroes as testified in *Against Apion* 1.12., the description of Saul as reminiscent of Homeric heroes was likely to be a deliberate strategy to make Saul seen as a Jewish equivalent of the great Greek heroes. See James A. Montgomery, "The Religion of Flavius Josephus," *Jewish Quarterly Review* 11 (1920–21): 277–305 (304, #45); Louis H. Feldman, "Josephus' View of Saul," in *Saul in Story and Tradition*, ed. Carl S. Ehrlich (Tübingen: Mohr Siebeck, 2006), 214–244 (227).
53 David Daube, "Typology in Josephus," *Journal of Jewish Studies* 31 (1980): 18–36 (26); Louis H. Feldman, *Josephus's Interpretation of the Bible* (Berkeley: University of California Press, 1998), 56.

plained sympathetically. For instance, Saul's sparing of Agag is defended on the basis of halakhic arguments, and for the massacre in Nob, David and Jonathan rather than Saul are blamed. His visit to the woman in Endor is also seen sympathetically, in that Samuel is depicted as a hypocrite, while Saul as one accepting his destiny.[54] In short, according to some rabbinic and midrashic interpretations, Saul was a "righteous" and innocent king who accepted his destiny.[55]

Of course, there were other early interpretations that understood Saul negatively. The Chronicler reports only his death, and justifies the death and the transfer of the kingdom to David, by commenting that Saul was "unfaithful to YHWH in that he did not keep the command of YHWH", and that "he had consulted a medium, seeking guidance, and did not seek guidance from YHWH (1Chr 10:13–14)". Although it is not true that Saul did not seek guidance from YHWH,[56] these verses epitomize how the Chronicler understood the Saul-David narrative in the books of Samuel which had been handed over to him.[57] Psalm 79 and the hymns in Ben Sirach (ch. 44ff) reflect a similar view, by excluding Saul from the *Heilsgeschichte* of Israel,[58] and later in the 1st century C.E., Saul is portrayed negatively in *Pseudo-Philo* as "paradigmatic for the bad leader".[59] Considering the Chronicler's tendency to glorify David, and the importance of David at the time of the rising messianic hope,[60] however, it is worthwhile to give more attention to the existence of pro-Saulide interpretations than to anti-Saulide ones. No one would deny that 1Sam prefers David to Saul, but the impor-

---

54 Leviticus Rabbah 26:7. For the English translation, see *Midrash Rabbah,* trans. J. Israelstam & J. J. Slotki; ed. H. Freedman and M. Simon, 10 vols (London: Soncino, 1939–1992), IV (1951), 335–6.

55 Hanna Liss, "The Innocent King. Saul in Rabbinic Exegesis," in *Saul in Story and Tradition,* ed. Ehrlich, 245–260.

56 "When Saul inquired of YHWH, YHWH did not answer him, not by dreams, or by Urim, or by prophets." (1Sam 28:6)

57 Graeme Auld holds that the Chronicler did not have the books of Samuel, but there was a common source both for the Chronicler and for the author of the books of Samuel. Although the view is not totally unconvincing, I follow the view of the majority scholars that the Chroniclers wrote their version of the Israelite history on the basis of the books of Samuel. See Graeme Auld, *Kings without Privilege* (Edinburgh: T&T Clark, 1994); Y.S. (Craig) Ho, "Conjectures and Refutations: Is 1 Samuel xxxi 1–13 really the source of 1 Chronicles x 1–12?" *VT* 45 (1995): 82–106.

58 Von Rad, *Old Testament Theology,* I, 327.

59 Frederick J. Murphy, *Pseudo-Philo: Rewriting the Bible* (New York: Oxford University Press, 1993), 186, 205–219.

60 For instance, in *Testaments of the Twelve Patriarchs,* the original of which is from the 1st century BCE, non-Davidic king is severely criticised, and the hope of the restoration of the Davidic monarchy is clearly envisaged. See especially, Text XII, Jud 22:2f. Cf. Walter Dietrich, *David: Der Herrscher mit der Harfe* (Leipzig: Evangelische Verlagsanstalt, 2006), 335–341.

tant question is how the point is made. Does the text make its point by presenting Saul totally negatively? My view is that it does not, and should warn us against seeing the story as propaganda. It is possible, as Brettler argues, that pro-Saulide interpretations were due to the then existing but now lost pro-Saulide traditions,[61] or, as Liss claims, the less anti-Saulide interpretations reflect the efforts of the rabbis who wanted neither pro-monarchic nor anti-monarchic ideals at the time when they were endeavouring to establish a Jewish nation on the basis of Torah.[62] However, although one should admit that some rabbinic literature evidently shows elements of over-interpretation, it seems that the biblical narrative itself is open to those less anti-Saulide interpretations. And if both ancient and modern readers can read the narrative not as straightforwardly anti-Saulide, we may well ask whether the purpose of the narrative was propagandistic or apologetic, because it is less likely that propaganda/apology would describe the opponent with such sympathy and respect.

### 1.2.2.2 Is the HDR unambiguously pro-Davidic?

Even if one adopts the interpretation less hostile to Saul, the view can still stand that the HDR is Davidic propaganda, because the focus of the propaganda might have been more sophisticated and less antagonistic. That is, the pro-Davidic party might have wanted to argue that David was the legitimate successor to the great but unfortunate king, and their focus was to convince readers that a brighter future was ahead with the new king. If this were the case, there would have been no need to vilify Saul. It needed only to show how worthy David was to be the successor to the previous king, and how blessed he was by God, and we can easily find such elements in the Saul-David story. However, even such a modified view cannot stand sensitive reading of the text, because it seems obvious that the narrative allows the reader to glimpse the darker side of David.

Above all, the characterization of David in the Saul-David narrative is not always conducive to presenting David as an ideal successor to Saul; indeed sometimes, the narrative sounds almost anti-Davidic. In contrast with Saul who was tragic but always transparent and heroic, or in contrast with Jonathan who was innocent and selfless, David is often depicted as passively calculating, ambitious, secretive, unloving, and potentially violent. This is made most evident in the Jonathan passages, because here the too virtuous picture of Jonathan cre-

---

**61** Brettler, *Creation*, 111.
**62** Liss, 256.

ates such a stark contrast that David's negative traits are made to stand out. For example, in contrast with Jonathan who loves David at the risk of his own life, David is never said to love anyone. If the subject in וַיֶּאֱהָבֵהוּ (1Sam 16:21) is David, it would be the only exception. However, the context suggests that the subject is more likely to be Saul, and even if David were the subject, it seems merely an expression of the treaty bond of David to Saul.[63] Besides, in contrast with the ever-communicative Jonathan, David is always secretive. He only once speaks to Jonathan in chapter 20, and that is solely for his own security. Lastly, the repetition of the covenant making between Jonathan and David leads us not only to see Jonathan's great love of David, but also nudges us to ask the reason for the unusual repetition. And not a few readers would see it as an indication of David's unreliable personality: Jonathan keeps making and renewing the covenant, precisely because David is not so reliable! Indeed, as Polzin points out, David's request of Jonathan to lie to his father in chapter 20 already hints that "David can dissemble when it is in his own interest to do so".[64]

One might protest that this overstretches the meaning of the text, and reads too much into it. However, it seems that over-interpretation is also prevalent for those who think the HDR to be propaganda. For instance, the "overkill" or "over-stress" in the story has often been regarded as the sign of the propagandistic or apologetic nature of the narrative. Too emphatic a denial of David's involvement with Abner's and Ishbaal's deaths, it is often argued, indicates that the historical fact was the opposite, and thus the text is propagandistic or apologetic.[65] If "over-stress" was a literary device as Wesselius claims, however, is it impossible that the author used it deliberately to express an anti-Davidic sentiment? That an ancient author devised a hidden signal in the text might sound too speculative at first, but there are several indications that warn us not to dismiss the possibility too quickly. For instance, the twice-mentioned arrow-shooting in chapter 20 has no immediate function in the narrative. David is informed by Jonathan *in person*

---

63 For the discussion about the subject of וַיֶּאֱהָבֵהוּ, see Fokkelman, *Narrative Art and Poetry in the Books of Samuel*, II, 140; McCarter, *I Samuel*, 281–2; Edelman, *King Saul in the Historiography of Judah*, 122; S. D. Walters, "The Light and the Dark," in *Ascribe to the Lord: Biblical and Other Studies in Memory of Peter C. Craigie*, eds. L. Eslinger & G. Taylor (Sheffield: JSOT Press, 1988), 567–89.

64 Polzin, *Samuel and the Deuteronomist*, 192.

65 VanderKam thinks that "the zeal of the editor to exonerate David" leads us to suspect David's complicity in Abner's and Ishbaal's deaths. Similarly, Wesselius suggests that the device of "over-stress" is "an indicator that what is told is but part of the truth and that other aspects of the events can easily be detected." See James C. Vanderkam, "Davidic Complicity", 533; J. W. Wesselius, "Joab's Death and the Central Theme of the Succession Narrative (2 Samuel IX – 1 Kings II)," *VT* 40 (1990): 336–351 (339–340).

of Saul's ultimate resolution to kill him (20:41–42), and this makes the arrow-shooting sign unnecessary. Nonetheless, the author went on for as many as 10 verses to repeat what is apparently unnecessary, and we are led to wonder what its precise function is. Of course, they might be a later addition designed to embellish the story and to make the friendship between them look more genuine.[66] Yet, it is interesting that the arrow-shooting episode finishes with the following sentence: "But the boy knew nothing; only Jonathan and David knew the arrangement (20:39)." With this concluding report, the reader might well be encouraged to notice that there is something cryptic in the narrative, and some – not all – will recognize the hidden message in the text. The possibility of such literary signals is acknowledged even by those who think that the HDR is an apology. For instance, in connection with the anti-Davidic verses in the narrative, Meir Malul writes, "[i]t is our impression, that this author or editor, though commissioned to write a certain 'history', nevertheless was clever enough to insert here and there subtle hints which reveal the true nature of the 'history' he wrote or rather was commissioned to write."[67]

In fact, it is not historically impossible that a scribe of northern origin in the Davidic court sneaked his own ambivalence about, or distrust of, David into an official document. Just as the Russian composer Dmitri Shostakovich parodied Stalin's oppression with the exaggeratedly glorious finale in his 5th Symphony, so the writer or compiler of the Jonathan passages could have attempted a similar effect by repeatedly mentioning David's old covenant with Jonathan. Absalom's revolt was supported both by northern Israel and Judah, and surely there were a considerable number of people who were discontented with David.[68] This makes it plausible that a similar sentiment was expressed covertly in the HDR. If the HDR was not composed by the core members of the royal court, the probability is higher. We can imagine for instance that the young man who first recommended David to Saul in 1Sam 16:18 was given an insignificant position later by the new regime, and wrote a court history with the sense of disappointment and grumble at David's unreliability! This in turn raises an interesting question about

---

66 Ralph W. Klein, *1 Samuel* (Waco: Word Books, 1983), 209.

67 Meir Malul, "Was David involved in the Death of Saul on the Gilboa Mountain?" *RB* 103 (1996): 517–545 (520, #10).

68 The union between the northern tribes and Judah was vulnerable, and so the discontent of the northerners is easily understandable. As to the southern discontent, two reasons can be mentioned: first, David moved the capital to Jerusalem from Hebron; second, David introduced the Ark, a cultic object of the northern tribes that had been contaminated by the Philistines, to Jerusalem. See Albrecht Alt, *Kleine Schriften zur Geschichte des Volkes Israel III*, 2nd edition (München: Beck, 1968), 243–257.

genre-recognition: If the author, although he was commissioned to write propaganda, only pretended to do so and expressed his resistance covertly in the writing, is the text propaganda or something else? In any case, the existence of the less pro-Davidic or mildly anti-Davidic passages in the narrative should rather be interpreted as indicating that the *Tendenz* of the narrative is less apparent than many scholars have argued.

In addition to the potentially anti-Davidic passages, some unnecessarily negative reports about David in the narrative also make us suspect that the author did not aim at writing propaganda. The scene in chapter 17 where the boy David repeatedly asks about the reward for killing Goliath gives the impression that David was an ambitious man from his boyhood,[69] and David's confession in 22:22 that he knew Doeg's presence when he visited Ahimelech unnecessarily betrays that he was careless and culpable for the deaths of the priests in Nob. In narrating the political deals between David and Abner in 2Sam, the author even tells of Michal's husband weeping for losing his wife (3:16). This unnecessarily poignant scene highlights David's cold-bloodedness, because the narrative does not say that the request of Michal was made out of David's love of Michal, and Michal's relationship with David later in the narrative indicates that David's motive was more political.[70] The narrative implicitly tells the reader that David did not hesitate to destroy the husband-wife relationship of the one who saved him in the past for the sake of his own political benefit. A propagandistic author would not have wanted to include such a description.

Again, the less pro-Davidic interpretation might be accused of being an overclever reading influenced by modern literary criticism, but such an interpretation is found among the interpretations of early readers. Most noticeably, the Babylonian Talmud blames David for the massacre in Nob, and for the death of Saul and his sons. It says, "the Holy One, blessed be He, had said to David, 'How long will this crime be hidden in thy hand [i.e., unpunished]. Through thee Nob, the city of Priests, was massacred [...] and through thee Saul and his three sons were slain'."[71] Were the Jewish sages aware of the sophisticated skills like "over-stress" to discover the truth behind the text? Is it not more plausible

---

69 We do not know how old he was exactly, so it is possible that David was not a boy at the time. However, he was too young to follow his elder brothers for war, and this indicates that David was quite young.

70 John Kessler, "Sexuality and Politics: The Motif of the Displaced Husband in the Books of Samuel," *CBQ* 62 (2000): 409–23 (416); Ellen White, "Michal the Misinterpreted," *JSOT* 31 (2007): 451–64.

71 *The Babylonian Talmud: Sanhedrin*, trans. I. Epstein; ed. H. Freedman (London: Soncino, 1935), 95a (640).

that the text itself allows the interpreter to read the text in that way? If so, does not this mean that the text is not intended to cover up David's faults?

### 1.2.2.3 The Parallels with the Ancient Near Eastern Literature

All things considered then, Alter's evaluation does much to commend the view that David depicted in the narrative is "one of the most unfathomable figures of ancient literature",[72] and such a characterization of the main hero makes it doubtful that the HDR can be labelled as pro-Davidic propaganda or apology. Some might still want to raise the question whether such a conclusion is due to an anachronistic interpretation. Probably, they would argue, that was how the parallel literature in the ancient Near East propagated the royal ideologies, and the HDR was just following or has developed the style or form that had been handed down for ages. Against such a view, I would like to show that the parallels between the HDR and the ancient Near Eastern royal apologies are not as close as has been argued.

Above all, the way in which David and Saul are described in the HDR is markedly different from the way the defendant and the opponent are described in other ancient Near Eastern apologies. This point is succinctly made by David A. Bosworth who, on the basis of Dietrich's previous studies, points to the differences between the David narratives and other ancient Near Eastern literature. According to his observation, there are five areas where the comparison is possible: (i) nearness of the king to the divinity; (ii) the king's personal merits; (iii) the king's dynastic descent or popular support, or both; (iv) the king's success against foreigners; and (v) the king's success at home. In each area, the biblical portrait of David has some propagandistic or apologetic elements, but it also allows criticisms of David not common in the wider literature. For instance, (i) David's relationship with God is not always "sunny", and this is not a standard part of the ancient Near Eastern presentations of royalty; both (ii) the mentioning of David's weakness, grief, and humiliation, and (iii) the frank admissions of David's unpopularity are very unusual in ancient Near Eastern royal propaganda; (iv) David's military campaigns against the foreigners were not totally successful; and (v) his success at home is not perfect either. Consequently, Bosworth concludes, "[t]he biblical portrait of David does include elements characteristic of propaganda; it presents David in positive ways that tend to legitimate his rule. The narrative also includes, however, negative aspects that cast doubt on David's

---

72 Alter, *David Story*, xviii.

moral quality (and therefore his legitimacy). In other words, the text is not as simple as 'royal propaganda'."[73]

Even if we narrow down the comparison, and compare the HDR with the Hittite apologies, which are regarded as the closest parallels, the differences are quite remarkable. True, there are lots of elements that the HDR shares with the Telepinu Proclamation and the Apology of Hattušili III. Both the HDR and the Hittite apologies attempt to justify the usurpation by emphasizing the unworthiness of their predecessors, by describing the victors as merciful, and above all, by appealing to the divine will. However, the following features make the connection less than reliable. First, as already pointed out by commentators, there is a radical formal difference between the Hittite apologies and the HDR. The former were written in the first person, whereas the latter is in the third. This formal difference, in my view, is too great to be explained as a development of the genre, especially because later apologies such as that of Nabonidus still maintain the first person form. Secondly, it is remarkable that despite such evident apologetic tones, the Hittite apologies do imply that the kings did indeed usurp the throne. In the Telepinu Proclamation, "Telepinu drove them [king Huzziya and his five brothers] away." In the Apology of Hattušiliš, Urhiteshub is reported to have battle with Hattušiliš, and finds himself trapped in the town of Shamuha "like a pig in a sty" or "like a fish in a net".[74] By contrast, contradicting the usual frankness about David's fault, the HDR never says that David actually confronted Saul, and usurped the throne. Thirdly, as admitted by Hoffner and McCarter, it is difficult to attempt a genre comparison on the basis of only two works. Hoffner claims that it might be because there were not many usurpations.[75] However, considering the continuous coups d'état in the Northern Kingdom, it is remarkable that we have nothing else to compare with the Hittite apologies. Finally, the suggestion that the HDR is royal propaganda presupposes quite an early dating, because after the collapse of the northern kingdom, antipathy against the northerners decreased. However, the argument for the early dating of the HDR in David's or Solomon's time is less than clear.[76]

A more fundamental difficulty in comparing the ancient Near Eastern "apologies" with the David narratives is that it is arguable whether the literature

---

**73** David A. Bosworth, "Evaluating King David: Old Problems and Recent Scholarship," *CBQ* 68 (2006): 191–210 (204–209); Walter Dietrich, "Das biblische Bild der Herrschaft Davids," in idem, *Von David zu den Deuteronomisten: Studien zu den Geschichtsüberlieferungen des Alten Testaments* (Stuttgart: Kohlhammer, 2002), 9–31.

**74** Hoffner, "Propaganda and Political Justification," 53–54.

**75** Hoffner, "Propaganda and Political Justification," 50.

**76** Dietrich, *Early Monarchy*, 248, 263.

which scholars draw on to find a parallel with the HDR can be safely called "propaganda" or "apology" anyway. For instance, as to the understanding of the inscription of Idrimi, Van Seters pointed out that "[t]he work is not propagandistic in the narrow sense of trying to win public support for any specific actions of the king, but it has a general political function in projecting an image of the founder of a new dynasty".[77] The similarities with the HDR are very general indeed, and it seems inappropriate to think of any common literary tradition between them.[78] Even the Hittite apologies, which scholars regard almost as the archetype of the genre of royal apology, are not totally free from generic ambiguity. The difficulty in categorizing the apology of Hattušili III as to its genre has been long recognized,[79] and Cancik in particular is convinced that the genre of the document is that of an "endowment document (*Stiftungsurkunde*)", and the "apology" functions only as a historical introduction.[80] The introduction is unusually long and literarily creative, but it is not solid enough to base the whole genre of royal apology on such an ambiguous ground.

An additional difficulty is that whereas "propaganda" and "apology" nowadays imply some sort of untruth – whether it be total distortion or shrewd manipulation – it is not always easy to tell whether a certain ancient text intended to tell the truth or not. For instance, it is generally agreed that Hattušili's religious piety was not completely unfounded.[81] He indeed believed that his god led him to the kingship, and he recorded what he believed to be true. Can we call such a writing propaganda, and say that he was writing it to justify his illegitimate usurpation through religion? The writer might have written what was untrue, but if the writer believed that he was writing truthfully, was he writing propaganda or a historical record? The existence of different or conflicting accounts of the same event can be helpful, because it can at least confirm that the account could be deceptive. For instance, I am less reluctant to call the re-

---

77 Van Seters, *In Search of History*, 190.

78 Similarly, Longman III, *Fictional Akkadian Autobiography*, 73.

79 Th. P. J. van den Hout, "Apology of Hattušili III," in *COS*, I, 199; Alfonso Archi, "The Propaganda of Hattušili III," *Studi Miceni ed Egeo-Anatolici* 14 (1971): 185–215 (186); Hubert Cancik, *Grundzüge der hethitischen und alttestamentlichen Geschichtsschreibung* (Wiesbaden: Harrassowitz, 1976), 41–44; Hans H. Güterbock, "Hittite Historiography: a Survey," in *History, Historiography, and Interpretation*, eds. Hayim Tadmor and Moshe Weinweld (Jerusalem: Magnes, 1983): 21–35 (30).

80 Cancik, *Grundzüge der hethitischen und alttestamentlichen Geschichtsschreibung*, 43. Cancik's view is accepted by Van Seters and Fischer. See Van Seters, *In Search of History*, 119–120; Alexander A. Fischer, *Von Hebron nach Jerusalem: Eine redaktionsgeschichtliche Studie zur Erzählung von König David in II Sam 1–5* (Berlin: de Gruyter, 2004), 189.

81 Archi, "The Propaganda of Hattušili III", 197–200.

cord of Hattušili III royal propaganda or apology, because his son's historical accounts and his own correspondence with the royal courts of Assyria, Babylon, and Egypt tell us that the reality was quite different from what is written in the Apology.[82] But the David story has no such extrabiblical materials to compare with and offer a different view. This indicates that we should be doubly careful in labelling the Davidic narrative propaganda. We do not know whether the writer was deliberately distorting the facts or was writing what he believed to be true.[83]

All these discussions perhaps bring us back to the issue about the definition of propaganda/apology. What is propaganda? What does it mean to be apologetic? In fact, all our objections to labelling the HDR as "propaganda" can be circumvented by defining the term "propaganda" as "an extremely subtle form of communication".[84] There might be a kind of "Richter scale" of propaganda techniques,[85] and the ambiguity found in the David story might reflect the superb propaganda techniques used by the author. Indeed, one of the standard textbooks on propaganda lists several different kinds of propaganda.

> White propaganda comes from a source that is identified correctly, and the information in the message tends to be accurate [...] Black propaganda is when the source is concealed or credited to a false authority and spreads lies, fabrications, and deceptions [...] Gray propaganda is somewhere between white and black propaganda.[86]

According to this categorization, the David narrative might come under the category of "gray propaganda", and this might justify labelling the HDR as propaganda. However, the same authors distinguish "persuasion" from propaganda, and say that the distinction between "propaganda" and "persuasion" lies in the fact that the propagandist is concerned to benefit only the view of the writer, whereas "persuasion" aims at mutual understanding and benefit. Now a difficulty arises, because we are not sure whether the David story was written to benefit

---

**82** Th. P. J. van den Hout, "Khattushili III, King of the Hittites," *Civilizations of the Ancient Near East*, ed. Jack Sasson, 4 vols (New York: Scribner, 1995), II: 1107–1112 (1108).

**83** A similar point is made by Sparks when he discusses the genre-recognition of some ancient near eastern literature. He writes, "'lthough modern scholars are fairly confident that the authors of the Weidner Chronicle and the Synchronistic History invented many aspects of their histories, it is impossible to know whether they really believed their invented stories (reified fiction) or whether they merely used them to achieve pious aims (generic ruse or generic deception)." See Sparks, *Ancient Texts*, 410–411.

**84** Whitelamn, "The Defence of David," 65–68.

**85** Rex Mason, *Propaganda and Subversion in the Old Testament* (London: SPCK, 1997), 170–174.

**86** Garth S. Jewett and Victoria O'Donnell, *Propaganda and Persuasion*, 3rd edition (London: Sage, 1999), 16–20.

only the Davidic monarchy and his supporters,[87] or was also aimed at helping the people of Israel to come to terms with the tragic events surrounding Saul or later tragedies. All this makes it inappropriate to explain the less anti-Saulide and less pro-Davidic elements in the HDR by appealing to some modified definitions of the term "propaganda". In fact, if we can fiddle with the definition of propaganda, anything can be seen as some sort of propaganda. Is there any text – text in the broadest sense – which does not propagate the ideology of the writer? Probably, deliberate untruthfulness is most characteristic in propaganda, and if we want to label the HDR as such, we should be able to demonstrate that the HDR deliberately relates what is not true for a particular – most likely political – reason. This cannot be demonstrated however, and the less anti-Saulide and less pro-Davidic nature of the narrative should lead to the conclusion that the David narrative is not propaganda.

### 1.2.2.4 A Different Context of the Reader

I believe that I have shown sufficiently so far that the David narrative and the HDR, which cannot be separated completely when we interpret the whole, cannot be called "propaganda" or "apology". Yet, I add briefly the point that our reading context, i.e., the presuppositions which the current reader brings to the text, discourages us from conceding this widely held view about the HDR. Some might object to considering the reading context for genre-recognition. However, to a certain extent, genre is recognized by a process of abstraction,[88] and this is inevitably affected by the reader. In other words, when a text includes different voices, one must choose which of them is dominant, and this selection is very much influenced by the reader's situation. In fact, it is not difficult to see that "reading the HDR as propaganda" was heavily influenced by the reading context of the time. In the 1970–1980 s when the framework began dominating scholarship, there were several elements that encouraged such an interpretation. Firstly, it was widely held at the time that the David narratives in Samuel were an outstanding example of historiography that stood comparison only with the later Greek ones. The David narratives were fundamentally a historical record, and

---

**87** Lemche applies here the principle used in Roman criminal cases, *cui bono*, and the fact that David greatly benefits from all the events leads him to conclude that it was written to support David's cause. Ishida expresses a similar view. However, I think that there is a logical leap in drawing such a conclusion. For instance, in the Joseph story, despite all the obstacles, Joseph always comes out on top, but no one calls the Joseph story propaganda. See Lemche, "David's Rise", pp. 2–25; Fischer, *Von Hebron nach Jerusalem*, 183–193.
**88** Richter, 132.

scholars were keen to discover historical facts from the books of Samuel. In short, "reading the HDR as history" was a scholarly tradition with which any discussion should converse, whether one sees it as a correct or mistaken one. Secondly, the overstretched "hermeneutics of suspicion" was becoming more popular, and there was a growing tendency to analyze the given text with exaggerated suspicion. No benefit of the doubt was allowed when it came to dealing with traditions, and authoritative texts such as the biblical narratives were more likely to be seen as including untruth to bolster the position of those in power.[89] Finally, the political milieu of the cold war in which capitalists and communists were fighting each other with propagandas, along with Stefan Heym's novel *King David Report* that ingeniously captured such an atmosphere were great stimuli for discovering a similar work going on in the David narratives. I am not sure whether the David narrative was composed in an "era of competing royal ideologies in ancient Israel" as Brettler argues,[90] but the 1970 – 80 s were certainly an era of competing political ideologies. Moreover, although it is hardly possible to demonstrate the influence of Heym's novel on biblical scholarship, it is quite extraordinary that so many biblical scholars cite the novel when they present their views.[91] They might have done so just for reference or for interest, but the unusual nature of such fascination makes us wonder whether the novel contributed somehow to the scholarly interpretation of the David story, or at least to the confirmation of their provisional impression.[92]

The current reading context however is markedly different, and above all, reading the David narratives as history is not a widely accepted view any

---

**89** It is interesting that many scholars who think that the David narratives are propaganda apply the hermeneutics of suspicion to every bit of the text, while they have no difficulty in accepting the historical existence of David. I am of the view that David's historical existence is quite plausible, given the evidence available. Nonetheless, the plausibility of David's existence is not dramatically higher than David's murder of all his rivals, and yet, scholars build up hypotheses about the historical David (i.e. David's murders), on the basis of the not yet totally certain fact (i.e. David's existence).

**90** Brettler, *Creation*, 109.

**91** For instance, Hoffner, "Propaganda and Political Justification", 50; Brettler, *Creation*, 91–93; McKenzie, *King David*, 25–26; Halpern, *David's Secret Demons*, 96. The novel was published in 1972. For more focused discussion about Heym's novel, see Walter Dietrich, "Von einem, der zuviel wußte: Versuch über Stefan Heyms 'König David Bericht'," in *Von David zu den Deuteronomisten*, 100–112.

**92** It is noteworthy that Van Seters recently mentioned the influence of Heym's novel on Halpern's *David's Secret Demon* in his article, "A Response to G. Aichelle, P. Miscall and R. Walsh, 'An Elephant in the Room': Historical-Critical and the Postmodern Interpretations of the Bible," *JHS* 9 (2009) < http://www.arts.ualberta.ca/JHS/Articles/article_128.pdf> [accessed 8 November 2010] (10–13)

more. Ranke's "noble dream" of writing *wie es eigentlich gewesen* has turned out to be unachievable,[93] and hardly anyone thinks now that the purpose of the biblical narratives was to write history as it actually happened. Rather, reading the David narratives as propaganda or apology is the dominant view now, and that is where any scholarly discussion and critical dialogue about the HDR begins. Moreover, the cold war era has long finished, and the so-called post-modern thoughts and ideas have made people less interested in politics. If the political manipulation of information shocked people in the 20th century, now people are more likely to respond simply by saying: "so, what is new?" Finally, the hermeneutics of suspicion also seems to have lost much of its magic spell, especially as it is now often misappropriated to impose what the interpreter already had in their mind upon the text, or to create a very counter-intuitive interpretation. The clearest example of such an excessive use of the hermeneutics of suspicion is found in Baruch Halpern's *David's Secret Demons: Messiah, Murderer, Traitor, King*, and for recognizing the inappropriateness of the interpretation, the conclusion of his 480 page book is worthy of rather a long citation:

> The preceding investigations indicate that David's enemies regarded him as a non-Israelite. Specifically, they thought of him as the Gibeonite agent of Philistine masters. They accused him of importing a foreign icon, the ark, as his state symbol. He consistently allied with foreign powers to suppress the Israelites whom he dominated. He spent most of his career as a brigand-king, and where he ruled, he did so by employing murder and mayhem as tools of statecraft. In fact, the only murder in the books of Samuel of which he was probably innocent is the one murder of which he stands accused in the apology. His enemies considered him a mass murderer [...] The real David was not someone whom it would be wise to invite to dinner. And you certainly would not be happy to discover he was marrying your daughter, or even a casual acquaintance [...] The biblical story of David is indeed mythic in nature. But the myth was made necessary, though not by his glory, but his gore.[94]

Ironically, however, the prevailing hermeneutics of suspicion in scholarly discussion undercuts its own ability to persuade, because when suspicion is made too evident, it is not suspicion any more. And consequently, this brings about a question which produces exactly the opposite effect: How can suspicion play the role of uncovering the hidden truth, if the truth is already known to almost everybody? How can one be sure that the HDR was written as an apology for David, when everyone can see the defendant's murderous and treacherous nature on the basis of what is written?

---

**93** Cf. Elizabeth A. Clark, *History, Theory, Text: Historians and the Linguistic Turn* (Cambridge, MA: Harvard University Press, 2004), 9–28.
**94** Halpern, *David's Secret Demons*, 479–480.

To conclude, neither a literary reading of the Saul-David narrative, nor a closer investigation of the ancient Near Eastern parallels, nor our reading context encourages us to read the HDR as propaganda or royal apology.[95] In fact, we may well wonder whether we still have the problem which prompted us to read the HDR as propaganda, because the irreconcilable thematic disunity between the Saul Cycle and the HDR, and between the HDR and the "Succession Narrative" does not seem to exist anymore. All these narratives narrate the stories of great men's rise and fall, and the emphasis in each case is not so different that we need to come up with a hypothesis of Davidic propaganda to explain it.[96] They are different of course, but the degree of distinctiveness is not the kind that justifies labelling the HDR as propaganda. Now that we have come to the conclusion that "propaganda" or "apology" is not a valid framework for reading the HDR any more, we will attempt to find an alternative framework.

### 1.3 An Alternative Framework

What is then the most appropriate framework for reading the HDR at this point of interpretative history? What is the label with which we can describe the whole HDR best? These questions do not admit any simple answer which we might wish to obtain through a certain methodical procedure, and require us to carry out critical dialogues with different views. As we saw above, the dominant view of reading the HDR as propaganda is not satisfactory for telling us what the HDR is all about. The HDR as a whole is too subtle and sophisticated, and shows interests that go beyond what we would normally expect from propaganda. Re-

---

**95** More recent commentators such as Walter Dietrich, David T. Tsumura, Alexander A. Fischer, and David Bosworth expressed their reluctance to accept the widely held view. I discussed the issue more extensively however, because most scholars seem to mention it just in passing, expecting others to accept their presuppositions about the text. Probably, it is due to the difficulty of demonstrating what the genre of the HDR is, or because they think that such an issue does not make much difference. However, I am of the view that the genre-recognition or the understanding of the whole is crucial to further discussions, and through a dialogical process, we can achieve a better understanding of the text and find a better framework of reading the HDR. See Dietrich, *The Early Monarchy in Israel*, 249; Tsumura, *The First Book of Samuel*, 412; Fischer, *Von Hebron nach Jerusalem*, 193; Bosworth, "Evaluating King David," 209.

**96** This certainly urges us to draw more attention to the view represented by Schulte, Friedman, and Dietrich that rejects the hypothesis of the HDR. See Hannelis Schulte, *Die Entstehung der Geschichtsschreibung im alten Israel* (Berlin: de Gruyter, 1972); Richard Elliot Friedman, *The Hidden Book in the Bible* (London: Profile, 1999); Walter Dietrich, *The Early Monarchy in Israel: The Tenth Century B.C.E.* (Atlanta: Society of Biblical Literature, 2007).

cent studies thus tend to draw the conclusion that the HDR is more or less a fiction, and the literary artistry of the narrative, which has often been pointed out by literary critics, has supported such a view. Let us take a closer look at such views, and see how much it fits as the genre of the HDR. Here again, we may have to rely very much on "indirect constructive inference", and our literary competence.

### 1.3.1 Myth or Allegory

Klaus-Peter Adam, in one of the most recent studies on the Saul-David narrative, suggests that the HDR is properly understood as "mythische Vorzeitüberlieferung mit legitimatorischer Funktion [...] aus moderner Sicht [...] 'Fiktion'".[97] The main impetus for such a conclusion is as follows. First, the narrative shows almost a systematic contrast in the descriptions of the two main heroes, Saul and David. In depicting David, there are so many allusions to Saul that it cannot be a completely separate tradition put together,[98] and Saul in the narrative exists almost only in relationship with David, which indicates that there must be some intended connection between the two characters. Adam regards such a stereotypically contrastive characterization as an indication that both Saul and David are representatives or types rather than historical figures. David is a paradigmatic figure of the founder of the dynasty, and Saul is the same for the first Israelite monarchy. Thus the whole narrative may well be called "allegory",[99] and if we follow Moye's definition of myth that the term refers to "an independent, closed, symbolically rich narrative about some archetypal character whose story, which takes place in the primeval time of the beginning, represents some universal aspect of the origins or nature of humanity in its relation to the sacred or the divine",[100] the Saul-David story is to be called a (historicized) myth. Second, the narrative has traces of literary embellishment. For instance, the vivid descriptions of the characters and the existence of a *Funktionträger* like Joab betray the fictional nature of the narrative. The later parts in the "synchronic chronicle" of Judah and Israel, which Adam believes shows more neutral *Tendenz*, do not show much interest in such artistic descriptions of the characters, and this makes evident the generic difference between them. Third, the narrative has a clear pro-Davidic *Tendenz*. This gives us the hint that purpose of such an allegory

---

**97** Adam, *Saul und David*, 15.
**98** Adam, *Saul und David*, 3.
**99** Adam, *Saul und David*, 21.
**100** Richard H. Moye, "In the Beginning: Myth and History in Genesis and Exodus," *JBL* 109 (1990): 577–598 (578).

or historicized myth was the legitimation of the Judean dynasty.[101] It grounds Israel's collapse on the paradigmatic incompetence of Saul, and the person of David symbolizes the continuously surviving dynasty in Judah. Adam points out that it was a widely used custom in Mesopotamia to create a pre-history with a view to legitimate and glorify later kings. The Saul-David narrative was written for a similar purpose to preface the "synchronic chronicles" of Israel and Judah. The author created this mythical fiction on the basis of what really happened later in the history of the two kingdoms, (i.e. the conflict between the two kingdoms, the treaty and its transgression, and the fall of Israel and the survival of Judah), in order to provide the paradigmatic introduction of the work.

A paradigmatic element in the description of David is recognized also by Walter Brueggemann. Unlike Adam, however, he thinks that David does not symbolize the Judean dynasty, but personifies the social transformation in which the marginal ones become the legitimate holders of power. The narrative tells how a bandit called David survived all the hardships and rose to the highest position, and David in the narrative functions as "a paradigm for all those who yearn for such social transformation [...] a model for the last becoming first, and the story should only be told when we intend to make that subversive claim". Therefore, the HDR is "survival literature", or "partisan literature" written for those who identify themselves with a David figure, to encourage the necessary social transformation.[102] Bruggemann does not label the David stories as myth or allegory, but has a similar understanding in the sense that it is more symbolic or paradigmatic than historical.

Despite some useful insights, Adam's and Brueggemann's understanding do not do justice to the HDR, and the reason for their inadequate labelling is that both of them see the narrative as clearly pro-Davidic and anti-Saulide with a clearly tilted tendency, whether it was for the Judean dynasty or the marginalized. As I have shown, the narrative does not betray such a black and white judgement either on Saul or on David. Saul is a tragic hero with a disappearing glimpse of glory, and David is God's beloved, but often on the brink of falling into darkness. Neither of them can be an embodiment of a single value or group, and neither of them can be seen as an archetype. This certainly weakens Adam's view that Saul and David are merely allegorical figures created to prefigure the later events in the history of Israel and Judah. Similarly, it is doubtful that

---

**101** Adam, *Saul und David*, 213.
**102** Walter Brueggemann, *David's Truth: In Israel's Imagination and Memory*, 2nd edition (Minneapolis: Fortress Press, 2002), 8–13.

such a subtle literature can function as "survival literature" or "partisan litera-ture" to support one particular social class. Labelling the narrative as myth or allegory is based on a simplistic interpretation of the text, and this is not ade-quate for finding out the best reading framework for the HDR.

### 1.3.2 Traditional Story or Saga

By contrast, David Gunn draws attention to the innate ambiguities and openness of the narrative, and argues that the narrative is a traditional story whose pri-mary purpose is "serious entertainment". The word "entertainment" gives the impression that the narrative was written for fun. However, Gunn thinks that there is also "serious" entertainment which "grips one and challenges one to self- or social-reassessment", and this is what the Saul-David story is all about.[103] One might think of "novel" as the genre of the narrative, and Gunn is sympathetic to reading it as a novel or a short story. However, he prefers the term "traditional story", because the term novel implies "an essentially writ-ten as opposed to an oral genre, and it implies also a particularly high degree of autonomy of the author over his style and subject matter". For Gunn, the David story is closer to a traditional composition, and not easily differentiated from leg-ends or sagas in the Hebrew Bible.[104] Gunn does not discuss the genre of the story of Saul in much detail, because he apparently believes that he has already made the point convincingly enough. But from the fact that he labelled the story of Saul also as "serious entertainment", it is reasonable to conclude that he does not differentiate the Saul narrative and the David narrative in terms of genre. Both of them are traditional stories for serious entertainment.

Gunn's understanding of the HDR as a whole and indeed all of the David sto-ries has much to commend it. In particular, his understanding of the purpose as "serious entertainment" seems to fit best with the literature we are dealing with. Nonetheless, his labelling the narrative as "traditional story" is not a very attrac-tive option, because neither his conviction that the narrative is fundamentally an oral composition nor his denial of the author's autonomy has much to support it. As Susan Niditch argued, the distinction between orality and literacy may not have been so sharp as Gunn imagines, and in ancient literary convention, written works could have oral elements without becoming an oral composition. As Van Seters more recently pointed out, the stock scenes or traditional motifs, and the repetition of the same motif do not necessarily reflect oral tradition, but they

---

103 Gunn, *The Fate of King Saul*, 11; *The Story of King David*, 61.
104 Gunn, *The Story of King David*, 38.

could be "either the result of direct literary imitation of an earlier example or the invention and repetition of a particular motif by the same author".[105] Furthermore, the author's creativity in the David narratives cannot be dismissed. One cannot imagine that an author who was so much restricted by the oral tradition he inherited could write "the finest work of Hebrew narrative art". Finally, the term "tradition" is highly ambiguous, and does not tell us much about its genre.[106]

In agreement with Gunn's view that the purpose of the David narratives is "serious entertainment", but not with his labelling the narrative as "traditional story", Van Seters proposes "the term *saga* in the specific meaning of the Icelandic and Norse sagas as the most appropriate comparative literature for the David story". And he lists the following features to support his judgement. First, both the David story and the Icelandic sagas "deal with the principal figures and families of the founding age of the nation and extend over more than a single generation of that period". Second, both are "based on an older written historical record". Third, in both cases, authors are anonymous, and try to persuade their audience that they are giving a true portrayal of the past. Fourth, both works are intended as serious entertainment. Fifth, both works use a number of literary conventions, above all, rivalry and feud, to integrate numerous episodes over an extended period of time and to motivate the action of the story. Sixth, both seem to parody and subvert the literary tradition. Therefore, "the story of David from his first introduction into the service of Saul to the final transfer of power to Solomon (1Sam 16–2 Sam 20; 1Kings 1–2) is a saga in form and intention".[107]

Saga understood in this way might be a much better label than others. However, despite Van Seters's effort to distinguish it from the German *Sage*, the term "saga" can be confusing, bearing the connotation that the narrative is basically unhistorical, oral, and poetic.[108] Even if we successfully dispose of *Sage* and replace it with a more narrowly defined category such as the Icelandic saga, inadequacy still remains, because it implies that the narrative is fundamentally a fictional story. The label is mainly used for the narratives in Genesis such as the Abraham cycle (12:1–25:18), or the Jacob cycle, and even if one admits a generic

---

**105** John Van Seters, *The Biblical Saga of King David* (Winona Lake: Eisenbrauns, 2009), 40–41.
**106** Susan Niditch, *Oral World and Written Word* (Louisville: Westminster John Knox Press, 1996), 108–130; Van Seters, *In Search of History*, 286–287 (#167).
**107** Van Seters, *The Biblical Saga of King David*, 42–49.
**108** Cf. Robert W. Neff, "Saga," in *Saga, Legend, Tale, Novella, Fable. Narrative Forms in Old Testament Literature*, ed. G. W. Coats (Sheffield: JSOT Press, 1985): 17–32; Hermann Gunkel, *Genesis*, 6th edition (Göttingen: Vandenhoeck & Ruprecht, 1964), viii-xiii.

similarity between the Saga of Abraham and the David story, it is not acceptable to categorize them under the same heading, because the latter has much more historical elements. Of course, this is not a problem for Van Seters, since he believes that the David story is a complete fiction. However, this is ungrounded, and as we will see shortly, the David story is not properly understood without taking its historical elements seriously. Finally, the "(Icelandic) saga" is basically about one hero, and for Van Seters, the hero is David as the title of his recent book *The Biblical Saga of King David* indicates. As I have argued earlier, however, the HDR is not only about David, but also about Saul. And if we remove 2Sam 2:8–4:12 as Van Seters does, the point is made clearer, because the story ends with rather a long report of Saul's death and a brief notice about David's enthronement. All this suggests that the label "saga", even if it is narrowed down to mean the "Icelandic saga", is not appropriate for the David narratives, and the HDR in particular.

### 1.3.3 *Novelle* and Novel

Among those who recognized the fictional element and literary artistry of the David narrative, a more favoured label for the narrative has been *Novelle* (novella in English) or novel. Wilhelm Caspari already regarded some narratives in the books of Samuel as *Novellen*,[109] and more recently, Humphreys included the David narratives in the biblical novellas, the best example of which he thinks is the Joseph story in Genesis and the story of Esther and Mordecai in Esther.[110] Some scholars went further to connect the David story to the modern concept "novel". For instance, R. N. Whybray recognized the novelistic elements in the "Succession Narrative", and listed them as follows: thematic and structural unity; convincing and lively dialogue; credible characters, corresponding in their complexity to the experienced realities of human nature (though this is not true of all the characters); and a lively and flexible style, conveying to the reader mood, feelings, atmosphere, irony and humour.[111] Hans-Jürgen Dallmeyer, another recent reader of the David narrative and a psychiatrist by profession, labels the David narrative as an *Entwicklungsroman* that fundamentally deals with David's inner growth. According to his reading, David's encounter with Bathsheba is a decisive turning point that brings David's inner journey into motion. In the earlier part of the David story, David is depicted as preoccupied with

---

**109** Wilhelm Caspari, "Der Stil des Eingangs der israelitischen Novelle," *ZWT* 53 (1911): 218–253.
**110** W. L. Humphreys, "Novella," in *Saga, Legends, Fable, Tale, Novella*, ed. Coats, 82–96.
**111** R. N. Whybray, *The Succession Narrative, a Study of II Samuel 9–20; I Kings 1 and 2* (London: SCM, 1968), 19–47.

successes and achievements, and solely oriented toward power and victory, so much so that he does not hesitate to take advantage of other human beings for his own credit. But he meets Bathsheba, the "contrast figure" of his belligerent temperament, and the whole event around the affair awakens his inner potential for maturity, and turns him into a different man. He becomes now less "impulsively belligerent" than "observantly enduring, open to advisers, and above all, with emotions".[112] Dietrich, the co-author of Dallmeyer's book and his apparent biblical advisor, expresses his general approval of Dallmeyer's interpretation, and the books of Samuel may well be read as a novel that traces the spiritual growth of an unknown man.[113]

The label "novella" or "novel" indeed captures very well some of the remarkable features of the Saul-David story. The narrative shows all the elements essential to the novella/novel, such as the character development, the trace of literary artistry, and the purpose of reflective entertainment. And, in terms of genre, it is closer to the Joseph story than to the "Saga of Abraham". Nevertheless, the label is not totally satisfactory, because it does not do justice to the narrative's indelible historical interest. One might argue that the historical elements are meant to embellish the story and to make it more entertaining. The main purpose of the narrative is to "seriously" entertain the reader, one would argue, and the historical interest serves such a main purpose, and for the sake of which fabrication of historical data is not forbidden. However, some of the historical information that is isolated from the context and useless for the flow of the story speaks against it. Often historical inaccuracy is brought forward as evidence that the narrative is not interested in history. However, "bad history" is not necessarily a non-history or a fiction. It is certainly possible that the author got many things wrong when it comes to the precise topography and chronology, but this cannot be used to make a case against the historical purpose of the text, because the author or the compiler might have believed that what he "knew" was correct. Besides, as Wellhausen pointed out a century ago, it is very unlikely that the author fabricated all those names that have no consequence whatsoever in the story.

One might also contend that the purpose of the David story cannot be historical, because the obvious interest in literary artistry, the apparent ideological preference for David and the Davidic monarchy, God's interference in the course of events, and the superhuman achievements of the main characters show us clearly that the narrative does not have any pretention of "objectivity". All

---

**112** Walter Dietrich and Hans-Jürgen Dallmeyer, *David – ein Königsweg. Psychoanalytisch-theologischer Dialog* (Göttingen: Vandenhoeck & Ruprecht, 2002), 173–178 (178).
**113** Dietrich, *David: Der Herrscher mit der Harfe*, 37–8.

these objections however can be met if we accept the recent change in the way we understand what "history" or historiography is. More and more scholars now maintain that history is not an objective record of a historical event, but always includes interpretation and evaluation. It is often presented in a narrative form with great literary artistry, and this makes the position that sees "history" and "narrative" as antithetical obsolete. Therefore, there is no reason to deny the historical nature of the David narratives, on the basis of its interest in narrative art. Furthermore, the peculiarity in biblical historiography or even in Jewish mentality should be taken into account for fairer evaluation of the materials in the Bible. For the Israelites, history is not just what happened in the human world. As Dietrich points out, "the interconnection between human activities with their consequences and the actions of God" is "a unique quality of Old Testament history writing",[114] and what appears to be "impure" in biblical historiography does not mean that the intention of the text is not historical. Biblical historians "do not want to depict past reality; instead, they intend to communicate the truth of history to their readers (which also includes communicating the truth *through* history)".[115]

Then do we have to return to the older view that sees the narrative more or less as historiography or history writing? Indeed, although the label was unpopular for a while, due to a rather positivistic differentiation between literary aspect and historical interest, several more recent scholars reaffirm the label for the David narratives, with the help of a more flexible understanding of history. For instance, Dietrich is convinced that "the authors of the books of Samuel and Kings undoubtedly intend to write *history* – and this is what they actually do",[116] and Robert Alter expresses his view that the author of the David story understood himself as a historian.[117] If one thinks that the term "history" still carries the positivistic connotation of the 19th century, we could clarify the term, and call the David story "history writing",[118] or "narrative history", as these highlight both historical and literary interests of the narrative.[119]

---

**114** Dietrich, *Early Monarchy*, 107. A similar view was already made in James Barr, "Story and History in Biblical Theology," in *Journal of Religion* 56 (1976): 1–17.

**115** Dietrich, *Early Monarchy*, 108; cf. Gerhard von Rad, "The Beginnings of Historical Writing in Ancient Israel," in *The Problem of the Hexateuch and other essays*, trans. E. W. Trueman Dicken (Edinburgh/London: Oliver & Boyd, 1966), 166–204 (170–171).

**116** Dietrich, *Early Monarchy*, 106.

**117** Alter, *David Story*, xxi-xxii.

**118** Sparks, recognizing the taxonomic problem distinguishes historiography from history writing, and writes, "[i]n my nomenclature, *historiography* refers to any text that presents the past on the basis of its author's source inquiry, and the term *history writing* is a still narrower category that includes historiographies that define the significance of past events through an

### 1.3.4 Popular History or Jewish Historical Novel

Despite the undeniable historical nature of the David narratives, the label "narrative history" or "history writing" does not seem best for the HDR, because these place the primary emphasis on its historical elements rather than on its novelistic ones. Now it sounds as if I am contradicting myself, because I have objected to the labels such as saga and *Novelle*, on the grounds they do not take into account the historical elements of the David narratives. However, even if the HDR has both elements, the novelistic elements are greater than the historical ones, and the purpose of "serious entertainment" is dominant. Furthermore, "narrative history" or "history writing" is still too broad, and it can include almost all historical narratives in the Hebrew Bible, failing to express the distinctiveness of the HDR. Certainly, the HDR feels different from 2Kings and from the Chronicles. Then, how should we label it? How can we come up with a label whose main purpose is "serious entertainment" that is replete with literary artistry, but not without historical interest? Perhaps, we could start from Eissfeldt's observation that there was in Israel "what may be termed unofficial, popular historical narrative or historical writing".[120] We do not accept the label in Eissfeldt's sense, because he is convinced, despite the "epic features", that the HDR intends to narrate what happened and how. And yet, the label "popular history" seems to fit very well with the narrative we are dealing with.[121] It seems to hit the right balance, in the sense that the HDR looks less formal and more stylistic than the Chronicler's history, and less fanciful and more historical than the Patriarchal narratives in Genesis. More importantly, with the label "popular his-

---

extended, selective, and chronologically sensitive narrative." See his *Ancient Texts for the Study of the Hebrew Bible*, 362. For the development of the concept of historiography and history writing, see André Heinrich, *David und Kilo. Historiographische Elemente in der Aufstiegsgeschichte Davids und im Alten Testament* (New York/Berlin: de Gruyter, 2009), 25–39.

**119** Cf. Hans M. Barstad, "History and the Hebrew Bible," in *Can a 'History of Israel' Be Written?*, ed. Lester L. Grabbe (Sheffield: Sheffield Academic Press, 1997), 37–64; idem, *History and the Hebrew Bible: Studies in Ancient Israel and Ancient Near Eastern Historiography* (Tübingen: Mohr Siebeck, 2008), 15–17.

**120** Eissfeldt, *Introduction*, 50.

**121** According to Reinhard Kratz, unlike the ancient near eastern historical writing that was largely interested in the legitimation of the kingdom and the ruling dynasty, the biblical historical narratives are interested in overcoming the *status quo*. This may indicate that one of the peculiarities in the Hebrew historical narratives is their "unofficial" character, and I think, the HDR epitomizes such distinctiveness of the biblical historical narratives. See Reinhard Kratz, "Memoria, Memorabilia, and Memoirs: Notions of the Past in Northwest Semitic Inscriptions of the First Millennium BCE," in *The Past in the Past: Concepts of Past Reality in Ancient Near Eastern and Early Greek Thought*, eds. Hans M. Barstad and Pierre Briant (Oslo: Novus Press, 2009): 111–131 (130–131)

tory", we can trace the development of the genre in the wider biblical literature. In the Hellenistic period, we have a series of what might be called "Jewish historical novels", and in this sense, the HDR may well be seen as an early example, or even prototype of the later "Jewish historical novel". The term "historical novel" might well give the impression that the genre is basically a fiction. However, if we follow Lawrence Wills's understanding of the term, it is not necessarily so. According to Wills,

> *historical novel* is often used to refer to a work of fiction that makes use of a historical personage or setting, rather than to history that is told with novelistic flourishes. One is clearly fiction; the other is considered history, if poor history. By *historical novel* I am referring to the latter only. These works could be assimilated to the history category as, say, 'novelistic histories' or 'popular histories', but I am convinced that, despite their assumption of a historical referent for the action, they are more closely associated with the other novels.[122]

This seems to allow for our concern to make the label accommodate both elements – mainly novelistic, and secondarily historical.

There are indeed similarities between the Saul-David narrative and the Jewish novels. First, both of them have the purpose of "serious entertainment".[123] Second, both have an element of binary opposition of values. In the former, David is depicted antithetical to Saul, and in the latter, the Jewish heroes are placed against foreign kings or officials. Third, the motif of female debasement and prayer is important in both. Susanna in the Greek addition to Daniel and Abigail in 1Sam 25 will be the parallel examples. Fourth, in both, "the social network in which the protagonists are situated is always the extended family."[124] Tobit is narrated within the extent of his family, and in the Saul-David narrative, the story is centred upon Saul's court that is largely made of Saul's family and relatives. Fifth, in both, we can find the motif of psychological transformation from the most vulnerable to the most worthy, which is regarded by Wills as "the new syntax of the Jewish novel".[125] Esther matures from a mere replacement of the abdicated queen to a national hero, and David, as Dallmeyer observed, matures from a success-oriented fighter to an empathically all-accepting

---

**122** Lawrence M. Wills, *The Jewish Novel in the Ancient World* (Ithaca: Cornell University Press, 1995), 185.
**123** Cf. Philip R. Davies, *Scribes and School. The Canonization of the Hebrew Scriptures* (Louisville: Westminster John Knox Press, 1998), 142–151.
**124** Wills, 212.
**125** Wills, 233.

father.[126] Sixth, the primary audience in both cases seem to be lower than the ruling class. "The Jewish novels clearly have a literary function at a somewhat different level of society [...] In terms of social level, the Jewish novels look up at the Greek novels from below."[127] Similarly, the success of a fugitive might well have delighted the less privileged class, as Brueggemann observed. Seventh, both reshape legend into history with a view to strengthening the message. In 2Maccabees, the legendary figure Onias is made into "a positive paradigm of how a pious Jewish ruler should interact with Greek kings and generals, in strong contrast with villains".[128] In the Saul-David narrative, a legend about Jonathan is reshaped into stories about the friendship between Jonathan and David,[129] and this makes clear that the reader should look after the descendants of Jonathan.

Of course, differences between the HDR and the Jewish (historical) novels cannot be underestimated. Unlike the HDR, the narrator in the Jewish historical novels sometimes makes himself known in the narrative as in 2Maccabees, and the emotional descriptions are rather exaggerated. Besides, in the Jewish novels, the subject of transformation is normally female, and there are signs of deliberate manipulation of historical facts. Finally, the Jewish novels are, unlike the Saul-David narrative that has a "mosaic" character, more or less a unified story. However, these differences can be explained as an evolution of the genre or adaptation to a different context. For instance, the appearance of the narrator and the "pathetic" character are definitely due to Hellenistic influence, and the attraction to the female characters reflects the general atmosphere of the Hellenistic world.[130] As to the "mosaic" character, it is not totally alien in the Jewish novels, because the Tales of the Tobiads or Tobiad Romance[131] seems to have originated as a collection of legends that gathered around the Tobiad

---

126 The HDR does not tell us about David's emphatic fatherhood. However, as Gordon has shown, we can notice the transformation of David's character in 1Sam 24–26. See Gordon, "David's Rise and Saul's Demise".

127 Wills, p. 27.

128 Sara Raup Johnson, *Historical Fictions and Hellenistic Jewish Identity* (Berkeley: University of California Press, 2004), 40.

129 Kaiser thinks that only a couple of verses can be attributed, even vaguely, to the historical figure of Jonathan. See Otto Kaiser, "David und Jonathan: Tradition, Redaktion, und Geschichte in 1 Sam. 16–20. Ein Versuch," *Ephemerides Theologicae Lovanienses* 66 (1990): 281–296.

130 But in historical novels, it is male characters. For instance, Izates in *Royal Family of Adiabene.*

131 The original text has not been found. The text is available in Josephus's *Judean Antiquities*, Book 12 (4.1–11).

family.[132] Some might claim that the deliberate manipulation of historical facts in the Jewish novels might be the greatest difference between the two. But how deliberate the manipulation of historical facts in the Jewish novels is is far from clear, and Jewish historical novels normally do not show the signs of manipulation.

In short, among the various possibilities for describing the HDR as a whole, the label "popular history", or "Jewish historical novel" seems to tell us best what kind of text the HDR is. Of course, this cannot be proved or demonstrated unambiguously. However, it is inevitable in genre-recognition that we have to rely very much on indirect inferences, and our literary competence. And, at this time of interpretative history, it seems that the best label to name the HDR as a whole is "popular history", or "Jewish historical novel".

## 2 The Theme and Function of the HDR

Now, to understand the nature of the HDR as a whole, we are left with the question of its theme and its function. The "mosaic" character of the HDR makes it difficult to know the theme, because it may well have been the case that the HDR did not have any one unified theme. Indeed, insights from literary study have helped us realize that the idea of one unified theme of a literary work might well have been alien to the ancient people.[133] Nonetheless, it is not totally impossible to talk about the theme of the HDR, if we do not pretend to pursue one definite answer, but take it as a part of the interpretative process. In fact, understanding a theme cannot be separated from the process of genre-recognition, because this essentially involves the consideration of both the content and the form. Theme and genre illuminate each other, and as long as we maintain that genre-recognition is not only possible but also necessary, so is the understanding of the theme. Likewise, just as genre-recognition is not an attempt for a definite answer but a provisional reading framework, so is the theme.

Then what can we say when asked what is the theme of the HDR? We can start with the least controversial point that the story is above all about a historical person, David. As the title "History of David's Rise" indicates, the work tells a story about how David rose from a shepherd boy to king of Israel and Judah. He is at the centre of the whole narrative, and moves the narrative forward. But

---

**132** Johnson, 81.
**133** Cf. Barton, "Historical Criticism and Literary Interpretation," 13; Van Seters, *In Search of History*, 320–21.

in the course of his rise, there is an antagonist, or more appropriately, the second protagonist, Saul. In the contrapuntal development of the narrative, Saul's fall is counterbalanced by David's rise, and the contrast between them may well justify the widely shared impression that Saul was a foil to the main hero David, and functions only to highlight the glorious rise of the young upstart. However, it is remarkable that the way in which David rises copies closely the way Saul rose in the past. The secret anointing, the test-like achievement against Nahash and Goliath respectively, the war against their archenemies the Philistines and the Amalekites, and so on, are found in both rises, so that one may well see in David a better version of Saul. Moreover, the tragedy that Saul goes through is so poignantly depicted, that one cannot easily forget about the declining king and rejoice with David's rise without certain reservation. Saul and David are narratologically intertwined so closely that they look sham twins in the whole narrative, and this makes us reconsider the view that the HDR is merely a story of David's rise. Of course, Saul does not appear in 2Sam 1–5. But even in these chapters, which some commentators readily strike out from the HDR, the figure of Saul looms behind the figure of Ishbosheth, the non-son[134] who is patronized by a hero from the previous generation Abner, just as Saul was by Samuel. Although David is certainly the focus of the story, the author's interest never departs completely from the figure of Saul. And this makes the view inadequate that the HDR is a story of David, and Saul is merely a foil to David's rise.

The story of a more active but declining Saul, and a more passive but rising David, however, soon makes us realize that the ultimate focus of the Saul-David narrative is not either on Saul or David, but on God who is implied in the whole narrative as the master of all human events. In the narrative, Saul is described as one who struggles desperately to maintain his power, but the more he tries, the worse he becomes. David on the other hand stays quiet and passive, but he is led to high position by an invisible power. The point of this contrasting description, however, is not to praise David unconditionally, or legitimate his succession to Saul, and this is shown most clearly by how Saul and David share both glory and shadow. In the narrative, Saul is described as the one disappearing in the shadow. It is as if he were swallowed up by his own shadow – his gloomy sentiment, jealousy, and violent temperament. By contrast, David stands in the opposite position. He shines under the brightest sun, and is described as pure, innocent, and successful. And yet, the text sporadically allows the reader to glimpse

---

**134** Ishbosheth is not mentioned in I Samuel 31 where Saul's sons are reported to have been killed in the battle.

the shadow behind the figure of growing greatness, and we know, from his coun-
ter-hero Saul, that the shadow that grows as the figure grows might eventually
swallow up David as well. The possibility is more than real, because the reader
knows that David rose in the way his predecessor rose. David followed Saul's
path toward the throne, so why not toward a similar end?

Indeed, we know that the later pictures of David found in the "Succession
Narrative" confirm that the glorious David also disappears into the shadow created by himself. Following his affair with Bathsheba, he is in decline, and not
capable of controlling things anymore. Things always worked for David while
Saul was in decline, but now David is dragged along by the events over which
he has no control, being forced to accept what he does not want. One might
say that David's decline is only found outside the HDR, but it is not. David's re-
pressed murder instinct in 1Sam 25, the long list of his sons in 2Sam 3:2–5;
5:13–14, and the acknowledgement of his own helplessness before the sons of
Zeruiah in 2Sam 3:39 – all these anticipate later events such as David's murder
of Uriah, his sons' bloody strife for the throne, and his impotence (1Kings 1:1–4).
Neither Saul nor David is the winner after all, and both of them disappear in
their frailties. We do not know of course all of these from the HDR without reading the "Succession Narrative". Nonetheless, the shadow that begins to grow pre-
vents the reader from being indulged in the figure of glorious David, because
there is almost no one who does not have at least indirect knowledge about David's later life, or about what happened to the Israelite kings who had disputes
with other civilians, and who had many sons. And the reader eventually comes
to realize that David is not that different, even if he is a better one, and that the
ultimate protagonist of the story is God who raises and brings down human beings. In short, the message that the HDR intends to get across may well be "God
is behind the rise and the fall of all human beings. God is the master of human
fate".

As to the function of the HDR, we start with the question of the purpose,
and we have already mentioned that the purpose of the HDR may be better described as "serious entertainment". The narrative skill which has been pointed
out by many commentators indicates that the narrative certainly has an intention
to entertain the reader. In other words, the work expects the reader to find the
story fascinating and enjoyable, and it has been proved that it truly does. The
HDR however is not merely a story for fun, and as Gunn pointed out, it "grips
one and challenges one to self- or social-reassessment".[135] It challenges the reader, lest they should be too dependent on the power of human beings, and teach-

---

**135** Gunn, *The Fate of King Saul*, 11; *The Story of King David*, 61.

es that God is the one on whom we can rely. Neither a black-and-white viewpoint nor any extreme position is encouraged, and it is made clear that no one has the last word except God. In fact, the mixture of narrative and instruction is not alien in the ancient Near Eastern literary culture, as the examples such as the story of Ahiqar from Elephantine and the Egyptian *Instruction of Onkhsheshonq* from the 5th-4th century B.C.E. show.[136] Both of them are stories surrounding a royal court whose main function is to teach in the form of narrative, and although the Joseph story looks more similar, the HDR may well be compared to these narratives of serious entertainment.

To conclude, a close reading of the text, comparison with other literature, comparison between different scholarly views, and the consideration of our place in the interpretative history, suggest that the HDR is to be read as a "popular history" or an early Jewish historical novel. Its theme is God's mastery over human rise and fall, or indeed human lives, and it functions to entertain and instruct the reader. This is what we get through "understanding the HDR as a whole", and I believe that this can provide us with the foundation on which we can build historical hypotheses. Of course, as I have consistently argued, this understanding is not *the* correct interpretation, but is open to revision. In particular, when we go through literary-critical investigation about the redactional history of the HDR, our understanding may well be modified. Nonetheless, the genre, theme, function of the HDR as here understood helps us to deal with the unevenness of the narrative more coherently and sensibly in the following chapters, and to speculate what the socio-historical settings for the composition were. Now we turn to the question of the redactional history, and revisit our initial question, the question of the beginning and the end of the HDR.

---

**136** Both of these are didactic stories whose main characters are courtiers. For earlier ancient near eastern examples, see Lawrence Wills, *Jews in the Court of a Foreign King: Ancient Jewish Court Legends* (Minneapolis: Fortress, 1990), 39 – 74 (43).

# Chapter 4
# The Beginning and the Ending of the HDR Revisited

In the previous chapters, we have seen how the question of the beginning and the ending of the HDR is inevitably related to our understanding of the HDR as a whole, and it is proposed that the whole of the HDR is best understood or "labelled" as a "Jewish historical novel". We expect that such a conclusion will have significant implications for the initial question of the beginning and the ending of the HDR, and now we shall attempt to identify the different layers in the HDR on the basis of such an understanding of the whole. This of course does not mean that the label decides everything about where the HDR begins and ends. However, it guides us to make reasonable decisions about conflicting or equally persuasive evidence. Since it is presumed that the HDR is basically a pre-deuteronomistic work, in this chapter, we will attempt to exclude the deuteronomistic and post-deuteronomistic verses from 1Sam 15–2Sam 8.[1] We start with a discussion of the additions to the shorter LXX[B], and then discuss the possible deuteronomistic additions. Finally, we shall attempt to identify some other additions.

## 1 The Additions to the Shorter Version of 1Sam 17–18

Although absolute certainty cannot be guaranteed, textual differences can be one of the most important clues for unearthing the different layers, especially when the differences are found among the oldest versions. Promisingly, we have two strikingly different textual witnesses in 1Sam 17–18: Whereas the Masoretic Text (MT) on which most modern translations are based has 88 verses in chapters 17 and 18, the Old Greek version as found in the Septuagint Codex Vaticanus (LXX[B]) has only about 59 verses, omitting 17:12–31,41,48b,50; 17:55–18:6a,10–12,17–19,21b,30. There has been an ongoing debate among scholars as to how to explain the discrepancy between the two major witnesses. Some have argued that the longer version was original, and the LXX translator or a Hebrew scribe abridged the proto-MT for harmonization. Others have held that

---

1 Almost all those who maintain the hypothesis of the HDR agree that the HDR does not go beyond 1Sam 15–2Sam 8, and it seems reasonable to start the discussion from the largest possible option.

there were two independent traditions of the David and Goliath story. One of them is found both in MT and LXX, and the other one is only in MT. This hypothesis argues that the additional verses in MT, probably another independent source itself, were added later to the shorter version for some reason, and consequently, MT has both traditions mixed up in one narrative, and thus with many repetitions and inconsistencies. Although the issue may seem relevant only to the two chapters in 1Sam, I believe that it can guide us to an important insight as to our whole discussion. Therefore, I will investigate the question at some length.

### 1.1 Two Versions of 1Sam 17–18: MT & LXX[B]

If we read 1Sam 16–18, several tensions in the narrative are easily noticeable. Among many of them, the following are the most evident. First, David is twice introduced to Saul and his courtiers. In 16:14–23, he is brought to Saul as a lyre-player and armour-bearer. In 17:55–18:5, however, Saul does not know who David is, and David is summoned to the court as an unknown shepherd who miraculously killed a Philistine giant. Second, David is introduced at least twice to the audience or the reader. In 16:1–11, David is first introduced when he is anointed by Samuel, and in 17:12–14, David is once more introduced in a similar manner to Samuel (1:1ff) and Saul (9:1ff). Third, Goliath is twice introduced in 17:4 and 17:23 using similar patterns. Both verses designate first Goliath's military role as "a champion (הַבֵּנַיִם)", and give his regiment (Philistine army), name (Goliath), and origin (from Gath). Fourth, Goliath's head is brought to Jerusalem in 17:54, but David still has it in his hand when he meets Saul in the court or, more likely, in the headquarters near the battle field (17:57).

In addition to these tensions created by doublets, the overall characterizations of David are also rather contradictory. On the one hand, David is depicted as an experienced courtier and warrior who has already been around and made himself known in the court. Thus one of Saul's servants recommends David to Saul as "skilful in playing, a man of valour, a warrior, prudent in speech, and a man of good presence" (1:23). On the other hand, David is also painted as an inexperienced shepherd. He is left with his father's sheep while his brothers go out for battle, and when he comes to the battlefield, his brother assumes that David has come just "to see the battle" (17:28). Besides, he is incapable of wearing Saul's armour because he "was not used to it" (17:39).

If we get rid of what we have only in MT (hereafter, the MT pluses), however, most of these inconsistencies seem to be removed and a more coherent picture emerges. According to the shorter version found in LXX, David is first introduced when he is called in to play the lyre for Saul (16:18–23), and stays in the court until he leaves in order to escape Saul's murder attempts in chapter 19. David is introduced to the audience/reader in chapter 16, and Goliath as a champion who proposes a single combat at the very beginning of the battle in 17:4. After the battle, David takes his head to Jerusalem, and is praised by women in 18:7. Above all, in the shorter version, David is consistently a lyre-player and warrior who is already experienced in battle and court life.

### 1.1.1 Hypothesis A: MT as an Expansion

The fact that the shorter version presents us with an independent and complete story has led a number of scholars to conclude that the LXX translator had a different Hebrew text from the proto-MT. According to this hypothesis, two different traditions circulated independently, and the translator of the *Vorlage* of the LXX had one of them (the shorter version) at hand which he translated into Greek. By contrast, another tradition which included the MT pluses was also available to the scribe of the proto-MT, and was added to the shorter version.

This hypothesis is first of all text-critically supported, and Emanuel Tov, one of the supporters of the hypothesis, presents his argument on the basis of translation technique. In a series of articles, most elaborately in the paper written for the joint research on the David and Goliath story in 1986, he compared MT with LXX of 1Sam 17–18, and demonstrated that (1) exegetical renderings were very limited in the translation – in other words, the translator was very cautious in departing from the Hebrew account for exegetical reasons; (2) the translator kept the word-order of the Hebrew version as much as possible; (3) the translator made great efforts to use the same number of Greek words in translating Hebrew words; (4) the translation contains lots of expressions which reflect particular characteristics of the Hebrew language. All these led him to conclude that the translation technique of the LXX translator was "relatively literal," and that what we have in LXX is not an abridgement of MT, as it is unlikely that a translator who was so loyal to the parent text would have omitted about 45 % of it. More likely, LXX represents an independent tradition on its own.[2] Similarly, Johann Lust points out that such a dramatic shortening of a Hebrew text as we find in 1Sam 17–18 has no parallel in the other parts of the book, and thus, abridge-

---

2 Emanuel Tov, "The Composition of 1 Samuel 16 – 18 in the Light of the Septuagint Version," in *Empirical Models for Biblical Criticism*, ed. Jeffrey H. Tigay (Philadelphia: University of Pennsylvania Press, 1985): 99–130; D. Barthélemy, D.W. Gooding, J. Lust, and E. Tov, *The Story of David and Goliath: Textual and Literary Criticism* (Göttingen: Vandenhoeck & Ruprecht, 1986), 33–39.

ment by the translator is very unlikely. Lust also believes that the agreement of 4QSam[A] with LXX in 17:4 which has "four" instead of "six" also supports the hypothesis.[3]

Moreover, the supporters of the hypothesis question whether the purpose of a supposed abridgement was harmonization, as often argued. If the purpose was harmonization, why did LXX leave some contradictions untouched, whereas it removed some verses which do not have contradictions? For example, although the single combat in chapter 17 where David is the only hero, and the song of women in chapter 18 which praises both David and Saul, seem contradictory, why did the translator not harmonize them? Or why were 18:1–4, which cause no contradictions, removed? In fact, does not the removal create disagreement with 20:8 which presupposes the covenant between David and Jonathan?

Finally, the hypothesis is supported by literary analysis of the shorter version (Version 1) and the longer version (Version 2). For instance, Lust reads 17:1–11,32–54; 18:1b,(3)4 as a well balanced composition, whereas most of the MT pluses interrupt the narrative creating tensions. Thus he concludes, "the editor used an existing story, or parts of it, as an insert. He adapted it so as to avoid major contradictions. But he did not succeed in avoiding all of them." Furthermore, the form of 17:12 indicates that it belonged to another tradition, which has elements of a "fairy tale" or of a "romantic epic" with political overtones."[4] Tov also believes that Version 1 is more logical than Version 2 in the flow of the story. Therefore, Version 1 is more original, and MT as we have it now is an expansion of Version 1.[5]

### 1.1.2 Hypothesis B: LXX as an Abridgement of the MT *Vorlage*

In a literary perspective, the hypothesis that LXX had a different Hebrew text from MT maintains that there are several inconsistencies and tensions in MT, whereas LXX presents us with a more coherent version of the story. And this has been a part of the argument of those who favour Hypothesis A. However, it has been pointed out that coherence or unity in chapters 17–18 can be

---

3 Van der Kooij, quoting Tov, points out that there are important differences between 4QSam[A] and LXX, and says that we should not rely too much on the agreement between them in 17:4. However, although not all the details are reliable, Tov reaffirms the close relationship between 4QSam[A] and LXX. See Barthélemy, et al., *The Story of David and Goliath*, 7–11. Arie van der Kooij, "The Story of David and Goliath: The Early History of Its Text," *ETL* 68 (1992): 118–131 (122); Emanuel Tov, "The Textual Affiliation of 4QSam[a]," *JSOT* 14 (1979): 37–53 (40).

4 Barthélemy, et al., *David and Goliath*, 12–13.

5 Barthélemy, et al., *David and Goliath*, 41–42.

found differently from the way the supporters of Hypothesis A find it. And this has led a group of scholars to claim that the coherence we find in the shorter version is the result of the abridgement by the LXX translator who did not quite see the flow of the original narrative or who saw it quite differently. For example, D. Barthélemy argues that the figure of David in 17:12–31 agrees very well with that in 17:32–54, and there is no break in the narrative flow between 17:12–31 and 17:32–54.[6] Similarly, Arie van der Kooij claims that there is no break between 17:31 and 17:32, as LXX witnesses, and indeed, 17:12–58 constitutes an independent coherent story, which describes David as a shepherd boy who astonishingly kills the Philistine giant. He adds that this original or "basic" story went through a couple of redactions, and concludes that this long version represented in MT was shortened by a Hebrew scribe or, possibly, by the translator of LXX.[7] As to the question of why the shorter version is not always consistent in removing the discrepancies, it is argued that the scribe or translator removed the obvious and disturbing contradictions and duplications but left some contradictions inextricably woven into the basic story,[8] and that the removal of the encounter of David and Jonathan can be seen as the result of *parablepsis*, i. e. "The eye of the scribe may have wandered from 17:54 to 18:6."[9]

Walter Dietrich is also one of those who see the demarcation of the two distinct traditions in MT differently. According to his view, in MT, one strand (17:1–9,48b,50,51b-53) presents David as a slinging soldier, and another strand (17:12–14a,15b,17–18,20–23aα,24–34a,36,40,42abα,43,49,51,54–58) depicts David as a shepherd boy. The composite nature of the MT text is acknowledged, but there is no break in the narrative flow between 17:31 and 17:32 as the supporters of Hypothesis A maintain. Therefore, he holds that the compilation of two different traditions happened before the translation, and LXX is an abridgement of the original Hebrew text.[10] The purpose was to emphasize the theme of the confrontation between Israel and the Philistines (= between Israel and a foreign power), which, he believes, was a pressing issue in the Hellenistic era. This was done by

---

6 Barthélemy, et al., *David and Goliath*, 48–50.

7 Van der Kooij, "David and Goliath," 127–130.

8 Alexander Rofé, "The Battle of David and Goliath: Folklore, Theology, Eschatology," in *Judaic Perspectives on Ancient Israel*, eds. J. Neusner, B. A. Levine, and E. S. Frerichs (Philadelphia: Fortress Press, 1987): 117–151 (121).

9 Barthélemy, et al., *David and Goliath*, 9.

10 More recently, Erik Aurelius presented a similar view, although he saw the demarcation differently. See Erik Aurelius, "Wie David ursprünglich zu Saul kam (1Sam 17)," in *Vergegenwärtigung des Alten Testaments: Beiträge zur biblischen Hermeneutik; Festschrift für Rudolf Smend zum 70. Geburtstag*, eds. Christopher Bultmann, Walter Dietrich, and Christoph Levin (Göttingen: Vandenhoeck & Ruprecht, 2002): 44–68.

removing another theme in the story, the theme of the tension between Saul and David (= between the Northern kingdom and Judah).[11]

The most striking difference in understanding coherence in the narrative can be found in David Gooding's reading. He denies first of all that the doublets in the narrative create discrepancies. For instance, there are no two contradictory descriptions of David as a warrior (16:18) and as a shepherd (17:12ff), because 17:33 does not deny that David is *also* a warrior. David is not introduced again in 17:12ff, because 17:12–16 does not serve the function of presenting the *dramatis personae* for the first time. 17:55–58 does not present the first encounter of Saul with David, but David's permanent transfer from Jesse's household to Saul's.[12] All these doublets indeed move the narrative forward to a dramatic climax, and there is no break between 17:1–11 and 17:12ff as Hypothesis A argues. The narrative in MT is "a highly-wrought, sophisticated, narrative-sequence, that everywhere makes excellent sense",[13] and the shorter version is an abridgement of the longer one by a "very literalistic, unimaginative mind" who thought "to improve it by removing doublets and discrepancies".[14] An attempt to read these chapters as an artfully constructed whole is made more boldly by Robert Polzin who reads 16:1–19:24 as a unit, and sees 17:1–24 as an "artful composition".[15]

Those who support this hypothesis also argue that Hypothesis A is not as strong as it first seems even in text-critical perspective, because the general translation technique of the LXX translator does not exclude completely the possibility that there were truncations. In fact, there are some expansions (especially in 17:43) in LXX, and possible exegetical renderings such as we might find in the change of עבדים of Saul into Εβραιοι of Saul in 17:8.[16] Concerning the argument that the abridgement found in LXX has no parallel, it is claimed that neither such a considerable expansion in the Hebrew text tradition nor a very complicated pre-history of both versions has its parallel.[17]

To summarize the two different views we have looked at so far, the proponents of Hypothesis A believe that (1) text-critically, such a dramatic abridgement as we find in 1Sam 17–18 is very unlikely; (2) in literary perspective, there are inconsistencies in MT, whereas there is an overall unity and coherence

---

11 Walter Dietrich, "Die Erzählungen von David und Goliat in 1 Sam 17," *ZAW* 108 (1996): 172–191 (179).
12 Barthélemy, et al., *David and Goliath*, 56–61.
13 Barthélemy, et al., *David and Goliath*, 75.
14 Barthélemy, et al., *David and Goliath*, 82.
15 Polzin, *Samuel and the Deuteronomist*, 164–67.
16 Van der Kooij, "David and Goliath," 123.
17 Dietrich, "Erzählungen," 177.

in LXX. Thus, MT is a later expansion of the Hebrew version which the translator of LXX used. By contrast, those who support Hypothesis B hold that (1) from a literary point of view, there are no serious inconsistencies in 1Sam 17–18 as Hypothesis A argues, or at least, coherence or unity can be found differently from the way in which LXX presents the story; (2) text-critically, although the abridgement of the Hebrew text in translation is not common, we cannot exclude the possibility in principle, and we do find some cases of possible exegetical renderings in the text. Therefore, it was at the level of the translation or the work of a Hebrew scribe that the longer version was shortened to that in LXX.

## 1.2 Toward the Solution

From the above summary, it is clear that the following questions are crucial in opting for one or the other solution. First, where do we put more emphasis: on textual-critical evidence or on literary-rhetorical evidence? Second, how do we see inconsistencies or coherence in the narrative? Is the narrative as presented in MT coherent? Or is it full of discrepancies? The importance of these questions is evident from the fact that at the end of the Joint Research made by four leading scholars on the David and Goliath Story, the methodological issue came to the fore. In fact, those who started with textual criticism went for the hypothesis of MT as an expansion (Lust, Tov), whereas those who started with the final form of MT opted for the hypothesis of LXX as an abridgement (Barthélemy, Gooding). Similarly, concerning the coherence or unity of the narrative, they question each other about the way in which the opposite side reads and understands the unity of the narrative.

Concerning the first issue, I think that textual criticism should be considered prior to literary criticism in this case, because the question of the composition history of 1Sam 17–18 arose out of the very fact that we have two significantly different textual witnesses. And if I am right in this, it seems quite clear that the translators of LXX did not shorten the text available to them. In this respect, I am very much in agreement with Emanuel Tov that the translation technique of LXX was rather literal. Of course, there still remains the possibility of exegetical modifications, and thus we cannot be absolutely sure that the translator never shortened the text. However, as long as we work with limited evidence, which is unavoidable in the study of ancient texts, nothing can be absolutely sure. We work toward higher probability, and if the possibility is reasonably high, we can regard a hypothesis as acceptable. In fact, Anneli Aejmelaeus's recent textual study of the books of Samuel confirms that the dramatic abridgement is unlikely. In a series of lectures given as the Oxford Grinfield Lectures in

2009, she showed that a good number of Hebrew words were either transliterated or mistranslated, and suspected that the translators were rather sloppy and/or did not fully understand what was going on in the Hebrew text.[18] Therefore, it would be extremely unusual for such an incompetent translator to venture to abridge the text with great care. Furthermore, although exegetical renderings are not unheard of in early Judaism, it is difficult to decide whether it was an exegetical rendering or a variant reading in our case. For example, the change of "servants" into "Hebrews" in 17:8 might be an example of exegetical rendering in the light of its context, as van der Kooij argues. However, the understanding of the context can be subjective, and the change may well have been a variant reading as it is quite possible to confuse עבדים with עברים. We do not have enough evidence at hand to choose one reading or another, and in that case, we should rather rely on the quantitative analysis which argues against the idea of abridgement.

Lastly, some would claim with Dietrich that neither considerable expansion in the Hebrew text tradition nor a very complicated pre-history of both versions has a parallel.[19] But we may well be reminded that "the Bible evolved very much through addition and supplementation in the same mould as midrashic supplementation of the biblical text".[20] It may be true that large expansion of a text is not common either. Yet, considering what we know about the transmission of Hebrew tradition, it is still more probable than large abridgement of a text. In a culture in which more than 85 letters of the biblical text were regarded as a property of holy books,[21] the removal of about 30 verses – whether by a Hebrew scribe or by a translator – seems too extraordinary. Therefore, it is reasonable to conclude, from a text-critical point of view, that it is more probable that the translator of LXX did not shorten the text.

Of course, one might still argue with Barthélemy that a Hebrew scribe, not the translator, abridged the text. The suggestion does not seem very convincing to me, not only because it is not an economical explanation, but also because it

---

**18** For instance, הַגִּישֵׁנוּ in 1Sam 14:9 is translated into ἀπαγγείλωμεν, apparently connecting it with the verb נגד, and וְנָגְלִינוּ in 1Sam 14:8 into κατακυλισθησόμεθα, relating it to the verb גלל. The noun מַצָּב in 1Sam 14:11 is transliterated as μεσσαβ, and חרם in 1Sam 15:3,8 is related to Ιεριμ. More examples are given in Anneli Aejmelaeus, "Text-History of the Septuagint and the Hebrew Text in the Books of Samuel," Grinfield Lecture Note (Oxford, February 17–26, 2009).
**19** Dietrich, "Erzählungen," 177.
**20** John Barton, "What is a Book? Modern Exegesis and the Literary Conventions of Ancient Israel," in *Intertextuality in Ugarit and Israel,* ed. Johannes C. de Moor (Leiden: Brill, 1998): 1–14 (6).
**21** Barton, "What is a Book?" 1–2. This, of course, is a late development. Nonetheless, the general attitude toward the tradition could not have been very different.

seems to tell against the general attitude of ancient people to their traditions. However, we leave the possibility open, and move to the literary aspect of the discussion. The issue related to literary aspect is very delicate and requires careful treatment, because the understanding of coherence in a narrative is inevitably subject to certain relativity. Whether a text is coherent or not largely depends on culture and time, and no one can establish a universal law about it. Indeed, we know from recent developments in biblical scholarship that the question has become more vivid. One clear example would be Robert Alter's reading of Genesis 38. Contrary to the widely held view, he reads the story of Judah and Tamar not as an interpolation, but as a part of the highly artistic composition of the author. Doublets and repetitions are not seen as the sign of later additions, but as literary devices enhancing dramatic effect.[22] Now unity is understood in a wider context, and as the understanding of the wider context can be even more variable, we find it difficult even to talk of higher probability. And indeed, the different understanding of coherence and unity has led to the division of current biblical scholarship into two camps: historical-critical method on the one side, literary criticism on the other.

In the discussion about the composition history of the David and Goliath story, to a certain extent we are struggling with a similar issue about different understandings of unity and coherence in a narrative. Hypothesis A sees the story presented in MT as full of repetitions and discrepancies and that in LXX as coherent, and concludes that it must have been expanded into the longer version. Hypothesis B, by contrast, sees the story presented in MT as more or less unified and that in LXX as too tidy, and concludes that the longer less tidy one was shortened into the shorter tidier one. Coherence and unity matter for both positions, but since there is no one to make an objective judgement about it, each is allowed to choose a position according to their taste, and we may have to accept that whether we support Hypothesis A or Hypothesis B is just a matter of taste.

But what if ancient people had a very different attitude toward coherence or inconsistencies in narrative? What if they did not care much about those issues when they compiled their traditions or even when they composed a text?[23] Or, what if, as Herbert Donner has argued, the foremost task for the ancient redactor was neither infusing a theological idea nor creating literary art, but preserving the already semi-sacrosanct sources as fully as possible, losing as little as

---

22 Alter, *The Art of Biblical Narrative*, 3–10.
23 Benjamin D. Sommer, "The Scroll of Isaiah as Jewish Scripture, Or, Why Jews Don't Read Books," *Society of Biblical Literature 1996 Seminar Papers*, 225–242, quoted from Barton, "What is a Book?", 3.

possible?[24] Although we cannot be too certain about the motives of the ancient redactors, this certainly undermines the argument that the longer version was abridged for harmonization. If consistency and coherence were not the most important criteria for ancient people, it is very unlikely that they took such trouble to excise carefully the verses that might interrupt the text. But at the same time, this also weakens the argument of Hypothesis A. For example, Tov and Lust believe that the LXX's story is more original than the MT's story, because the former is more logical than the latter. However, in a culture where consistencies and coherence did not matter much, a writer could have composed a text full of inconsistencies.[25] Therefore, we cannot conclude from the impression that the LXX's story is more coherent than MT, that LXX's story was original and MT's story was its expansion. Indeed, it can be argued that the LXX's story is the later version, precisely because it shows more concern about coherence.[26]

After all, what the discussion about the coherence issue tells us is that (1) we cannot decide which one is original between MT and LXX on the basis of its coherence, and that (2) it is very unlikely that ancient people made a dramatic abridgement to make their text more coherent, i.e. for harmonization. Again, this leads us to go for the expansion hypothesis as more probable. One might still argue that although abridgement was very unusual, a clear ideological purpose might have prompted the translator or the Hebrew scribe to venture the task. For instance, as Dietrich proposed, the abridgement might have been carried out to make clearer the theme of the conflict between Israel and a foreign power in the Hellenistic era when the question of whether Israel could survive among the foreign powers was most pressing.[27] The argument is quite attractive – though there are other reasons why such a late date seems unlikely, but its weakness is that Dietrich considered only chapter 17, and neglected the fact that the conflict between Saul and David – which he believes the Greek translator removed from chapter 17 – continues to be a main concern in chapter 18 onwards. If the abridgement had been designed to remove such a central theme, it was an impossible task from the beginning unless most of the so-called "History of David's Rise" is removed. Therefore, the abridgement of the text for such a reason is unlikely.

In fact, even when it comes to examining the purpose, the expansion hypothesis seems to have more to say. As suggested by a number of scholars, an-

---

24 Donner, "Der Redaktor," 27–28.
25 Barton, "What is a Book?", 7– 8.
26 For instance, Chronicles shows concerns about coherence when it is developing Kings. Cf. Barton, "What is a Book?", 12.
27 Dietrich, "Erzählungen," 179.

cient people may well have been willing to incorporate whatever traditions they acquired into their collections.[28] And the further elaboration of the greatest hero may well have been a legitimate reason for the expansion. As McCarter observed, it is very plausible that "once the tale of victory over the Philistine was introduced into the older narrative about David's rise to power [...] it began to attract more material from the same circle of tradition".[29] However, one might still argue that the extent of the expansion is nonetheless too unusual. Furthermore, one might wonder whether the compiler would incorporate a tradition even if it introduced not just a double perspective, but a contradictory picture of the hallowed hero. For example, what was the point of introducing a passage that describes David as an ambitious and reward-seeking person? Why did the compiler want to tell the readers or the audience that David was said to have an "evil heart" by his own brother, even if the term "evil" is always attributed to David's counter hero, Saul? This presses us further to elaborate the purpose of the expansion.

## 1.3 Purpose and Date of the Expansion

As to the purpose of the rather bold expansion, L. Krintezki suggests that the editor wanted to make his kerygma clearer that "not the king, but the unknown, young hero was the suitable instrument, through whom YHWH saves His people".[30] Although it seems evident that the redactor wanted to convey such a message, it is less likely that it was the main purpose for the expansion, because the theological motif is less obvious in the MT pluses. Ralph Klein argued that the additions and the alterations were made to "heighten the hostility of Saul for David, or to magnify the virtues of David".[31] However, the MT pluses in chapter 17 show no interest in Saul, let alone in vilifying him, and do not hide David's negative or at least vulnerable character. Graeme Auld & Y. S. Ho proposed that the expansion was made to contrast David with Saul, and that David's success in his errand in contrast to Saul's failure is one example.[32] However, it is not clear whether David was successful in the errand, because, although

---

28 McCarter, *I Samuel*, 296; Barthélemy, et al., *David and Goliath*, 10, 42.
29 McCarter, *I Samuel*, 308–9.
30 L. Krintezki, "Ein Beitrag zur Stilanalyse der Goliathperikope (1 Sam. 17, 1–18, 5)," *Bib* 54 (1973): 187–236 (200).
31 Klein, *1 Samuel*, 186–7.
32 A. Graeme Auld and Y.S. Ho, "The Making of David and Goliath," in *Samuel at the Threshold* (Hants: Ashgate, 2004), 81–97 (87–88, 95).

Jesse tells David to bring back a "token (עֲרֻבָּה)" of his brothers' well-being (1Sam 17:18), he fails to do so. In fact, if we look at only the eventual outcome, it is Saul who succeeds in the errand, because the lost asses are found any way (1Sam 9:20), whereas the text does not say that Jesse received the "token".

In my view, a more likely purpose for a rather bold expansion is a literary one. That is, the redactor wanted to make the David story more like the Joseph story. The similarity between the two has been pointed out by several scholars,[33] and attempts have been made to explain the connection. For instance, Grønbaek suggested that the author might have wanted to present the relationship between Joseph and Benjamin as the prototype of the relationship between David and the Benjaminites, so that David might be seen as the carer of the Benjaminites and worthy of being king over both Judah and Israel.[34] Dietrich and Naumann, by contrast, proposed that the David story was modelled on the Joseph story, and was a sort of Judahite national epic created "in conscious contrast to the corresponding Northern model", the Joseph Story.[35] Westermann suspects that the Joseph story itself came into being to deal with the question, "May and ought a brother rule over his brothers (Gen 37:8)?", and Berges proposes that the author of the HDR responded to the same question by saying, "Wie Josef Israel als מֹשֵׁל am Leben erhält, so errettet David Israel als מֶלֶךְ."[36] Plausible though they may be, all these views presuppose that both the Joseph story and the David story were written during the monarchical period, while this is far from clear. In fact, several scholars think that the Joseph story is from the exilic period,[37]

---

33 Hans Joachim Stoebe, "Die Goliathperikope 1 Sam. XVII 1–XVIII 5 und die Textform der Septuaginta," *VT* 6 (1956): 397–413 (403–4); Donald B. Redford, *A Study of the Biblical Story of Joseph (Genesis 37–50)* (Leiden: Brill, 1970), 89; Claus Westermann, *Genesis 37–50* (Minneapolis: Fortress, 2002), 28–29; Grønbaek, *Aufstieg*, 96–100; Alter, *The Art of Biblical Narrative*, 117; Moshe Garsiel, *The First Book of Samuel: A Literary Study of Comparative Structures, Analogies and Parallels* (Ramat Gan: Bar Ilan University Press, 1985), 120–21; Ulrich Berges, *Die Verwerfung Sauls: Eine thematische Untersuchung* (Würzburg: Echter, 1989), 235–38.

34 Grønbaek, *Aufstieg*, 100.

35 Dietrich and Naumann, *Samuelbücher*, 59.

36 Westermann, *Genesis 37–50*, 24–5; Ulrich Berges, *Die Verwerfung Sauls*, 237.

37 Heaton argues that the Joseph story cannot be pre-exilic, because the Joseph story has the following exilic or post-exilic traces: (1) the association of wisdom and understanding with the spirit; (2) the motif of dreams and their interpretations; (3) the foreknowledge of Yahweh; (4) the theme of the Divine providence, and (5) the context of the Jews among the Gentiles. Redford, on the basis of grammar and syntax, its difference from the patriarchal narratives, and the silence about Joseph in the Former/Latter prophets, dates the Joseph story between the mid-seventh and mid-fifth B.C.E., and his dating is accepted by Meinhold and Gnuse who label the Joseph story "*Diasporanovell*". See E. W. Heaton, "The Joseph Saga," *The Expository Times* 59 (1947/48): 134–136; Redford, *A Study of the Biblical Story of Joseph*, 252–3; Arndt Meinhold, "Die Gattung

and McCarter is convinced that even if the MT pluses were an early composition, they "did not find its [their] way into the text of the primary narrative until at least the fourth century B.C.E.".[38] Stoebe thinks that the similarity is due to the same theological message, that is, God gives life and salvation to the Israelites through a hero who is despised and has to live in a foreign land.[39] This is plausible in the exilic or post-exilic period, and the story of David and Goliath on the whole does express such a message. However, as in the case of Krintezki's suggestion, we are reminded again that the MT pluses show less theological interest than the shorter version in which David repeatedly attributes his victory to YHWH. This tempts us to consider that the similarity between the Joseph story and the David story is to do with their common literary background. The Joseph story has been long called a "short story" or *Novelle*,[40] and shares several features with some Aramaic and Hellenistic novella and the later Jewish novels.[41] The novelistic flavour found in the Joseph story might well be to do with the expansion of the shorter version of the David story. In other words, what Wills calls the "Jewish novelistic impulse" encouraged the compiler to venture rather a bold expansion.[42] The following points can support the possibility.

---

der Josephsgeschichte und des Estherbuches: Diasporanovelle I," *ZAW* 87 (1975): 306–324 (316); Robert Gnuse, "From Prison to Prestige: The Hero Who Helps a King in Jewish and Greek Literature," *CBQ* 72 (2010): 31–45 (42).

**38** McCarter, *I Samuel*, 308.

**39** Stoebe, *Das erste Buch Samuelis*, 328.

**40** Redford and Meinhold, following Gunkel, think that the Joseph narrative and the narratives in Esther, Judith, and Tobit are similar. Westermann however emphasises the difference between them, and disagrees with the common designation of the Joseph story as a *Novelle*, because Joseph was a historical figure and the focus of the story is not just an individual, but the family of Jacob. For Westermann, the Joseph story is better labelled as "belles lettres", but with some reservation as the Joseph story is not a form of fiction separable from the relationship of the family form of community to political society and with God's action in both. See Redford, *A Study of the Biblical Story of Joseph*, p. 67; Meinhold, "Gattung I," 316; Westermann, *Genesis 37–50*, 25–6.

**41** Cristiano Grottanelli, "Biblical Narrative and the Ancient Novel," in idem, *Kings and Prophets: Monarchic Power, Inspired Leadership, and Sacred Text in Biblical Narrative* (New York: OUP, 1999), 147–171.

**42** Wills terms it as "the tendency under certain social conditions for authors to transfer oral stories over to a written medium, to embellish them and create others, using description, interior psychological exploration, dialogue, and other narrative devices that can be easily manipulated in written prose but are not as often utilized in oral." Wills, *Jewish Novel*, 5.

Firstly, it is easy to notice that the motifs used in the MT pluses are common in the "ancient novel".[43] For instance, they have the motifs of travel (from Jesse to his brothers), adventure and excitement (David's volunteering to fight the giant), warfare (the fight against the giant Goliath), and court life and intrigue (the encounter with Jonathan and popularity in the court).[44] More specifically, the MT pluses share with the Jewish novels the motif of the clever young man who wins the favour of the king (1Sam 17:55–18:5 of David who "has insight, is wise" יַשְׂכִּיל; Dan 1:20 of Daniel; Tales of the Tobiads, *AJ* 12.172–79 of the young Joseph; 12.190–220 of the young Hyrcanus), and the motif of the jealousy of the worthless elder brothers (*AJ* 12.190, 195,197,221; 1Sam 17:28). True, the theme of sibling jealousy and the errand motif were not unusual,[45] and both the David story and the Jewish novels might have just followed common folkloristic motifs such as dispatching, reward, marvellous means, and false heroes.[46] However, it needs to be asked what prompted the redactor to incorporate such folkloristic motifs into the more sober historiographical narrative, and we are reminded that the editorial work that resembles such a process is found in the composition of Tobit and of Daniel. The book of Tobit and Daniel 1–6 are not written as Jewish novels per se, but as a compilation of legends and folklore with a Jewish novelistic flavour. It is well known that the Book of Tobit used the folkloric motifs such as "The Grateful Dead" and "The Monster in the Bridal Chamber",[47] and the introduction of Mordecai in Es 2:5 is reminiscent of the formula in 1Sam 9:1. The authors of the Jewish novel certainly played with folkloristic elements, and a similar process might well have happened in the expansion. Indeed, a number of scholars see the ancient novel as history that degenerated by the addition of adventures and sub-plots.[48]

Secondly, the description of the main hero David shows resemblance to that in the Jewish novels. Above all, David as a boyish/ feminine, and thus vulnerable character in the MT pluses reminds us of a feature common in the Jewish novels. In 1Sam 17:42, David is described as having יפה מראה. This is a very unusual description for men, because in the Hebrew Bible, with the exception of Joseph

---

**43** It is commonly called the "romance". But I use the term "novel", because as Pervo wrote, "'Novel' appears preferable to the once-fashionable 'romance', since the latter is more narrow in range and pejorative in connotation." See Richard I. Pervo, *Profit with Delight* (Philadelphia: Fortress Press, 1987), 103.

**44** Pervo, *Profit with Delight*, 106–8.

**45** McCarter, *I Samuel*, 304; Tsumura, *The First Book of Samuel*, 449.

**46** Cf. H. Jason, "The Story of David and Goliath: A Folk Epic?" *Bib* 60 (1979): 36–70.

**47** Wills therefore calls the book a "novelized" folklore. Wills, *Jewish Novel*, 76.

**48** See E. Schwartz, *Fünf Vorträge über den griechischen Roman* (Berlin, 1896), 147, cited from Pervo, *Profit with Delight*, 91.

(Gen 39:6) other than David, the phrase, "appearance" (מראה) coupled with "beautiful" (יפה), always refers to beautiful women (Sarah in Gen 12:11; Rachel in Gen 29:17; Tamar in 2Sam 14:27; cf. Es 2:7). However, Joseph and David are reported exceptionally to have such feminine handsomeness. Of course, the phrase is not only in the MT pluses, but also in LXX. However, the Greek version has μετὰ κάλλους ὀφθαλῶν which seems to reflect עִם־יְפֵה עֵינַיִם and is different from עִם־יְפֵה מַרְאֶה of MT. We are not certain whether LXX knew 16:12 and copied the wording, whereas MT did not know the verse (it has been often argued that 16:1–13 was rather late), or MT knew the wording in 16:12 but intentionally changed it. But in either case, the point is clear that the one who expanded the text wanted to present David as rather a vulnerable – as femininity often symbolizes – hero. The appearance of feminine and vulnerable heroes is, as Wills points out, a characteristic of the Jewish novel.[49] Neither Esther nor Judith are typical heroes, but vulnerable human beings whom no one expects to bring salvation to their people.[50] However, they astonishingly overcome the enemy of the nation, and confirm that God does not save "with sword, and with spear, and with javelin [...] but in the name of YHWH of Hosts" (cf. 1Sam 17:45). The picture of the vulnerable David in the MT pluses fits better with such protagonists in the Jewish novels, than with that of the typical hero of legend who is "normally invulnerable and is not buffeted by events".[51] In fact, the scene where David is humiliated by his brother Eliab in 17:28–29 might have been intended to magnify the dramatic effect of the salvation through the vulnerable hero. Contrary to the common view, the scene may not be so much to do with the motif of the jealousy of the worthless elder brothers as to do with the hero or heroine's experience of social shame that brings about the audience's sympathy, and reminds

---

**49** Wills, *Jewish Novel*, 225.

**50** Levenson draws attention to the fact that Mordecai is a descendant of Kish, and argues that the story implicitly refers to Mordecai as the "worthier" successor of Saul. More recently, Amit argues that the book of Esther was written by a post-exilic pro-Saulide author with a view to rehabilitating the descendants of Saul. This is an interesting idea, but I think, at least in 1Sam 17–18, the analogy better works in a different way. Just as David (the unexpected vulnerable hero), instead of Saul (the expected hero) saved the people of Israel, so did Esther (David's avatar as a vulnerable hero), instead of Mordecai (a descendant of Kish and Saul's avatar). Indeed, the verbal similarity of Esther 1:19 with 1Sam 15:28 confirms that the narrator thought Esther – not Mordecai – to be David revividus. The direct influence in any direction cannot be proved, but the pattern shares the feature popular in the Jewish novels. See Jon Levenson, *Esther* (Louisville: Westminster John Knox, 1997), 56–7; Yairah Amit, "The Saul Polemic in the Persian Period," in *Judah and the Judeans in the Persian Period*, eds. Oded Lipschits and Manfred Oeming (Winona Lake: Eisenbrauns, 2006): 647–661 (653–655).

**51** Wills, *Jewish Novel*, 45.

them of their own vulnerability. The humiliation of the vulnerable hero(ine) is another popular motif in the Jewish novel – most evidently in the Susanna story,[52] and it is likely that the MT pluses use the same motif to stress the message.

Furthermore, the characterization of David as a success-oriented and self-promoting figure also shows a similarity with the Jewish novels. As mentioned above, the MT pluses have David keep asking about the reward for the killing of Goliath, and in contrast with the shorter version where David is promoted solely by others and by YHWH, the focus of the achievement is more on the individual David rather than on YHWH. This is the point where the MT pluses become closer to Esther than to the Joseph story. In the latter, the hero overcomes the crisis only because of YHWH's being with him, while in the former, YHWH is not mentioned, and the initiative is taken by Esther or by Mordecai.[53] Additionally, the picture of a crafty hero who saves his people is reminiscent of the book of Judith, where the heroine, having reproached all those fearing to confront the enemy, defeats the enemy through deception, and comes back with the severed head as David does in the MT pluses (1Sam 17:57; Judith 13:15). And the picture of the "calculating" David who manipulates Jonathan may well be compared with Mordecai who manipulates Esther.

Thirdly, the motif that David was loved by all others (18:1–5), apart from the evil king and his closest allies, is worth drawing attention to. Grønbaek argues that David's popularity among the courtiers is to do with the author's intention to legitimate David further by giving a "*demokratischen Gehalt*" to the narrative.[54] However, we are reminded that it was also a popular motif in the Jewish historical novel such as 3Macc and Artapanus's work. For instance, Artapanus, in rewriting the Exodus episode, stresses Moses' popularity with the Egyptians (3 Fragment 27:6,10),[55] and 3Macc has the scene where the Greeks show sympathy to the Jews, and try to help them (3Macc 3:8–10). The motif might have been favoured by the authors of the Jewish historical novels who were struggling with the pressing issue about Jewish identity in a foreign world, and who wanted to claim that the relations between the Jews and the gentiles were fundamentally harmonious, and the persecution was a deviation from the norm.[56] The one responsible

---

52 Wills, *Jewish Novel*, 60.

53 Arndt Meinhold, "Die Gattung der Josephsgeschichte und des Estherbuches: Diasporanovelle II," *ZAW* 88 (1976): 72–93 (79).

54 Grønbaek, *Aufstieg*, 102–3.

55 James H. Charlesworth, ed., *The Old Testament Pseudepigrapha* (London: DLT, 1985), II, 898–90 (899).

56 Johnson, *Historical Fictions and Hellenistic Jewish Identity*, 166.

for the expansion might have wanted to present his monarchical hero as having experienced a similar situation: David was persecuted by an evil ruler, although most people loved him.

Fourthly, the duplication by the MT pluses in 18:10–11 and in 18:17–19 also suggests that the novelistic impulse was at work in the author's mind. Unlike the additions in chapter 17, these two pluses have less to do with the hero David, and they are rather isolated from the main narrative. McCarter suspects that Saul's first murder attempt was inserted to make clear that the offer of Michal comes after the estrangement between Saul and David, and the offer of Merab was the consequence of Saul's promise to David.[57] However, Saul's uneasiness with David is already expressed twice in the shorter version where Saul's fear of David is reported to be so great that he had to remove him from his presence (18:12–14). Thus, the duplication is not necessary. One might argue that the offer of Merab was the natural follow-up of the preceding story in the MT pluses. But according to 18:17b, the offer is not the reward for the past action, but for the future. Therefore, the duplication was more to do with its rhetorical effect. It is well known that duplication is often used to slow down the pace of the action, and thus to heighten the dramatic effects. Indeed, since 18:10–11 make clear that Saul's tragedy is to do with the work of the evil spirit, the additional account of Saul's murder attempt brings about "an understanding sympathy" for Saul.[58] Similarly, David's additional self-degradation in 18:18 helps to highlight the surprising outcome of the event that David does become Saul's son-in-law. These duplications affect the emotions of the reader, arousing sympathy toward the helpless hero caught up in fate, and magnifying the wonder of God's work – common motifs in ancient novels.

Fifthly, there are linguistic and stylistic traces of lateness in the MT pluses, and if it is late, the literary milieu of the expansion coincides with the time when the Jewish novel was beginning to sprout. Although the dating of the MT pluses cannot be certain, Alexander Rofé has pointed out that there are several features that indicate the lateness of the David-Goliath story, or at least, of the MT pluses. For instance, the length is unusually great for a classical Biblical story, and the highly paradigmatic quality is much closer to the Persian-period works such as Dan 1–6 than to the earlier narratives. The traces of late orthography as *plene* spelling in דּוֹז in 17:34,36, and the use of the denominative verb ערב in the Hiphil in 17:16 also point to the late authorship. The use of a definite demonstrative pronoun together with an indefinite noun in וַעֲשָׂרָה לֶחֶם הַזֶּה (17:17) is only common in

---

**57** McCarter, *I Samuel*, 306–7

**58** Hertzberg, *I & II Samuel*, 158; Grønbaek, *Aufstieg*, 110–111.

Rabbinic Hebrew, and the introduction of temporal clauses at the beginning of the sentence (17:55,57) is a characteristic of late biblical Hebrew.[59] If these indications are taken seriously,[60] the composition is located much later, and even if the composition was early, it is more likely that the MT pluses were written or at least added in the Persian period.

Finally, it is noteworthy that although the Jewish novels were set in almost the entire span of Israelite history, there is no work set in the period of monarchy. 3Macc, the *Letter of Aristeas*, 2Macc, *Alexander Romance*, and *the Tale of the Tobiads* are set in the Hellenistic period, while the book of Tobit is in the Assyrian. Daniel is set in the neo-Babylonian period, and Esther and Judith are in the Persian exilic setting. Patriarchal narrative is rare, but we still have the fragments of Artapanus and *Joseph and Aseneth*. Surprisingly, however, there is no romance or novel about the popular king David, and we can easily imagine that the redactor wanted to make something similar, whether he created it or borrowed it from an independent tradition – perhaps, from a more evidently novelistic one about David.

To summarize, the similarity between the MT pluses and the Jewish novel, together with the signs of lateness in the style of the MT pluses, suggests that the purpose for the bold addition to the shorter version, or the *Vorlage* of LXX was to do with the literary milieu of the time. That is, in addition to the long-held tendency to put together as many traditions as possible, what Wills calls the "Jewish novelistic impulse" was an important factor for the expansion. Of course, the MT pluses are too little to establish the relationship between the Jewish novels and the one responsible for the expansion, and this should and will be pursued more in detail later. For the moment, however, such a possibility can be at least an answer to those who question the expansion hypothesis on the basis of its unusual boldness. And consequently, we are now convinced that the MT pluses are certainly post-deuteronomistic – probably, added in the Persian period; and they are excluded from the HDR proper.

---

**59** Rofé, "The Battle of David and Goliath," 126–131; Cf. Driver, *Notes*, 148.

**60** Rofé argues that these rather miniscule evidences should be taken seriously to date the composition, because "the classical diction of biblical texts was zealously preserved." Rofé, "The Battle of David and Goliath," 125.

## 2 The Deuteronomistic Additions

### 2.1 The Deuteronomostic hypothesis

Since Martin Noth published *Überlieferungsgeschichtliche Studien* in 1943, the discovery of the Deuteronomistic history has been regarded as one of the greatest achievements in modern biblical scholarship. In contrast to the traditional division between Pentateuch and the Former Prophets, the hypothesis held that the division existed after the first four books, and an exilic editor gave an overarching unity to the collection that extends from Deut–2Kings. Noth's view was not totally new, as the Deuteronomistic redaction in the Former Prophets was already recognized by W. M. de Wette as early as 1805, and the advocates of the Documentary Hypothesis also acknowledged the existence of the deuteronomistic layers in Judges–2Kings.[61] Noth, however, made two very important arguments in his book. First, he rejected the idea of the Hexateuch, which had been dominant since Wellhausen, and argued that Deuteronomy is not the ending of the Pentateuch, but the beginning of the historical books. Second, he argued that the deuteronomistic redaction was not sporadic, but much more organized, giving an overarching unity to diverse books.[62]

Despite some objections at the beginning, Noth's suggestion was soon accepted as standard, and the majority of biblical scholars still accept the hypothesis. Of course, the hypothesis is not accepted without modification. In particular, Noth's view of the purpose of the writing was challenged by many. For example, against Noth's pessimistic reading of the whole, von Rad recognized the importance of the Davidic dynasty, and saw a trace of hope, especially in the release of Jehoiakin at the end.[63] Wolff, although his reading was not as optimistic as von Rad's, also saw a note of grace, and held that there is a trace of hope in that the Lord will restore the repentant Israelites.[64] Such a different reading of the whole Deuteronomistic History, not surprisingly as this monograph consistently argues, affected scholars' view about the redactional history, and Frank Moore Cross came up with an idea that the primary edition of the Deuteronomistic History was not so much historiography as propaganda to support the Josianic reform. The work was not from the exilic period as Noth argued, but from the time of Josianic reform. As to the evidently anti-monarchic and pessi-

---

**61** Thomas Römer, *The So-Called Deuteronomistic History* (Edinburgh: T&T Clark, 2007), 16–21.
**62** Noth, *ÜS*, 10–12.
**63** Von Rad, *Old Testament Theology*, I, 334–347.
**64** Wolff, "The Kerygma of the Deuteronomic Historical Work," in *Vitality of Old Testament Traditions*, ed. Brueggemann and Wolff, 83–100.

mistic passages, Cross and his followers posit a later redactor who updated the first Josianic edition, after the experience of the exile, with sermonic touches.[65]

There was also a group of scholars who understood the whole of the Deuteronomistic History not very differently from Noth, but still felt some discordance in it, and thus rejected the idea of one single editorial work. Rudolf Smend was the first of them, and he identified, mainly from Joshua and Judges, the passages that show interest in the Law, and acknowledge that the land was not fully conquered.[66] Smend's view was developed by Walter Dietrich who focused on the books of Kings, and demarcated the later deuteronomistic layer marked by its prophetic features as well as the DtrN in the books of Kings.[67] Finally, Timo Veijola extended the discussion into the books of Samuel, and distinguished DtrG, DtrP, and DtrN more systematically.[68] These scholars, often designated as the Göttingen School, and whose model is called *Schichtenmodell* (the "Layer-model") in contrast with Cross's *Blockmodell* (the "Block-model"), do not accept the pre-exilic edition of the Deuteronomistic History as Cross and his followers do. They think that the first edition (DtrG) was immediately after the exile or the fall of Jerusalem, and the DtrN was complete by 520 B.C.E., and the DtrP was between the two.[69]

Although many sympathized with the Göttingen School in that the double-redaction theory is too simplified, the increasing number of the layers threatened the idea of the Deuteronomistic History itself, to the extent that some scholars, most notably Auld and Knauf, seriously questioned the existence of the Deuteronomistic History.[70] By contrast, it led some others to reassert Noth's original idea of one single deuteronomistic edition,[71] while others attempted to synthe-

---

65 Cross, *Canaanite Myth*, 274–89 (287).

66 Rudolf Smend, "The Law and the Nations. A Contribution to Deuteronomistic Tradition History," in *Reconsidering Israel and Judah*, ed. Knoppers and McConville, 95–110.

67 Walter Dietrich, *Prophetie und Geschichte: eine redaktionsgeschichtliche Untersuchung zum deuteronomistischen Geschichtswerk* (Göttingen: Vandenhoeck & Ruprecht, 1972).

68 Veijola, *Die ewige Dynastie*; idem. *Das Königtum*.

69 Dietrich, *Prophetie und Geschichte*, 143–4.

70 A. Graeme Auld, "The Deuteronomists and the Former Prophets, or 'What Makes the Former Prophets Deuteronomisitic?'," in *Samuel at the Threshold*, 185–92; E. A. Knauf, "Does "Deuteronomistic Historiography" (DtrH) Exist?" in *Israel Constructs its History: Deuteronomistic Historiography in Recent Research*, eds. A. de Pury, T. Römer and J.-D. Macchi (Sheffield: Sheffield Academic Press, 2000): 388–98.

71 Steven L. McKenzie, *The Trouble with Kings: The Composition of the Books of Kings in the Deuteronomistic History* (Leiden: Brill, 1991); idem, "The Trouble with Kingship," in *Israel Constructs its History*, ed. de Pury, Römer and Macchi, 286–314; John Van Seters, *In Search of History*, 322–53.

size the *Blockmodell* and the *Schichtenmodell*.[72] Most recently, Thomas Römer has presented the view that there were three major deuteronomistic redactions. According to his view, there was a Josianic edition, but this was not so much a history as Josianic propaganda. This was reworked into the proper "Deuteronomistic History" in the exilic period, and finally, the work was modified in the Persian period.

Despite recent scepticism, I believe that there was a deuteronomsitic history. The end-of-era reflections, dual overlapping chronologies, and a prophecy-fulfilment schema certainly demonstrates that the Deuteronomistic history is a unified whole, and so do the leitmotivs such as "other gods" and "the exile".[73] As to whether it was written by a single redactor/author as Noth first suggested, it is difficult to give a definite answer. But it is worthwhile to revisit the methodological question, and hear what Richard Nelson recently said: "The most convincing historical-critical models are those that explain textual features on a large scale. We find ourselves more comfortable and more convinced when we 'zoom out', taking in more forest and fewer trees, working as much as possible with textual blocks rather than individual verses."[74] Apparently, Nelson argues that we should see the whole rather than the parts, and that such an approach supports the *Blockmodell*, as it is often argued that Cross started from the whole, whereas the *Schichtenmodell* started from the parts. However, it should not be overlooked that the so-called Göttingen School also started from the whole. They just accepted Noth's reading of the whole that the Deuteronomistic History is fundamentally pessimistic or at least "critical",[75] and thus it is more likely to have come to exist after a traumatic experience. This shows again that the decision on the redactional activity of the Deuteronomistic history largely depends on the interpretation of the whole, and without agreement on the theme and the purpose of the whole, we cannot reach an agreement as to the redactional history either. However, as I have consistently argued, we cannot produce the correct interpretation of the whole through certain mechanical procedures. As

---

72 Mark A. O'Brien, *The Deuteronomistic History Hypothesis: A Reassessment* (Göttingen: Vandenhoeck & Ruprecht, 1989); Iain W. Provan, *Hezekiah and the Book of Kings: A Contribution to the Debate about the Composition of the Deuteronomistic History* (Berlin: de Gruyter, 1988).

73 Richard Nelson, "The Double Redaction of the Deuteronomistic History: The Case is Still Compelling," *JSOT* 29 (2005): 319–337 (320–324); Thomas Römer, "The Form-Critical Problem of the So-Called Deuteronomistic History," in *The Changing Face of Form Criticism*, eds. Sweeney and Ben Zvi, 240–252 (247–8).

74 Nelson, "The Double Redaction," 333.

75 Walter Dietrich, "Martin Noth and the Future of the Deuteronomistic History," in *The History of Israel's Traditions: The Heritage of Martin Noth*, eds. Steven L. McKenzie and M. Patrick Graham (Sheffield: Sheffield Academic Press, 1994): 153–175 (157).

Campbell observed, "the overall decision results from a basically intuitive survey of the signals, under the influence of exegetical observations,"[76] and this means, as to the theme and the purpose of the whole Deuteronomistic History, that it is unlikely to have a definite answer that never changes. Just as we did with the HDR, we have to be satisfied with the most appropriate understanding of the whole at this time of interpretative history.

Then, what is the most appropriate interpretation of the whole Deuteronomistic History at this moment? We do not have enough space here to discuss the theme and the purpose of the whole Deuteronomistic History as thoroughly as we did for the HDR, but it seems that the importance of the promise to David has been a bit exaggerated. It is true that the phrase "for the sake of David my servant and for the sake of Jerusalem which I have chosen (1Kings 11:12,13,32,34,36; 14:4; 2Kings 8:19; 19:34)" sounds like a refrain, and indicates a pro-Davidic hand in the books of Kings. However, is it also true for the books of Samuel? Indeed, the inclusion of the "Succession Narrative", the Bathsheba episode in particular, has been a perplexing issue for those who want to hold that the primary edition was Josianic. Would the redactor, who wanted to argue that "in David and in his son Josiah is salvation",[77] include the "Succession Narrative" where David is depicted as a murderous, weak, and irresolute king?[78] One might want to get away from the problem by leaving out the "Succession Narrative" or at least the "scandalous chapters" from it, and maintain that the primary edition of the Deuteronomistic History was Josianic propaganda.[79] The problem remains unsolved however, because even the earlier part of the David story is not as glorious as often believed. As we have seen in the previous chapter, the story of David's rise is too balanced to be called "propagandistic", and this calls into question the view that "the extremely positive depiction of David in the HDR can easily be understood as a piece of Josianic propaganda".[80] The dominant tone of the Deuteronomistic History should be

---

**76** Antony F. Campbell, "Martin Noth and the Deuteronomistic History," in *The History of Israel's Traditions*, eds. McKenzie and Graham, 31–62 (47).

**77** Cross, *Canaanite Myth*, 284.

**78** Van Seters, *In Search of History*, 277–91 (290); idem. "The Court History and DtrH: Conflicting Perspectives on the House of David," in *Die sogenannte Thronfolgegeschichte Davids: Neue Einsichten und Anfragen*, eds. A. de Pury and T. Römer (Göttingen: Vandenhoeck & Ruprecht, 2000), 70–93.

**79** Römer, *The So-Called Deuteronomistic History*, 94–5; Fischer, *Von Hebron*, 317. McKenzie also strikes out the Bathsheba episode, but takes it as post-deuteronomistic. See McKenzie, "The So-called Succession Narrative," in *Die sogennante Thronfolgegeschichte*, eds. de Pury and Römer, 123–35;

**80** Römer, *The So-Called Deuteronomistic History*, 95.

found in the summarizing speeches, and they seem more like a theodicy or sermons for repentance than propaganda. This makes the exilic dating more likely, and Noth's initial insight seems still most convincing, although it should be acknowledged that there were further deuteronomistic redactions after the first DtrH. The DtrH collected various traditions, and put them together in order with some annalistic notes, and composed the important speeches to convey their own message. This does not necessarily rule out the possibility that there was a Josianic collection of traditions. But it is found mostly in the books of Kings, and thus it was a much shorter version.[81] It seems also likely that there were exilic and post-exilic redactions which intended to fit the previous tradition better to the historical context. For a clearer view about the redactional history, further research is needed. But we have sufficient background for us to discuss the deuteronomistic additions in the Saul-David narrative.

## 2.2 The deuteronomistic additions in 1Sam 15–2Sam 8

It is widely believed that the deuteronomistic historian inherited the old traditions about Saul and David, and thus only a few verses in the Saul-David narrative can be assigned to the deuteronomistic historian. However, there are not a few passages that one might well call deuteronomistic, and we need to identify them so that the shape of the HDR proper emerges more clearly. In order to do so, we have to apply various criteria, not least the linguistic and thematic features to the verses that are suspect. And when the signals are ambiguous, we need to weigh them against the background, that is, against our previous decisions about the context.

---

**81** Perhaps, as Kratz argues, only 1Sam–2Kings were included in the first edition of the Deuteronomistic History. See Reinhard Kratz, *Die Komposition der erzählenden Bücher des Alten Testaments* (Göttingen: Vandenhoeck & Ruprecht, 2000), 160–161; idem, "Der literarische Ort des Deuteronomiums," in *Liebe und Gebot. Studien zum Deuteronomium. Festschrift für Lothar Perlitt*, eds. Reinhard Kratz and H. Spieckermann, (Göttingen: Vandenhoeck & Ruprecht, 2000), 101–120; idem, "Der vor-und der nachpriesterschriftliche Hexateuch," in *Abschied vom Jahwisten. Die Composition des Hexateuch in der jüngsten Diskussion*, eds. J. Ch. Bertz, K. Schmid, & M. Witte (Berlin: de Gruyter, 2002), 295–323. See also Brian Peckham, "The Deuteronomistic History of Saul and David," *ZAW* 97 (1985): 190–209; E. Würthwein, *Studien zum deuteronomistischen Geschichtswerk* (Berlin: de Gruyter, 1994), 1–11;

### 2.2.1 1Sam 15

A good number of scholars do not see the deuteronomistic redaction in this chapter, and regard it more or less as a literary unity. For instance, Noth held that the chapter was incorporated into the Saul tradition, the earliest version of which included 1Sam 9:1–10:16; 10:27b–11:15.[82] Stoebe, in agreement with Weiser, holds that the chapter describes Saul caught up in the tension between the old piety/form and the new thought, and believes that there are no traces of the deuteronomistic redaction here, and the chapter is essentially a literary unity.[83] Grønbaek acknowledges the deuteronomistic hand in v. 2 and v. 6. Verse 2 is thematically reminiscent of Deut 25:17ff, and shares some stylistic features with the passage in Deuteronomy such as אשר עשה עמלך and מצרים (בצאתכם) בדרך בעלתו. As to verse 6, its formulation is similar to 1Sam 10:18; 12:6,8, where the Deuteronomist describes the Exodus, and the close relationship between the Kenites and the Israelites presupposed in the verse also indicates the deuteronomistic hand at work.[84] However, Grønbaek believes that the chapter as it stands is basically a unity that combined two ancient traditions. The Gilgal tradition about the rejection of Saul that highlights the superiority of the Ephraimite in Israel, was added to the even older Judean tradition about Saul's campaign against the Amalekites. The slightly ambiguous attitude toward Saul arose from the mixture of the anti-Saulide Gilgal tradition and the pro-Saulide Carmel tradition.[85] Recent scholars are more interested in the evidently prophetic element in this old tradition. Bruce C. Birch for instance suggests that the chapter was constructed around the oracle in 15:22–23 near the start of the period of the 8th century classical prophets.[86] McCarter holds that the old tradition of Saul's Amalekite campaign was reworked by a prophetic circle near the end of the eighth century B.C.E.,[87] while Campbell believes that an older story about Samuel's rebuke – not rejection – of Saul was reworked by a prophetic circle around Elisha into the story of God's rejection.[88]

Despite the apparent unity, however, it has been pointed out that certain elements do raise questions which may well signal the possibility of more complex

---

82 Noth, ÜS, 62–3.

83 Stoebe, *Das erste Buch Samuelis*, 278–282.

84 Grønbaek, *Aufstieg*, 46, 52; cf. Smith, *Samuel*, 131.

85 Grønbaek, *Aufstieg*, 64–68.

86 Bruce C. Birch, *The Rise of the Israelite Monarchy: The Growth and Development of 1 Samuel 7–15* (Missoula, Mont.: Scholars Press, 1976), 96, 107.

87 McCarter, *I Samuel*, 22, 270.

88 Campbell and O'Brien, *Unfolding the Deuteronomistic History*, 254–5; Antony F. Campbell, *Of Prophets and Kings: A Late Ninth-Century Document (1 Samuel 1–2 Kings 10)* (Washington: Catholic Biblical Association, 1986), 111–123.

redactions. For instance, Samuel rejects Saul's plea to return with him for having failed to "ban (חרם)" the Amalekites, and he does so to such an extent that Samuel's garment is torn by the desperately supplicating Saul.[89] But in vv. 23b–29, instead of putting Agag to the ban immediately, the prophet returns with Saul, and perhaps "offers" rather than "bans" Agag in Gilgal.[90] This certainly raises the question whether Samuel himself consistently obeys God's command. Moreover, how can v. 29 be reconciled with vv. 11 and 35, which use the same verb (נחם in niphal), but convey the exactly opposite message? Why do the Amalekites' past "sins" suddenly become a problem? Why is the Kenites' kindness toward the Israelites suddenly recalled? Why is there the unusual concentration on the word מאס "refuse" in vv. 23–26? Do not the phrases such as לָמָה לֹא־שָׁמַעְתָּ בְּקוֹל יְהוָה and וַתַּעַשׂ הָרַע בְּעֵינֵי יְהוָה sound deuteronomistic?[91] Why is the establishment of the monument in Carmel mentioned, when everything else seems to happen in Gilgal? And above all, why does Samuel suddenly become the centre stage, when the previous and the following chapters show no interest in him? These questions led not a few scholars to conclude that there are several layers in the text, and the most crucial of them is deuteronomistic. In particular, Walter Dietrich identifies four text layers in the chapter as follows: (i) the Gilgal narrative; (ii) the adaptation of the Gilgal narrative into an exemplary history of the relationship between king and prophet; (iii) the redactional work of this expanded version by the DtrP; (iv) the expansion by the DtrN to diminish Saul's and

---

**89** Grønbaek argues that both the subject in the verb וַיֶּחֱזַק, and the suffix in מְעִילוֹ in 15:27 refer to Samuel, and that Samuel tore his own robe. This is unlikely, however, and I think that the subject is Saul, and the suffix refers to Samuel. Since Samuel "turns around (סבב)", it is unlikely that he seizes Saul's robe and tears it. It is also implausible that Samuel tears his own robe, after he turns around. Why does he not allow Saul to see the very moment of tearing? The grammatical difficulty as to the change of the subject is not a big problem. In the series of *waw* consecutives, the subject needs not be the same in each clause (cf. Lev 1:1; Lambdin § 98). Indeed, both the ancient Versions (4QSam[A], LXX, Peshitta, and Josephus) and most commentators (McCarter, Klein, Tsumura) understand the verse in this way. See Grønbaek, *Aufstieg*, 40–42; Stoebe, *Das erste Buch Samuelis*, 289–90; McCarter, *I Samuel*, 264; Klein, *1 Samuel*, 145–6; Tsumura, *The First Book of Samuel*, 406.

**90** The word יְשַׁסֵּף (*piel* of שׁסף) does not occur elsewhere in the Hebrew Bible, but most Versions and commentaries agree that it means "to cut in pieces". Hertzberg, followed by Tsumura, holds that Samuel's action is the performance of the ban, while Grønbaek and McCarter think that the use of the word with "in the presence of YHWH" suggests "sacrificial butchering." In any case, it is clear that Samuel did not execute YHWH's commandment immediately, but delayed it. See Hertzberg, 129; Tsumura, 410; Grønbaek, 38; McCarter, *I Samuel*, 269.

**91** Both שמע בקול יהוה and עשה הרע בעיני יהוה are very frequent in deuteronomic literature. See Moshe Weinfeld, *Deuteronomy and the Deuteronomic School* (Oxford: Clarendon Press, 1972), 337, 339.

heighten Samuel's dominance.[92] The DtrP adapted the Gilgal tradition that had been circulated in prophetic circles to a wider biblical-historical context, with theological emphases,[93] and incorporated this revised prophetic narrative into the books of Samuel.[94]

All these views show us that there is a general agreement that we have a fairly old tradition in chapter 15 as we have it now, and that it was marked with prophetic elements. The difference in the views, albeit not exclusively, mainly comes from how critical of Saul one finds the prophet Samuel to be in the narrative. Is the figure of the prophet in this chapter closer to the zealous and harsh prophets like Ahijah (1Kings 14) or Elijah (1Kings 21)? Or is the prophet closer to the deuteronomistic redactor who is more reflective and wants to teach, rather than to condemn? As often mentioned, the oracle in vv. 22–23 does sound like the early "writing prophets" such as Hosea and Amos, and the harsh attitude of Samuel who repeatedly says that God rejected Saul might make us inclined to locate the author among the 9th century prophets. However, despite the harsh comments in these verses, Samuel on the whole is quite sympathetic to Saul, and such a tone is most evident in the fact that the narrative of the rejection is framed with Samuel's agony and sympathy for him. Samuel "cries out to YHWH all night" when he is first told that Saul is rejected in v. 11, and even after his delivery of the message, he grieves over Saul (v. 35). This suggests that the figure of the prophet on the whole is not totally hard-hearted towards the king. This impression is strengthened by the fact that the verses which include the harshest criticism sound rather discordant in the context, as the sudden concentration of the DtrN word "reject" and the rather abrupt touch of the classical prophets indicate.[95] The more thoughtful criticism of the prophet gives us the impression that the prophet's attitude is closer to the deuteronomistic redactor than to the early prophets, and such an impression is strengthened by the fact that the parallel between the Saul-David narrative and other pre-deuteronomistic prophetic narratives is not so strong as some scholars claim. For instance, the dismissal of the king such as in other pre-deuteronomistic prophetic narratives is extremely

---

92 Walter Dietrich, *David, Saul und die Propheten: Das Verhältnis von Religion und Politik nach den prophetischen Überlieferungen vom frühesten Königtum in Israel* (Stuttgart: Kohlhammer, 1992), 10–25 (24–5).

93 Dietrich, *David, Saul und die Propheten*, 17.

94 Dietrich, *David, Saul und die Propheten*, 51–2; Similar views are found in Georg Hentschel, *Saul*, 19–20, 100–102; F. Foresti, *The Rejection of Saul in the Perspective of the Deuteronomistic School: A Study of 1 Sm 15 and Related Texts* (Rome: Edizioni del Teresianum, 1984); E. Würthwein, *Studien zum deuteronomistischen Geschichtswerk*, 6.

95 Dietrich, *David, Saul und die Propheten*, 19 (#35).

severe. Both Jeroboam and Ahab are told of "evil" and "consumption", and the condemnation is simply a delivery of what God has already decided, following rather a strict format. By contrast, in Saul's rejection, the prophet converses with the king, and he, albeit sternly, instructs the king, rather than condemns him outright. This prophet is more like a reflective theologian than a zealous charismatic, and such a description of the prophet suggests that the dominant tone was infused by the deuteronomistic-prophetic redactor rather than by an earlier northern prophetic circle.

Indeed, it is worth asking whether the pre-deuteronomistic prophetic narrative, if it existed at all, was as extensive as some have argued. It is acknowledged that there is no prophetic intervention in the accession of Solomon and his decline. This led Campbell to posit that the pre-deuteronomistic prophetic narrative – which he calls "Prophetic Record" – had two parts, the first of which concludes with 2Sam 8:15, and the second of which resumes in 1Kings 11:26.[96] However, it is difficult to understand why there is a sudden lacuna in the middle, if the prophetic circle wants to produce a narrative about king and prophet from Samuel to Jeroboam. Furthermore, considering that the prophetic oracles were not made into a collection before the mid-8th century, it is very unlikely that the prophetic editors produced such a lengthy history in the 9th century.[97] It is more likely therefore that the "first part", i.e. the Saul-David narrative that had been revised by a prophetic circle, did not exist before the deuteronomistic redactor. Perhaps the prophetic narrative, even if it had been available before the exile, was first incorporated into the books of Samuel by the late exilic Deuteronomist, who might well have found it congenial to his own ideology.

To conclude, it is unlikely that the prophetically revised version of chapter 15 existed already before the Deuteronomistic historian's compilation of it into the history. The general depiction of the relationship between the prophet and the king is not totally hostile, and the tone of the criticism is more reflective than explosive. This brings us to conclude that it was the late exilic Deuteronomist rather than the pre-exilic prophetic circle, who introduced the chapter into the whole. The conclusion of course is far from certain, because there is no decisive hard evidence for us to know the precise composition history of the chapter. However, we can reach a reasonable conclusion by weighing the varied and sometimes conflicting evidence against the larger context. Indeed, our interpretation of the chapter – that the dominant attitude of Samuel toward Saul is sympathetic – is partly influenced by our interpretation of the whole Saul-David nar-

---

**96** Campbell and O'Brien, *Unfolding the Deuteronomistic History*, 30–31.
**97** Van Seters, *Biblical Saga*, 21–23.

rative as not anti-Saulide/pro-Davidic. Moreover, the reflective and more theological tone of Samuel's criticism is interpreted as deuteronomistic, because we had concluded earlier that the deuteronomistic redaction was essentially an exilic work designed to urge the reader/audience to return to God and obey the law. One might argue that such a procedure is too subjective and contextual. But our view is that such is what inevitably happens whenever we attempt to identify the different layers of the text, whether we admit it or not. The point is that we do it with as much transparency as possible, and this will help us to avoid obscuring what biblical criticism really does.

### 2.2.2 1Sam 16:1–13

According to Noth, 1Sam 16:1–13 is an even later addition than chapter 15 to the old Saul tradition, but it was still pre-deuteronomistic.[98] Weiser also regards the passage as pre-deuteronomistic, and submits more specifically that it was added to the older traditions about David's rise by the author of the HDR. The passage functions as the introduction to the whole narrative, and this is inferred from the fact that the theme and the *Tendenz* of the whole HDR are wonderfully compressed there.[99] Grønbaek holds a similar view, but thinks that the passage was rather created by the author of the HDR who wanted to provide not only a negative introduction to the HDR (chapter 15), but also a positive one. By providing a picture of David's anointing that is similar to Saul's anointing in 1Sam 9:1–10:16, the author contrasted David with Saul, and showed that David rightly replaced Saul.[100] Mettinger also ascribes 16:1–13 to the author of the HDR, but he connects it with 1Sam 10:17–27a rather than with 9:1–10:16.[101] This is taken up by McCarter, but as he is convinced that both 10:17–27a and 16:13 reflect prophetic reaction to the older tradition of Saul's election, he concludes that David's anointing here is "yet another major chapter in the prophetic reworking of the older materials about the early history of the monarchy".[102] Campbell also assigns the passage to the pre-deuteronomistic prophetic circle, although he sees the similarities rather with the anointing of Jehu, and argues that 16:1–13 is "the creation of the prophetic circles claiming their mandate to establish and dismiss kings".[103]

---

98 Noth, *ÜS*, 62 (#1).
99 Weiser, "Legitimation," 325 ff.
100 Grønbaek, *Aufstieg*, 68–76.
101 Mettinger, *King and Messiah*, 174–9.
102 McCarter, *I Samuel*, 277–8.
103 Campbell and O'Brien, *Unfolding the Deuteronomistic History*, 257.

Veijola, however, on the basis of the silence about David's secret anointing in other parts of the HDR, and of other deuteronomistic characters, suspects that 16:1–13 was post-DtrG,[104] and Dietrich more boldly assigns most of the verses to the DtrP. Dietrich's view is mainly based on his observation that the passage shows clear connections with the deuteronomistic verses (DtrP) in chapter 15. In particular, he draws attention to the use of מאס and בחר, which he regards as the "central concept of the deuteronomistic thought". He also points to the typically DtrP pattern found in the passage, according to which God's word is sent first to a prophet, made known to other people, and then fulfilled. All the verses that link 16:1–13 with chapter 15 can be attributed to the DtrP, and the older story simply narrates: God commands Samuel to anoint David in Bethlehem, and when Samuel comes to Bethlehem, the elders ask anxiously whether his visit means something bad. Samuel calms them down, saying that he came for sacrifice, and tells them to prepare themselves. He himself looks after the sanctification of Jesse and his sons, and when he comes to know about David, requires him to be brought. Samuel recognizes how handsome he looks, and anoints him in the midst of his brothers, and returns to Rama.[105]

We may not be able to identify the different layers in this passage as precisely as Dietrich attempts to. Nevertheless, it is reasonable to assume that the passage as we have it is not pre-deuteronomistic. The view that the passage was inserted by the pre-exilic prophetic circle is unlikely, because the way in which Samuel is depicted in the narrative – especially in v. 2 – does not fit with the picture of those charismatic and all-righteous prophets who deliver God's word without fear. Samuel in this passage is closer to the exilic prophets who not only condemned Israel for her sins but also lamented over God's too harsh punishment (Jer 8:18–21; Hab 1:2–4,13), than to the 9th century prophets such as Ahijah and Elijah. Furthermore, both in 2Sam 2:4 and 5:3, no prophet is mentioned for anointing, and this makes it difficult to understand the importance of Samuel in 16:1–13 without chapter 15 where Samuel's role of anointing is emphasized (15:1).[106] So, did the narrative of David's anointing also come from the same redactor of 1Sam 15, say from the DtrP, or the late exilic deuteronomistic circle? Perhaps, the original might well have come from them, and when Cyrus is called "shepherd"[107] (Isa 44:28) and YHWH's anointed (Isa 45:1), the depiction of David

---

104 Veijola, *Die ewige Dynastie*, 102 (#156).
105 Dietrich, *David, Saul und die Propheten*, 76–78.
106 Cf. Budde, *Samuel*, 114; Stoebe, *Das erste Buch Samuelis*, 302–3.
107 Some read רֵעִי (my friend) for רֹעִי (my shepherd) here. However, "my friend" does not fit in the context, and there is no reason to read against the MT. See Christopher R. North, *The Second*

as shepherd being anointed against human expectation may well have been an attempt to converse with the dominant political atmosphere of the time.[108] However, it seems that the passage was reworked by an even later redactor, and the trace of revision is found in the fact that there are two motifs running separately in the passage: the anointing motif and the sacrifice motif. Indeed, in the narrative, Samuel plays more the role of priest, and when he plays the role of prophet, he is depicted as a not totally reliable one. He misunderstands how God elects, and appears even "insensitive to the interests of God".[109] One might well feel that the figure of a prophet is slightly parodied here, and this distances the narrative from the prophetic Deuteronomist. Furthermore, it seems that the tone of the narrative is less pro-Davidic than the exilic Deuteronomist. In v. 12, even if Samuel is told that God does not look at appearances, the narrator does not talk about David's "heart", but his beauty. Together with all the allusions to Saul's anointing, the narrator seems to say that David is better than Saul, but not very different, because, after all, the first thing to be noticed is not his heart but his appearance, just as in the case of Saul! This allows us to glimpse the author's rather ambiguous attitude toward David's election, and suspect that the passage in its final form did not come from a zealously pro-Davidic party.

In brief, the dominant tone of the passage is cautious about the reliability of prophets and about the election of David, and this suggests that the reworking was done by a post-exilic redactor, who might have had a critical view of the restoration policy of the pro-Davidic Jerusalem-centred leaders. Indeed, David as shepherd in 16:1–13 is reminiscent of the MT pluses – 17:34ff in particular, and Psalm 151 mentions the David and Goliath story immediately after David's anointing. This indicates that there was a certain connection between the MT pluses in chapters 17–18 and David's anointing in chapter 16. Furthermore, David's anointing "in the midst of his brothers" might well be seen as revealing influence from the Joseph story,[110] and if we are correct in holding that the Joseph story influenced the MT pluses, this also supports the speculation that the re-

*Isaiah: Introduction, Translation and Commentary to Chapters XL-LV* (Oxford: Clarendon Press, 1967), 147; Jan L. Koole, *Jesaja III* (Kampen: Kok Pharos, 1997–2001), 425–6.

**108** Given the prevalence of "shepherd" imagery for ancient near eastern kings, this is hard to show. It is noteworthy, however, that in the Hebrew Bible, the symbol of shepherd as YHWH's regent is used first in the exilic literature such as Jeremiah and Ezekiel. See Veijola, *Die ewige Dynastie*, 65. For similarities between the story of Cyrus' rise in Herodotus' *Histories* and the HDR in the Hebrew Bible, see Katherine Stott, "Herodotus and the Old Testament. A Comparative Reading of the Ascendancy Stories of King Cyrus and David," *SJOT* 16 (2002): 52–78.

**109** Polzin, *Samuel and the Deuteronomist*, 153.

**110** Stoebe, *Das erste Buch Samuelis*, 304; Grønbaek, *Aufstieg*, 70.

working of 16:1–13 occurred in the post-exilic period, about the same time when the MT pluses were added.

### 2.2.3. 1 Sam 20

There are fairly obvious indications that chapter 20 is not a literary unity. Verses 11(or 12)–17 are disruptive to the narrative flow, and point toward the episode of sparing Mephibosheth in 2Sam 9 on the one hand, and refer back to 19:1–7 where David hides himself on the other. Furthermore, in contrast with the surrounding materials, it is now Jonathan who begs the favour from David, not the other way around.[111] Most likely, therefore, these verses were added later to form a bridge between the HDR and the "Succession Narrative", and scholars, on the basis of the terminologies, attribute them to the Deuteronomist, together with v. 42b which refers back to the oath in vv. 13 and 17.[112] One might argue that vv. 23,40–42a are also deuteronomistic, because v. 23 refers again to the covenant between Jonathan and David, and vv. 40–42a, although unnecessary after the arrow-signal in vv. 35–39, seem to be a prelude to 42b.[113] These seem to be secondary as well,[114] but whether they are deuteronomistic is arguable.

Then if we leave out all these secondary – possibly deuteronomistic – additions, could we regard all the rest as belonging to the HDR proper? Probably not, because it is difficult to reconcile the chapter with 19:9–12 where Saul's clear animosity does not require any further test of Saul's intention with regard to David.[115] Furthermore, the rest of the chapter does not fit well with the whole narrative which we interpreted as the story of Saul's decline and David's rise. In this chapter, Saul plays only a minor role, and Jonathan suddenly becomes the centre of the narrative. One might well argue that the passage is a literary embellishment to the main narrative about Saul's decline and David's rise. The chapter is about how David survived the threat from Saul with the help of the crown prince Jonathan, and such a story certainly enriches the main narra-

---

**111** Veijola, *Die ewige Dynastie*, 82–3.

**112** For instance, יהוה אלהי ישראל in v. 12, the oath formula with YHWH's name in v. 13, and the concept of עד עלם with absolute meaning "for always" in v. 15 are characteristic for the Deuteronomist. In fact, these verses were regarded as deuteronomistic already by the source critics like Smith and Budde. See Veijola, *Die ewige Dynastie*, 83–84; McCarter, *I Samuel*, 344; Klein, *1 Samuel*, 205–6; Budde, *Samuel*, 142, 163; Smith, *Samuel*, 187.

**113** McCerter, *I Samuel*, 342–43.

**114** Budde, *Samuel*, 140; Veijola, *Die ewige Dynastie*, 83; Otto Kaiser, "David und Jonathan," 281–96 (288).

**115** One might argue that it was just to enlighten naïve Jonathan. However, it is unlikely that Jonathan is ignorant about the matters around his father and sister and David.

tive. Plausible though it may be, such a literary embellishment with a touch of discordance with the larger narrative is more likely to be a secondary addition, and our impression is that it came from the late exilic or early post-exilic period, when the motif of salvation through an influential person favourable to the protagonist was popular in court narratives. In fact, the dynamic between David and Jonathan is reminiscent of the relationship between Mordecai and Esther in the book of Esther. Both David and Mordecai are calculating, while Jonathan and Esther are weak but after a moment of the deepest distress, save others. Moreover, it is interesting to notice that the rare phraseology "the evil is complete (כלתה הרעה)" that occurs three times in this chapter (vv. 7,9,33) appears elsewhere only in Esther 7:7 and 1Sam 25:17, and the expression "if I find favour in your eyes (אִם־מָצָאתִי חֵן בְּעֵינֶיךָ)" in 20:29 occurs elsewhere almost exclusively in Esther (5:8; 7:3; 8:5).[116] In both stories, the unexpected heroes (Jonathan and Esther) come at the centre of the story, and save the people in danger. As we saw above, this is one of the features in the Jewish novel, and we are led to suspect that the inclusion of chapter 20 in the books of Samuel was influenced by the "Jewish novelistic impulse". Of course, this makes it difficult to explain the "deuteronomistic" verses in the chapter. However, the use of the deuteronomistic phraseology does not mean that they were from the early Deuteronomist, or even from the Deuteronomist at all. The deuteronomistic redaction went on well into the Persian period, and it is possible that a late exilic or a post-exilic redactor, who had grown up not only with the orthodox ideology and style of the Deuteronomist, but also with novelistic stories, was responsible for the addition.

### 2.2.4 1Sam 25

Apart from v. 1, which is most likely a redactional insertion,[117] the chapter is seen by many as a literary unity. Yet, one might well notice that the narrative flow is interrupted by the rather elaborate speech of Abigail in vv. 28–31. The speech might have come from the author of the HDR,[118] but a certain deuteronomistic flavour is evident in the narrative. For instance, the expression מלחמות יהוה נלחם (to fight YHWH's wars) in v. 28, which does not fit with the immediate context, is a characteristic of the Deuteronomist, and the promise of the dynasty (v. 28) and of the election as נָגִיד (v. 30) occurs elsewhere in the deuteronomistic passages such as 1Kings 1:35; 2:24.[119] This led Veijola and McCarter to hold

---

**116** Schulte, *Entstehung*, 109, 122 (#45)
**117** Budde, *Samuel*, 163–4; Stoebe, *Das erste Buch Samuelis*, 451–2; McCarter, *I Samuel*, 388.
**118** Grønbaek, *Aufstieg*, 174; Mettinger, *King and Messiah*, 37–8.
**119** Veijola, *Die ewige Dynastie*, 51–2.

that Abigail's speech in vv. 28–31 is deuteronomistic. Veijola recognizes even more secondary additions. 23b cannot be original, because of the repetition in v. 24a. Verses 24b,25,28,31 are secondary, because אֲמָתֶךָ is used in these verses, whereas in v. 27, which he thinks is essential to the original narrative, שִׁפְחָתְךָ is used. These secondary verses are inseparable from vv. 26,29,30. Verses 21–22 disrupt the flow of the narrative; v. 39a (from וַיֹּאמֶר) is isolated, and closer to the later additions in terminology and content. Thus, he concludes that vv. 21–2,23b,24b–26,28–34,39a are secondary additions,[120] and ascribes all these to the DtrG.[121]

Although one cannot be sure of the precise extent of the expansion, the main story in chapter 25 seems to be a family story of David, or a story about "how David got such a wonderful wife". This is known from the fact that it is neither Saul nor David, but Abigail, who comes to centre stage in the story, and the tendency of the story is not to glorify or legitimate David, as the narrative does sound like "a proleptic glimpse, within David's ascent, of his fall from grace".[122] Possibly, the core narrative was related to other "family stories" as we find elsewhere in 22:1–5, or to a collection about David as an outlaw,[123] and to this core narrative, elaborate and sometimes theologizing verses were added, one of which is Abigail's speech. Since the core narrative does not contradict the whole Saul-David narrative, it might have been a part of the pre-deuteronomistic HDR. However, it is noteworthy that the story, even without the secondary additions, works so well, perhaps too well, as an allegory for the story of Saul and David. Nabal is depicted as a miniature Saul, and Abigail seems to represent the ideal Israelite in terms of the attitude toward David. Robert Gordon thus calls the story of Abigail and David a "narrative analogy", which he defines as "a device whereby the narrator can provide an internal commentary on the action which he is describing, usually by means of cross-reference to an earlier action or speech".[124] Together with the remarkable literary artistry pointed out by commentators,[125] this suggests that even the core story came to us with the reworking of a later redactor who knew the full implication of the conflict between Saul and David.

---

**120** Veijola, *Die ewige Dynastie*, 47–48.
**121** Veijola, *Die ewige Dynastie*, 51–54.
**122** Levenson, "1 Samuel 25," 24.
**123** Dietrich, *Early Monarchy*, 269–70.
**124** Gordon, "David's Rise and Saul's Demise," 42.
**125** Schulte, *Entstehung*, 38; Mark E. Biddle, "The Ancestral Motifs in 1 Samuel 25: Intertextuality and Characterization," *JBL* 121 (2002): 617–638.

Indeed, the wisdom and folly contrast, evident in the narrative, although influence from Egypt in the Solomonic period is not impossible, is more likely to be influenced from a culture more imperial and cosmopolitan. Indeed, it is interesting to notice that when she does not tell her husband Nabal (25:19), in whom there is senselessness (נְבָלָה in MT; ἀφροσυνη in LXX) like his own name (25. 25), Abigail follows exactly what the sage teaches in Sirach (22:13), "Do not talk much with a senseless person (ἀφρονος)". Moreover, in her quasi-prophetic declaration in v. 30, Abigail uses the title נָגִיד instead of מֶלֶךְ to describe David's future role, even though Saul has just acknowledged that David would become מֶלֶךְ in 24:21[20]. This may well be an indication that the author of the narrative had in mind a role in distinction from, or even in contrast with the political leader "king",[126] and if so, Abigail's prophecy that David will be נָגִיד rather than מֶלֶךְ reflects the situation where the Davidic monarchy is no more, or even the hope for it is discouraged or debated. Finally, certain elements in the narrative are reminiscent of the Jewish novels. In addition to the verbal similarity of "the evil is complete (כלתה הרעה)" in v. 7 with Es 7:7, the self-debasement of the heroine Abigail, which is evident in her calling herself repeatedly "your maidservant" and offering herself to wash the feet of David's servants,[127] may well remind the reader of the heroines such as Esther before the meeting with Ahasuerus, or Susanna before "all the people" for condemnation. Besides, the biblical character who shows similarity with Nabal is not only Saul, but also Belshazzar in Dan 5, who throws a drinking party in all his arrogance, is informed of what God is going to do with him by the wise Daniel, and is killed on the night of the party with no reason given. It is of course possible that these Jewish novels imitated the style of 1Sam 25. In that case, it should be asked why the Jewish novel imitated the rather a discordant section with unusual style of the biblical narratives. All this suggests that although the core of the tradition might well have come from an old legend about David, the whole Abigail narrative was reworked

---

126 Murray thinks that Abigail's use of the title נָגִיד can be seen as a polemic against מֶלֶךְ-ship. Van Wolde agrees with Murray, but does not seem them as antithetical, but as different: "*mœlœk* refers to military, constitutional, hereditary, leadership reflecting human relationships, whereas *nāgîd* refers to spatial, non-constitutional leadership reflecting the relationship between YHWH and his people." See Donald F. Murray, *Divine Prerogative and Royal Pretension. Pragmatics, Poetics and Polemics in a Narrative Sequence about David (2 Samuel 5.17–7.29)* (Sheffield: Sheffield Academic Press, 1998), 281–301 (294–5); Ellen van Wolde, "A Leader Led by a Lady: David and Abigail in 1 Samuel 25," *ZAW* 114 (2002): 355–375 (367–372).

127 One might see a sexual connotation in Abigail's self-characterization as maidservant. See Edelman, *King Saul*, 214, 220.

in the Persian period under the influence of the literary atmosphere of the time, and was incorporated into the books of Samuel.[128]

### 2.2.5 2Sam 3

If we regard 3:2–5 as the end of the previous section, whether it is an insertion or not,[129] 3:6–39 on the whole is more or less a literary unity, and there are no significant disruptions. It describes how Abner fell out with Ishbosheth, and attempted to hand over the kingdom of Saul to David, but failed because of Joab's old rancour. It is argued that certain verses in this section refer to a context that goes beyond the immediate concern. For instance, God's oath in v. 9 and in v. 18 are mentioned out of the blue, and so is Israel's elders' wish to make David their king in v. 17. Moreover, David's declaration of innocence and his curse on Joab's house in vv. 28–29 sound awkward unless one is aware of Solomon's liquidation of Abner in 1Kings 1–2. Similarly, David's acknowledgement of his own weakness and the condemnation of the sons of Zeruiah are out of context, and show clear connections with the "Succession Narrative". This has led several scholars to conclude that these verses – especially, vv 9–10,17–19,28–29 – are secondary, and probably deuteronomistic.[130]

Before we discuss to what extent secondary additions are found in this narrative, however, we have to ask why the narrative, or even the larger unit in 2Sam 2–5, gives us a strikingly different impression from what we understood to be the HDR. The story is not concerned with Saul and David any more, but with Saul's house and David's house. True, it is because Saul is no longer alive. However, after Saul and his sons are killed, it needs to be explained why the narrative drastically slows down before David takes over Saul's kingdom. One might argue that this describes the last stage of the decline of Saul's house. Yet, it is still unlikely that the "last stage" was written at such length and in such detail. Moreover, as McCarter points out, "Nowhere is the story of David's rise more insistent in its apologetic tone than here in its controversion of David's involve-

---

**128** From various connections of 1Sam 25 with patriarchal narratives, Biddle concludes that the chapter is a "literary parable skillfully composed on the basis of themes and motifs derived from existing literature", and cannot be pre-deuteronomistic. Lozovvy dates it even later in the 5th century. See Biddle, "The Ancestral Motifs in 1 Samuel 25," 636; Joseph Lozovvy, *Saul, Doeg, Nabal, and the "Son of Jesse"* (New York/London: T & T Clark, 2009), 169–177, 190.

**129** Cf. Noth, *ÜS*, 63 (#3); McCarter, *II Samuel*, 102.

**130** But there is difference in how much is secondary and/or deuteronomistic. See Veijola, *Die ewige Dynastie*, 30–32, 59–63; McCarter, *II Samuel*, 113–118, 121; Mettinger, *King and Messiah*, 40–44; Fischer, *Von Hebron*, 116–126.

ment in Abiner's death,"[131] the apologetic tone is too explicit here, and this does not agree with our understanding of the whole Saul-David narrative. Finally, the description of David is quite different from the previous narrative. David is no longer a young hero in these chapters, but a passive and weak king who cannot avoid being manipulated by others.

Several scholars therefore claim that the material in 2Sam 2–4 came from a different hand than that of the author of the HDR.[132] Van Seters, in particular, points out that the sudden appearance of Ishbosheth does not agree with the account in 1Sam 31 where all Saul's sons were killed in the battle against the Philistines, and 2:4b–7 is continued most naturally by 5:1 ff. Moreover, Jezreel is said to belong to Saul's territory in 2:9, whereas 1Sam 31:7ff reports that it was taken by the Philistines. The total ignorance of the Philistine problem in these chapters is another sign of a distinct origin.[133] Van Seters then argues that the account of the war with Ishbosheth belongs to the Court History, because (i) there are so many links between this section and the Court History, as we saw in the verses which scholars often regard as secondary; (ii) both 2:8–4:12 and the Court History show a special interest in the household of Saul and its relationship to David; (iii) in contrast to the HDR, both show distinctive literary qualities; (iv) Joab is a well-known figure in the account of the war with Ishbosheth, just like in the Court History, and the characterization is consistent in both; (v) both show the intricate development of the plot over the course of several scenes; (vi) both show more "secular" elements in distinction from the HDR. Therefore, 2Sam 2:8–4:12 belongs to the Court History, which Van Seters believes is an "antilegitimation story, referring to the same theme of divine promise but in an entirely different way".[134]

Although I am not totally convinced that the "Succession Narrative'" or the Court History is a later addition to the HDR, it is difficult to ignore the similarities of the account in 2:8–4:12 with the latter part of the David story, and its differences from the HDR. Of course, it is possible that this section was added to the HDR as an expansion that turned the story of Saul and David into the story of Saul's house and David's house, or even that of Israel and Judah. But this requires us either to posit additional redactional activity between the HDR and the deuteronomistic redaction, or to presuppose a third tradition that belongs neither to the HDR nor to the Court History. Considering the similarities that Van Seters points out, however, these options are less economical explanations than it is to hold

---

131 McCarter, *II Samuel*, 121.
132 Rendtorff, "Beobachtungen"; Schulte, *Entstehung*; Gunn, *King David*.
133 Van Seters, *In Search of History*, 281–2.
134 Van Seters, *In Search of History*, 282–9.

that 2:8–4:12 was a part of the Court History.[135] If we want to ascribe it neither to the HDR nor to the Court History, we should draw attention to Grønbaek's observation that the inclusive idea of Israel is characteristic to the whole of 2Sam 2–5. These chapters, although they do not cover up the conflict between David's house and Saul's house, attempt to present the conflict between them as "eigentlich unnatürlich und daher nur vorübergehend".[136] Such a tendency reminds us of the novelistic redactor whom we believe was unhappy about Judean exclusivism. This will be discussed later, but at least, regardless of how many verses in the narrative are secondary or deuteronomistic, it is untenable now that the account belongs to the HDR. The understanding of the whole Saul-David narrative as pro-Davidic propaganda might have pushed scholars to include these chapters in the HDR, despite their evidently distinctive character. However, once we have a different view about the whole, we should exclude II Samuel 2:8–4:12 from the HDR proper.

### 2.2.6 2Sam 5

There is an element of odd repetition or contradiction in vv. 1–3. Verse 1 reports that "all tribes of Israel" came to Hebron to designate David as נָגִיד of Israel, but according to verse 3, "all elders of Israel" came to Hebron to anoint David as "king over Israel". One might regard v. 1 as a preparatory step to the proper anointing in v. 3. However, v. 3 seems unaware of any previous arrangement. In fact, there are several other indications that vv. 1–2 are secondary. They refer back to 1Sam 18 (18:5 in particular) where David's military leadership is mentioned, and the shepherdship of David seems to allude to David's anointing by Samuel in 1Sam 16:1–13 and/or to Nathan's oracle in 2Sam 7, or more specifically to 7:7–8. Moreover, it is historically implausible that "all tribes of Israel" came to Hebron, whereas the visit of the elders in v. 3 for the anointment is quite possible. Grønbaek ascribes the addition to the author of the HDR, because it fits with what he thinks is the intention of the work. They highlight that David was a legitimate successor to Saul as king over both Judah and Israel.[137] But we

**135** For objections, see Veijola, *Die ewige Dynastie*, 162; E. Blum, "Ein Anfang der Geschichtschreibung?", in *Die sogenannte Thronfolgegeschichte Davids*, ed. de Pury and Römer, 4–37 (21, #74); Fischer, *Von Hebron*, 7–11.

**136** Grönbaek, *Aufstieg*, 247. A similar point is made more recently in Andreas Kunz, "'Soll das Schwert denn ewig fressen?' Zur Erzählintention von II Samuel 2. 8–32," in *Erzählte Geschichte: Beiträge zur narrativen Kultur im alten Israel*, ed. Rüdiger Lux (Neukirchen-Vluyn: Neukirchener, 2000): 53–79.

**137** Grønbaek, *Aufstieg*, 248–9.

have seen that this is a particular interpretation, and we cannot ascribe them to the author of the HDR on the basis of Grønbaek's own interpretation of the whole. Mettinger also thinks that they are from the author of the HDR, because they point back to 1Sam 16:1–13 and look ahead to 7:7–8, both of which he ascribes to the author of the HDR.[138] However, we have concluded that 1Sam 16:1–13 was incorporated in the exilic or post-exilic period, and 2Sam 7, even if it includes some old traditions, is basically an exilic deuteronomistic work.

On the basis of some "deuteronomistic" phrases in these verses, therefore, Veijola and McCarter hold that verses 1–2 are from the (early) Deuteronomist. Veijola argues that these verses are meant to make David fit with the DtrG's view of the ideal governance in which theological and political dimensions are integrated,[139] while McCarter thinks that they were added mainly to anticipate Nathan's oracle.[140] Both are possible, but it is less likely that such a discussion about ideal governance occurred soon after the end of the monarchy and the fall of the state. The issue might have been more pressing when the restoration looked possible, and this is supported by the fact that in comparison with v. 3, vv. 1–2 have a wider perspective, which fits better with the late exilic atmosphere. Moreover, it is noteworthy that the phrase "bone and flesh" occurs elsewhere in Gen 29:14 and in Judges 9:2, and in both cases, the outcome for those appealed to in such a way is not positive. Jacob is deceived repeatedly by Laban, and the people of Shechem are destroyed by Abimelech. It is unlikely that the phrase is used negatively here, considering the laudatory words in v. 2. However, it is possible that the verses came from a time when an appeal to "bone and flesh" was an important issue, and it was most likely the late exilic period or early post-exilic period when there was an attempt to redefine the identity of Israel according to the genealogical ground, i.e. "bone and flesh". The appeal to "bone and flesh" positively here and negatively in Genesis and Judges might well reflect the inner debate among the Jews in the Persian period.

Verses 4–5 have the stereotypical deuteronomistic notices on the accessions of the kings of Israel and Judah, and they are probably deuteronomistic. But it is also possible, since these verses are missing in the old witnesses such as the LXX[B] and 4QSam[A], and 1Chr 11, that the verses are "very late additions to the text in the spirit of the authentically deuteronomistic notices".[141] In vv. 6–8, we have the account of the conquest of Jerusalem, which appears to be irrelevant to the flow of the narrative. Grønbaek explains the awkwardness of the insertion

---

**138** Mettinger, *King and Messiah*, 44–5.
**139** Veijola, *Die ewige Dynastie*, 63–6.
**140** McCarter, *II Samuel*, 131.
**141** McCarter, *II Samuel*, 133.

by arguing that it emphasizes David's achievement even further.[142] These verses, however, do not make much sense without the list of David's sons from Jerusalem in vv. 13–15 or the latter part of the David story, the setting of which is Jerusalem. Thus vv. 6–8 were also a later addition that was attracted to the mention of Jerusalem when the account of David's early life was connected with the latter part. Verses 9–10 are regarded by many as marking the end of the HDR, and the motif of YHWH being with David is seen as clear evidence for such a conclusion. However, the *assertorisch* use of the so-called *Beistandformel* is found most frequently in later texts such as the Joseph story and Chronicles,[143] and it is far from clear that the verse belonged to the pre-deuteronomistic HDR. Verses 11–12 can be ascribed quite confidently to the later redactor, since they prepare the reader for 1Sam 7, which we regard as a late exilic text (see below).[144] The genealogical interest and the mention of Solomon indicate that vv. 13–16 also came from the Deuteronomist.

The provenance of vv. 17–25 is more difficult to decide. Grønbaek thinks that they originally belonged to the HDR, but the Deuteronomist relocated them in order to make a smoother transition to the following stories.[145] Mettinger sees the passage as the fulfilment of the prophecy in 3:17–19, and as he thinks the promise belongs to the HDR, rather than to the Deuteronomist, he argues that 5:17 also belongs to the HDR.[146] However, 3:17–19 is a part of the account of the war with Ishbosheth, and it is unlikely that 5:17–26 embodies the fulfilment of the prophecy in the passage that we do not regard as pre-deuteronomistic. Thus I maintain that they were first incorporated by the Deuteronomist, when the ancient traditions about David's war against the Philistines were put together with some materials in 2Sam 8. The deuteronomistic historian might have wanted to wrap up the rise of David here, just as he did for Saul in 1Sam 14:47–51, before 2Sam 6–7 was inserted. The redactor who inserted these chapters rather violently might have thought that the establishment of Jerusalem as political and cultic centre was necessary for securing the country from the neighbouring powers. To summarize what we have concluded so far, 2Sam 5 is a collection of later additions inserted primarily to make a smoother transition to the following

---

142 Grønbaek, *Aufstieg,* 256.

143 Preuß observes that the so-called *Beistandformel* is used (i) as promise through God; (ii) promise, petition or wish by human beings; (iii) as a statement by a human being, that is, not promisingly, but *assertorisch*. The *Beistandformel* in the HDR belongs to (iii). See Horst Dietrich Preuß, "… ich will mit dir sein!" *ZAW* 80 (1968): 139–73 (148–52).

144 Grønbaek, *Aufstieg,* 257–8; McCarter, *II Samuel,* 146.

145 Grønbaek, *Aufstieg,* 252–3.

146 Mettinger, *King and Messiah,* 42.

materials in 2Sam 6–20. Perhaps only v. 3 can be safely located in the pre-deuteronomistic HDR, and the fact that verses 4–5 are missing in the old witnesses such as the LXX[B] and 4QSam[A], and 1Chr 11 might support that there was a major division after verse 3.

### 2.2.7 2Sam 7

The ongoing discussions about the literary history of 2Sam 7 are extensive, but it is generally agreed that the chapter is basically a deuteronomistic work. Of course, there is a group of scholars who date the chapter – Nathan's oracle in particular – earlier. For example, Weiser, on the basis of Herrmann's form-critical analysis,[147] believes that it is a modification of an ancient genre and belongs to the HDR. Verses 8–11 form-critically correspond to the historical overview in the Egyptian *Königsnovelle*, and the allusions to the HDR in these verses clearly indicate that the author wrote the chapter with the materials of the HDR in hand. As to the dynastic interest that goes beyond the immediate context, Weiser argues that the HDR was written in Solomon's reign, and the legitimation of Solomon's succession by appealing to the dynastic promise made to David makes excellent sense.[148] More recently, the authorial unity of 2Sam 7:1–17 was defended by William M. Schniedewind.[149] He thinks that the perpetuity of the dynastic promise is so basic that it cannot be exilic, and the common rewriting of the promise in later literature suggests that the original text is from the united monarchy. Concerning the tensions between the two oracles in vv. 3–7 and vv. 8–17, he argues that they reflect the tensions within the early Israelite monarchy.[150]

It is not our concern at this point to identify the different layers in the chapter or figure out how old they are.[151] However, even if it is established that the chapter includes certain ancient traditions that probably came from the Davidic-Solomonic period, it does not necessarily mean that they were already compiled before the deuteronomistic redaction. Nor does that conclusion prove that

---

147 Siegfried Herrmann, "The Royal Novella in Egypt and Israel," in *Reconsidering Israel and Judah*, eds. Knoppers and McConville, 493–515.

148 Weiser, "Legitimation," 346–9.

149 William M. Schniedewind, *Society and the Promise to David: the Reception History of 2 Samuel 7:1–17* (Oxford: Oxford University Press, 1999), 30–39.

150 Schniedewind, *Society and the Promise*, 39.

151 For a survey of views of major scholars, see Dietrich and Naumann, *Samuelbücher*, 154. For a more recent survey, see Michael Pietsch, *"Dieser is der Sproß Davids..." Studien zur Rezeptionsgeschichte der Nathanverheißung im alttestamentlichen, zwischentestamentlichen und neutestamentlichen Schrifttum* (Neukirchen-Vluyn: Neukirchener, 2003), 1–30; Van Seters, *Biblical Saga*, 241–68.

they were available to the author of the HDR. As Weiser already pointed out, the decision depends on whether the chapter serves the *Grundanliegen* of the HDR,[152] and this implies that how we understand the larger context, i. e. the Deuteronomistic History and the whole HDR, is crucial here as well. As mentioned repeatedly, the HDR has been understood as the story of David's rise, and this led many scholars to expect the end of the story to mark the climax of the rise. Those who interpret the rise as more theological and of wider perspective might well see the climax in the promise of the eternal dynasty in 2Sam 7, in contrast with those who see the rise as more political and immediate, and see the climax in the enthronement in 2Sam 5. However, if we understand the HDR not merely as the story of "rise", but also as the story of "decline", the promise of an eternal dynasty looks a bit artificial and too glorious. It is possible that the original document was already available in the Davidic-Solomonic period. And yet, it is unlikely that the author of the HDR, who was interested in the "movement" of decline and rise rather than a definite status in glory, marked the end of the HDR with such a glorious promise. On the other hand, it is not easy to understand why the author of the HDR included the oracle that expresses such a strong objection to David's idea of building the temple.[153] Of course, the author might have wanted to emphasize that not only in David's rise, but also in the future, is the initiative in the hands of God. However, the tone of the objection is too strong to avoid the impression that it reflects a real issue of the time rather than that it makes a theological point. As Schniedewind rightly points out, "the rhetorical questions in verses 5–7 seriously question the need for a temple".[154]

How were these two rather conflicting visions handed down then? Were they already included in the pre-deuteronomistic HDR? In my view, it is unlikely that the author of the HDR marked the end of the HDR either with the too glorious dynastic promise, or with the too hostile anti-temple record. Rather, the compilation of these two is best explained as the work of someone who wanted to reconcile them somehow, and most likely, it was the Deuteronomist who incorporated them into the books of Samuel. In fact, historically, the clearest case of the debate around the building of the temple is found in the building of the Second Temple (cf. Isa 66). There was certainly a group of people who objected to building the temple, partly because they thought the time had not yet come, and partly because they were suspicious of religious nationalism that neglected

---

152 Weiser, "Legitimation," 346.

**153** The syntax of v. 5b "Are you going to build me a house…?" indicates that this is a rhetorical question that may suggest negative assertion, or a "surprised or indignant refusal". See G-K §150d.

**154** Schniedewind, *Society and the Promise*, 37–8.

the issue of social justice (Jer 7:1–15).[155] The Deuteronomist tried to deal with such issues,[156] and 2Sam 7 reflects the tension. Moreover, David's pious thought that "I am dwelling in the house of cedars, but the ark of God is dwelling in the midst of the curtain" reminds us of what the prophet Haggai says, "Is it a time for you to dwell in your panelled[157] houses, while this House is lying in ruins? (Hag 1:4)". Nathan's oracle as it stands now is an attempt at reconciliation of the dynastic promise and the suspicion about rebuilding the temple. Probably, the Deuteronomist in the late exilic period made use of two prophecies quoted by competing parties within the Jewish circle, and produced a kind of "document of compromise" that looks similar to the early deuteronomistic speeches, by adding 11b and 13a which play with the word בַּיִת, and David's prayer in vv. 18–29.[158]

## 3 The Persian-period Additions

We have seen so far that among the passages often designated as deuteronomistic, there are only a few DtrH additions, and most of the later additions seem to have come from the late exilic and post-exilic periods. The late exilic additions are close to the deuteronomistic view, but not always characterized by typically deuteronomistic features. They seem to have been dealing with various issues, such as the role of the prophet in the restored monarchy, the necessity of the Davidides for the restoration, and the choice of Jerusalem as the place for the Temple, and their answer was fairly deuteronomistic. In other words, they argued for the necessity of the Davidic monarchy, regulated by prophets, and supported the centralization of the cult in Jerusalem. So far we have identified the narratives of Saul's rejection (1Sam 15:1–35); David's anointing (16:1–13); David's conquest of

---

**155** Albertz, *Israel in Exile*, 128–9.

**156** Römer, *The So-Called Deuteronomistic History*, 146–7.

**157** The meaning of סְפוּנִים (passive participle plural of סְפַן "cover, panel") is not certain. Ackroyd sees the contrast between the richness and adornment of the houses of some returnees and the condition of the Temple. But Meyers hold that the word does not necessarily imply richness, and argue that the contrast is between the finished houses and the unfinished temple of God. In any case, the house of the returnees is contrasted with the devastated Temple, and the situation is seen as deplorable. See Peter R. Ackroyd, *Exile and Restoration* (London: SCM Press, 1968), 155–6; Carol Meyers and Eric Meyers, *Haggai, Zechariah 1–8* (Garden City, N.Y: Doubleday, 1987), 23–4.

**158** Eckhard von Nordheim, "König und Tempel: Der Hintergrund des Tempelbauverbotes in 2 Samuel VII," *VT* 27 (1977): 434–453 (447). For the view that the Deuteronomistic History was structured on the basis of three programmatic passages (Deut 31; Josh 23; 2Sam 7), see McCarthy, "II Samuel 7," 131–8.

Jerusalem (2Sam 5:6–16); Nathan's oracle (2Sam 7) as belonging to this layer. In addition to these, however, we suppose that there were also post-exilic additions which show the influence of the "Jewish novelistic impulse", and of less polemical tendency, and we have identified so far the revised version of David's anointing; the MT pluses of the David and Goliath story; the narrative of Jonathan and David; the Abigail episode; [the account of the war with Ishbosheth]; the report of Israel coming to David (2Sam 5:1–2) as belonging to this post-exilic layer. Now we examine further whether there are more additions in 1Sam 15–2Sam 8 that we might well ascribe to the late exilic or post-exilic period.

## 3.1 The shorter version of the David and Goliath story (1Sam 17)

We concluded earlier that the additional verses in MT which we do not find in LXX[B] were added to the shorter text, partly because the redactor wanted to collect as many materials about David as possible, and partly because he wanted to give a novelistic flavour to the story. The addition seems to have occurred in the early post-exilic period, and the MT pluses are certainly post-deuteronomistic. The shorter version, however, cannot be safely located in the pre-deuteronomistic HDR either. We saw above that the coherence in the shorter version does not prove that this narrative was more original and older than the MT pluses, because the concern for coherence might well have been later rather than earlier. Indeed, Rofé's linguistic analysis shows that the evidence of its lateness, such as the use of later vocabulary such as ברר for "choose", is found in the shorter version as well.[159] Furthermore, the highly theological and kerygmatic nature of the shorter version makes it unlikely that the story came from the monarchical period. In fact, David's proclamation that "You are coming to me with sword, and with spear, and with a javelin. But I am coming to you in the name of YHWH of Hosts (17:47)" reflects a similar theology to Zechariah's "Not by might, nor by power, but by my spirit" in Zech 4:6. Of course, this does not exclude the possibility that the basic story circulated for a long time in the monarchical period. However, the use of the derogatory expression "uncircumcised Philistine" and the designation of YHWH as the "living God" in v. 36 (cf. Isa 37:4,17; Jer 10:10;

---

**159** The form seems to come from ברה "eat", but this does not make sense here. LXX reads ἐκλέξασθε, and Targum reads בְחָר. Thus Budde, Driver, and Smith regard בְּרוּ as an error for בחרו לכם (cf. 1 Kings 18:25), while Ehrlich and McCarter revocalize it, and read בֹּרוּ from ברר "select". By contrast, Tsumura argues that ברה may be a bi-form of ברר, and no revocalization is necessary. See Budde, *Samuel*, 123; Driver, *Notes*, 140; Smith, *Samuel*, 155; McCarter, *I Samuel*, 287; Tsumura, *The First Book of Samuel*, 444; Rofé, "The Battle of David and Goliath," 126–31.

23:36; Dan 6:21,27 [ET. 6:20,26]), the expansion of the knowledge of YHWH to the "whole world" in v. 46, the reference to the "assembly (קָהָל)" in verse 47, and possible cultic elements in theses verses – all speak against the pre-deuteronomistic incorporation. Finally, as Yadin pointed out, Goliath's armour as described in the narrative might well reflect the "national awakening" of the Greek root in the region of Philistia in the 6th century B.C.E.[160] The accumulation of these signals makes it reasonable to conclude that the shorter version of the David and Goliath story came from not much earlier than the MT pluses.

## 3.2 The Duplications (1Sam 18:10–11; 26:1–25; 2Sam 1:5–10, 13–16)

It is interesting that the earlier part of the David narrative has a series of double accounts of more or less the same incident. Among others, the two accounts of Saul's murder attempt under the influence of the "evil spirit", David's sparing of Saul, and Saul's death are particularly noteworthy. One might think that the duplications were to include as many traditions as possible in the narrative collection about David's early life. But we must not overlook the fact that these duplications show a fairly consistent pattern, in that the older versions were augmented by the copies which are literarily richer and show a more positive, or at least more sympathetic, attitude toward the figure of Saul. For instance, we have two accounts of Saul's murder attempt in 18:10–11 and 19:9–10. The first account is missing in LXX[B], and it is generally agreed that it was added to the earlier version of the same story in 19:9–10. The purpose of the insertion might well have been a "redactional 'correction' of the primary narrative, in which the offer of Michal follows the beginning of David's estrangement from Saul".[161] Yet attention to some other features helps us to understand better why it was added, and by whom. In particular, we note that the addition of this episode functions to heighten the dramatic tension, by doubling the crisis situation. Besides, as we saw in Chapter 3, the positioning of this episode at the very beginning of the tension between David and Saul, leads the reader to be more sympathetic to Saul in the following narratives.[162] These features

---

160 Azzan Yadin, "Goliath's Armour and Israelite Collective Memory," *VT* 54 (2004): 373–95.
161 McCarter, *I Samuel*, 306.
162 Of course, one might well argue that the repetition of the murder attempt justifies David's flight from Saul, and the duplication puts Saul in an even more negative light. However, if one draws attention to the use of the word jlx, a word implying the irresistible possession by the spirit, and to its consequence that David is now unable to relieve Saul from the evil influence, the verses make the reader sympathetic to Saul rather than apologetic for David. Indeed, the

make it plausible that the duplicator was interested in literary artistry, and held a more reconciliatory attitude toward Saul. The plausibility becomes high, if we consider that it is also a part of the addition to the shorter version preserved in LXX[B]. We have seen above that the MT pluses in the David and Goliath story were partly influenced by the Jewish novelistic impulse. If the same person added 18:8–9 to the shorter version, our impression that the redactor was interested in literature is strengthened. Similarly, we saw that the one who added the MT pluses held a more realistic – if not critical – view of David, especially when the young hero was depicted as ambitious and called "insolent" (1Sam 17:12–31). It seems that the redactor who added the second account of Saul's murder attempt similarly did not support either David or Saul one-sidedly, but viewed the tension between them as unfortunate and tragic.

A similar pattern is recognizable in the two accounts of David's sparing of Saul. It is much debated whether chapter 24 is dependent on chapter 26,[163] or whether they were from independent traditions.[164] However, among many others, the following make it reasonable to conclude that chapter 24 is dependent on chapter 26. First, the concern for David's kingship and the whole of Israel in chapter 24 goes beyond the immediate context. Second, David's protest that he will not kill YHWH's anointed and Saul's poignant recognition of David's voice fit well with the context in chapter 26, but not in chapter 24. This, which

---

circumstantial clause 'David was playing with the lyre as usual' indicates that Saul's possession and prophesy occurred while David was playing (see G-K §156), and Sarah Nicholson interprets this as implying that David's performance was a partial reason for Saul's disturbance, and then, the text is seen as even anti-Davidic. However, I think that her reading goes beyond the limit of interpretation. What the text can mean is that the power of the evil spirit is now too strong, so that even David is unable to help Saul. The text is not anti-Davidic, but sympathetic to or less polemical against Saul. See Sarah Nicholson, *Three Faces of Saul: An Intertextual Approach to Biblical Tragedy* (Sheffield: Sheffield Academic Press, 2002), 104–5.

**163** The majority of scholars believed chapter 26 to be older, but several recent scholars argue the opposite. See Wellhausen, *Prolegomena*, 264–5; Smith, *Samuel*, 216, 231; Stoebe, *Das erste Buch Samuelis*, 431; McCarter, *I Samuel*, 386–7; Cynthia Edenburg, "How (Not) To Murder a King: Variations on a Theme in 1 Sam 24; 26," *SJOT* 12 (1998): 64–85. For the opposite view, see Walter Dietrich, "Die zweifache Verschonung Sauls (ISam 24 und 26). Zur 'diachronen Synchronisierung' zweier Erzählungen," in *David und Saul*, ed. Dietrich, 232–253; Klaus-Peter Adam, "Nocturnal Intrusions and Divine Interventions on Behalf of Judah. David's Wisdom and Saul's Tragedy in 1 Samuel 26," *VT* 59 (2009): 1–33 (24–5); John Van Seters, *Biblical Saga*, 180. Most recently, however, Steven McKenzie confirms the priority of chapter 26 in his article, "Elaborated Evidence for the Priority of 1 Samuel 26," *JBL* 129 (2010): 437–444.

**164** See Baruch Halpern, *The First Historians: The Hebrew Bible and History* (New York, 1988), 62; Klaus Koch, *The Growth of the Biblical Tradition: The Form-Critical Method* (New York: Charles Scribner's Sons/Macmillan, 1988), 142–147; Grønbaek, *Aufstieg*, 164–170.

Cynthia Edenburg calls "ungrammatical actualization", makes it more likely that the narrative of the cave incident (1Sam 24) was patterned on the camp raid narrative (1Sam 26).[165] Third, 1Sam 26 makes no explicit allusions to 1Sam 23–24. Fourth, it is unlikely that David hides a second time near the Ziphites after they have already betrayed him.

So what was the purpose of the duplication? We might figure it out from the fact that chapter 24 shows more interest in literary aspect, and is more sympathetic toward Saul. The author's literary interest has been widely recognized for its beauty and vividness,[166] "its expansive and flowery speeches"[167], and the use of the "contrastive dialogue".[168] The quotation of the proverbs, once by David and once by Saul, is also a sign of the author's literary interest. Rost regards the use of images and similes as evidence for the literary skill of the author of the "Succession Narrative",[169] and a similar taste is noticeable here, when the author quotes proverbs twice. The concentric structure of chapter 25 in the middle also indicates that the redactor was not just a collector of materials, but a literary artist. In terms of the *Tendenz*, although McCarter argues that the chapter degrades Saul in the extreme, and describes David as even more innocent and pious, I think that the chapter is more sympathetic to Saul, and invites the reader to hold a similar attitude to the founder of the northern kingdom. Unlike chapter 26, we have in this chapter the picture of Saul who "raised his voice and wept", and as Alter noted, "the brevity of Saul's 'is it your voice, David, my son?' reflects a character overwhelmed with feeling, forced to pull up short in the midst of his mad pursuit and to return to the point of origin of his bond with David."[170] One might well see a sign of Saul's genuine repentance here, and when read together with the duplication in 18:10–11, this certainly makes the reader feel sorry for Saul. Furthermore, David's passivity in this narrative is not so much the further glorification of David's virtue as an invitation to imitate David who embraces the weaker enemy. David's heroism is more evident in the second episode, and the picture of David hiding himself in a cave where one might want to "cover his feet" does not make David impressive.

Finally, Saul's death is reported twice in 1Sam 31 and 2Sam 1, and the second account apparently contradicts the first. In the former, Saul, while being pursued by archers, asks his weapon-bearer to finish him off, lest he should be humiliat-

---

165 Edenburg, "How (Not) To Murder a King," 76–7.
166 Hertzberg, *I & II Samuel*, 195.
167 McCarter, *I Samuel*, 386.
168 Alter, *The Art of Biblical Narrative*, 72–3.
169 Rost, *Succession*, 92. See also Schulte, *Entstehung*, 142; Gunn, *The Story of King David*, 77.
170 Alter, *The Art of Biblical Narrative*, 73.

ed by the "uncircumcised". But when the request is denied, he kills himself, and his three sons are killed in the battle. In the second account, however, Saul is overtaken not by "archers", but by "the chariotry and cavalry officers", and asks an Amalekite, not the weapon-bearer, who was passing by, for a sort of mercy killing. The Amalekite kills the wounded king, and instead of the three sons, only Jonathan is reported to have ended his life in the battle.[171] Source critics explained the contradictions by positing two different sources in 2Sam 1:1–16, ascribing vv. 1–4, 11–12 to J and vv. 5–10, 13–16 to E. This removes the evident contradictions, and the J source in 2Sam 1 follows smoothly from 1Sam 31.[172] This has been much challenged recently, and the majority of scholars now explain the contradictions as the result of the Amalekites' lies, and hold that both accounts came from the same hand.[173] However, this solution has weaknesses, because there is nothing much in the text that leads us to reach such a conclusion. Indeed, "David has no inkling that the man is not truthful, nor does the author suggest it,"[174] and it is unlikely that the Amalekite lied to gain a reward from David, because what he did is closer to a "mercy killing", and it would make his achievement less impressive to David.[175] Pamela Reis most recently responds to such criticism, and argues that the author makes it "abundantly clear" that the Amalekite is lying, by preceding the Amalekite's report with the account of Saul's suicide, and by depicting the Amalekite as disreputable and unreliable in the preceding narrative. She also claims that the Amalekite expected a reward, because he had thought that David was one of Saul's closest relatives.[176]

However, it is still unlikely that the Amalekite thought that David's being son-in-law to Saul would be still valid, and expected a reward for "his mercy killing", when it was well known that David was living under the protection of the Philistines, Saul's archenemy. Moreover, the fact that the two accounts *can be read* as a unity does not prove that they came from the same author, or were together originally. As in the case of the shorter version and the longer version in 1Sam 17–18, a highly interpretative strategy can get around even the most evident

---

**171** It is noteworthy that in 2Sam 21, which is believed by many to have come from the post-exilic period, only Saul and Jonathan are mentioned.
**172** Budde, *Samuel*, 193–4.
**173** McCarter, *II Samuel*, 63–4; Bill Arnold, "The Amalekite's Report of Saul's Death: Political Intrigue or Incompatible Sources?" *Journal of the Evangelical Theological Society* 32 (1989): 289–298; Pamela Tamarkin Reis, "Killing the Messenger: David's Policy or Politics?" *JSOT* 31 (2006): 167–191.
**174** Smith, *Samuel*, 254.
**175** John Mauchline, *I and II Samuel* (NCB; London: Oliphants, 1971), 197.
**176** Reis, "Killing the Messenger," 170–77.

contradictions in a narrative. The zeal to defend the integrity of the biblical text in its final form sometimes tempts us to devise rather unfounded interpretations. However, if we really want to take the Bible seriously, we should resist such a temptation, and accept the difficulties and try to explain them. Probably, it is more helpful to ask here why the author, despite the disruption it might cause, inserted or created the account of the Amalekite's lie and David's execution. McCarter claims that the purpose of the second story is to explain how Saul's diadem and bracelet came into David's hand. This fits with the whole picture of the HDR, whose purpose he believes is to exonerate David from Saul's death, and thus he ascribes the account to the author of the HDR.[177] However, if we read the whole differently, we might well wonder whether the second account of Saul's death can be explained by the author's apologetic intention. By contrast, it is noteworthy that an important motif in this account is that of deception, which is one of the central motifs both in the account of the war with Ishbosheth and in the "Succession Narrative".[178] This makes it possible that the account of David's killing of the Amalekite came from someone interested in playing with literary motifs, and this, together with the contradictions in the account, makes it more sensible to conclude that vv. 5–10,13–16 were an addition to the earlier account of Saul's death in 1Sam 31. Therefore, I hold that 2Sam 1:5–10,13–16 is another case of duplication, and a similar impulse, which we saw in the previous duplications, seems to work in duplicating the episode by adding those verses. Although the author's literary interest is not so evident here, the use of the deception motif clearly shows the author's literary skill. Moreover, the emphasis on Saul's status as YHWH's anointed in v. 16 and the depiction of David condemning the Amalekite who killed off Saul might well have been intended to urge the reader to embrace the descendants of Saul as David did. He might have said, "[t]he northerners are also the chosen people of God, and now in a deplorable situation. What is the point of being happy about it, and being so cruel to them?" If we posit that these verses were added together with the dirge for Saul and Jonathan in 2Sam 1:17–27, both the author's literary interest and the sympathetic attitude toward the Saulides are made even more evident.

To summarize, from a fairly coherent pattern in these duplications, we can conclude that they were all made by the same redactor who was interested in

---

177 McCarter, *II Samuel*, 64–5.
178 See H. Hagan, "Deception as Motif and Theme in 2 Sam 9–20; 1 Kgs 1–2," *Bib* 60 (1979): 301–26; Van Seters, *In Search of History*, 285; R.-J. Frontain, "The Trickster Tricked: Strategies of Deception and Survival in the David Narrative," in *Mappings of the Biblical Terrain: The Bible as Text*, eds. V. Tollers and J. Maier (Lewisburg, PA: Bucknell University Press, 1990): 10–192.

literary artistry and held a more sympathetic view toward the Saulides. McCarter is right in connecting chapter 24 with the author of the MT pluses, although his reading of the chapter as more apologetic and polemical is unconvincing.[179] Just like the one responsible for the MT pluses, the redactor shows greater interest in literary artistry, and is less polemical with regard to the conflict between David and Saul. The redactor also shows a similar taste as the one responsible for the account of the war with Ishbosheth in 2Sam 2–4. As we saw above, this author also shows more sophisticated literary style, and a conciliatory attitude toward the Saulides. This locates the one who made the duplications at the time when the rivalry between Israel and Judah was a distant issue, and when the northern kingdom was in a weaker position than Judah. This impression is further strengthened if we draw attention to the fact that chapter 24 includes David's promise not to destroy Saul's descendants (vv. 22–23). Evidently, the duplicator was urging the reader not to cut off the descendants of Saul from Israel, and it seems reasonable to locate the duplicator in the post-exilic period.

### 3.3 The Escape Episodes in 1Sam 19

There are four short episodes in chapter 19, and three of them, as they stand, narrate how David escaped from Saul with the help of important characters such as Jonathan, Michal, and Samuel. All these three episodes however are likely to be secondary, and the purpose of the addition seems to be literary, i.e. the redactor wanted to make the story more entertaining. First, 19:1–7 seems secondary, because 18:30 is smoothly followed by 19:8, and 19:5 presupposes chapter 17. Besides, vv. 2–3 betray that two different materials are merged into one. It is possible that there was old material about Jonathan's success in reconciling his father with David, but the confusion in vv. 2–3 seems to suggest that the material was influenced by chapter 20. The addition certainly heightens the dramatic tension, and the purpose seems mainly literary. Second, the Michal episode in 19:11–17 is also secondary, because (i) David's flight from Saul to Michal's house does not make sense; (ii) the expression וַיִּמָּלֵט in v. 12 sounds conclusive; and (iii) the allusions to the Jacob narrative in Genesis and the Rahab story in Joshua suggest that this episode cannot be an old tradition.[180] One might argue that the Teraphim mentioned in the passage indicate that the passage was pre-deuteronmistic, because it was rejected both in the Josianic reform

---

179 McCarter, *I Samuel*, 386–387.
180 Stoebe, *Das erste Buch Samuelis*, 361.

(2Kings 23:24) and in the Persian period (Zech 10:2). However, if the redactor was disputing with mainstream thoughts, it does not exclude its incorporation in the post-exilic period. Finally, 19:18–24 is also an addition, as (i) it contradicts 15:35 where Samuel is said to never meet Saul again; (ii) Samuel as the leader of ecstatic prophets is not found anywhere else; (iii) the thrice sending-out suggest a connection with the Elijah cycle in 2Kings 2; and (iv) it presupposes 15:35b–16:13, which we concluded to be a late exilic deuteronomistic addition, where David and Samuel get to know each other. The origin of the material is uncertain, but Grønbaek and Dietrich believe that the author of the HDR is responsible for the addition,[181] whereas Budde, Smith and McCarter think that they were much later additions.[182] More recently, Christophe Nihan has suggested that the story was explicitly directed against the charismatic ideal of 10:5–6,10–12 (14a) that was popular in the early Persian period, and was intended "to reassert the superiority of the classic (literary) prophets over the charismatic groups".[183] Whether the addition was as late as Nihan argues is to be investigated further, but it is more likely that three episodes in the chapter were added at the same time, and this suggests that 19:18–24 was added later, rather than earlier.

### 3.4 More Persian-period additions

#### 3.4.1 The Merab Offer (1Sam 18:17–19)
Saul's idea of "giving" his first daughter to David seems to fulfil the promise he made for the one who killed Goliath. This presupposes the MT pluses, and the style of duplication indicates that the passage is from the post-exilic redactor.

---

181 According to Grønbaek, the narrative is a reworking of the Gilgal tradition complex which includes 9:1–10:16 by the author of the HDR. The narrative is a kind of parody of 10:10–12, and functions to annul Saul's anointing. Similarly, Dietrich thinks that the author of the HDR transformed what was originally a counter aetiological account into a story about the divine protection for David. See Grønbaek, *Aufstieg*, 119; Dietrich, *David, Saul und die Propheten*, 81–9.
182 Budde, *Samuel*, 139; Smith, *Samuel*, 181; McCarter, *I Samuel*, 331.
183 Christophe Nihan, "Saul among the Prophets (1 Sam 10:10–12 and 19:18–24). The Reworking of Saul's Figure in the Context of the Debate on 'Charismatic Prophecy' in the Persian Era," in *Saul in Story and Tradition*, ed. Ehrlich, 88–118 (105).

### 3.4.2 David's Flight to Ahimelech and the massacre of the priests at Nob (1Sam 21:2–10; 22:1–23)

The section might well have contained originally independent traditions. But in the present shape, these episodes explain the survival of Abiathar in the "Succession Narrative", and describe the fulfilment of the prophecy about Eli's family in 1Sam 2:27–36. The emphasis on the election of Jerusalem and its priesthood, and the corresponding rejection of Shiloh and the house of Eli fit well with the deuteronomistic view.[184] Furthermore, it mentions Goliath's sword, and although it is not explained how the sword came to Ahimelech, it seems to be aware of the Goliath story. The narratives might well have come from the late exilic deuteronomistic redactor.

### 3.4.3 Jonathan's visit to David (1Sam 23:16–18)

This does not fit with the context, and it is highly unlikely that Jonathan made a journey just to encourage David in the middle of Saul's hot pursuit of David. The passage seems to have been added together with other Jonathan passages in the post-exilic period, in order to stress the bond between the Davidides and the Saulides. The redactor obviously argues that the bond is eternal, and the Davidides should look after the descendants of the Saulides.

### 3.4.4 David's sparing of Saul (1Sam 26)

This seems to be unaware of 23:19–28 which we believe belongs to the HDR proper, and the motif of David living in a foreign land seems to be related to the exilic experience.

---

**184** Cf. McCarter, *I Samuel*, 366–7; Klein, *1 Samuel*, 222. Hentschel however thinks that the narrator is sympathetic to the Elides in 1Sam 22:6–23, and speculates that the passages is pre-Josianic. By contrast, Conrad, on the basis of the distinction between "sacred" and "secular" in 1Sam 21:2–10, thinks that the passage is a post-exilic addition. See Georg Hentschel, "Die Verantwortung für den Mord an den Priestern von Nob," in *For and Against David. Story and History in the Books of Samuel*, eds. Graeme Auld and Erik Eynikel (Leuven: Peeters, 2010): 185–199 (196); Joachim Conrad, "David's Königtum als Paradoxi: Versuch zu I Sam 21,2–10," in *Gott und Mensch im Dialog. Festschrift für Otto Kaiser zum 80. Geburtstag*, Band 1, ed. Markus Witte (Berlin: de Gruyter, 2004): 413–424 (417).

### 3.4.5 David's flight to Achish (27:1–12) and David's life among the Philistines (28:1–2)

These do not seem to be aware of David's previous flight to Achish in 21:11b–16, which we believe belong to the HDR proper. The story of David living among the foreigners wisely but loyally might have been attractive to the exiles. However, a similar motif was popular in the Jewish novels in the post-exilic period. The habit of duplication and the late expression such as "if I find favour..." in 27:5 might also be evidence for the post-exilic redaction.

### 3.4.6 Saul's visit to the woman in En-dor (1Sam 28:3–25)

It has been believed that this section was inserted, as 28:1–2 seems to be smoothly followed by 29:1ff, and if we are right in holding that 27:1–28:2 belongs to the post-exilic layer, this section should have been added even later. However, it is not necessary that the appointment of David as Achish's bodyguard (28:1–2) should be immediately followed by a description about a specific battle at Aphek (29:1ff). Indeed, 28:3–25 functions to indicate to the reader that time had passed since the appointment, and gives a smoother flow to the narrative. Furthermore, the post-exilic redactor seems to have enjoyed structuring the narrative following what Tsumura calls "the AXBY pattern". In 1Sam 17:1–19, "two strands of dialog, AB and XY, are intertwined in an AXBY pattern (A: 1–11; X: 12–15; B: 16; Y: 17–19)."[185] Similarly, 1Sam 28:1–31:13 was structured in the same pattern of 28:1–2 (A); 28:3–25 (X); 29:1–30:31 (B); 31:1–12 (Y),[186] and this suggests that the passage belongs to the same post-exilic layer.

One might object, of course, and point to Samuel's severe rebuke to Saul in vv. 1–19 which does not fit with the less polemical tone of the post-exilic novelistic addition. However, it is arguable whether vv. 17–19 is meant to shed even more negative light on Saul. The overall context is sympathetic to Saul, and in fact Samuel's harsh words add to the reader's sympathy, because the recapitulation of the words in 1Sam 15 seems to indicate that the redactor was parodying the previous deuteronomistic passage. We have seen above that the DtrP's story of David's anointing was reworked by the post-exilic redactor, and Samuel was turned into someone ignorant of God's will. Similarly, here the post-exilic redactor might have picked up the justifiable criticism of the prophet Samuel in 1Sam 15,[187] and exaggerated it, so that the reader might feel Samuel's too harsh atti-

---

185 Tsumura, *The First Book of Samuel*, 446.
186 Tsumura, *The First Book of Samuel*, 615–7
187 Cf. Schulte, *Entstehung*, 106–108.

tude in 1Sam 28 to be unreasonable, and feel even more sympathetic to Saul. Indeed, the prophecy about the defeat of Israel in v. 19 is not mentioned in 1Sam 15, and the addition may have been intended to say that although God's messenger in 1Sam 15 announced that God rejected only Saul, but others would see the endurance (נצח) of Israel (15:29), these hardliners went too far, and talked not about "the endurance of Israel" but of the defeat of the whole Israel! Historically, it is plausible that the post-exilic redactor who was against the Judah-centric exclusivism wanted to say, "Claim for Judean priority is understandable, but exclusivism is ridiculous!"

### 3.4.7 The Philistine warlords' rejection of David (29:1–11); David's campaign against the Amalekites (30:1–25); the list of the distribution of the spoil (30:26–31)

These episodes tell the reader how wisely and faithfully David behaved in the foreign land. Certainly, this was a popular motif in the Persian period, especially for the leaders of the restoration project who were close to the foreign rulers, but managed to get what their people needed. One might also notice a tone of anti-exclusivism in 1Sam 30:22–25, where David establishes the custom of distributing the war booty to the non-military people.

### 3.4.8 The transfer of the Ark to Jerusalem (2Sam 6)

Whether this originally belonged to the so-called Ark Narrative in 1Sam needs extensive discussion.[188] The chapter may well include pre-exilic traditions, but the author of the Michal episode seems to be aware of the entire Samuel. Dietrich recently expressed the view that this author fits well with the picture of his *Höfische Erzähler* from the 8th–7th century BCE who emphasized the importance of the king's humility and Judah's elected status.[189] However, these features togeth-

---

188 For more detailed discussion, see Rost, *Succession*, 6–34; Campbell, *Ark Narrative*; P. D. Miller Jr. and J. J. M. Roberts, *The Hand of the Lord. A Reassessment of the "Ark Narrative" of 1 Samuel* (Baltimore/London: Johns Hopkins, 1977); McCarter, *II Samuel*, 183–4; Peter Porzig, *Die Lade Jahwes im Alten Testament und in den Texten vom Totem Meer* (Berlin: de Gruyter, 2009), 136–176.

189 Walter Dietrich, "Die Überführung der Lade nach Jerusalem (2 Sam 6): Geschichten und Geschichte," in *For and Against David*, eds. Auld and Eynikel, 235–253.

er with the cultic interest of the chapter fits better with the late exilic concern about the question whether the Temple is necessary for the restoration.[190]

### 3.4.9 David's Wars and His Cabinet (2Sam 8)

As mentioned above, 2Sam 8 seems to have been added by the deuteronomistic historian together with 2Sam 5:17–25.[191] As Smith writes, "[t]he tone of the whole chapter is the tone of a summary – the author would give us a brief sketch of David's wars and pass on to something more important."[192] Before 2Sam 7 was incorporated in the books of Samuel later in the Persian period, the deuteronomistic historian might have wanted to make a similar juncture here before David's decline starts, just as he did in 1Sam 14:47–51 before the beginning of Saul's decline.

## 4 Conclusion and Remaining Questions

In this chapter, we attempted to identify the sections that do not belong to the pre-deuteronomistic HDR. In 1Sam 15–2 Sam 8, there are later additions to the shorter version in 1Sam 17–18, deuteronomistic additions, and late exilic and post-exilic additions, and without these, we are left with 1Sam 16:14–23[193] (the introduction of David to Saul's court); 18:6–9[194] (the beginning of the tension be-

---

**190** Smelik, "Hidden Messages in the Ark Narrative," in *Converting the Past: Studies in Ancient Israelite and Moabite* Historiography (Leiden: Brill, 1992), 35—58 (55—58); Berges, *Verwerfung*, 35. It is worth pointing out that Porzig suggested in one of the most recent literature on the Ark Narrative that the expansions in 2Sam6 point toward the chronicler's theology. See Porzig, *Die Lade Jahwes*, 171—173.

**191** Alt, "Zu II Samuel 8,1," 149–52; Noth, *ÜS*, 65; McCarter, *II Samuel*, 251.

**192** Smith, *Samuel*, 305.

**193** אֲשֶׁר בַּצֹּאן in v. 19 seems to be aware of 16:1–13. However, it might have been added by a later redactor to accommodate the popular tradition that David was a shepherd. In fact, its artistic quality and summarizing element raise the possibility that 16:14–23 was reworked by the post-exilic redactor.

**194** Most likely, בְּשׁוּב דָּוִד was added. It does not make sense with the precedent בְּבוֹאָם, and breaks the usual syntax of בְּ + וַיְהִי + infinitive construct, followed by *waw* consecutives. Besides, the song of the dancing women suggests that both Saul and David were the heroes, even if David was surprisingly more, or equally impressive in the battle. In LXX[B], the entire v. 6a is missing, and one might be tempted to strike out the whole v. 6a. However, if the entire chapter 17 is a later addition as argued above, it is odd that v. 6b follows 16:23 immediately. There must have been some indication of victory in a battle. The definite article before הַפְּלִשְׁתִּי might suggest that the specific battle against Goliath is meant here. However, the article in Hebrew can be used to

tween Saul and David); 18:12–16[195],20 – 30[196] (the worsening of the tension through David's successes); 19:8–10 (Saul's murder attempt under the influence of the evil spirit); 21:11b–16 (David's flight to Achish); 22:1–5 (David's flight to Adullam and grouping of the militia); 23:1–14 (David's deliverance of the people of Keilah and their betrayal); 23:19–28 (Ziphites' betrayal and Saul's pursuit); 1Sam 31:1–2Sam 1:4,11–12 (Death of the Saulide); 2:1–4a (David's rise to the Judahite throne); 2:4b–7; 5:3 (David's rise to the Israelite throne). The identification of the pre-deuteronomistic passages in 1Sam 15–2Sam 8 enables us to find where the HDR begins and ends. That is, we now see that the narrative begins with the introduction of David into Saul's court in 1Sam 16:14, and ends with David's rise to the throne over both Judah and Israel in 2Sam 5:3. The unifying theme of the narrative is the decline of Saul and the rise of David, and the tendency is pro-Davidic, although not completely anti-Saul. The plausible setting for the composition might be the time of Hezekiah. This king from the late 8th–early 7th century B.C.E. was keen on incorporating the people of the northern kingdom,[197] and might well have wanted to say to the northerners, "Your kingdom declined and fell, but God is raising a new one, which is better than the former!" In fact, one might well imagine that Hezekiah delivered a similar message to that ringing at the very end of the HDR proper: "Now let your hands be strong, and become valiant soldiers, because your lord Saul is dead, and the house of Judah anointed me as your king (2Sam 2:7)." And Hezekiah might have wanted to have the same happy ending in his effort to restore the kingdom of David as in the end of the HDR proper. "And then all the elders of Israel came to the king to Hebron, and made a covenant with the king David in Hebron in the presence of YHWH. They anointed David as king over Israel (2Sam 5:3).[198]

The question of the beginning and the ending of the so-called HDR however is not solved satisfactorily yet, because there are still a couple of questions which remain to be answered. First, we have to explain the still existing connections

---

determine the class. In particular, it is used with gentillic names (G-K, §126 l-m) as in the Canaanite הַכְּנַעֲנִי in Gen 13:7, the Kenite הַקֵּינִי in Gen 15:19 f. In v. 8, וְעוֹד לֹא אַךְ הַמְּלוּכָה is missing, and most likely was added later.

**195** Verses 12–14 may be a later addition to make the narrative more like the Joseph story.
**196** Verse 21b seems to be a redactional expansion to facilitate the interpolation of vv. 17–19. See McCarter, *I Samuel,* 316.
**197** Bustenay Oded, "Judah and the Exile," in *Israelite & Judaean History,* eds. John H. Hayes and J. Maxwell Miller (London: SCM Press, 1977): 435–86 (441–44).
**198** Cf. Joachim Conrad, "Zum geschichtlichen Hintergrund der Darstellung von Davids Aufstieg," *TLZ* 97 (1972): 321–332. Dietrich, although he has a longer narrative history extending from Saul to Solomon, also dates what he calls the "Narrative History of the Early Monarchy" soon after the fall of Samaria. See Dietrich, *Early Monarchy,* 309.

between the HDR proper and the other parts of the books of Samuel. At the beginning of this chapter we limited the discussion to 1Sam 15–2Sam 8, and we reach the conclusion that the HDR proper begins in 1Sam 16:14 and ends in 2Sam 5:3. However, it is not ruled out completely that the beginning might be found earlier than 1Sam 15, and the ending later than 2Sam 8. Indeed, even after the removal of all the late additions, some connections with other parts of the books of Samuel are noticeable. For instance, without 1Sam 11, it is difficult to understand why the people of Jabesh-Gilead showed such loyalty to Saul in 1Sam 31:11–13, and without the knowledge of Jonathan's prominence and popularity from 1Sam 14, it sounds odd that the people fasted only "for Jonathan his son", among his sons in 2Sam 1:12, even if 1Sam 31:2 mentions two other sons, Abinadab and Malchishua. A similar question can be raised as to the ending. The HDR proper describes how Saul declines and David rises, and the "Succession Narrative" has a similar pattern in the sense that this describes the decline of David and the rise of Solomon. And if we agree with Alberto Soggin when he said, "*mutatis mutandis*, what happened to David was very similar to what had once happened to Saul, a feature which we can perhaps also see as a didactic aim of the 'succession narrative'," we have to explain why the HDR proper should be separate from the "Succession Narrative" when the same pattern continues. In the next chapter, therefore, we will extend our discussion to the so-called Saul cycle and the "Succession Narrative", and examine whether the one responsible for the HDR proper left more materials in other parts of the books of Samuel. The discussion also will help us to find out more about the late exilic and post-exilic redactors who contributed not a little to the final shape of the David story.

# Chapter 5
# The Composition of the Books of Samuel

We have excavated the pre-deuteronomistic HDR, and as a result, reached a conclusion that the HDR proper begins in 1Sam 16:14 and ends in 2Sam 5:3. To consolidate such a conclusion, we need to show that no trace of the HDR is found elsewhere in the books of Samuel. However, this is not an undisputed question, and not a few scholars have expressed the view that there is obvious continuity between the HDR and the surrounding materials, namely, the so-called Saul Cycle and the so-called Succession Narrative. Therefore, in order to secure the hypothesis that there was a pre-deuteronomistic HDR that had existed as an independent written source and extended from 1Sam 16:14 to 2Sam 5:3, we are left with the task of showing that the continuity and the connections are only apparent. Otherwise, we would have to come up with a different hypothesis.

## 1 The Relationship with the so-called Succession Narrative

### 1.1 The so-called Succession Narrative and the Disputes

Since Leonhard Rost published his monumental work in 1926, the existence of a pre-deuteronomistic source in 2Sam 9–20; 1Kings 1–2 has been regarded as one of the few certainties in the study of the books of Samuel. More recently, however, the canonical status of his theory has been seriously questioned. Objections were raised of course soon after the publication of Rost's *magnum opus*, but the recent scepticism is more extensive and fundamental, raising questions in almost all aspects. For example, it is now questioned whether the theme of the narrative is indeed to do with Solomon's succession to the throne. Rost ingeniously argued that the whole story deals with the question "who shall sit on the throne (1Kings 1:20,27)", and the issue of Solomon's succession to David's throne is the unifying theme of the whole.[1] Anticipating the objection that the succession issue is not that obvious except in 1Kings 1–2, Rost labelled 2Sam 10–12 as "a story of the background to the succession (*Vorgeschichte der Thronfolge*)", and 2Sam 13–20 as a story of the background of "the one who was to succeed (*Vorgeschichte des Thronfolgers*)".[2] Not persuaded by this, however,

---

1 Rost, *Succession*, 89.
2 Rost, *Succession*, 73.

some scholars read the narrative differently, and suggested alternative views. For instance, Blenkinsopp identified two themes in the narrative as "the legitimisation of David's own claim, and the struggle for the succession to his throne brought on by his determination to start a dynasty".[3] Flanagan went further to argue that the theme of succession is only a small part of the whole story, and the main narrative is concerned with David's reign, and better named as "Court History".[4] Although the materials in 2Sam may well be interpreted as a long prelude to Solomon's eventual succession to David, it is now widely accepted that Rost's solution to include those materials under a single theme of succession has lost its magic spell.

The genre of the "SN" is also disputed. For a long while, the narrative has been labelled a "historical work". On the basis of the unusual number of historical names, Wellhausen was convinced that the narrative is history,[5] and this was reaffirmed by Rost who wrote "real historical facts are related here, but in a strongly stylized dress [...] this is an historical narrative which rushes along with the excitement of a drama; it is based on actual events".[6] This was accepted by the majority of scholars, and von Rad's celebrated declaration that the "SN" marked the beginning of history writing became part of the ABC of biblical studies.[7] However, the unusual quality of its artistry led more and more scholars to conclude that it was a literary creation by someone enormously talented in narrative art. Even before Rost's work was published, several prominent scholars such as Caspari and Gressmann related it to novella or novel, and later scholars like Whybray and Humphreys saw it as a carefully constructed political novel or a novella.[8] After the emergence of the New Critics in biblical scholarship, the literary quality of the narrative drew even more attention. In particular, Gunn un-

---

3 Joseph Blenkinsopp, "Theme and Motif in the Succession History (2 Sam XI, 2ff) and the Yahwist Corpus," in *Volume du Congrèss, Genève 1965* (Leiden: Brill, 1966): 44–57 (47).

4 J. W. Flanagan, "Court History or Succession Narrative? A Study of 2 Sam 9–20 and 1 Kings 1–2," *JBL* 91 (1972): 172–181.

5 Wellhausen, *Composition*, 259.

6 Rost, *Succession*, 104.

7 It should be noted, however, that already in 1906, Eduard Meyer called the narrative sections in Judges and in Samuel "Trümmer eines grossen Geschichtswerks," and classified them as the first historiographical work in the ancient near east. See Eduard Meyer, "Die Israeliten und ihre Nachbarstämme," in *Die Israeliten und ihre Nachbarsämme. Alttestamentliche Untersuchungen von Eduard Meyer. Mit Beiträgen von Bernhard Luther* (Halle, 1906), 207–561. Quoted from André Heinrich, *David und Klio. Historiographische Elemente in der Aufstiegsgeschichte Davids und im Alten Testament* (New York/Berlin: de Gruyter, 2009), 17–18.

8 Whybray, *Succession*, 11–19; Humphreys, "Novella," in *Saga, Legend, Fable, Tale, Novella*, ed. Coats, 82–96.

derstood the purpose of the narrative as "serious entertainment" which is meant to grip one and challenge one to self- or social-reassessment,[9] and suggested that its genre is "traditional story". Most recently, Van Seters, although he largely agrees with Gunn's view, labels the David story as "saga", and writes, "The story of David from his first introduction into the service of Saul to the final transfer of power to Solomon (1Sam 16–2Sam 20; 1Kings 1–2) is a saga in form and intention."[10]

As it is widely accepted that the work is not history in the strictest sense, more attention has been drawn to the *Tendenz* of the narrative, and its social setting. However, there is no agreement on this either, rather there is perhaps a very great diversity in opinion. For Rost, the whole text was written "in majorem gloriam Salomonis" by an eyewitness of the whole event in "the beginning of the Solomonic period".[11] The apologetic motifs that one might find in David's generosity to Mephibosheth and David's lament over Absalom's death made some believe that the narrative was originally pro-Davidic, while others do not overlook the passages that are evidently critical of David such as Nathan's oracle in 2Sam 12. Sometimes, the same passage is interpreted as anti-Davidic by some, and as pro-Davidic by others. For instance, David's dealing with his sons is seen by some as meant to criticise David's weak and irresolute character, while by others it is understood as showing his tender and caring personality. Whether the narrative is pro-Solomonic as Rost argued is also debated. Some saw Solomon's liquidation of his enemies as a sign of his political competence, while others think that it was written to bring about disgust from the readers, expressing an anti-Solomonic perspective. Attempts have also been made to explain the ambiguous *Tendenz* of the narrative by assuming different layers in the narrative. However, there is also disagreement in deciding the "original" *Tendenz* of the narrative, although more scholars think that the original was anti-monarchical, and was later made into a pro-monarchical one. Different understanding of the *Tendenz* of course has led to different views about the dating and social setting of the composition.

Finally, like the HDR, there is no agreement about the precise extent of the source. According to Rost's initial view, the source is traceable in 2Sam 6:16,20–23; 7:11b,16; 9–20 + 1Kings 1–2, and this was put together with older materials such as the Ark Narrative and the story of the Ammonite War. But the word עַד in 9:1 seems to presuppose background material for the following vers-

---

**9** Gunn, *The Story of King David*, 61.
**10** Van Seters, *Biblical Saga*, 40–49 (49).
**11** Rost, *Succession*, 105–6.

es, and David's generosity to Mephibosheth in 2Sam 9 is not understandable without 2Sam 21. Therefore, some scholars include 2Sam 21, and speculate that it was removed from where it originally had been for some reason. Others want to include 2Sam 7 because, without the promise of the dynastic succession, the theme of succession is not comprehensible. This was already noticed by Rost, and led him to include 2Sam 7:11b,16 in his "Succession Narrative". But later scholars asked why the whole chapter cannot be included, as so many connections with the following narratives are recognizable.[12] As we saw above, not a few scholars see clear continuity between 2Sam 2–4 and the "Succession Narrative", and hold that the beginning is found somewhere in 2Sam 2. There is also a group of scholars who see the beginning later, believing that the early chapters seem quite isolated from the main topics in the later ones. For instance, Würthwein and Veijola think that the narrative begins in chapter 10,[13] while Campbell and Bar-Efrat see a "greater unity" in 2Sam 11–20.[14] Conroy and Flanagan believe that it starts with 2Sam 13,[15] and Mildenberger argues for an even later beginning in 2Sam 15.[16] The difficulty in finding a proper beginning of the source led Wellhausen and Whybray to suspect that the original beginning was lost in the course of merging different sources.[17]

Although there is less disagreement about the ending, that too is a matter of dispute. For Rost, "the succession story comes to a definite conclusion in 1Kings 2:46," where the narrator reports that the Davidic dynasty was established by Solomon's hand.[18] Later scholars however recognized the deuteronomistic hand in 1Kings 1–2. Noth, believing that 2:13–35,36–46 was a later insertion to the pre-deuteronomistic "SN", held that the narrative finishes in 1Kings 1:53, and a sim-

---

12 G. P. Ridout, "Prose Compositional Techniques in the Succession Narrative (2 Sam 7, 9–10; 1 Kings 1–2) (unpublished doctoral thesis, GTU, 1971); F. Polak, "David's Kingship – A Precarious Equilibrium," in *Politics and Theopolitics in the Bible and Postbiblical Literature*, eds. Yair Hoffman, Henning Reventlow Graf, and Benjamin Uffenheimer (Sheffield: JSOT Press, 1994): 119–147 (142–147).

13 E. Würthwein, "Die Erzählung von der Thronfolge Davids – theologische oder politische Geschichtsschreibung?" in *Studien zum Deuteronomistischen Geschichtswerk*, 29–79 (58); Timo Veijola, "David und Meribaal," *RB* 85 (1978): 338–361 (358).

14 Campbell, *Of Prophets and Kings*, 82–84; Shimon Bar-Efrat, *Narrative Art in the Bible* (Edinburgh: T & T Clark, 2004), 136.

15 Charles Conroy, *Absalom, Absalom! Narrative and Language in 2 Sam. 13–20* (Rome: Pontifical Biblical Institute, 1977), 5–6; Flanagan, "Court History," 173–176.

16 F. Mildenberger, "Die vordeuteronomistische Saul-Davidüberlieferung" (unpublished doctoral thesis, University of Tübingen, 1962).

17 Wellhausen, *Composition*, 256; Whybray, *Succession*, 8.

18 Rost, *Succession*, 113.

ilar view was taken by Gray and Mettinger.[19] Those who see the beginning later in 1Sam 11–15 tend to see the ending earlier in 2Sam 20, as the theme of succession in 1Kings 1–2 seems unrelated to the David materials in 2Sam.

## 1.2 Understanding of the "SN" as a Whole

The disputes around the "SN" are enormous, and it seems hopeless to discuss anything which could be connected with it. Moreover, our concern is the relationship between the "SN" and the HDR, and therefore, one might argue that we should not worry about the larger picture, but narrow down the focus on the composition and redaction of the "SN". However, as we have consistently argued, this is only possible when we have understood the nature of the literature. This makes it inevitable to discuss the complex issues surrounding the genre, *Tendenz*, and theme of the "SN", even if this will look only cursory and superficial. Only then, will we be able to present our views on the composition of the 'SN' and the relationship between the "SN" and the HDR.

### 1.2.1 Genre

The question of genre can be dealt with very briefly, not because genre recognition is straightforward, but because we have discussed a similar issue quite extensively in Chapter 3. And we believe that the "SN" also can be labelled as a "Jewish historical novel". Perhaps, the historical flavour is slightly stronger in the "SN" than in the HDR, and Wellhausen's observation that 'aus keiner Periode der israelitischen Geschichte haben wir so viele historische Namen'[20] cannot be overlooked, especially as some names such as Chimham in 2Sam 19:37 do not have any function in the story. Nevertheless, this is still a matter of degree, not of kind. We cannot explain the degree of literary artistry evident in the work, by referring to "a strongly stylized dress" as Rost and many others do, and Würthwein's claim that the "SN" is historical in its entirety, albeit not in its parts, does not seem convincing.[21] Historical information is only scattered, while the whole "SN" mainly consists of narrative blocks. Again, this does not mean that the author of the "SN" intended to write a "historical novel". The au-

---

**19** Noth, *Könige 1–16* (Neukirchen-Vluyn: Neukirchener Verlag des Erziehungsvereins, 1968), 9–11; John Gray, *I & II Kings: A Commentary*, 3rd fully revised edition (London: SCM Press, 1977), 105; Mettinger, *King and Messiah*, 28.
**20** Wellhausen, *Composition*, 259.
**21** Würthwein, "Erzählung," 29–79 (79).

thor might well have thought that he was writing history as Alter and Dietrich believe.[22] However, talk of what exactly the author intended to write is no more fruitful than talk of the authorial intention in a text. Just as it is more fruitful and reliable to discuss the intention of the work, so it is better to think about the guiding framework for reading the text. And the best way at this moment of interpretative history is to label it as a "historical novel", even if this assessment may change in the future.

### 1.2.2 Tendenz

The identification of the *Tendenz* of the work is more complicated. As we saw above, the wild disagreement on this issue seems to suggest that biblical criticism is futile. However, if we carefully clarify the surrounding issues, and the underlying presuppositions, we can make an honest, but quite a plausible case. For this, we begin with the two crucial sections in the "SN", namely, the Bathsheba episode in 2Sam 11–12 and the account of Solomon's ascension in 1Kings 1–2. Delekat already picked out these two episodes, when he argued that the text was basically anti-Davidic, anti-Solomonic, and anti-monarchical, and that the "SN" was meant to show that David and Solomon's kingship was not willed by God.[23] Würthwein also discusses these two sections, and claims that they express anti-Solomonic and anti-Davidic tendencies respectively.[24] More recently, Van Seters has presented his interpretation of the whole "SN" as an anti-messianic fiction on the basis of these two narratives. Therefore, we should look at these two in more detail.

### 1.2.2.1 The Bathsheba Episode

The existence of the Bathsheba episode has puzzled scholars for its evidently negative depiction of David. Even if we yield to the explanation that the deuteronomistic historian was loyal to the materials which he had inherited, "[t]here is no other instance in the traditions on the early monarchy where David and Solomon are portrayed so negatively."[25] The incident is so embarrassing to the Davidic dynasty that it is hard to imagine that the Deuteronomist included it in the

---

**22** Alter, *The David Story*, xxi-xxii; Dietrich, *Early Monarchy*, 106–109.

**23** L. Delekat, "Tendenz und Theologie der David-Salomo-Erzählung," in *Das ferne und nahe Wort: Festschrift Leonhard Rost zur Vollendung seines 70. Lebensjahres am 30. November 1966 gewidmet*, ed. F. Maass (Berlin: Alfred Töplemann, 1967): 26–36 (30–36).

**24** Würthwein, "Erzählung," 33–53.

**25** Dietrich, *Early Monarchy*, 291.

History, and if we hold that the Deuteronomistic History was written as Josianic propaganda, the difficulty becomes insuperable. The unlikelihood of its inclusion in the Deuteronomistic History seems even more strengthened by the fact that the description of David in the episode is very similar to that of Ahab in the Naboth episode in 1Kings 21. According to Van Seters's observation, the two episodes share the following points: both of them desire property near his palace (vineyard and Bathsheba), and try to acquire it through non-violent means. When this does not succeed, they use violent and illegitimate means, and achieve what they want. In both cases, this leads to a prophet's condemnation, and the kings are given the sentence. They show repentance, and their punishment is mitigated. These similarities make David's sin seem as evil as Jeroboam's cultic sins, and this is unthinkable for the Deuteronomist. Thus Van Seters concludes that the whole "SN", or the Court History as he calls it, is anti-Davidic, anti-messianic, and post-deuteronomistic.[26] McKenzie is of the same view, and argues that not only the inclusion of the crime, but also the entire tone is "exactly the opposite of apologetic for David". In distinction from Van Seters, however, McKenzie thinks that only these chapters, not the entire "SN", were a post-deuteronomistic insertion, perhaps by the same circle who included the Elijah-Elisha cycle.[27]

Despite these anti-Davidic interpretations, I do not think that the Bathsheba episode is incompatible with the pro-Davidic tendency of the Deuteronomistic History. It is true that the depiction is negative, and might well have scandalized the reader and the audience. Moreover, we cannot shake off the negative impression by limiting David's exemplary character to cultic matters as Gordon does.[28] As Van Seters pointed out, in the books of Kings the positive view of David is not restricted to cultic matters.[29] Nevertheless, the degree of negativity is not such that the portrait of David in the episode is incompatible with that in the David story as a whole and the Deuteronomistic History. Here again, we are faced with the question about presupposition on the wider issues, more precisely, how our views about surrounding issues can affect our judgement on a particu-

---

**26** Van Seters, *In Search of History*, 287–291; idem. "The Court History and DtrH," in *Die sogenannte Thronfolgegeschichte*, eds. de Pury and Römer, 72–73; idem, *Biblical Saga*, 287–301, 327–340.

**27** McKenzie, "The So-Called Succession Narrative," in *Die sogennante Thronfolgegeschichte*, eds. de Pury and Römer, 123–135 (133).

**28** Robert P. Gordon, "In Search of David: The David Tradition in Recent Study," in *Faith, Tradition and History: Old Testament Historiography in its Near Eastern Context*, eds. A. R. Millard, J. K. Hoffmeier, and D. W. Baker (Winona Lake: Eisenbrauns, 1994): 285–298 (289).

**29** Van Seters, "The Court History and DtrH," 72.

lar issue. Were we to hold that the Deuteronomistic History is closer to Josianic pro-Davidic propaganda, the Deuteronomistic History as a whole could not contain the Bathsheba episode within itself. The degree of negativity is indeed too high. But if we take the Deuteronomistic History as an exilic reflection that came about after a long experience of Davidic monarchy, the degree of negativity that the work can contain grows substantially. And if the version of the Deuteronomistic History came from the period when political issues surrounding David and his dynasty were less polemical or explosive, it could contain even more negative elements, capable of containing a dramatic mixture of negative and positive descriptions of David. How we understand the whole HDR also affects how much negativity the whole Deuteronomistic History can hold. And if we understand the whole HDR as not one-sidedly pro-Davidic, the contrast between David in the HDR and the same in the Bathsheba episode reduces to the point where we can assume that the picture of David in 2Sam 11–12 was not intolerable to the Deuteronomist. After all, the views about the Deuteronomistic History and the HDR that we have presented in the previous chapters allow us to include the Bathsheba episode in the "SN'. The sinfulness of David in these chapters might well have given a greater sense of hope to the exiles. They might have thought that even David committed a hideous crime, but was forgiven, and thus they could also be forgiven and restore the kingdom despite their unfaithfulness in the past (cf. Ps 51).

In fact, the apparent similarities of the Bathsheba episode with 1Sam 15 serve only to prepare the reader for the sharpness of the difference, and make it more than plausible that the Bathsheba episode was included with other parts of the "SN" by the exilic Deuteronomist. Van Seters briefly mentions the similarities between the two, and regards them as the sign of the author's familiarity with 1Sam 15 (but not the other way around).[30] However, the fact that the structural similarities lead to a dramatically different ending seems to refute Van Seters's anti-Davidic interpretation, and reveals its fundamentally pro-Davidic *Tendenz*. True, the similarities are quite remarkable. Both Saul's and David's sins were committed after successful – but unfinished – military campaigns, the Amalekite war (1Sam 15:1–9) and the Ammonite War (2Sam 10:1–11:1) respectively. The military successes are followed by the sins of the kings, namely, Saul's disobedience (1Sam 15:8–9) and David's adultery and murder (2Sam 11), and these threaten their kingship. Both of them are confronted by their prophets, Samuel (1Sam 15:10–11) and Nathan (2Sam 12:1), but do not understand that they have committed sins (1Sam 15:13 and 2Sam 12:5–6). The prophets rebuke them

---

30 Van Seters, "The Court History and DtrH," 74–75.

with more explanation (1Sam 15:14–16; 2Sam 12:7–10), and give them sentences (1Sam 15:17–19; 2Sam 12:11–12), which finally lead both kings to acknowledge their sins with one word חָטָאתִי ("I sinned") (1Sam 15:24; 2Sam 12:13a). Despite all these similarities, the response to the confession of the two kings is markedly different. Saul is not forgiven and he is told that he will lose his kingship, while David is forgiven instantly. Of course, Saul is partly forgiven in the sense that he remains king and the prophet goes with him to offer sacrifice, while David is partly not-forgiven in that he is told that his child will die. However, the punishment for David does not affect his kingship and his dynasty. Besides, even the punishment mentioned in 12:10–12, although Van Seters thinks that it completely contradicts the promise of eternal dynasty in 2Sam 7, turns out to be anticipating Absalom's rebellion in the following chapters. By contrast, the punishment for Saul is irretrievable, even if Saul looks more repentant than David: Saul pleads for forgiveness, but is cruelly rejected. David, by contrast, does not plead for forgiveness, but is immediately forgiven.

Similarly, in the Ahab story in 1Kings 21, the difference with the Bathsheba episode is more obvious than the similarity, because Ahab is never told that his sin is forgiven. The response to his repentance is only a postponement of the unavoidable disaster, whereas a short-term disaster is inflicted on David without endangering the eternal promise. Van Seters's recognition of the similarity between the two accounts is commendable, but he seems to have overlooked very important differences. This is quite a serious mistake, because as Alter pointed out, in similar structures, or in "type-scenes", the meaning of the text is often found in a minuscule difference. To figure out the *Tendenz* of an apparently ambiguous text, "one must be alert even to the shift of a single word in what may first seem a strictly formulaic pattern."[31]

### 1.2.2.2 Solomon's succession to David

Solomon's accession and the liquidation of his political enemies in 1Kings 1–2 have led some commentators to suspect that the "SN" was anti-Solomonic, or even anti-monarchical. According to these, the author of these chapters described Solomon's succession to David as a palace intrigue that took advantage of the old and weak king David, making clear that it had nothing to do with God's will. Solomon's accession was built on the falsehood of Nathan's party that David had promised to make Solomon succeed him, and was confirmed by brutal assassinations based on the suspicious testament of David. Therefore,

---

**31** Alter, *The Art of Biblical Narrative*, 100–102 (102).

the account of Solomon's succession to David must be anti-Solomonic or anti-monarchical in intent.[32] However, Adonijah's affirmation of the legitimacy of the Davidic succession in 2:15 makes it unlikely that the text is anti-Solomonic or anti-Davidic. One might argue that at least David's testament in 1Kings 2:5–9 was a later addition to shed a negative light on David or offer an apology for Solomon. But McKenzie is probably right here in seeing the purpose of the testament as more to do with the preservation of the dynasty. "The continuation of David's line through Solomon in fulfilment of Yahweh's promise was a major interest of his [the author] [...] The account of Solomon's accession in 1Kings 1–2 resolves the tension and shows Yahweh's faithful completion of his promise to David."[33] This means that 1Kings 1–2 including David's testament is compatible with the pro-Davidic deuteronomistic view. Indeed, there are several indications that one might identify the chapters as deuteronomistic. As McKenzie has shown, deuteronomistic language is scattered all over these chapters (1:48; 2:1–4,10–12,15bb,24,27b,31b-33,44 – 45), and it is impossible to excise these verses from earlier material: 1Kings 1–2 is not properly understood without knowing the stories in 1–2Sam such as the oracle against Eli (2:27), Joab's assassinations (1:5–6,31–33), Barzillai's loyalty (2:7), and Shimei's cursing (2:8–9,44–45).[34] To conclude, neither the Bathsheba episode nor the account of Solomon's accession is incompatible with the pro-Davidic and pro-dynastic view. They certainly do not idealise the Davidic dynasty, but the overall *Tendenz* can be said to be "cautiously in favour of the Davidic dynasty".

### 1.2.3 Theme
Although Rost was convinced that the whole "SN" is concerned with the issue of who will sit on David's throne, it seems difficult now to hold the "SN" together under the theme of succession. If we leave out 1Kings 1–2, the narrative may well be understood as "a record of how David maintained the powers of office and continued to be the legitimate king of Israel and Judah".[35] But with 1Kings 1–2, it is difficult to narrow down the focus to the story of David, because in these chapters, David is only a minor character who provides Solomon with a footstep to the throne, and the time gap between 2Sam 20 and 1Kings 1–2 is rather dramatic. If we do not restrict the focus to the character of David, and expand

---

**32** Delekat, "Tendenz und Theologie der David-Salomo-Erzählung," 30–36; Würthwein, "Erzählung," 33–39.
**33** McKenzie, "The So-Called Succession Narrative," 131.
**34** McKenzie, "The So-Called Succession Narrative," 129.
**35** Flanagan, "Court History," 131.

it to the Davidic dynasty, however, a more or less unifying theme for the whole "SN" emerges. It deals with how the Davidic dynasty is sustained in spite of troubles and difficulties, and how God's promise of the Davidic dynasty is eventually fulfilled.

## 1.3 Composition and Redaction

Rost argued that the "SN" is one of the earliest records about the monarchy in Israel, and that it is a self-contained work written by an eyewitness of the event. Although this was accepted by most scholars, not a few have recognized the difficulty in ascribing the "SN" to a single author. Some separate 1Kings 1–2 from the "SN", because these chapters are concerned with totally different issues from 2Sam 9–20, and others strike out the Bathsheba episode, because the story of Absalom's rebellion seems unaware of 2Sam (10)11–12. Some want to isolate the so-called Benjaminite episodes from the "SN", as these are coloured with an unusually apologetic character. The extreme diversity on the question of the beginning and the ending of the "SN" betrays how difficult it is to embrace all the stories in the "SN" at once. Two different solutions have been suggested to explain the unevenness of the "SN": either different blocks of tradition might have been put together by one redactor/compiler, or some sort of *Ur-form* has gone through redactional stages. As in the case of the Deuteronomistic History, the latter solution has been favoured by German scholars, and the most developed, or extreme case can be found in Thilo Alexander Rudnig's recent study. In his monograph published in 2006, Rudnig attempts to reveal all the different layers in the "SN", and identifies eight stages of redaction. The earliest document was what he calls "Gründungsdokumente der davidischen Dynastie", and this was redacted by a pro-dynastic redactor in the 9th century, BCE. About 300 hundred years later in the early exilic period, the document went through a deuteronomistic edition, and soon in the late exilic period, perhaps in the late 6th–early 5th century, the Absalom narrative went through an additional redaction that linked the exilic experience to David's flight. This edition is soon revised by a "dynastic-critical" redactor in the 5th century, whose literary artistry has been praised ever since Rost as the finest in Hebrew narrative art. After this anti-Davidic redaction, several minor redactions followed in the 5th–3rd century, that include what Rudnig calls "David-Biographie Schicht", "Ratgeber-Bearbeitung", "Nachrichtendienst-Bearbeitung", and "Theodizee-Bearbeitung".[36]

Rudnig's study is thorough and has many insights, and I agree with him in that (i) there was a late exilic redaction that attempted to make some connection between the David story and the exilic experience; (ii) there was a post-exilic redaction that expressed a certain unease about the Davidic dynasty, a characteristic of which is its literary artistry. However, I find it difficult to accept his eight-stage redaction for the "SN", because I am not sure whether the ancient scribe could fiddle with the hallowed text so often. Even if it was possible, I do not think that we can excavate the different layers with such precision as Rudnig claims. There must have been several additional redactions after its first incorporation into the Deuteronomistic History. But unlike in the HDR, the "SN" seems to have endured only a little revision.

Another way of explaining the unevenness of the "SN" is similar to the Block model in the Deuteronomistic History Hypothesis, and it holds that one author compiled the different materials together. For instance, McCarter believes that the author of the Solomonic apology collected different written sources such as the HDR, the Absalom narrative (2Sam 13–20); the story of the Gibeonites' revenge and David's patronage of Meribaal (2Sam 21:1–4 + 9:1–13), and composed his own story on the basis of these earlier materials and combined them all together. Therefore, the "SN" is basically a compilation of one author, although 1Kings 1–2 was a new creation by the author.[37] While McCarter believes that the "SN" was a pre-deuteronomistic work, recent representatives for a similar view tend to maintain that the compilation and creation was done by the Deuteronomist. For instance, Steven McKenzie, who believes that the "SN" was "not a single narrative but a complex of stories", draws attention to the fact that the deuteronomistic language is scattered throughout the narrative collection, and concludes that the "SN" was a Deuteronomist's creation. The overall message also confirms the deuteronomistic authorship, as the "SN" is concerned with "the continuation of David's line through Solomon in fulfilment of Yahweh's promise".[38] Similarly, Serge Frolov denies the existence of one single narrative written by one author. Having observed that 2Sam 1–1Kings 2 is "fairly homogeneous, with chaps. 21–24 being the only exception", Frolov shows that the author of the narrative collection expresses the view that (i) kingship is the only conceivable type of political organization; (ii) only David and his descendants are

---

**36** Thilo Alexander Rudnig, *Davids Thron: Redaktionskritische Studien zur Geschichte von der Thronnachfolge Davids* (Berlin/New York: Walter de Gruyter, 2006).
**37** McCarter, *II Samuel*, 12–13.
**38** McKenzie, "The So-Called Succession Narrative," 131.

eligible to rule over Israel; (iii) God is firmly on the king's side. This fits largely with the view expressed in Nathan's oracle and deuteronomistic ideology discernible in Deut 17:13–20; 1Kings 9:3–9; 2Kings 21:11–15, and consequently, Frolov concludes with McKenzie that the narrative traditionally called "SN" did not exist independently before the deuteronomistic work.[39]

On the whole, I agree more with McKenzie's and Frolov's view than with Rudnig's, although I do not deny that there were some minor redactions. The separation of 2Sam 21 from 2Sam 9 suggests that the compiler of the "SN" worked with several written materials, and the higher integrity of the Absalom narrative compared with other materials seems to suggest that the author of the "SN" built around the Absalom tradition. Concerning the author, the exilic Deuteronomist seems most plausible. Indeed, it is difficult to explain why and when the "SN" was created before the deuteronomistic work. Too early a date is improbable, because the existence of such a long and extensive narrative in the $10^{th}$–$9^{th}$ century seems unlikely.[40] One might want to date the composition soon after the fall of Samaria, but I do not find that convincing either, because the "SN" is not sufficiently pro-Davidic for a Hezekian or Josianic author. The degree of positivity about David and the Davidic dynasty seems just right for the exilic Deuteronomist, and we have seen above that instances of deuteronomistic language are not missing in the "SN". There might have been some minor redactions, but as I mentioned above, the pre-deuteronomistic redactions are impossible to excise, and the post-deuteronomistic redactions were relatively insignificant. One might object by pointing out that the style of the "SN" is quite distinctive when compared with the Deuteronomistic History. However, as I will argue below, the late exilic revision of the Deuteronomistic History seems to have incorporated various narrative materials, turning the genre of the work from a theological chronicle to a popular history. This late exilic Deuteronomist shows more openness to different styles, and this explains how the "SN" was incorporated into the Deuteronomistic History.

If we hold the author of the "SN" to be the late exilic Deuteronomist, it is unnecessary to exclude the Bathsheba episode from the "SN" as both McKenzie and Frolov do. Perhaps for them the story is "too" negative with regard to David,

---

**39** Serge Frolov, "Succession Narrative: A 'Document' or a Phantom?" *JBL* 121 (2002): 81–104 (101–102).

**40** Cf. David W. Jamieson-Drake, *Scribes and Schools in Monarchic Judah: A Socio-Archaeological Approach* (Sheffield: Almond, 1991). Dietrich thinks that his "history of the early monarchy" could not have been written in 10–$9^{th}$ centuries, because this is too early for a large-scale literary product. In my view, even the "SN" is too large for such an early period. See Dietrich, *Early Monarchy*, 263.

and the negativity goes beyond the limit of the deuteronomistic view. However, if we date the addition of the "SN" to the Deuteronomistic History in the late exilic period, the negativity is held within that limit. In fact, when it was questioned after the experience of its disastrous past whether the restored Israel needed the Davidic monarchy, the underlying concept expressed in the "SN" might well have helped the reader to give the Davidic monarchy another chance. The author might well have said, "Yes! David, like any other king, was a sinner. But he was forgiven, while others like Saul and Ahab were not! Although the Davidic monarchy was sinful, God is still in favour of it. Therefore, the restoration of the Davidic monarchy is the best option!"

## 1.4 Relationship between the HDR and the "SN"

Now we turn to our initial question about the relationship between the HDR and the "SN". Since Rost separated the "SN" from the earlier part of the David story, the HDR and the "SN" have been regarded as two independent entities. However, a good number of scholars have pointed out that there is undeniable continuity between the two. For instance, Schulte believes that the same *Tendenz* runs through both the HDR – or *Saul-David Überlieferung* as she calls it – and the "SN", and the following motifs are found in both: the motif of the "untouchability of the king" (2Sam 16:9; 19:22 in the "SN" / 1Sam 22:17; 24; 26 in the HDR); of the king's innocence (2Sam 3:39*; 16:10; 19:23 in the "SN" / 1Sam 25 in the HDR); of the pious king, especially appeal to YHWH's revenge (2Sam 3:39; 16:12 in the "SN" / 1Sam 24:20 in the HDR); of the king's generosity (2Sam 2:4b–7 in the HDR / 2Sam 9:9; 14; 18; 19 in the "SN"); David's sin (2Sam 12 in the "SN" / 1Sam 25 in the HDR). The characters also run through both the HDR and the "SN". For instance, Abner introduced in 1Sam 14:50 appears in 17:55–8; 2Sam 2:3. Abiathar appears in 1Sam 22:20; 30:7; 2Sam 8; 17; 1Kings 1:7,19; 2:26; Joab in 1Sam 26:6; 2Sam 2:13ff; 3:24–27; 1Kings 2:5, Abigail in 1Sam 25; 29:5; 2Sam 2:2; 3:2, Michal in 2Sam 3:15; 2Sam 6.[41] Similarly, Fritz Stolz draws attention to the continuity between the HDR and the "SN", and points out that the theme of Jonathan's descendants and the negative characterisation of the sons of Zeruiah are found both in the HDR and the "SN".[42] Dietrich adds to these points that the sudden appearance of the ark (2Sam 11:11; 15:24–25) and the tent in which it is located (1Kings 2:28–30) seems to presuppose 2Sam 6, and the motif of "shedding inno-

---

**41** Schulte, *Entstehung*, 140–165.
**42** Fritz Stolz, *Das erste und zweite Buch Samuel* (Zürich: Theologischer Verlag Zürich, 1981), 18.

cent blood" binds together the HDR and the "SN" (1Sam 25:26,31,33; 2Sam 1:16; 4:11; 16:7–8; 1Kings 2:5–6,32–33,37).[43] All these and many other pieces of evidence[44] make Stolz's observation not unwarranted that the connection between the "SN" and the HDR is not just redactional.[45]

It is noticeable, however, that many of the continuities are found in what we identified as deuteronomistic or post-deuteronomistic HDR. 2Sam 2:8–4:12 seems to be a later addition to the HDR proper – whether it belongs to the "SN" or not, and therefore the connection with this section does not guarantee that the HDR and the "SN" belonged to the same source before the deuteronomistic work.[46] All other linking points can be assigned to later additions to the HDR proper. The theme of Jonathan's descendants is from the Persian-period additions, and the negative characterisation of the sons of Zeruiah seems to be from the late exilic period. The motif of "shedding innocent blood" has been assigned to the late exilic, or more likely to the post-exilic addition. 2Sam 6, which might well provide the sudden appearance of the ark with a background, seems to have come from the late exilic period, and the motifs such as "the untouchability of the king", "the king's innocence", "the pious king", "the king's generosity", and "David's sin" all appear only in the later additions, as do the bridging characters like Abner, Abiathar, Joab, Abigail, and Michal. All the connections are only apparent, and there is nothing to suggest that the HDR without the deuteronomistic and post-deuteronomistic addition has any literary connection to the "SN".

## 2 The Relationship with the so-called Saul Cycle

### 2.1 The Saul-Tradition in 1Sam 9–14

Scholars have suspected that there was an old Saul-Tradition or "Saul Cycle" in 1Sam, and this included the story of the lost asses, Saul's victory over the Ammonites, and Saul's wars against the Philistines. The precise extent is not yet established. Noth for example thinks that the old *Saul-Überlieferung* which the Deuteronomist incorporated into his History is found in 1Sam 9:1–10:16 +

---

**43** Dietrich, *Early Monarchy*, 239–240.
**44** For more evidence for the literary connection, see also Ficker, "Komposition und Erzählung," 273–282; Johannes Klein, *David versus Saul. Ein Beitrag zum Erzählsystem der Samuelbücher* (Stuttgart: Kohlhammer, 2002), 140–196; Ina Willi-Plein, "1 Sam 18–19 und die Davidshausgeschichte," in *David und Saul im Widerstreit*, ed. Dietrich, 138–177.
**45** Stolz, *Samuel*, 18.
**46** Cf. Fischer, *Von Hebron*, 269–291.

10:27b–11:15 + 13–14, and 15:1–16:13,[47] while Schulte includes part of 1Sam 28 and the whole of 1Sam 31, expanding it to include 1Sam 9:1–10:16; 11:1–11; 13:3–7a,15b–18,23; 14:1–31,36–46,52; 28:3–15,19aβb–25; 31.[48] Instead of 1Sam 28 and 31, McCarter includes the account of Saul's birth which he believes was turned into an account of Samuel's birth on the basis of the apparent word-play around שאל, and holds that it was a loose collection of materials that was similar to the Samson cycle in Judges 13–16 and the stories of "major judges".[49] Humphreys thinks of an even larger work that includes 9:1–10:16; 11:1–11; 13–14; 15 (now recast); 17–22 (again recast); 26; 28; 31,[50] while Kratz, although he speaks of "an originally independent Saul tradition" that includes 1Sam 1:1–20 + 9:1–10:16 + 11:1–15 + 13–14 (without later additions), believes that it did not exist independently, but only as part of a larger whole.[51] It is generally accepted that the Tradition was favourable to Saul, although it might not have idealized him. McCarter thinks that prophetic or anti-monarchical elements were later additions, and the original Saul cycle just explained the rise of kingship as having evolved out of the "saviour" tradition.[52] The date and the location of the composition of the Saul Traditions are hard to tell, but it is likely to have originated in the Benjaminite region. It seems to have been transmitted orally for a while, and some suggest that the collection was already made as early as the Solomonic period[53] or the latter part of the 9th century.[54]

Despite uncertainty about the "original" Saul-Tradition, it is clear that the collection was redacted by later editors. Wellhausen thought of an anti-monarchical redactor who had attached 1Sam 8; 10:17–27; [11]; 12 to 1Sam 7, and dated it later in the exilic period.[55] Noth had a similar view, but assigned Wellhausen's anti-monarchical strand to the Deuteronomist,[56] while Veijola recognized both pro-monarchical and anti-monarchical strands within the deuteronomistic redaction, and assigned the anti-monarchical strand to the DtrN.[57] More and more scholars however hold that the Cycle is not easily divided into pro-mo-

---

**47** Noth, *ÜS*, 62 (# 1).
**48** Schulte, *Entstehung*, 105.
**49** McCarter, *I Samuel*, 26–27.
**50** W. Lee Humphreys, "The Rise and Fall of King Saul: A Study of an Ancient Narrative Stratum in 1 Samuel," *JSOT* 18 (1980): 74–90 (76).
**51** Kratz, *Komposition*, 170–180 (Eng: 174).
**52** McCarter, *I Samuel*, 27.
**53** Humphreys, "The Rise and Fall of King Saul," 87.
**54** McCarter, *I Samuel*, 27.
**55** Wellhausen, *Composition*, 240–243.
**56** Noth, *ÜS*, 57–60.
**57** Veijola, *Königtum*, 115–122.

narchical and anti-monarchical layers, and some argue that although there are anti-Saulide passages, the whole text is not particularly anti-monarchical. But one gets an impression that even Saul is always treated with some respect in the Cycle, and it is difficult to identify the *Tendenz* unambiguously. Perhaps it is reasonable to assume that the original Saul Tradition was pro-Saulide, and this was redacted to serve the David story in the following chapters. The composer seems to have been pro-Davidic and pro-monarchical, but not totally hostile to the Saulides.

## 2.2 Relationship between the HDR and the Saul Cycle

At first, it seems unlikely that there is any literary connection between the HDR and the Saul Narrative, because unlike the "SN", the Saul Narrative is not about David, but about Saul and Samuel. It deals with how Saul became king with the help of Samuel, and how successful (and unsuccessful) he was as king over Israel. David does not appear in the narrative, and there seems to be no reason to consider any literary connection between them. However, we are reminded that Saul is a very important figure in the HDR, and without the Saul Narrative in 1Sam 9–14, his character and narrative function in the HDR is not properly understood. Above all, the report that the Spirit left Saul (1Sam 16:14) presupposes that Saul received the Spirit in the first place (1Sam 10:6; 11:6), and the loyalty of the people of Jabesh-gilead to Saul after his death is difficult to understand without 1Sam 11. Similarly, Jonathan's appearance in 1Sam 18:1 and his preeminent position during Saul's reign and his independent character require pre-knowledge of 1Sam 13–14. Moreover, David's rise seems to be modelled on Saul's rise, and how David is different from Saul cannot be properly understood without the Saul Narrative. For instance, the motif of the consultation of YHWH appears both in the HDR (1Sam 23:2,4; 28:6; 2Sam 5:19) and in the Saul Cycle (1Sam 14:37), and without Saul's failure to receive YHWH's oracle, the meaning of David's success in doing so is not sufficiently understood. Finally, there seem to be some linguistic connections. The expression "to uncover the ear (גלה את אזן)" in 1Sam 9:15 appears in the HDR in 1Sam 20:2,(12),13; 22:8,17; 2Sam 7:27, and the expression "at the time tomorrow (כָּעֵת מָחָר)" in 1Sam 9:16 is found in 1Sam 20:12. The verb ענה in the sense of "giving an oracle" in 1Sam 9:17; 14:37 is found in 1Sam 23:4; 28:6,15.[58]

---

58 Schulte, *Entstehung*, 109–110 (# 27).

All the points of connection, however, seem to have come from later additions, and therefore the HDR was originally separate from the Saul Tradition. We have assigned David's anointing and the Jonathan passages to the exilic addition, and the expression "to uncover the ear" and "at the time tomorrow" occur mainly in the exilic additions such as 1Sam 20 and 2Sam 7.[59] The verb ענה in the sense of "giving an oracle" does occur in the HDR proper, but it is only one occasion in 1Sam 23:4, and we cannot establish a literary connection on the basis of one example. Although there is no linguistic connection, the report of Saul's death in 1Sam 31 might well have come from the Saul Cycle, because the overall tone is quite different from the surrounding David materials, and the sudden appearance of the people of Jabesh-gilead is incomprehensible without the Saul Tradition. However, this does not necessarily mean that the HDR and the Saul Tradition belong to the same literary work. It might well have been the case that the author of the HDR had the Saul Tradition to hand, and relocated the account of Saul's death where it is now.

In brief, the connections of the HDR with the "SN" and the Saul Tradition are only apparent, because all of them are found in what we have identified as exilic or post-exilic additions. This means that there is nothing against the view that the HDR proper existed as an independent source, and its extent is 1Sam 16:14–2Sam 5:3.[60] The fact that the account of Saul's death, which may well have belonged to the Saul Tradition, and the old core of the En-dor episode are found in the HDR proper suggests that the author had to hand both the Saul Tradition and old materials about David, and composed the HDR proper

---

59 According to Cross, "to uncover ear" is deuteronomistic. However, the expression elsewhere occurs in Ruth 4:4; Job 33:16; 36:10,15, and this might suggest that the expression was popular in the late exilic and post-exilic period. See Cross, *Canaanite Myth*, 256.

60 Recently, the argument that the HDR was not an independent source, but was composed to connect the tradition about Saul with the tradition about David is gaining momentum, especially among German-speaking scholars. Although it is certainly a viable alternative to the traditional views, I have some reservations. Considering the duplications, it seems reasonable to believe that there was an original layer. One might call the original layer "core" traditions, and if there were such "core" traditions about David's early years, the next question to be asked is whether they were just fragments or a self-contained narrative. If they were merely fragments, it seems more likely that the HDR was created to bridge the Saul Cycle and the "SN" by incorporating bits and pieces about David. If, however, the "core" traditions were sufficiently self-contained, one may well regard it as an independent source. And in my view, they were a self-contained narrative, because (1) even without the later additions that I marked out above, the narrative has a fairly clear structure. It begins with the introduction of the hero in chapter 16, followed by the growing tension between the hero and the anti-hero, reaches its climax at Saul's death, and ends with the enthronement of the hero; (2) and as I consistently argue that there was a good reason Hezekiah wanted to create such a narrative.

out of these. The old materials about David might have been a story of a nobody who overcame hardships and became king of Judah, and this might well have originated in the Davidic-Solomonic period, as a heroic saga of David. This however was combined with the story of Saul's fall, and the result was a story of David's rise and Saul's fall. Now this has become a sort of "persuasion literature" that advertises David and his kingdom as a replacement for the fallen king and his kingdom, and this might well have been first written down in the Hezekian period. As I already suggested in the previous chapter, this story fits well with Hezekiah's policy of embracing the northern kingdom, and expanding his territory. Although the mass immigration of the northerners to Jerusalem is now less certain than it used to be,[61] there is a high probability that the Saul tradition was brought in by the northerners, and the Jerusalem court scribe created the HDR proper with it. The HDR as we have it is however quite different from this HDR proper, because the former is adorned with literary embellishments, and infused with a generally, but not exaggeratedly pro-Davidic tone. And I believe that the "History of David's Rise" is a fitting title for this final form of the HDR rather than for the HDR proper, and in this sense, the HDR was given its dominant tone in the Persian period. A later redactor, who was interested in storytelling and less polemical in political debates, added materials and revised some of the original ones, and turned the HDR proper into something closer to the prototype of the Jewish novel that was to flourish about a century later.

## 3 Composition of the Books of Samuel

We have concluded that the HDR proper was independent from the so-called Saul Cycle and from the "SN", and was incorporated into the Deuteronomistic History together with other narrative traditions. The books of Samuel were basically a creation of the Deuteronomist, whose History covered the entire period of the monarchy in Israel from the first king to the last. This does not necessarily mean, however, that the first edition of the Deuteronomistic History had all the narrative sections. In fact, the Deuteronomist's formulaic and straightforward style – most clearly expressed in the "sermons" and in the evaluation of kings – fits ill with the rich and multi-dimensional narratives in the books of Samuel, and makes us wonder whether the same Deuteronomist would have combined such very different materials. Indeed, one can hardly get away from the

---

61 N. Na'aman, "When and How Did Jerusalem Becomes a Great City? The Rise of Jerusalem as Judah's Premier City in the Eighth-Seventh Centuries B.C.E.," *BASOR* 347 (2007): 21–56 (35–38).

impression that the books of Samuel are closer to the patriarchal narratives than the books of Kings or the Chronicles, while the latter two look quite similar. Furthermore, the peculiarity of the Saul and David narratives is not only generic/stylistic, but also theological. As Rainer Albertz observes, unlike any other period, the period of the united monarchy is treated as "a new period of pure, unadulterated faith in Yahweh".[62] The peculiarity can be explained through the Deuteronomist's vital interest in the Davidic monarchy and the Jerusalem temple, as well as the law and the land.[63] However, if the first edition of the Deuteronomistic History was composed soon after the fall of Jerusalem as we maintain, one may well wonder whether such an optimistic picture of the monarchy was likely to have any place in the literature that was imbued with a repentant and lamenting tone.

Noth explained the existence of the extensive narratives in rather a formulaic DtrH, by positing that the Deuteronomist inherited them, and his loyalty to the old source left the unevenness uncompromised. This is still accepted by the majority of scholars, and recent scholars have strengthened this idea by emphasizing the "compiler" side of the Deuteronomist rather than the "author" side, i.e. by clarifying the nature of the pre-deuteronomistic source. For instance, Walter Dietrich argues that before the deuteronomistic work, there was already a self-contained narrative history on the early monarchy in Israel, whose extent is 1Sam 1–1Kings 12 at most, or 1Sam 9–1Kings 2 at least.[64] Therefore, the Deuteronomist had no choice but to endure the generic and ideological distinctiveness. The appeal to the alleged loyalty of the Deuteronomist to the old sources however should have some limits. Otherwise, one can argue that the whole Bible was compiled on a single day by a single compiler who was loyal to the old traditions. The question is whether there was an acceptable reason why the author of the DtrH was willing to include the long narrative in the History, even if it might obscure its clear message. And I cannot see why the Deuteronomist was so keen to do so, when the monarchy had just ended tragically. One might argue that he wanted to persuade the reader that the monarchy as such was not a problem, but later kings did not live up to the great examples of David and Solomon. However, this is unlikely, not only because the Deuteronomist was likely to have been more occupied in dealing with the disaster itself than with the discussion about the institution of monarchy, but also because the history of the early monarchy as we have it in the Deuteronomistic History does not

---

**62** Rainer Albertz, *Israel in Exile: The History and Literature of the Sixth Century B.C.E.* (Atlanta: Society of Biblical Literature, 2003), 290–291.
**63** Albertz, *Israel in Exile*, 291.
**64** Dietrich, *Early Monarchy*, 298 f.

seem to present the reader with an idealistic picture of Israel. From the very beginning of monarchy until Solomon's succession, the internal strife within the royal family is endless, and this could not have suggested to those who had just witnessed the national disaster that the restoration of the Davidic monarchy would be a good idea. Possibly the HDR proper was included in the DtrH, and the ambiguous character which we now find in the Saul and David narratives came from the expansion of the HDR proper and the addition of the "SN". This becomes plausible, considering that most kings of Judah are evaluated rather positively in the DtrH, whereas kings of Israel are almost unanimously condemned. However, as I mentioned above, it is curious that the Deuteronomist in the books of Kings shows no interest at all in how David overcame all the difficulties and became king of Israel.

Furthermore, it seems doubtful that there was development from the rich and more sophisticated narrative to a rigid and simplistic chronicle-like history as Dietrich holds. Development in the opposite direction is more plausible: the first Deuteronomist created a "synchronistic chronicle" with a clear theological message, and this was expanded by narratives of diverse views. Examples from the ancient Near East also support such a direction of generic development. As Adam observes, the king lists in Mesopotamia were often expanded by the addition of "*Vorzeitüberlieferung*" about mythical kings. For instance, the so-called king list of Lagaš,[65] or the Neo-Babylonian Etana Epic[66] annexed mythical stories about legendary kings before the list proper, in order to legitimate later kings who actually existed. Adam thinks that the "evidently legitimating tendency" of the Saul-David narrative makes clear that the narrative was added to the synchronistic chronicle found in the books of Kings, in order to provide the chronicle with a proper pre-history.[67] I do not agree with Adam that the Saul-David Tradition shows a clearly legitimating *Tendenz*, and that Saul and David are only mythical figures. But a direction of generic development from chronicles to narrative history seems much more plausible. Besides, we are reminded that the dominant literary genre in the Neo-Babylonian period was chronicles, while narrative genre – court history in particular – became popular in the Persian period. If the Deuteronomistic History was composed in the exilic period, the literary convention of the time then makes development from theological chronicle to narrative history more likely. The theological and ideological distinctiveness of the David narratives is also better explained in this way. The repentant treatise

---

**65** Edmond Sollberger, "The Rulers of Lagaš," *JCS* 21 (1967): 279–291, (279–280); Sparks, *Ancient Texts*, 348.
**66** Translation of the text is in *ANET* 114–118, 517. See also Sparks, *Ancient Texts*, 286–287.
**67** Adam, *Saul und David*, 13–21.

on Israel's history might well have come immediately after the exile, and the "vital interest" in the Davidic monarchy and the Temple came later, when the restoration looked viable.

Together with the late exilic and the post-exilic additions that we identified in the previous chapter, all these considerations urge us to conclude that the narratives about the early monarchy were added later as an expansion to the first edition of the Deuteronomistic History. Probably the DtrH was composed not long after the catastrophic experience as theological reflection, and this followed more or less the format of the Neo-Babylonian chronicles, or was based on the pre-deuteronomistic "synchronistic chronicles". And later in the exilic period, when the restoration of the Davidic monarchy and the Jerusalem temple became a real possibility, there was the debate about whether they are necessary for the restored Israel. This prompted narratives about David, that might have been kept in a royal archive or the "deuteronomistic library",[68] to be incorporated into the History with a view to support the Davidic monarchy. A growing interest in narratives in the late Neo-Babylonian and Persian periods stimulated the process of narrative expansion even further, and even narratives which are non-monarchical, such as the Elijah-Elisha Cycle, were introduced into the History. Consequently, literature, which had been very much like a chronicle, turned into a mixture of history and novel. Now I trace a possible process of composition of the books of Samuel. This is very speculative, but may help us to take a fresh look at the composition history of the books of Samuel.

## 3.1 Pre-deuteronomistic Traditions

Despite my reservation in acknowledging the existence of an extensive narrative before the exile, there were certainly pre-exilic materials in the books of Samuel. As Dietrich observed, a few songs and proverbs seem to have originated in the early monarchical period. For instance, David's lament over Saul and Jonathan (2Sam 1:19–27), and David's lament over Abner (2Sam 3:33–34) may well have come from David himself, and the famous song "Saul killed his thousands, David his tens of thousands (1Sam 18:7; 21:12; 29:5)" might have been popular during David's reign or even earlier. Sheba's call, "We have no share in David, and we have no inheritance in the son of Jesse" (2Sam 20:1) also looks ancient.

---

68 Nadav Na'aman, "Sources and Composition in the History of David", in *The Origin of the Ancient Israelite States*, eds. Volkmar Fritz and Philip R. Davies (Sheffield: Sheffield Academic Press, 1996): 170–186 (180–182); Römer, "The Form-Critical Problem," 251.

It is used in 1Kings 12:16 in a more extended form, but this might have been an adaptation of the earlier expression that had been known from the united monarchy. In addition to these songs or proverbs, we can see lists that might well have been old and whose historicity cannot be doubted. Na'aman enumerates them as follows: the list of towns in which Samuel worked (1Sam 7:16); the list of countries with which Saul fought (1Sam 14:47); the list of Saul's kinsmen (1Sam 14:49–51); the list of cities and villages that received gifts from David while he was in Ziklag (1Sam 30:27–30); the list of regions and towns belonging to the kingdom of Eshbaal (2Sam 2:9); the list of David's sons (2Sam 3:2–5; 5:13–16); the list of David's high officials (2Sam 8:16–18; 20:23–26); the list of the so-called Thirty, David's elite military unit (2Sam 23:24–39); the list of the boundary points of David's kingdom (2Sam 24:5–8).[69] Several small narratives such as the report of David's war in 2Sam 8 and the anecdotes of David's heroes in 2Sam 21:15–22; 23:8–17,18–23 also seem to have come from the early period, and so do the short notes such as we find in 1Sam 22:1–5.[70] Of course, we do not have proof of their antiquity, and Van Seters questions the historicity of many of these lists, mainly on the basis of their apparent anachronism.[71] Nonetheless, their irrelevance to the surrounding materials and their fragmentary style lead us to believe that they were indeed old materials that might have been kept in the royal archive.

Although their early dating is more difficult than the short materials mentioned above, several fairly long narrative materials also can be dated before the fall of Jerusalem. Above all, the story of David's early days as a fugitive may well have come from quite an early period, and the Saul Tradition possibly originated not long after the northern kingdom was separated from Judah. The Absalom narrative as we have it may be too complex and developed for us to think that it was produced long before the exile. However, the core part might well have been an old tradition that was handed down to the Deuteronomist. Similarly, the story of Saul's rejection (1Sam 15) and the Abigail episode (1Sam 25) were likely to be in their original form pre-deuteronomistic (oral?) traditions. Whether the HDR proper and the "SN" existed before the exile is more difficult to establish, although I am more convinced about the pre-exilic existence of the HDR proper than that of the "SN". The stylistic distinctiveness of the "SN" however does not rule out the possibility that the proto-SN existed before the deuteronomistic work. We cannot be sure how all these ancient materials were kept and

---

**69** Na'aman, "Sources and Composition," 170–186.
**70** Dietrich, *Early Monarchy*, 264–267.
**71** Van Seters, *Biblical Saga*, 90–99.

handed down, although one might speculate that they were kept in the royal library or the "deuteronomistic library". Neither does it seem possible to excise the pre-deuteronomistic sections from the Deuteronomistic History, because the deuteronomistic redaction was bolder than we have thought, especially during the expansion in the late exilic period.

### 3.2 The First Edition of the Deuteronomistic History (DtrH)

It is totally plausible that a group of intellectuals or a single author composed a history of the Israelite monarchy after the deportations of two Davidic monarchs (Jehoiachin in 597 and Zedekiah in 587). From the tone of the Deuteronomist, as I concluded in the previous chapter, the exilic composition of the first edition of the Deuteronomistic History is more plausible than a Josianic or Hezekian composition.[72] It is likely to have been written in Babylonia soon after the third deportation in 582, following the style of the Babylonian Chronicles.[73] Possibly, the author of the DtrH based his work on what Jepsen identified as "synchronistic chronicles" of Israel and Judah,[74] and added post-Hezekian chronological information and post-traumatic theological comments to the chronicles. A remaining question then is how extensive it was, and I suggested above that it was much shorter, and only the HDR proper, or more likely, none of the David materials were included in the first edition of the Deuteronomistic History.

This obviously raises many questions, not least how the repeated praise of David in the books of Kings was possible without some record about Saul and David in the History. However, the apparent awareness of the Saul and David story may well have come from general knowledge about them, rather than from concrete knowledge of the story. Moreover, the praise of David in the books of Kings does not necessarily require the existence of an extensive narrative about David within the History. Indeed, the David narrative, which is not unambiguously pro-Davidic, does not fit well with the unconditional praise of

---

72 For Josianic composition, see Cross, *Canaanite Myth*; Nelson, "Double Redaction". For Hezekian, see Helga Weippert, "Die 'deuteronomistischen' Beurteilung der Könige von Israel und Juda und das Problem der Redaktion der Königsbücher," *Bib* 53 (1972): 301–339; Provan, *Hezekiah and the Book of Kings*.

73 Noth argued for its origin in Palestine, but I find it more plausible that it was composed in Babylonia, because (i) it is more likely that literary activities flourished in the imperial centre than in Judah; (ii) it was not impossible that the exiles carried some archival materials to Babylonia. See Noth, *ÜS*, 110; Ackroyd, *Exile and Restoration*, 65–68; Albertz, *Israel in Exile*, 282–284.

74 Alfred Jepsen, *Die Quellen des Königsbuches* (Halle: Max Niemeyer, 1953), 30–40.

David as a perfect and ideal king. Furthermore, the David mentioned in the books of Kings is more iconic than realistic, and the praise of David is too formulaic to assume the knowledge of a well-narrated story of David. For instance, although the DtrH repeatedly mentions that God said to David that He would make David a lamp for his descendants forever, nothing is mentioned of the lamp in the David narratives. By contrast, David's other virtues such as tenderness, loyalty, and courage in the HDR and the "SN" are never mentioned in the DtrH. In fact, the Deuteronomist's habit of quoting the past event without including the actual record of it is also found in his repeated mention of the exodus event in the DtrH. Although the Deuteronomistic History repeatedly mentions the event (1Kings 6:1; 8:9,16,21,51,53; 9:9; 12:28; 2Kings 17:36; 21:15), it does not start with exodus, and the event of exodus remains merely an iconic event throughout the DtrH, as David's life and the promise of an eternal dynasty do.[75] Of course, this does not rule out the possibility that some form of David narratives existed before the deuteronomistic work, and I suspect that they were kept in a royal archive or in the deuteronomistic library. However, it is more likely that the Deuteronomist did not include them in the first edition of the Deuteronomistic History, which was mainly narrating the history of kings of Judah and Israel with a straightforward message to the exiles who had just experienced the terrible end of the monarchy.

## 3.3 The Deuteronomistic Expansion (DtrE)

After the release of Jehoiachin at the earliest, but more likely after Cyrus's military successes,[76] the hope of restoration seems to have infected the Israelites in Babylonia. Naturally, interest in the person of David increased as we see in Ezekiel, and this may well have attracted the materials about David into the Deuteronomistic History. However, the restoration of the Davidic monarchy was not accepted without hesitation and doubts, because the exiles had learned from the

---

75 Schmid solves the problem of the frequent allusions to the exodus in the deuteronomistic texts by arguing that the history begins with Exodus 2. Römer however finds it unconvincing, because it makes the recapitulation of the events in Exodus and Numbers in Deut 1–3 redundant. See Konrad Schmid, *Erzväter und Exodus: Untersuchungen zur doppelten Begründung der Ursprünge Israels innerhalb der Geschichtsbücher des Alten Testaments* (Neukirchen-Vluyn: Neukirchener, 1999), 162–165; Thomas Römer, "Form-Critical Problem," in *Changing Face*, eds. Sweeney and Ben Zvi, 246–247.

76 Albertz argues that Cyrus's Lydian campaign in 547/546 first signalled a change in the political climate. See Albertz, *Israel in Exile*, 284–5.

DtrH that the experiment of monarchy was after all a great failure. Therefore, it is possible that there was a group that was critical or suspicious of the restoration of the monarchy, and some responded to such a critical stance with apologetic remarks about David and his dynasty.[77] The so-called Göttingen School rightly recognized different voices in the History, and attempted to assign them to different groups. Inspiring it may be, but it is unlikely that we can distinguish the different schools within the expanded Deuteronomistic History with any confidence. Indeed, the disagreement within the Göttingen School about the extent and the *Tendenz* of the different deuteronomistic schools has proved such an attempt to be less than promising. We would rather agree with Rainer Albertz who "find[s] it more appropriate to ascribe such revisions to ongoing debate within the larger Deuteronomistic circle rather than attempt to identify clearly distinct Deuteronomistic authors and circles".[78]

One feature that has not drawn proper attention from the Göttingen School, or indeed any scholars, however, is that the deuteronomistic expansion in the late exilic period showed increasing interest in storytelling. It is noteworthy that the so-called DtrP expressed their view not through some clear statements or homilies as the DtrH did, but through the introduction and revision of narratives. According to Dietrich, the DtrP collected prophetic stories that had not been included in the DtrH, and introduced them into the Deuteronomistic History. Dietrich is very keen on identifying the ideological feature of the DtrP layer, and discovers its "sharply anti-monarchical accent" and its claim that kings should obey God's will and reign accordingly.[79] He fails however to notice a more evident fact, namely, that the DtrP was interested enough in storytelling to take the trouble to collect the old stories and revise them. The deuteronomistic revision in the later exilic period reflects diverse debates within the larger deuteronomistic school, and it is impossible to differentiate different schools on the basis of literary analysis. Yet, I believe that the growing interest in narratives is the most visible characteristic in this redactional stage. The richness found in the late exilic expansion of the Deuteronomistic History keeps us from labelling the

---

77 Most scholars see some strands in the book of Zechariah which defend the restoration of the Davidic monarchy. It has been also argued that the rivalry between David and Saul was a live issue during the early Persian period. See Diana Edelman, "Did Saulite-Davidic Rivalry resurface in early Persian Yehud?" in *The Land That I Will Show You: Essays on the History and Archaeology of the Ancient Near East in Honour of J. Maxwell Miller*, ed.s J. Andrew Dearman and M. Patrick Graham (Sheffield: Sheffield Academic Press, 2001): 69–91; Joseph Blenkinsopp, "Benjamin Traditions Read in the Early Persian Period," in *Judah and the Judeans in the Persian Period*, eds. Oded Lipschits and Manfred Oeming (Winona Lake: Eisenbrauns, 2006): 629–645.
78 Albertz, *Israel in Exile*, 276.
79 Dietrich, *Prophetie und Geschichte*; idem, *David, Saul und die Propheten*, 152.

whole redactional stage as "narrative expansion", but it seems evident that the interest in narratives was one of the clearest features in the process. The pervading popularity of stories in the Neo-Babylonian and the Persian period may well have been an impetus to such a move.

One might ask why the DtrE needs to be separate from the DtrH, since if we date the redactional work slightly later than Noth first imagined (c.a. 562 BCE),[80] both the "cautiously Davidic" tendency and the interest in narratives can be explained. However, we can still distinguish the DtrE from the DtrH, because they show a number of fairly evident differences. First, stylistically or generically, they are clearly different. One is chronicle and formulaic, and the other is narrative and free. Secondly, they are also different theologically. One is rigid and straightforward, and the other is more open and contains diverse views. Thirdly, the attitude to the exilic experience is different. One is more immediate and traumatic, and the other is rather reflective and didactic or sapiential. Fourthly, the way in which David is depicted is different. One is rather iconic and symbolic, and the other is realistic (albeit not historical) and multi-faceted. Fifthly, the significance of the (cultic) law is different. One is very strict, and the other shows little interest. There is also literary-redactional evidence that can separate the DtrE from the DtrH, but I will not list the evidence here, because that has already been done by German scholarship for several decades. In brief, these evident differences indicate the existence of two quite different editions, and I find it more likely that the original DtrH, which was simpler, shorter, and more straightforward, was expanded through the addition of various narratives.

## 3.4 Post-exilic Novelistic Redaction

Although earlier scholars believed that the Deuteronomistic History was finalized in the exilic period, more recent scholarship recognizes that the redactional work continued in the post-exilic period. The so-called Göttingen School revised the previous view and dated the DtrN in the post-exilic period,[81] and more recently, Römer proposed that there was a Persian deuteronomistic edition that may well be compared with the DtrN. According to Römer, the returnees brought the exilic edition of the Deuteronomistic History with them, and revised it, in order to make it fit the new situation. In particular, he argues, the Deuteronomist

---

**80** For instance, Albertz dates it between 547–522 BCE. See Albertz, *Israel in Exile*, 285.
**81** Rudolf Smend, *Die Entstehung des Alten Testaments* (Stuttgart: Kohlhammer, 1984), 124; Dietrich, *David, Saul und die Propheten,* 152.

in the Persian period emphasized the need of segregation from foreign influen-
ces, developed the monolatry into monotheism, and legitimated the possibility
that the "true Israel" might live outside the province of Yehud. The Persian redaction is hardly noticeable in Samuel-Kings, and Römer suspects that it was because they were mostly interested in introducing the theme of segregation into
the law book and the conquest story.[82] Lester L. Grabbe, however, doubts that
there was serious conflict between those who returned and those who remained
in Jerusalem soon after the return in the late 6th century,[83] and if he is right, the
characteristic of the literary activity in the early post-exilic period is elusive.

More evident literary development with regard to the books of Samuel occurred in the mid-5th century, when Nehemiah's nationalistic policy stimulated certain unease, and the "novelistic impulse" began to emerge. In the previous chapter, I argued that in the HDR, we often come across passages that are less
polemical and show more literary interest. These passages seem to reject the tendency to demonize Saul and idealize David, and discourage any unnecessary
conflict by creating pictures that are less pro-Davidic, but more sympathetic to
Saul. For instance, David's ambitious character is already spotted from his
youth through the addition of 1Sam 17:12–31, and his calculating and unloving
character in his dealing with Jonathan in 1Sam 20. By contrast, Saul is shown
more sympathy. The repetition of the evil spirit's influence on Saul makes the
troubled king look like a victim of certain power beyond his control, and Samuel's overreaction against Saul in 1Sam 28:16–19 seems to make the reader
see the pointlessness of being severe and unforgiving to someone in a weaker
position. The introduction of the Jonathan passages on the other hand extends
the story of Saul and David to that of the Saulides and the Davidides, and
makes the point that the unnecessary conflict between the descendants of
Saul and those of David is silly and tragic.[84]

Earlier, I also suggested that there are passages in the HDR that show greater
literary interest. The author duplicated several stories, so that the dramatic tension heightens, and added songs (2Sam 1:19–27) and proverbs (1Sam 24:14) in

---

**82** Römer, *The So-Called Deuteronomistic History*, 169–78 (172).
**83** Lester L. Grabbe, *Yehud: A History of the Persian of Judah*, vol. 1, *A History of the Jews and
Judaism in the Second Temple Period* (London/New York: T & T Clark, 2004), 285–288.
**84** If we assign the account of the battle between Abner and Joab in 2Sam 2:8–32 to this
novelistic revision, the point is made even clearer. As Kunz has pointed out, the whole account
characterizes the battle between the two army leaders, who symbolize Israel and Judah respectively, as pointless bitterness. For Kunz's interpretation and its similarities with *Illiad*, see
"'Soll das Schwert denn ewig fressen?' Zur Erzählintention von II Samuel 2. 8–32," in *Erzählte
Geschichte: Beiträge zur narrativen Kultur im alten Israel*, ed. Rüdiger Lux (Neukirchen-Vluyn:
Neukirchener, 2000): 53–79.

order to embellish the work. Above all, the new poetics that we find in the later Jewish novels is traceable in the revised HDR. We see main characters burst into tears – David in 1Sam 20 and Saul in 1Sam 24, and the expression of intense emotion such as this distinguishes the HDR from the "SN" that is written in "deadpan style".[85] The importance of female characters that we witness in 1Sam 19:11–17 (Michal); 25 (Abigail); 28 (the woman at En-dor) is also peculiar in comparison with earlier narratives, but common in the later Jewish novels.

The combination of these characteristics that we find in the HDR makes the possibility real that the books of Samuel, the HDR in particular, were revised by someone who was uneasy about Nehemiah's nationalistic and intolerant policies. We have seen above that one of the DtrE's characteristics is its growing interest in narratives and willingness to accommodate different views, while the post-exilic Deuteronomist focused more on the issue of the identity of "true Israel" with a more rigid, or "nomistic" stance. Nehemiah was perhaps a conservative interpreter of such a post-exilic deuteronomistic view, and attempted to actualize it. This however caused a certain discontent among those who were less dogmatic about the "true Israel" and enjoyed the openness of the DtrE even more. And it is imaginable that these people, when an opportunity arose, revised the Deuteronomistic History in such a way that the nationalistic policy is not always based on their authoritative text. For instance, we hear from Neh 2:10 that there was a tension between Sanballat, the governor of the province of Samaria and Nehemiah, and Nehemiah's confrontational and insensitive attitude was the main reason for such a conflict.[86] Through the introduction of the Jonathan passages, the author of the revised HDR might have wanted to make a point that the confrontational and intolerant attitude of Nehemiah and his followers is silly and even tragic. The possibility is also confirmed from a literary point of view. The interest in storytelling kept increasing in the Persian period, and the court stories and narrative histories earned great popularity both in the ancient Near East and in ancient Greece in Nehemiah's time. This makes it reasonable to suspect that some Jewish intellectuals in Yehud were familiar with such a literary genre, and attempted a similar literary work.

True, there is no linguistic evidence that suggests that the HDR was revised in the Persian period. But this can be explained in two ways. First, the Persian revision does not mean that the author wrote a new work from scratch. The author might have revised it in such a way that the classical Hebrew style is not

---

**85** John Barton, "Dating the 'Succession Narrative'," in *In Search of Pre-exilic Israel*, ed. John Day (London/New York: T & T Clark, 2004): 95–106 (102).
**86** Grabbe, *A History of the Jews and Judaism*, 298–301.

disrupted too much, and managed to make his own hand unnoticed. Furthermore, the revised section of the HDR is not long enough to make any reliable judgement about when it was written simply on a linguistic basis. Therefore, the absence of particularly "Persian" language in these chapters does not rule out that the final revision was done in that period. Second, there are indeed several pieces of linguistic evidence. For instance, the unusual expression, "the evil is finished (כלתה תרעה)" in the HDR (1Sam 20:7,9,33; 25:17) occurs elsewhere only in Esther 7:7, and signs of late Hebrew are seen all over 1Sam 17:1–18:5.[87] The words based on the root נבל in the HDR (1Sam 25:19,25) occur elsewhere mostly in late texts such as Proverbs, Job, and Psalms.[88] There are also some indirect linguistic evidences. It is now widely accepted that the stories from the Elijah-Elisha Cycle are post-exilic, and we discover some phrases that often pop up in the cycle in the HDR.[89] For example, "at this time tomorrow (כָּעֵת מָחָר)" (1Kings 19:2; 20:6; 2Kings 7:1,18; 10:6) occurs in 1Sam 20:12, and the combination of two verbs "know (ידע)" and "see (ראה)" (1Kings 20:7; 20:22; 2Kings 5:7) occurs in 1Sam 24:12; 25:17; 2Sam 24:13. I do not think for a minute that the occurrence of these possibly late expressions can prove that the HDR was revised in the Persian period. However, these can at least leave the possibility open. As I argued earlier, the linguistic evidence alone cannot prove much, but when interpreted along with other evidences, it can help to confirm a certain point.

Some people might question whether it is possible to separate this novelistic redactor from the DtrE, because the former might have been at the end of the DtrE stage, and may well have accepted the Deuteronomistic ideology as orthodoxy. Besides, if we admit that the deuteronomistic work went on to the Persian period, the novelistic redactor cannot be easily differentiated from the DtrE. Despite the continuity, however, the following makes the novelistic edition distinct from the DtrE. First, unlike the DtrE, the novelistic edition reveals more clearly the characteristics of the later Jewish novels. As I mentioned above, the revised HDR not only shows literary artistry, but also something that might well be called the poetics of the Jewish novels. Indeed, it is interesting to notice that the characterisation of women shows a certain coherent development from the DtrE to the novelistic edition, and finally to the Jewish novels. The motif of the wise women appears in the Tamar episode and the woman from Tekoa ("SN"), and in the Abigail episode (the revised HDR), and we have assigned the former to the DtrE and the latter to the novelistic edition. The continuity be-

---

**87** Rofé, "The Battle of David and Goliath," 126–131.
**88** Schulte, *Entstehung*, 92.
**89** Steven McKenzie, *The Trouble with Kings*, 81–100; Albertz, *Israel in Exile*, 277–8; Römer, *The So-Called Deuteronomistic History*, 153–155.

tween these two is affirmed by the similarity between Abigail's speech and Tamar's and their mentioning *nabal*,[90] but there are important differences between Abigail and Tamar. Although some commentators have argued that Tamar is the main character – "the Wise Woman" of the episode – she remains mostly a passive character. She protests Amnon's נְבָלָה, but is unable to do anything against him. The woman from Tekoa is more active in that she challenges the king with clever stories, and yet, it is Joab who put all the words into her mouth (2Sam 14:19). Besides, Würthwein takes the episode as "wisdom-insertion (*weisheitlicher Einschub*)", while R. Bickert speculates that it is a post-DtrN addition.[91] There is therefore a possibility that the story of the Tekoite was a post-exilic addition, perhaps by the same novelistic redactor. In any case, Abigail shows a clear difference from both Tamar and the woman from Tekoa. She takes the initiative in doing what is necessary, and her husband Nabal does not know anything. She truly comes at the centre of the stage, and the development of female characters reaches its climax when the Jewish novels created characters like Esther and Judith. Possibly, although it is not sensible to give a precise dating, we might be able to speculate that the development of female characterization was as follows: Tamar in the "SN" was the earliest, and the woman from Tekoa was an insertion from the late Babylonian period (DtrE). Abigail and Esther came from the early Persian period, and Judith from the late Persian or Greek period. In the Greek period, the story of the wise women is followed by the popularity of the personified "Lady Wisdom" in Proverbs 8–9 and Wisdom of Solomon.

The HDR's novelistic character can also be made clearer, if we understand why the revision was done mostly to the HDR, while both the "SN" and the HDR are wonderful stories about David that might well have attracted the reader. It is indeed curious why the novelistic redactor left the "SN" almost untouched, and one may well argue that one should either hold that both the HDR and the "SN" went through a novelistic revision, and thus both are basically Persian works, or abandon the whole idea of the Persian revision. However, there are a couple of reasons for the limited revision. First, the "SN" was already a well-structured story that does not allow much interference. The reviser may well have recognized that this was a work of genius, on which he could not

---

**90** See J. Hoftijzer, "David and the Tekoite Woman," *VT* 20 (1970): 419–444 (424–427); Gunn, *The Story of King David*, 42–43; R. Bickert, "Die List Joabs und der Sinneswandel Davids. Eine dtr bearbeitete Einschaltung in die Thronfolgeerzählung 2 Sam 14,2–22," in *Studies in the Historical Books of the OT*, ed. John A. Emerton (Leiden: Brill, 1979): 30–51 (42ff).
**91** Würthwein, "Erzählung," 67–68; Bickert, "Die List Joabs und der Sinneswandel Davids," 50–51.

do much to improve. Secondly, if the author was someone who was uneasy about Nehemiah's nationalistic policies, as we have proposed, and wanted to get his message across through the revision, he must have felt less need to work on the "SN", because David here is already a mixture of virtue and vice. For his intention, the author would do better by advertising the "SN" rather than fiddling with it. Finally and more importantly, the revision was limited to the HDR, because the author thought that the HDR looked more congenial to the literary conventions of the time, and would be more appealing to his contemporaries. In the Persian period, stories about someone who rose from the bottom to high rank in the court were popular, and in the biblical literature, we find examples like Joseph, Daniel and Mordecai/Esther. Since the "success story" was a popular theme in the Persian period, the reviser might well have thought that the story of David's rise to the throne would be more enjoyable to the potential reader. Moreover, after the DtrE, the HDR already had several elements that would be appealing to a contemporary. For instance, it had a *senex iratus* or "blustering old man"[92] like Samuel (1Sam 15) or Saul (1Sam 22:7–8), and the motif that "everybody loves David (1Sam 18:12–16)".[93] It was much easier and more promising for the reviser to work on the HDR rather than on the "SN", and that was another reason why the HDR, not the "SN" received more novelistic revision.

Another characteristic of this redactor from the mid-5th century that makes the redactional work distinct from the DtrE is that the redactor seems to have brought back the materials that had been removed or left out by the DtrE, even if this would water down the pro-Davidic tendency. For instance, the MT expansion in 1Sam 17–18 might have been available for the DtrE, but as we saw earlier, the DtrE either did not include it, or even deliberately omitted it. It seems that it only came back to where it is now, when the novelistic editor brought it back again. This explains well why the MT-plus looks older, but not included in the shorter version found in the LXX.[94] Similarly, 2Sam 21 might

---

**92** According to Wills, Nebuchadnezzar in Daniel uses the motif of a *senex iratus*. See Wills, *Jewish Novel*, 48–49.

**93** See above, 138 –139.

**94** The following process can be speculated. Before Hezekiah created the original HDR, there were at least two different David traditions: one begins with 16:14, and the other with 17:12. Hezekiah took the former (David Tradition A) for his HDR, and left the tradition beginning with 17:12 (David Tradition B) in the library. Perhaps, Hezekiah took the David Tradition A for the introduction of his HDR, in order to highlight the initial friendship between David and Saul, not the least the image of David helping troubled Saul. At any rate, during the deuteronomistic expansion, the David Tradition B was taken up again, but the redactor smoothed out the combined one by excluding certain verses. Then this shorter version was translated into Greek.

have been removed by the DtrE from where it originally had been, to avoid the impression that David killed all the descendants of Saul except Jonathan's lame son Mephibosheth. This however was brought back in the post-exilic period along with another narrative that is not so favourable to David (2Sam 24).[95] The reviser was even more interested in collecting as many narratives as possible than the DtrE who rather selectively incorporated narratives into the History.

Finally, the novelistic edition shows an even more open perspective than the DtrE in both religious and political terms. The DtrE, although it tries to accommodate the opposition on the importance of the cultic centre and religious rules, basically followed the deuteronomistic law. The novelistic redactor, however, shows less interest in such things, and also some caution against too much reliance on cultic matters. In fact, through the addition and the revision of earlier traditions, the novelistic redactor seems to suggest that even religious practice that transgresses the deuteronomic law can do some good. For instance, Michal uses Teraphim that were condemned from the Josianic reform (2Kings 23:24) and even in the Persian period (Zech 10:2), but saves the future king David. The woman at En-dor, although Deut 18:11 forbade any consultation of the spirits of the dead (אוב), is described rather humanely, especially when she offers a motherly care to the terrified king. If there was a post-exilic revision of the Ark Narrative as Van Seters argues, the point is made even clearer. The novelistic reviser added the account of Uzzah's incomprehensible death in 2Sam 6:6–14 and the identification of Obededom as a Gittite, and sent the message to the reader that too much focus on cultic matters could be dangerous, and God blesses even foreigners if He wants. I would not go, however, as far as Van Seters who interprets this as an anti-messianic tendency of the redactor.[96] Nonetheless, it seems fairly clear that the redactor was from among those who were uncomfortable with the Davidic/Judean exclusivism that we come across in Ezra/ Nehemiah and in the DtrN. This author was neither anti-Davidic nor anti-Nehemiah, but certainly disapproving of a nationalistic and narrow-minded mentality.

Then, who was this novelistic redactor? As often is the case, the answer to this question will be an intellectual guess at best, and often sheer fantasy. Nonetheless, I would like to propose, to stimulate further discussion, that the author came from the "nobles (חורים)" mentioned in Neh 4:8,13–15; 5; 6:17–19; 13:15–17.

---

Finally, the novelistic redactor brought in all the omitted, and the longer version which we find in MT was created. Cf. Aurelius, "Wie David ursprünglich zu Saul kam (1Sam 17)," 60–64.

**95** Campbell assigns 2Sam 21–24 to what he calls "the third wave" in the traditions about David, and he believes that this brought "a critical edge" to the picture of David. See Campbell, "2 Samuel 21–24. The Enigma Factor," in *For and Against David*, eds. Auld and Eynikel, 347–358.
**96** Van Seters, *Biblical Saga*, 238–241.

These nobles were in the leading position of Yehud, and when Nehemiah launched his nationalistic policy, they showed willingness to work with him. Nehemiah was not totally happy with these nobles, especially because they continued to correspond with Nehemiah's enemy Tobiah. Nonetheless, they maintained a relationship, and from time to time the nobles tried to reconcile Nehemiah and Tobiah (Neh 6:17–19). As Grabbe noted, the nobles "attempted to get along with individuals so different as Nehemiah and Tobiah. This fits their role as a group who took seriously their responsibility of leadership in the community. On the whole, they appear to have taken a rather more cosmopolitan view of matters than Nehemiah and his followers."[97] Indeed, the theme which runs through the HDR as we have it seems to be compatible with such a cosmopolitan and sapiential character of the author. The author might have thought that neither Nehemiah nor Tobiah is perfect, and attempted to show that "the decline and fall" is an essential human condition, and any kind of black-and-white view is to be avoided.

But were the nobles able to do such redactional work, when they were careful not to displease Nehemiah and his followers? Here we are reminded that there was a time slot when the redactional work was actually possible. According to Neh 5:12; 13:6, Nehemiah stayed in Jerusalem for 12 years, and left Jerusalem in 433 BCE. When he came back to Jerusalem again, he discovered that a certain Eliashib prepared a room for Tobiah "in the courts of the house of God". This infuriated Nehemiah on his return; the household furniture of Tobiah was thrown out, and the chambers were cleansed (Neh 13:7–9). This incident indicates that when Nehemiah left Jerusalem in 433, the nobles attempted to overturn or mitigate Nehemiah's confrontational policy, and brought Nehemiah's enemies back to the centre of the scene. One may well imagine that the nobles' reconciliatory measures included literary work, and Eliashib and his circle might have attempted a revision of the HDR and even of Samuel-Kings.

The novelistic revision of the HDR and other parts in the books of Samuel seems to have had greater consequences than the reviser had imagined. For these revisers, the redactional work was just a re-touch to the Jewish tradition to alleviate Nehemiah's exclusivism. However, their work was followed by two totally different responses. The first is the birth of the Jewish novel in its proper sense. The poetics whose seed we discovered in the revised HDR now became the central motif in Daniel, Esther, Tobit, and others. The story of a vulnerable hero (ine) who overcomes difficulties in a hostile environment and saves the nation was so popular that no story could do without it. One might see the difference

---

97 Grabbe, *A History of the Jews and Judaism*, 310–11.

between the revised HDR and the Jewish novels of course. In these Jewish novels, the relationship between Jews and foreigners is depicted as more dangerous, while in the HDR, the perspective is more universalistic. Nonetheless, the default position in these Jewish novels is still that Jews and pagans get along, and the tension is seen as an exception. Otherwise, one cannot imagine that a Jew becomes the highest official (Daniel) or the queen (Esther) in the courts of the foreign power. The universalistic perspective of the novelistic HDR might have gone through some adaptation due to the growing hostility, but it continued to underlie the Jewish novels.

A development in the opposite direction is the creation of an alternative history of Israel by the Chronicler. It is still curious why the Chronicler wrote the whole history over again, and it is not sufficient to say that the intention was to explain the older traditions to the people in the 4th century. I find it more plausible that an elitist group in the 4th century found the Deuteronomistic History contaminated with entertaining narratives, and its ideology too obscured. The Chronicler's discontent with the novelistic HDR can be read from his almost complete omission of the record of David's early years, and his unambiguously pro-Davidic and pro-cultic view is from numerous additions, not least of the cultic passages. He might have thought that the "official" history has lost its proper sense of history and ideology, and having been frustrated by the revised Deuteronomistic History, decided to write a new one.[98]

---

98 Except in the case of the Torah, the concept of scriptural authority in the Second Temple Period was open, and some biblical stories were rewritten. In rewriting, the author's intention was one of the main reasons for omissions, changes, and additions. See Sidnie White Crawford, "The Rewritten Bible at Qumran," in *The Hebrew Bible and Qumran*, ed. James H. Charlesworth (Texas: Bibal Press, 1998):173–195; Erkki Koskenniemi and Pekka Lindqvist, "Rewritten Bible, Rewritten Stories: Methodological Aspects," in *Rewritten Bible Reconsidered. Proceedings of the Conference in Karkku, Finland, August 24–26 2006*, eds. Antti Laato and Jacques van Ruiten (Åbo Akademi University: Eisenbrauns, 2008): 11–39.

# Conclusion

To summarize the outcomes of our studies in this monograph, the pre-deutero-nomistic HDR begins with 1Sam 16:14 and ends with 2Sam 5:3, and this was per-haps composed in the Hezekian period as "persuasion literature" with a view to supporting Hezekiah's attempt to incorporate the northern kingdom into Judah, not long after the fall of Samaria. The composition might have been intended to persuade the northerners that they should join Judah in fighting against, or in seeking independence from, the Assyrians, especially because Hezekiah, a de-scendant of David, is the legitimate successor of the founder of the northern kingdom. Additionally, I have proposed that this work, which I have also called "the HDR proper", was incorporated into the Deuteronomistic History by the late exilic Deuteronomist, in order to make the point that the restoration of the Da-vidic monarchy and the Jerusalem temple were essential for the restored Israel. This late exilic deuteronomistic redaction was initiated by the hope of restora-tion, and influenced by a growing interest in storytelling in the literary atmos-phere of the time. Perhaps, this is when the attempt to create a story about David covering his entire life span was made for the first time. Finally, I suggest-ed the possibility that in the post-exilic period, the story of David's rise went through another major redaction and was given its final shape. The redactional work seems to have been motivated, partly by a certain unease among a group of leaders about Nehemiah's nationalistic policy, and partly by the "novelistic im-pulse" that was sprouting at the time. The redactor may have attempted to pro-duce a more enjoyable and less partisan story about the founder David, in order to counterbalance Nehemiah's exclusivism.

It is worth mentioning at this point that these conclusions are reached through a number of judgements on the relevant issues. First, my interpretation of the HDR as a whole was that the *Tendenz* is not unambiguously pro-Davidic, and therefore the work is not propagandistic, and this made it impossible that the HDR as we have it now can be distinguished from the "SN" without further clarification. The David story cannot be divided into two independent self-con-tained sources on the basis of their clearly distinct *Tendenzen*. Second, the HDR as a whole however is stylistically different from the "SN", in that the latter is characterized by its more or less coherent, "deadpan style", while the former shows a mixture of rather a simple report-like style and a novelistic style. This made it reasonable to assume the literary independence between the HDR and the "SN", although the stylistic mixture found in the HDR needs an explanation. Third, the novelistic style found in the HDR resembles the later Jewish novels, and this made it plausible that there was a redactional work whose literary quality might anticipate later works such as Esther and the story of Susanna. Fourth, thematically, both the HDR and the "SN" deal with the fall and rise of a king, and this made it likely that a redactional work was attempted to combine them into one continuous narrative about David; and its pro-Davidic and pro-Jerusalem position makes it most likely that the redactional work was deuteronomistic.

Several judgments on the issues that are not directly related to our concern also affected our decisions – our dating in particular, and the way in which the issues are discussed. First, it is assumed that the composition of an extensive narrative work as early as the 10th–9th century, or even the 8th–7th century B.C.E. is unlikely. This prompted us to date the creation of the David story that expands from his rise to his death later rather than earlier. Second, it is taken into consideration that the historical evidence for the existence of David is very thin. Although it seems more plausible that David did exist, the insufficiency of the evidence made us more cautious about believing in the existence of a historically reliable narrative about David in a very early period. Third, it is surmised that a genre develops in such a way that shorter and more straightforward works develop into complex and ambiguous works. This enabled us to posit that there was a major expansion of the Deuteronomistic History which transformed a theological chronicle into a narrative history. Fourth, it is also presumed that an extraordinarily artistic and rich piece of literature was less likely to have arisen in a small marginal part of the world than in the great powers of the world of the time. This inclined us to conjecture that the sophisticated literary artistry in the books of Samuel came after similar literature became popular in Neo-Babylonia or in Persia, and that the narrative expansion is more likely to have begun in the late exilic period. Finally, it is assumed that the meaning of a text is very much determined by the text in its final form. This made us focus more on the nature of the novelistic redaction than on the pursuit of the original document. Indeed, since it is not denied in this monograph that there were some very early materials in the narrative, one may wonder why the Persian redaction, which is relatively insignificant, is given such weight. However, the interest in the "original" document is partly based on the presupposition that the meaning of a text is basically found in the "original" text and later additions are less important, or even corrupt the correct meaning. But if one accepts a more flexible view about the meaning, and holds that the overall meaning of a text can change rather dramatically even by small changes in detail, it can be recognized that too much emphasis on the "original" form is not only futile, but also allows hidden presuppositions to impinge on the scientific investigation. In other words, one may persuade oneself that what one already believed is discovered in the "original" form of the text, and the irregularities or ambiguity of the final form that do not fit with one's previous belief is an outcome of a secondary work that is not worth much attention. Therefore, interest in the final form is important not only for recent literary criticism, but also for historical criticism, as it provides us with a safer entrance to further historical investigations.

The fact that these indirect presuppositions, whose truth value is difficult to estimate unambiguously, affected my decision about the extent of the HDR, led us to think about the nature of historical criticism, and of biblical criticism. Indeed, the need of having an idea about the larger picture, or the "whole", inevitably opens doors to a certain degree of subjectivity, and our studies which consistently emphasise its importance could give the impression that objectivity and scientific rigour are seriously compromised here. One might point more concretely to the fact that the HDR is labelled in this thesis as a "Jewish historical novel", not through a rigorous application of certain methods, but through consideration of various (circumstantial) evidences. The decision was not so much methodical as intuitive, and according to the common view of "science", one might argue, this is a compromise that justifies the postmodern accusation that historical criticism is another type of myth making.

If we look closer at what biblical criticism actually has been doing, and aims to do, however, the impression that objectivity or scientific rigour is seriously compromised in this thesis will fade away. The claim that historical critics aim to give out absolutely objective knowledge – knowledge that is acquired solely from a logical inference – to ordinary people is a misrepresentation of what they, or any scientific researchers, are trying to do. Although a common image of scientific researchers or biblical critics is such that they separate themselves from the object, and describe it with absolute objectivity, it has been long acknowledged that observation cannot be free from the observing subject. In particular, when evidences are ambiguous or conflicting, the decision depends very much on the intuitive judgement of the competent observer, and such a situation is more normative in interpretation of literary texts. Indeed, the 19th century English theologian John Henry Newman already pointed this out, and while discussing the notion of "illative sense", argued that knowledge is often arrived at by a process of inference which is neither inductive nor deductive. Very often, "the practised and experienced mind is able to make a sure divination that a conclusion is inevitable, of which his lines of reasoning do not actually put him in possession."[1] A similar point is made about a century later by Hans-Georg Gadamer, who argued that a competent reader does not interpret a text by applying rules, but perceives the "truth" of the text on the basis of his or her practical

---

[1] John Henry Newman, *An Essay in Aid of a Grammar of Assent*, 3rd edition (London: Burns, Oates, & Co., 1870), 314.

knowledge.[2] In science and biblical criticism, the picture of the subject detaching itself from the object to produce completely neutral knowledge is indeed a myth, and this is not a secret any longer.

The fact that historical critics do not understand themselves as excavators of absolutely objective facts can be shown more clearly, if we look at how source criticism arose and what it was trying to. When biblical scholars started to talk about literary sources, although they were dealing with "brute facts", i.e. objectively existing literary sources, it was neither from empirical observation, such as the archaeological discovery of the sources, nor from historical interests. Rather, it was an explanatory theory designed to explain the apparent inconsistencies and contradictions in biblical narratives.[3] In other words, source-critical statements are not so much concerned with the ontological status of literary sources as with their explanatory function. They were accepted to be true inasmuch as they explained the difficulties in the text, and it is perfectly possible to discern whether a source-critical statement can explain the difficulties better. After all, what biblical critics aim at is not so much to instruct as to "convert" the reader, so that the reader makes better sense out of the text.[4] Biblical critics have tried to provide intellectual guesses on the basis of a limited range of evidence, in order that the readers may understand the biblical text better and not manipulate the meaning for their own benefit. This of course involves the indirect presuppositions of the critics, and the judgement at the end may well largely depend on their personal intuition. As long as biblical critics are transparent about their arguments, however, this cannot be a problem, and most biblical scholars are always open to revision of their own views. As Van Seters recently responded to the postmodern critique of historical criticism,

> [c]ontrary to the (implied) assertion that contemporary historians claim to be "in possession of the Truth," and that it is only postmodernists that give up this claim, nothing could be a greater distortion of what science and historical criticism is all about. Indeed, it was precisely historical criticism who centuries ago challenged the final Truth of the biblical literalists and has continued to do so to this day.[5]

In short, historical critics do not aim at creating a different type of myth, nor at enlightening the ignorant reader with absolute knowledge. They provide various tools to help the reader to make sense of the ancient texts which have been enor-

---

**2** Gadamer, *Truth and Method*, 19–20.
**3** Barton, *Nature*, 22, 62–63.
**4** Thomas S. Kuhn, *The Structure of Scientific Revolutions*, 2nd edition (Chicago: University of Chicago Press, 1970), 148, 151–152.
**5** Van Seters, "A Response," 8–9.

mously significant to many people, and allow therefore their theories to be modified and sometimes discarded completely. Admittedly, the common misunderstanding about historical criticism and biblical criticism was caused, or at least worsened, by insufficient theoretical reflection on what they are actually doing, and I hope that this monograph is an example of self-reflective historical criticism, by making various direct and indirect presuppositions more transparent.

Since the monograph has two foci – theoretical and historical-critical – the limitations are evident, and further investigations are necessary. In particular, further research and reflection is needed on whether some of the "indirect presuppositions" could be clarified. For instance, one needs to investigate more about scribal practice in ancient Israel, especially in the 10th–8th century. If the composition of an extensive narrative was indeed possible at this time period, our late dating should be reconsidered. It is also essential to do more research on the narratives in the Neo-Babylonian and in the Persian period. The study on their characteristic features and narrative techniques will help us to clarify the development of the biblical narratives. Finally, since we concluded that the pre-deuteronomistic HDR existed, more study on this Hezekian work is necessary. Although it requires a very careful approach, the composition of the HDR proper can be another topic for further research. Despite these shortcomings, however, the monograph attempted to deal with a series of difficult issues surrounding the composition of the books of Samuel, and I hope that it will enhance further discussions about one of the finest Hebrew narratives in the Bible.

# Bibliography

Ackerman, Susan. "The Personal is Political: Covenantal and Affectionate Love ('ĀHĒB, 'AHĂBÂ) in the Hebrew Bible." *VT* 52 (2002): 437–458.

Ackroyd, Peter R. *Exile and Restoration.* London: SCM Press, 1968.

Adam, Klaus-Peter. *Saul und David in der judäischen Geschichtsschreibung. Studien zu 1 Samuel 16–2 Samuel 5.* Tübingen: Mohr Siebeck, 2007.

——, "Nocturnal Intrusions and Divine Interventions on Behalf of Judah. David's Wisdom and Saul's Tragedy in 1 Samuel 26." *VT* 59 (2009): 1–33.

Aejmelaeus, Anneli. "Text-History of the Septuagint and the Hebrew Text in the Books of Samuel." Grinfield Lecture Note (Oxford, February 17–26, 2009).

Ahlström, G. W. "Was David a Jebusite Subject?" *ZAW* 92 (1980): 285–287.

Albertz, Rainer. *Israel in Exile: The History and Literature of the Sixth Century B.C.E.* Atlanta: Society of Biblical Literature, 2003.

Alt, Albrecht. "Zu II Samuel 8:1." *ZAW* 13 (1936): 149–52.

——, *Kleine Schriften zur Geschichte des Volkes Israel III*, 2nd edn. München: Beck, 1968.

Alter, Robert. *The Art of Biblical Narrative.* New York: Basic Books, 1981.

——, *The David Story. A Translation with Commentary of 1 and 2 Samuel.* New York: W. W. Norton, 1999.

Amit, Yairah. "The Saul Polemic in the Persian Period." In *Judah and the Judeans in the Persian Period*, edited by Oded Lipschits and Manfred Oeming, 647–661. Winona Lake: Eisenbrauns, 2006.

Apel, Karl-Otto. "Scientistics, Hermeneutics, Critique of Ideology: An Outline of a Theory of Science from an Epistemological-Anthropological Point of View." In *The Hermeneutical Reader*, edited by Kurt Mueller-Vollmer, 321–345. Oxford: Basil Blackwell, 1986.

Archi, Alfonso. "The Propaganda of Hattušili III." *Studi Miceni Ed Egeo-Anatolici* 14 (1971): 185–215.

Arnold, Bill. "The Amalekite's Report of Saul's Death: Political Intrigue or Incompatible Sources?." *JETS* 32 (1989): 289–298.

Athas, George. *The Tel Dan Inscription: a reappraisal and a new interpretation.* London: T. & T. Clark, 2005.

Auld, A. Graeme. *Kings without Privilege.* Edinburgh: T&T Clark, 1994.

——, *Samuel at the Threshold.* Hants: Ashgate, 2004.

——, and Erik Eynikel, eds. *For and Against David. Story and History in the Books of Samuel.* Leuven: Peeters, 2010.

Aurelius, Erik. "Wie David ursprünglich zu Saul kam (1 Sam 17)." In *Vergegenwärtigung des Alten Testaments: Beiträge zur biblischen Hermeneutik; Festschrift für Rudolf Smend zum 70. Geburtstag*, edited by Christopher Bultmann, Walter Dietrich, and Christoph Levin, 44–68. Göttingen: Vandenhoeck & Ruprecht, 2002.

Bar-Efrat, Shimon. *Narrative Art in the Bible.* Edinburgh: T & T Clark, 2004.

Barr, James. *Comparative Philology and the Text of the Old Testament.* Oxford: Clarendon, 1968.

——, "Story and History in Biblical Theology." *Journal of Religion* 56 (1976): 1–17.

Barton, John. *Reading the Old Testament: Method in Biblical Study*, New Edition. London: DLT, 1996.

——, "Reading the Bible as Literature: Two Questions for Biblical Critics." *Journal of Theology and Literature* 1 (1987): 135–153.

——, "Historical Criticism and Literary Interpretation." In *Crossing the Boundaries*, edited by Stanley E. Porter, Paul Joyce, and David E. Orton, 3–15. Leiden: Brill, 1994.

——, "What is a Book? Modern Exegesis and the Literary Conventions of Ancient Israel.' In *Intertextuality in Ugarit and Israel*, edited by Johannes C. de Moor, 1–14. Leiden: Brill, 1998.

——, "Dating the 'Succession Narrative.'" In *In Search of Pre-exilic Israel*, edited by John Day, 95–106. London/New York: T & T Clark, 2004.

——, *The Nature of Biblical Criticism*. Louisville/London: Westminster John Knox Press, 2007.

Barthélemy, D, and others, *The Story of David and Goliath. Textual and Literary Criticism.* Göttingen: Vandenhoeck & Ruprecht, 1986.

Barthes, Roland. "From Work to Text." In *Textual Strategies. Perspectives in Post-Structuralist Criticism*, edited by Josué V. Harari, 73–81. London: Methuen, 1980.

Barstad, Hans M. "History and the Hebrew Bible." In *Can a 'History of Israel' Be Written?*, edited by Lester L. Grabbe, 37–64. Sheffield: Sheffield Academic Press, 1997.

——, *History and the Hebrew Bible: Studies in Ancient Israel and Ancient Near Eastern Historiography*. Tübingen: Mohr Siebeck, 2008.

Berges, Ulrich. *Die Verwerfung Sauls: Eine thematische Untersuchung*. Würzburg: Echter, 1989.

Bernstein, Richard. *Beyond Objectivism and Relativism*. Philadelphia: Univeristy of Pennsylvania Press, 1983.

Betti, Emilio., "Hermeneutics as the general methodology of the Geistes-wissenschaften." In *Contemporary Hermeneutics: Hermeneutics as Method, Philosophy, and Critique*, edited by Josef Bleicher, 51–94. London: Routledge & Kegan Paul, 1980.

Bickert, R. "Die List Joabs und der Sinneswandel Davids. Eine dtr bearbeitete Einschaltung in die Thronfolgeerzählung 2 Sam 14,2–22." In *Studies in the Historical Books of the OT*, edited by John A. Emerton, 30–51. Leiden: Brill, 1979.

Biddle, Mark E. "The Ancestral Motifs in 1 Samuel 25: Intertextuality and Characterization." *JBL* 121 (2002): 617–638.

Birch, Bruce C. *The Rise of the Israelite Monarchy: The Growth and Development of 1 Samuel 7–15*. Missoula, Mont.: Scholars Press, 1976.

Blenkinsopp, Joseph. "Theme and Motif in the Succession History (2 Sam XI, 2ff) and the Yahwist Corpus." In *Volume du Congrèss, Genève 1965*, 44–57. Leiden: Brill, 1966.

——, "Benjamin Traditions Read in the Early Persian Period." In *Judah and the Judeans in the Persian Period*, edited by Oded Lipschits and Manfred Oeming, 629–645. Winona Lake: Eisenbrauns, 2006.

Blum, Erhard. "Ein Anfang der Geschichtschreibung?" In *Die sogenannte Thronfolgegeschichte Davids: Neue Einsichten und Anfragen*, edited by A. de Pury and T. Römer, 4–37. Göttingen: Vandenhoeck & Ruprecht, 2000.

——, "Von Sinn und Nutzen der Kategorie 'Synchronie' in der Exegese." In *David und Saul im Widerstreit – Diachronie und Synchronie im Wettstreit*, edited by Walter Dietrich, 16–30. Göttingen: Vandenhoeck & Ruprecht, 2004.

Bosworth, David A. "Evaluating King David: Old Problems and Recent Scholarship." *CBQ* 68 (2006): 191–210.

Braaten, Carl E., and Robert W. Jenson, eds. *Reclaiming the Bible for the Church*. Edinburgh: T. & T. Clark, 1996.

Brettler, Marc Zvi. *The Creation of History in Ancient Israel.* London: Routledge, 1995.

—, "The Structure of 1 Kings 1—11." *JSOT* 49 (1991): 87–97.

Brown, F., S. R. Driver, and C. A. Briggs, *A Hebrew and English Lexicon of the Old Testament with an Appendix Containing the Biblical Aramaic.* Oxford: Clarendon Press, 1907.

Brueggemann, Walter. *David's Truth: In Israel's Imagination and Memory,* 2nd edn. Minneapolis: Fortress Press, 2002.

Buccellati, G. *Cities and Nations of Ancient Syria: An Essay on Political Institutions with Special Reference to Israelite Kingdoms.* Rome, University of Rome, 1967.

Budde, Karl. *Die Bücher Samuel.* Tübingen: J.C.B. Mohr, 1902.

Bunimovitz, Shlomo. "How Mute Stones Speak: Interpreting What We Dig Up." *BAR* 21 (1995): 58–67, 96–100.

Campbell, Antony F. *Of Prophets and Kings: A Late Ninth-Century Document (1 Samuel 1–2 Kings 10).* Washington: Catholic Biblical Association, 1986.

—, "Martin Noth and the Deuteronomistic History." In *The History of Israel's Traditions: The Heritage of Martin Noth,* edited by Steven L. McKenzie and M. Patrick Graham, 31—62. Sheffield: Sheffield Academic Press, 1994.

—, *1 Samuel.* Grand Rapids, Michigan: W.B. Eerdmans, 2003.

—, "Form Criticism's Future." In *The Changing Face of Form Criticism for the Twenty-First Century,* edited by Marvin A. Sweeny and Ehud Ben Zvi, 15—31. Grand Rapids: Eerdmans, 2003.

—, "2 Samuel 21–24. The Enigma Factor." In *For and Against David,* edited by Auld and Eynikel, 347–358.

—, and Mark A. O'Brien. *Unfolding the Deuteronomistic History: Origins, Upgrades, Present Text.* Minneapolis: Fortress Press, 2000.

Cancik, Hubert. *Grundzüge der hethitischen und alttestamentlichen Geschichtsschreibung.* Wiesbaden: Harrassowitz, 1976.

Caspari, Wilhelm. "Der Stil des Eingangs der israelitischen Novelle." *ZWT* 53 (1911): 218–253.

Charlesworth, James H., ed. *The Old Testament Pseudepigrapha,* 2 vols. London: DLT, 1985.

Childs, Brevard S. "Interpretation in Faith: The Theological Responsibility of an Old Testament Commentary." *Interpretation* 18 (1964): 432–449.

—, *Biblical Theology in Crisis.* Philadelphia: Fortress Press, 1970.

—, *Introduction to the Old Testament as Scripture.* Philadelphia: Fortress Press, 1979.

Clark, Elizabeth A. *History, Theory, Text: Historians and the Linguistic Turn:* Cambridge, MA: Harvard University Press, 2004.

Conrad, Joachim. "Zum geschichtlichen Hintergrund der Darstellung von Davids Aufstieg." *TLZ* 97 (1972): 321–332.

—, "David's Königtum als Paradoxie: Versuch zu I Sam 21,2—10." In *Gott und Mensch im Dialog. Festschrift für Otto Kaiser zum 80. Geburstag.* Band 1, edited by Markus Witte, 413—424. Berlin: de Gruyter, 2004.

Conroy, Charles. *Absalom, Absalom! Narrative and Language in 2 Sam. 13–20.* Rome: Pontifical Biblical Institute, 1977.

Craig, Hugh. "Stylistic Analysis and Authorship Studies." In *A Companion to Digital Humanities,* edited by Susan Schreibman, Ray Siemens, and John Unsworth, 273—288. Oxford: Blackwell, 2004.

Crawford, Sidnie White. "The Rewritten Bible at Qumran." In *The Hebrew Bible and Qumran,* edited by James H. Charlesworth, 173—195. Texas: Bibal Press, 1998.

Cross, Frank M. *Canaanite Myth and Hebrew Epic.* Cambridge, Mass.: Harvard University Press, 1973.

Crüsemann, Frank. "Zwei alttestamentliche Witze. I Sam 21:11–15 und II Sam 6:16, 20—23." *ZAW* 92 (1980): 215–227.

Cryer, Frederick H. "On the Recently-Discovered 'House of David' Inscription." *SJOT* 8 (1994): 3–19.

——, "King Hadad." *SJOT* 9 (1995): 223–35.

Daube, David. "Typology in Josephus." *JJS* 31 (1980): 18–36.

Davies, Philip R. *Scribes and School. The Canonization of the Hebrew Scriptures.* Louisville: Westminster John Knox Press, 1998.

Day, John, ed. *In Search of Pre-exilic Israel.* London/New York: T & T Clark, 2004.

Delekat, L., "Tendenz und Theologie der David-Salomo-Erzählung." In *Das ferne und nahe Wort: Festschrift Leonhard Rost zur Vollendung seines 70. Lebensjahres am 30. November 1966 gewidmet,* edited by F. Maass, 26—36. Berlin: Alfred Töplemann, 1967.

Derrida, Jacques. "Signature Event Context." In *A Derrida Reader,* edited by Peggy Kamuf, 80—111. New York: Columbia University Press, 1991.

Dick, Michael B. "The 'History of David's Rise to Power' and the Neo-Babylonian Succession Apologies." In *David and Zion: Biblical Studies in Honour of J.J.M. Roberts,* edited by Bernard F. Batto and Kathryn L. Roberts, 12—19. Winona Lake: Eisenbrauns, 2004.

Dietrich, M., O. Loretz, and J. Sanmartin, eds. *Die keilalphabetischen Texte aus Ugarit.* Neukirchen-Vluyn: Neukirchener, 1976.

Dietrich, Walter. *Prophetie und Geschichte: eine redaktionsgeschichtliche Untersuchung zum deuteronomistischen Geschichtswerk.* Göttingen: Vandenhoeck & Ruprecht, 1972.

——, *David, Saul und die Propheten: Das Verhältnis von Religion und Politik nach den prophetischen Überlieferungen vom frühesten Königtum in Israel.* Stuttgart: Kohlhammer, 1992.

——, "Martin Noth and the Future of the Deuteronomistic History." In *The History of Israel's Traditions: The Heritage of Martin Noth,* edited by Steven L. McKenzie and M. Patrick Graham, 153—175. Sheffield: Sheffield Academic Press, 1994.

——, "Die Erzählungen von David und Goliat in 1 Sam 17." *ZAW* 108 (1996): 172–191.

——, *Von David zu den Deuteronomisten: Studien zu den Geschichtsüberlieferungen des Alten Testaments.* Stuttgart: Kohlhammer, 2002.

——, "Die zweifache Verschonung Sauls (ISam 24 und 26). Zur "diachronen Synchronisierung" zweier Erzählungen." In *David und Saul im Widerstreit – Diachronie und Synchronie im Wettstreit,* edited by Walter Dietrich, 232—253. Göttingen: Vandenhoeck & Ruprecht, 2004.

——, ed. *David und Saul im Widerstreit – Diachronie und Synchronie im Wettstreit.* Göttingen: Vandenhoeck & Ruprecht, 2004.

——, *David: Der Herrscher mit der Harfe.* Leipzig: Evangelische Verlagsanstalt, 2006.

——, *The Early Monarchy in Israel: The Tenth Century B.C.E.* Atlanta: Society of Biblical Literature, 2007.

——, "Die Überführung der Lade nach Jerusalem (2 Sam 6): Geschichten und Geschichte." In *For and Against David,* edited by Auld and Eynikel, 235–253.

——, and Hans-Jürgen Dallmeyer. *David – ein Königsweg. Psychoanalytisch-theologischer Dialog.* Göttingen: Vandenhoeck & Ruprecht, 2002.

——, and Thomas Naumann. *Samuelbücher.* Darmstadt: Wissen-schaftliche Buchgesellschaft, 1995.

Dilthey, Wihelm. "The Development of Hermeneutics." In *Wilhelm Dilthey: Selected Writings,* edited and translated by Hans Peter Rickman, 246–263. Cambridge: Cambridge University Press, 1976.

Dines, Jennifer M. *The Septuagint.* London: T & T Clark, 2004.

Donner, Herbert. "Der Redaktor. Überlegungen zum vorkritischen Umgang mit der Heiligen Schrift." *Henoch* 2 (1980): 1–29.

Driver, S. R. *Notes on the Hebrew Text and the Topography of the Books of Samuel.* Oxford: Clarendon Press, 1913.

Eagleton, Terry. *Literary Theory: An Introduction,* 2nd edition. Minnesota: The University of Minnesota Press, 1996.

Edelman, Diana V. *King Saul in the Historiography of Judah.* Sheffield: Sheffield Academic Press, 1991.

——, "Did Saulite-Davidic Rivalry resurface in early Persian Yehud?" In *The Land That I Will Show You: Essays on the History and Archaeology of the Ancient Near East in Honour of J. Maxwell Miller,* edited by J. Andrew Dearman and M. Patrick Graham, 69–91. Sheffield: Sheffield Academic Press, 2001.

Edenburg, Cynthia. "How (Not) To Murder a King: Variations on a Theme in 1 Sam 24; 26." *SJOT* 12 (1998): 64–85.

Ehrlich, Carl S., ed. *Saul in Story and Tradition.* Tübingen: Mohr Siebeck, 2006.

Eissfeldt, Otto. *The Old Testament: an introduction, including the Apocrypha and Pseudepigrapha, and also the works of similar type from Qumran; the history of the formation of the Old Testament,* trans. Peter Ackroyd. Oxford: Basil Blackwell, 1965.

——, "Text-, Stil-, und Literarkritik in den Samuelbüchern." *OLZ* 30 (1927): 657–664.

——, "Noch einmal: Text-, Stil-, und Literarkritik in den Samuelbüchern." *OLZ* 31 (1928): 801–812.

Exum, J. Cheryl. *Tragedy and Biblical Narrative: Arrows of the Almighty.* Cambridge: Cambridge University Press, 1992.

Feldman, Louis H. *Josephus's Interpretation of the Bible.* Berkeley: University of California Press, 1998.

——, "Josephus' View of Saul." In *Saul in Story and Tradition,* edited by Carl S. Ehrlich, 213–244. Tübingen: Mohr Siebeck, 2006.

Ficker, Rudolf. "Komposition und Erzählung: Untersuchungen zur Ladeerzählung (1 S 4–6; 2 S 6) und zur Geshichte vom Aufstieg Davids (1 S 15–2 S 5)." Unpublished thesis. University of Heidelberg, 1977.

Fischer, Alexander A. *Von Hebron nach Jerusalem: Eine redaktionsgeschichtliche Studie zur Erzählung von König David in II Sam 1–5.* Berlin: de Gruyter, 2004.

Fish, Stanley. *Is There a Text in this Class?* Cambridge, Mass.: Havard University Press, 1980.

Flanagan, J. W. "Court History or Succession Narrative? A Study of 2 Sam 9–20 and 1 Kings 1–2." *JBL* 91 (1972): 172–181.

Fokkelman, J. P. *Narrative Art and Poetry in the Books of Samuel,* 4 vols. Assen: Van Gorcum, 1981–1993.

Foresti, F. *The Rejection of Saul in the Perspective of the Deuteronomistic School: A Study of 1 Sm 15 and Related Texts.* Rome: Edizioni del Teresianum, 1984.

Fowler, Alastair. *Kinds of Literature: an Introduction to the Theory of Genres and Modes.* Oxford: Clarendon, 1985.

Freedman, David Noel., ed. *The Leningrad Codex: A Facsimile Edition*. Grand Rapids, Michigan: Wm. B. Eerdmans, 1998.

Friedman, Richard Elliot. *The Hidden Book in the Bible*. London: Profile, 1999.

Frolov, Serge. "Succession Narrative: A 'Document' or a Phantom?" *JBL* 121 (2002): 81–104.

Frontain, R.-J. "The Trickster Tricked: Strategies of Deception and Survival in the David Narrative." In *Mappings of the Biblical Terrain: The Bible as Text*, edited by V. Tollers and J. Maier, 10–192. Lewisburg, PA: Bucknell University Press, 1990.

Frye, Northrop. *The Great Code: the Bible and Literature*. London: Routlegde & Kegan Paul, 1982.

Gadamer, Hans-Georg. *Truth and Method*. 2$^{nd}$ edn; London: Continuum, 1989.

——, "The Universality of the Hermeneutical Problem." In *Philosophical Hermeneutics*, translated & edited by David E. Linge, 3–17. Berkeley: University of California Press, 1976.

——, "On the Scope and Function of Hermeneutical Reflection." In *Philosophical Hermeneutics*, translated & edited by David E. Linge, 18–43. Berkeley: University of California Press, 1976.

Gadd, C. J. "The Harran Inscriptions of Nabonidus." *Anatolian Studies* 8 (1958): 35–92.

Garsiel, Moshe. *The First Book of Samuel: A Literary Study of Comparative Structures, Analogies and Parallels*. Ramat Gan: Bar Ilan University Press, 1985.

Gesenius, W. *Gesenius' Hebrew Grammar*, trans. A. E. Cowley. Oxford: Oxford University Press, 1910.

Gnuse, Robert. "From Prison to Prestige: The Hero Who Helps a King in Jewish and Greek Literature." *CBQ* 72 (2010): 31–45.

Gordon, Cyrus H. *Ugaritic Textbook*. AnOr 38, Rome: Pontifical Biblical Institute, 1965.

Gordon, Robert P. "David's Rise and Saul's Demise." *TynB* 31 (1980): 37–64.

——, *I & II Samuel*. Exeter: Paternoster, 1986.

——, "In Search of David: The David Tradition in Recent Study." In *Faith, Tradition and History: Old Testament Historiography in its Near Eastern Context*, edited by A. R. Millard, J. K. Hoffmeier, and D. W. Baker, 285–298. Winona Lake: Eisenbrauns, 1994.

Grabbe, Lester L. *Yehud: A History of the Persian of Judah*. Vol. 1, *A History of the Jews and Judaism in the Second Temple Period*. London/New York: T & T Clark, 2004.

Gray, John. *I & II Kings: A Commentary*, 3$^{rd}$ fully revised edition. London: SCM Press, 1977.

Gressmann, Hugo. *Die älteste Geschichtsschreibung und Prophetie Israels: von Samuel bis Amos und Hosea*. Göttingen: Vandenhoeck & Ruprecht, 1921.

Grønbaek, Jakob H. *Die Geschichte vom Aufstieg Davids (1.Sam.15–2.Sam.5): Tradition und Komposition*. Copenhagen: Prostant Apud Munksgaard, 1971.

Gross, Walter, Hubert Irsigler, and Theodor Seidl, eds. *Text, Methode und Grammatik: Wolfgang Ricther zum 65. Geburtstag* . St. Ottilien: EOS, 1991.

Grottanelli, Cristiano. *Kings and Prophets: Monarchic Power, Inspired Leadership, and Sacred Text in Biblical Narrative*. New York: OUP, 1999.

Gunkel, Hermann., *Genesis*, 6$^{th}$ edition. Göttingen: Vandenhoeck & Ruprecht, 1964.

Gunn, David. *The Story of King David: Genre and Interpretation*. Sheffield: JSOT Press, 1976.

——, *The Fate of King Saul: An Interpretation of a Biblical Story*. Sheffield: JSOT Press, 1980.

Gütterbock, Hans H. "Hittite Historiography: a Survey." In *History, Historiography, and Interpretation*, edited by Hayim Tadmor and Moshe Weinweld, 21–35. Jerusalem: Magnes, 1983.

Habermas, Jürgen. "A Review of Gadamer's *Truth and Method*.' In *The Hermeneutic Tradition. From Ast to Ricoeur*, edited by Gayle L. Ormiston and Alan D. Schrift, 213—244. New York: SUNY, 1990.

Hagan, H. "Deception as Motif and Theme in 2 Sam 9 – 20; 1 Kgs 1 – 2." *Bib* 60 (1979): 301 – 26.

Hagelia, Hallvard. *The Dan Debate: the Tel Dan Inscription in recent research*. Sheffield: Sheffield Phoenix, 2009.

Hallo, William W., ed. *The Context of Scripture: canonical compositions, monumental inscriptions, and archival documents from the biblical world*, 3 vols. Leiden: Brill, 2003.

Halpern, Baruch. *The First Historians: The Hebrew Bible and History*. New York, 1988.

——, *David's Secret Demons: Messiah, Murderer, Traitor, King*. Grand Rapids, Michigan: W.B. Eerdmans, 2001.

Hardmeier, Christof. "Hermeneutik und Grammatik. Zum Zusammenhang von Sprachbeschreibung und Textwahrnehmung." In *Text, Methode und Grammatik: Wolfgang Richter zum 65. Geburtstag*, edited by Walter Gross, Hubert Irsigler, and Theodor Seidl, 119—140. St. Ottilien: EOS, 1991.

Hasel, G. F. "נָגִיד." In *TDOT*, IX, 187 – 202.

Hausmann, J. "צלח", In *TDOT*, XII (2003), 382 – 385.

Hayes, John H., and J. Maxwell Miller, eds. *Israelite & Judaean History*. London: SCM Press, 1977.

Heaton, E. W. "The Joseph Saga." *ET* 59 (1947/48): 134 – 136.

Heidegger, Martin. *Being and Time*. Oxford: Blackwell, 1962.

Heinrich, André. *David und Klio. Historiographische Elemente in der Aufstiegsgeschichte Davids und im Alten Testament*. New York/Berlin: de Gruyter, 2009.

Hentschel, Georg. *Saul: Schuld, Reue und Tragik eines "Gesalbten"*. Leipzig: Evangelische Verlagsanstalt, 2003.

Herrmann, Siegfried. "The Royal Novella in Egypt and Israel. A Contribution to the History of Genre in the Historical Books of the Old Testament." In *Reconsidering Israel and Judah*, edited by Knoppers and McConville, 493 – 515.

Hertzberg, Hans Wilhelm. *I & II Samuel: a Commentary*. London: SCM Press, 1964.

Hirsch, Jr., E. D. *Validity in Interpretation*. New Haven: Yale University Press, 1967.

——, *The Aims of Interpretation*. Chicago: University of Chicago Press, 1976.

——, "Meaning and Significance Reinterpreted." *Critical Inquiry* 11 (1984): 202 – 225.

Ho, Y.S. (Craig). "Conjectures and Refutations: Is 1 Samuel xxxi 1 – 13 really the source of 1 Chronicles x 1 – 12?" *VT* 45 (1995): 82 – 106.

Hoffner, Jr., Harry A. "Propaganda and Political Justification in Hittite Historiography." In *Unity and Diversity: Essays in the History, Literature, and Religion of the Ancient Near East*, edited by H. Goedicke and J. J. M. Roberts, 49—62. Baltimore/London: Johns Hopkins, 1975.

Hoftijzer, J. "David and the Tekoite Woman." *VT* 20 (1970): 419 – 444.

Hoy, David Couzens. *The Critical Circle: Literature, History, and Philosophical Hermeneutics*. Berkeley: University of California Press, 1978.

——, "Heidegger and the hermeneutic turn." In *The Cambridge Companion to Heidegger*, edited by Charles B. Guignon, 170—194. Cambridge: Cambridge University Press, 1993.

Humphreys, W. Lee. "The Tragedy of King Saul: A Study of the Structure of 1 Samuel 9—31." *JSOT* 6 (1978): 18 – 27.

——, "The Rise and Fall of King Saul: A Study of an Ancient Narrative Stratum in 1 Samuel."
    *JSOT* 18 (1980): 74–90.
——, "From Tragic Hero to Villain: A Study of the Figure of Saul and the Development of 1
    Samuel." *JSOT* 22 (1982): 95–117.
——, "Novella." In *Saga, Legend, Fable, Tale, Novella*, edited by Coats, 82–96.
Iser, Wolfgang. *The Act of Reading*. London: Routledge & Kegan Paul, 1978.
Ishida, Tomoo. *The Royal Dynasties in Ancient Israel: A Study on the Formation and
    Development of Royal Dynastic Ideology*. Berlin/New York: W. de Gruyter, 1977.
——, "The Succession Narrative and Esarhaddon's Apology: A Comparison." In *Ah, Assyria:
    Studies in Assyrian History and Ancient Near Eastern Historiography Presented to Hayim
    Tadmor*, edited by Mordechai Cogan and Israel Eph'al, 166–173. Jerusalem: Magnes,
    1991.
Jamieson-Drake, David W. *Scribes and Schools in Monarchic Judah: A Socio-Archaeological
    Approach*. Sheffield: Almond, 1991.
Jarick, John. *2 Chronicles*. Sheffield: Phoenix, 2007.
Jason, H. "The Story of David and Goliath: A Folk Epic?" *Bib* 60 (1979): 36–70.
Jepsen, Alfred. *Die Quellen des Königsbuches*. Halle Salle: M. Nierneyer, 1953.
Jewett, Garth S., and Victoria O'Donnell. *Propaganda and Persuasion,* 3rd edition. London:
    Sage, 1999.
Jobling, David. *1 Samuel*. Collegeville: The Liturgical Press, 1998.
Johnson, Sara Raup. *Historical Fictions and Hellenistic Jewish Identity*. Berkeley: University of
    California Press, 2004.
Josephus, Flavius. *Judean Antiquities,* Books 5–7. Translation and Commentary by Christoper
    Begg. Leiden: Brill, 2001.
Kaiser, Otto. "David und Jonathan: Tradition, Redaktion, und Geschichte in 1 Sam. 16–20.
    Ein Versuch." *Ephemerides Theologicae Lovanienses* 66 (1990): 281–296.
Kessler, John. "Sexuality and Politics: The Motif of the Displaced Husband in the Books of
    Samuel." *CBQ* 62 (2000): 409–23.
Klein, Johannes. *David versus Saul. Ein Beitrag zum Erzählsystem der Samuelbücher*.
    Stuttgart: Kohlhammer, 2002.
Klein, Ralph W. *1 Samuel*. Waco, Texas: Word Books, 1983.
Knauf, E. A. "Does 'Deuteronomistic Historiography' (DtrH) Exist?" In *Israel Constructs its
    History: Deuteronomistic Historiography in Recent Research*, edited by A. de Pury, T.
    Römer and J.-D. Macchi, 388–98. Sheffield: Sheffield Academic Press, 2000.
Knoppers, Gary N. "Greek Historiography and the Chronicler's History: A Reexamination." *JBL*
    122 (2003): 627–650.
——, and J. Gordon McConville, eds. *Reconsidering Israel and Judah: Recent Studies on the
    Deuteronomistic History*. Winona Lake: Eisenbrauns, 2000.
Koch, Klaus. *The Growth of the Biblical Tradition: The Form-Critical Method*. New York:
    Charles Scribner's Sons/Macmillan, 1988.
Kooij, Arie van der. "The Story of David and Goliath: The Early History of Its Text." *ETL* 68
    (1992): 118–131.
Koole, Jan L. *Jesaja III*. Kampen: Kok Pharos, 1997–2001.
Korpel, Marjo C. A., and Josef M. Oesch, eds. *Delimitation Criticism: A New Tool in Biblical
    Scholarship*. Assen: Van Gorcum, 2000.
Koskenniemi, Erkki, and Pekka Lindqvist, "Rewritten Bible, Rewritten Stories: Methodological
    Aspects." In *Rewritten Bible Reconsidered. Proceedings of the Conference in Karkku,*

*Finland, August 24–26 2006,* edited by Antti Laato and Jacques van Ruiten, 11–39. Åbo Akademi University: Eisenbrauns, 2008.

Kratz, Reinhard, *Die Komposition der erzählenden Bücher des Alten Testaments.* Göttingen: Vandenhoeck & Ruprecht, 2000.

——, "Der literarische Ort des Deuteronomiums." In *Liebe und Gebot. Studien zum Deuteronomium. Festschrift für Lothar Perlitt,* edited by Reinhard Kratz and H. Spieckermann, 101–120. Göttingen: Vandenhoeck & Ruprecht, 2000.

——, "Der vor-und der nachpriesterschriftliche Hexateuch." In *Abschied vom Jahwisten. Die Composition des Hexateuch in der jüngsten Diskussion,* edited by J. Ch. Bertz, K. Schmid, & M. Witte, 295–323. Berlin: de Gruyter, 2002.

——, "Memoria, Memorabilia, and Memoirs: Notions of the Past in Northwest Semitic Inscriptions of the First Millennium BCE." In *The Past in the Past. Concepts of Past Reality in Ancient Near Eastern and Early Greek Thought,* edited by Hans M. Barstad and Pierre Briant, 111–131. Oslo: Novus Press, 2009.

Krintezki, L. "Ein Beitrag zur Stilanalyse der Goliathperikope (1 Sam. 17, 1–18, 5)." *Bib* 54 (1973): 187–236.

Kristeva, Julia. *Revolution in Poetic Language.* New York: Columbia University Press, 1984.

——, *The Kristeva Reader,* edited by Toril Moi. Oxford: Basil Blackwell, 1986.

Kuhn, Thomas S. *The Structure of Scientific Revolutions,* 2nd edition. Chicago: University of Chicago Press, 1970.

Kunz, Andreas. "'Soll das Schwert denn ewig fressen?' Zur Erzählintention von II Samuel 2. 8–32." In *Erzählte Geschichte: Beiträge zur narrativen Kultur im alten Israel,* edited by Rüdiger Lux, 53–79. Neukirchen-Vluyn: Neukirchener, 2000.

Lapsely, Jacqueline E. "Feeling Our Way: Love for God in Deuteronomy." *CBQ* 65 (2003): 350–369.

Lateiner, Donald. "Historiography: Greco-Roman." In *ABD,* III, 212–219.

Lawton, Robert B. "Saul, Jonathan, and the 'Son of Jesse'." *JSOT* 58 (1993): 35–46.

Lemche, Niels Peter. "David's Rise." *JSOT* 10 (1978): 2–25.

——, *Prelude to Israel's Past: Background and Beginnings of Israelite History and Identity.* Peabody: Hendrickson, 1998.

Levenson, Jon D. "1 Samuel 25 as Literature and as History." *CBQ* 40 (1978): 11–28.

——, *Esther.* Louisville: Westminster John Knox, 1997.

Lindström, Fredrik. *God and the Origin of Evil: A Contextual Analysis of Alleged Monistic Evidence in the Old Testament.* Lund: CWK Gleerup, 1983.

Liss, Hanna. "The Innocent King." In *Saul in Story and Tradition,* edited by Carl S. Ehrlich, 245–260. Tübingen: Mohr Siebeck, 2006.

Longman III, Tremper. *Fictional Akkadian Autobiography.* Winona Lake: Eisenbrauns, 1991.

Lozovvy, Joseph. *Saul, Doeg, Nabal, and the "Son of Jesse".* New York/London: T & T Clark, 2009.

Lux, Rüdiger, ed. *Erzählte Geschichte: Beiträge zur narrativen Kultur im alten Israel* (Neukirchen-Vluyn: Neukirchener, 2000).

Malul, Meir. "Was David involved in the Death of Saul on the Gilboa Mountain?" *RB* 103 (1996): 517–545.

Mason, Rex. *Propaganda and Subversion in the Old Testament.* London: SPCK, 1997.

Mauchline, John. *I and II Samuel.* NCB. London: Oliphants, 1971.

Mayer, W. "Die historische Einordnung der 'Autobiographie' des Idrimi von Alalah." *UF* 27 (1995): 333–350

McCarter, Jr., P. Kyle. *I Samuel*. Anchor Bible 8. New York: Doubleday, 1980.

——, "Apology of David." *JBL* 99/4 (1980): 489–504.

——, *II Samuel*. Anchor Bible 9. New York: Doubleday, 1984.

McCarthy, Dennis. "II Sam 7 and the Structure of the Deuteronomistic History." *JBL* 84 (1980): 131–138.

McKenzie, Steve L. *The Trouble with Kings: The Composition of the Books of Kings in the Deuteronomistic History*. Leiden: Brill, 1991.

——, *King David: A Biography*. Oxford: Oxford University Press, 2000.

——, "The So-Called Succession Narrative." In *Die sogennante Thronfolgegeschichte*, edited by de Pury and Römer, 123–135.

——, "The Trouble with Kingship." In *Israel Constructs its History,* edited by de Pury, Römer and Macchi, 286–314.

——, "Elaborated Evidence for the Priority of 1 Samuel 26." *JBL* 129 (2010): 437–444.

——, and M. Patrick Graham, eds. *The History of Israel's Traditions: The Heritage of Martin Noth*. Sheffield: Sheffield Academic Press, 1994.

Meinhold, Arndt. "Die Gattung der Josephsgeschichte und des Estherbuches: Diasporanovelle I." *ZAW* 87 (1975): 306–324.

——, "Die Gattung der Josephsgeschichte und des Estherbuches: Diasporanovelle II." *ZAW* 88 (1976): 72–93.

Mettinger, Tryggve N. D. *King and Messiah: the Civil and Sacral Legitimation of the Israelite Kings*. Lund: Gleerup, 1976.

Meyers, Carol, and Eric Meyers. *Haggai, Zechariah 1–8*. Garden City, N.Y: Doubleday, 1987.

Mildenberger, F. "Die vordeuteronomistische Saul-Davidüberlieferung.' Unpublished doctoral thesis. University of Tübingen, 1962.

Miller, Jr., P. D., and J. J. M. Roberts. *The Hand of the Lord. A Reassessment of the "Ark Narrative" of 1 Samuel*. Baltimore/London: Johns Hopkins, 1977.

Moberly, R. W. L. *The Bible, Theology, and Faith: A Study of Abraham and Jesus*. Cambridge: Cambridge University Press, 2000.

Montgomery, James A. "The Religion of Flavius Josephus." *JQR* 11 (1920–21): 277–305.

Moor, Johannes C. de., ed. *Intertextuality in Ugarit and Israel*. Leiden: Brill, 1998.

Moran, William L. "Ancient Near Eastern Background of the Love of God in Deuteronomy." *CBQ* 25 (1963): 77–87.

——, "Assurbanipal's Message to the Babylonians *(ABL 301)*, with an Excursus on Figurative *Biltu*." In *Ah, Assyria,* edited by Mordechai Cogan and Israel Eph'al, 305–336.

Moye, Richard H. "In the Beginning: Myth and History in Genesis and Exodus." *JBL* 109 (1990): 577–598.

Mueller-Vollmer, Kurt, ed. *The Hermeneutics Reader*. Oxford: Basil Blackwell, 1986.

Murphy, Frederick J. *Pseudo-Philo: Rewriting the Bible*. New York: Oxford University Press, 1993.

Murray, Donald F. *Divine Prerogative and Royal Pretension. Pragmatics, Poetics and Polemics in a Narrative Sequence about David (2 Samuel 5.17–7.29)*. Sheffield: Sheffield Academic Press, 1998.

Na'aman, Nadav. "A Royal Scribe and his Scribal Products in the Alalakh IV Court." *Oriens Antiquus* 19 (1980): 107–116.

——, "Sources and Composition in the History of David." In *The Origin of the Ancient Israelite States*, edited by Volkmar Fritz and Philip R. Davies, 170—186. Sheffield: Sheffield Academic Press, 1996.

—, "When and How Did Jerusalem Becomes a Great City? The Rise of Jerusalem as Judah's Premier City in the Eighth-Seventh Centuries B.C.E." *BASOR* 347 (2007): 21–56.

Neff, Robert W. "Saga." In *Saga, Legend, Tale, Novella, Fable. Narrative Forms in Old Testament Literature,* edited by G. W. Coats, 17–32. Sheffield: JSOT Press, 1985.

Nelson, Richard. "The Double Redaction of the Deuteronomistic History: The Case is Still Compelling." *JSOT* 29 (2005): 319–337.

Newman, John Henry. *An Essay in Aid of a Grammar of Assent,* 3rd edition. London: Burns, Oates, & Co., 1870.

Nicholson, Sarah. *Three Faces of Saul: An Intertextual Approach to Biblical Tragedy.* Sheffield: Sheffield Academic Press, 2002.

Niditch, Susan. *Oral World and Written Word.* Louisville: Westminster John Knox Press, 1996.

Nihan, Christophe. "Saul among the Prophets (1 Sam 10:10–12 and 19:18–24). The Reworking of Saul's Figure in the Context of the Debate on 'Charismatic Prophecy' in the Persian Era." In *Saul in Story and Tradition,* edited by Ehrlich, 88–118.

Nissinen, Martti. "Die Liebe von David und Jonatan als Frage der modernen Exegese." *Bib* 80 (1999): 250–263.

Nordheim, Eckhard von. "König und Tempel: Der Hintergrund des Tempelbauverbotes in 2 Samuel VII." *VT* 27 (1977): 434–453.

North, Christopher R. *The Second Isaiah: Introduction, Translation and Commentary to Chapters XL-LV.* Oxford: Clarendon Press, 1967.

Noth, Martin. *Überlieferungsgeschichtliche Studien,* 3rd edition. Tübingen: Max Niemeyer, 1967.

—, *Könige.* Neukirchen-Vluyn: Neukirchener Verlag des Erziehungsvereins, 1964-.

O'Brien, Mark A. *The Deuteronomistic History Hypothesis: A Reassessment.* Göttingen: Vandenhoeck & Ruprecht, 1989.

Oded, Bustenay. "Judah and the Exile." In *Isarelite & Judaean History,* edited by John H. Hayes and J. Maxwell Miller, 435–86. London: SCM Press, 1977.

Oesch, Josef M. *Petucha und Setuma: Untersuchungen zu eine überlieferten Gliederung im hebräischen Text des Alten Testaments.* Göttingen: Vandenhoeck & Ruprecht, 1979.

Oller, Gary H. "The Inscription of Idrimi: A Pseudo-autobiography?" In *DUMU-Ł²-ĐUB-BA-A,* edited by Hermann Behrens, Darlene Londing, and Martha T. Roth, 411–417. Philadelphia: Samuel Noah Kramer Fund, University Museum, 1989.

Palmer, Richard E. *Hermeneutics: Interpretative Theory in Schleiermacher, Dilthey, Heidegger, and Gadamer.* Evanston: Northwestern University Press, 1969.

Peckham, Brian. "The Deuteronomistic History of Saul and David." *ZAW* 97 (1985): 190–209.

Pietsch, Michael. *"Dieser is der Sproß Davids…" Studien zur Rezeptionsgeschichte der Nathanverheißung im alttestamentlichen, zwischentestamentlichen und neutestamentlichen Schrifttum.* Neukirchen-Vluyn: Neukirchener, 2003.

Pervo, Richard I. *Profit with Delight.* Philadelphia: Fortress Press, 1987.

Polak, F. "David's Kingship – A Precarious Equilibrium." In *Politics and Theopolitics in the Bible and Postbiblical Literature,* edited by Yair Hoffman, Henning Reventlow Graf, and Benjamin Uffenheimer, 119–147. Sheffield: JSOT Press, 1994.

Porzig, Peter. *Die Lade Jahwes im Alten Testament und in den Texten vom Totem Meer.* Berlin: de Gruyter, 2009.

Polzin, Robert. *1 Samuel.* Part 2, *Samuel and the Deuteronomist: A Literary Study of the Deuteronomic history.* Bloomington: Indiana University Press, 1989.

Popper, Karl R. *The Logic of Scientific Discovery,* Revised Edition. London: Hutchinson, 1968.

Porter, Stanley E., and others, eds. *Crossing the Boundaries: Essays in Biblical Interpretation in honour of Michael D. Goulder.* Leiden: Brill, 1994.

Preuß, Horst Dietrich. "... ich will mit dir sein!" *ZAW* 80 (1968): 139–173.

Pritchard, J. B., ed. *The Ancient Near Eastern Texts Relating to the Old Testament,* 3$^{rd}$ edition. Princeton: Princeton University Press, 1969.

Provan, Iain W. *Hezekiah and the Book of Kings: A Contribution to the Debate about the Composition of the Deuteronomistic History.* Berlin: de Gruyter, 1988.

Pury, A. de., T. Römer and J.-D. Macchi, eds. *Israel Constructs its History: Deuteronomistic Historiography in Recent Research.* Sheffield: Sheffield Academic Press, 2000.

——, and T. Römer, eds. *Die sogenannte Thronfolgegeschichte Davids: Neue Einsichten und Anfragen.* Göttingen: Vandenhoeck & Ruprecht, 2000.

Rad, Gerhard von. "The Beginnings of Historical Writing in Ancient Israel." In *The Problem of the Hexateuch and other essays,* trans. by E. W. Trueman Dicken, 166–204. Edinburgh/London: Oliver & Boyd, 1966.

——, *Old Testament Theology,* 2 vols. London: SCM Press, 1975.

Redford, Donald B. *A Study of the Biblical Story of Joseph (Genesis 37–50).* Leiden: Brill, 1970.

Reis, Pamela Tamarkin. "Killing the Messenger: David's Policy or Politics?" *JSOT* 31 (2006): 167–191.

Rendtorff, Rolf. "Beobachtungen zur altisraelitischen Geschichtsschreibung anhand der Geschichte vom Aufstieg Davids." In *Probleme biblische Theologie,* edited by Hans W. Wolff, 428–439. München: Chr. Kaiser, 1971.

Revell, E. J. "Masoretic Text." in *ABD,* IV, 597–599.

Richter, Wolfgang. *Exegese als Literaturwissenschaft. Entwurf einer alttestamentlichen Literaturtheorie und Methodologie.* Göttingen: Vandenhoeck & Ruprecht, 1971.

Ridout, G. P. "Prose Compositional Techniques in the Succession Narrative (2 Sam 7, 9–10; 1 Kings 1–2)." Unpublished doctoral thesis. GTU, 1971.

Roberts, Jim. "Legal Basis for Saul's Slaughter of the Priests of Nob (1 Samuel 21–22)." *JNSL* 25 (1999): 21–29.

Rofé, Alexander. "The Battle of David and Goliath: Folklore, Theology, Eschatology." In *Judaic Perspectives on Ancient Israel,* edited by J. Neusner, B. A. Levine, and E. S. Frerichs, 117–151. Philadelphia: Fortress Press, 1987.

Römer, Thomas. *The So-Called Deuteronomistic History: A Sociological, Historical and Literary Introduction.* London: T&T Clark, 2007.

——, "The Form-Critical Problem of the So-Called Deuteronomistic History." In *The Changing Face of Form Criticism,* edited by Sweeney and Ben Zvi, 240–252.

Rost, Leonhard. *Die Überlieferung von der Thronnachfolge Davids.* Stuttgart: W. Kohlhammer, 1926. ET, *The Succession to the Throne of David.* Sheffield: Almond Press, 1982.

Rudnig, Thilo Alexander. *Davids Thron: Redaktionskritische Studien zur Geschichte von der Thronnachfolge Davids.* Berlin/New York: Walter de Gruyter, 2006.

Sasson, Jack M. "On Idrimi and Šarruwa the Scribe." In *Studies on the Civilization and Culture of Nuzi and the Hurrians in Honor of Ernest R. Lacheman on His Seventy-fifth Birthday,* edited by M. A. Morrison and D. I. Owen, 188–191. Winona Lake: Eisenbrauns, 1981.

Schleiermacher, Friedrich. *Hermeneutics: The Handwritten Manuscripts.* Missoula: Scholars Press, 1977.

Schmid, Konrad. *Erzväter und Exodus: Untersuchungen zur doppelten Begründung der Ursprünge Israels innerhalb der Geschichtsbücher des Alten Testaments.* Neukirchen-Vluyn: Neukirchener Verlag, 1999.

Schniedewind, William M. *Society and the Promise to David: The Reception History of 2 Samuel 7:1–17.* Oxford: Oxford University Press, 1999.

Schroer, Silvia, and Thomas Staubli. "Saul, David und Jonatan – eine Dreiecksgeschichte? Ein Beitrag zum Thema 'Homosexualität im Ersten Testament'." *BuK* 51 (1996): 15–22.

Schulte, Hannelis. *Die Entstehung der Geschichtsschreibung im alten Israel.* Berlin: de Gruyter, 1972.

Seitz, Christopher R. *Word without End: The Old Testament as Abiding Theological Witness.* Grand Rapids: Eerdmans, 1998.

Smelik, K. A. D. "Hidden Messages in the Ark Narrative." In *Converting the Past: Studies in Ancient Israelite and Moabite Historiography.* Leiden: Brill, 1992, 35—58.

Smend, Rudolf. "The Law and the Nations. A Contribution to Deuteronomistic Tradition History." In *Reconsidering Israel and Judah*, edited by Knoppers and McConville, 95–110.

——, *Die Entstehung des Alten Testaments.* Stuttgart: Kohlhammer, 1984.

Smith, Henry P. *A Critical and Exegetical Commentary on the Books of Samuel.* Edinburgh: T&T Clark, 1899.

Sollberger, Edmond. "The Rulers of Lagaš." *JCS* 21 (1967): 279–291.

Sparks, Kenton. "Propaganda." In *Dictionary of the Old Testament: Historical Books*, edited by Bill T. Arnold and H. G. M. Williamson, 819—825. Leicester: Inter-Varsity, 2005.

——, *Ancient Texts for the Study of the Hebrew Bible. A Guide to the Background Literature.* Peabody: Hendrickson, 2005.

Steiner, R. C. "Papyrus Amherst 63: A New Source for the Language, Literature, Religion, and History of the Arameans." In *Studia Aramaica*, edited by M. J. Geeler, J. C. Greenfield, and M. P. Weitzman, 204—205. New York: Oxford University Press, 1995.

——, and C. F. Nims. "Ashurbanipal and Shamash-shum-ukin: A Tale of Two Brothers form the Aramaic Text in Demotic Script." *RB* 92 (1985): 60–81.

Sternberg, Meir. *The Poetics of Biblical Narrative. Ideological Literature and the Drama of Reading.* Bloomington: Indiana University Press, 1987.

Steuernagel, Carl. *Lehrbuch der Einleitung in das Alte Testament.* Tübingen: J.C.B. Mohr, 1912.

Stoebe, Hans Joachim. "Die Goliathperikope 1 Sam. XVII 1 – XVIII 5 und die Textform der Septuaginta." *VT* 6 (1956): 397–413.

——, *Das erste Buch Samuelis.* Gütersloh: Gütersloher Verlagshaus, 1973.

——, *Das zweite Buch Samuelis.* Gütersloh: Gütersloher Verlagshaus, 1994.

Stolz, Fritz. *Das erste und zweite Buch Samuel.* Zürich: Theologischer Verlag Zürich, 1981.

Stott, Katherine. "Herodotus and the Old Testament. A Comparative Reading of the Ascendancy Stories of King Cyrus and David." *SJOT* 16 (2002): 52–78.

Sturtevant, E.-H., and G. Bechtel, eds. *A Hittite Chrestomathy.* Philadelphia: Linguistic Society of America, 1935.

Sweeney, Marvin A., and Ehud Ben Zvi, eds. *The Changing Face of Form Criticism for the Twenty-First Century.* Grand Rapids: Eerdmans, 2003.

Tadmor, Hayim. "Autobiographical Apology in the Royal Assyrian Literature." In *History, Historiography, and Interpretation*, edited by Hayim Tadmor and Moshe Weinfeld, 36—57. Jerusalem: Magnes, 1983.

Taggar-Cohen, Ada. "Political Loyalty in the Biblical Account of 1 Samuel XX-XXII in the Light of Hittite Texts." *VT* 40 (2005): 251–268.

Tengström, S. "נוּחַ", *TDOT*, XIII, 365–402.

Thiselton, Anthony C. *New Horizons in Hermeneutics: The Theory and Practice of Transforming Biblical Reading*. Grand Rapids, Michigan: Zondervan Publishing House, 1992.

Thompson, J. A. "The Significance of the Verb Love in the David-Jonathan Narratives in 1 Samuel." *VT* 24 (1974): 334–338.

Thompson, Thomas L. "'House of David': An Eponymic Referent to Yahweh as Godfather." *SJOT* 9 (1995): 59–74.

——, "Dissonance and Disconnections: Notes on the Bytdwd and Hmlk.hdd Fragments from Tel Dan." *SJOT* 9 (1995): 236–240.

Tollers, V., and J. Maier, eds. *Mappings of the Biblical Terrain: The Bible as Text*. Lewisburg, PA: Bucknell University Press, 1990.

Tov, Emanuel. "The Textual Affiliation of 4QSamᵃ." *JSOT* 14 (1979): 37–53.

——, "The Composition of 1 Samuel 16–18 in the Light of the Septuagint Version." In *Empirical Models for Biblical Criticism*, edited by Jeffrey H. Tigay, 99—130. Philadelphia: University of Pennsylvania Press, 1985.

Tropper, Josef. *Ugaritische Grammatik*. Münster: Ugarit-Verlag, 2000.

Tsumura, David Toshio. *The First Book of Samuel*. Grand Rapids, Michigan: W.B. Eerdmans, 2007.

Ulrich, Eugene Charles. *The Qumran Text of Samuel and Josephus*. Ann Arbor, MI: Scholar Press, 1978.

——, ed. *The Biblical Qumran Scrolls. Transcriptions and Textual Variants*. Leiden/Boston: Brill, 2010.

VanderKam, James C. "Davidic Complicity in the Deaths of Abner and Eshbaal: A Historical and Redactional Study." *JBL* 99/4 (1980): 521–539.

Vanhoozer, Kevin J. *Is There a Meaning in this Text?* Leicester: Apollos, 1998.

Van den Hout, Th. P. J. "Khattushili III, King of the Hittites." In Vol. 2, *Civilizations of the Ancient Near East*, edited by Jack Sasson, 1107—1112. New York: Scribner, 1995.

——, "Apology of Hattušili III." In Vol. 1, *The Context of Scripture: canonical compositions, monumental inscriptions, and archival documents from the biblical world*, edited by William W. Hallo and K. L. Younger, 199. Leiden: Brill, 1997–2002.

Van Seters, John. *In Search of History*. New Haven: Yale University Press, 1983.

——, "The Court History and DtrH: Conflicting Perspectives on the House of David." In *Die sogenannte Thronfolgegeschichte Davids: Neue Einsichten und Anfragen*, edited by A. de Pury and T. Römer, 70—93. Göttingen: Vandenhoeck & Ruprecht, 2000.

——, *The Biblical Saga of King David*. Winona Lake: Eisenbrauns, 2009.

——, "A Response to G. Aichelle, P. Miscall and R. Walsh, 'An Elephant in the Room': Historical-Critical and the Postmodern Interpretations of the Bible." *JHS* 9 (2009) < http://www.arts.ualberta.ca/JHS/Articles /article_128.pdf> [accessed 8 November 2010].

Veijola, Timo. *Die ewige Dynastie: David und die Entstehung seiner Dynastie nach der deuteronomistischen Darstellung*. Helsinki: Suomalainen Tiedeakatemia, 1975.

——, *Das Königtum in der Beurteilung der deuteronomistischen Historio-graphie: eine redaktionsgeschichtliche Untersuchung*. Helsinki: Suomalainen Tiedeakatemia, 1977.

——, "David und Meribaal." *RB* 85 (1978): 338–361.

Walters, S. D. "The Light and the Dark." In *Ascribe to the Lord: Biblical and Other Studies in Memory of Peter C. Craigie*, edited by L. Eslinger & G. Taylor, 567—89. Sheffield: JSOT Press, 1988).

Warnke, Georgia. *Gadamer: Hermeneutics, Tradition and Reason.* Oxford: Polity Press, 1987.

Weinfeld, Moshe. *Deuteronomy and the Deuteronomic School.* Oxford: Clarendon Press, 1972.

Weippert, Helga. "Die 'deuteronomistischen' Beurteilung der Könige von Israel und Juda und das Problem der Redaktion der Königsbücher." *Bib* 53 (1972): 301–339.

Weiser, Artur. "1 Samuel 15." *ZAW* 13 (1936): 1–28.

——, "Die Legitimation des Königs David: Zur Eigenart und Entstehung der sogen. Geschichte von Davids Aufstieg." *VT* 16 (1966): 325–354.

Wellhausen, Julius. *Der Text der Bücher Samuelis.* Göttingen: Vandenhoeck & Ruprecht, 1871.

——, *Die Composition des Hexateuchs und der Historischen Bücher des Alten Testaments*, 3rd edition. Berlin: Georg Reimer, 1899.

Wesselius, J. W. "Joab's Death and the Central Theme of the Succession Narrative (2 Samuel IX – 1 Kings II)." *VT* 40 (1990): 336–351.

Westermann, Claus. *Genesis 37–50.* Minneapolis: Fortress, 2002.

White, Ellen. "Michal the Misinterpreted." *JSOT* 31 (2007): 451–64.

Whitelam, Keith W. *The Just King: Monarchical Judicial Authority in Ancient Israel.* Sheffield: JSOT, 1979.

——, "The Defence of David." *JSOT* 29 (1984), 61–87.

Whybray, R. N. *The Succession Narrative: A Study of II Samuel 9–20; I Kings 1 and 2.* London: SCM Press, 1968.

Willi-Plein, Ina. "1 Sam 18–19 und die Davidshausgeschichte." In *David und Saul im Widerstreit*, edited by Dietrich, 138–177.

Williamson, H. G. M. *1 and 2 Chronicles.* London: Marshall & Scott, 1982.

Wills, Lawrence M. *Jews in the Court of a Foreign King: Ancient Jewish Court Legends.* Minneapolis: Fortress, 1990.

——, *The Jewish Novel in the Ancient World.* Ithaca: Cornell University Press, 1995.

Wolde, Ellen van. "A Leader Led by a Lady: David and Abigail in 1 Samuel25." *ZAW* 14 (2002): 355–375.

Wolf, Herbert M. "The Apology of Hattushilish Compared with Other Political Self-Justifications of the Ancient Near East." Unpublished doctoral thesis. Brandeis University, 1967.

Wolff, Hans W. "The Kerygma of the Deuteronomistic Historical Work." In *The Vitality of Old Testament Traditions*, edited by Walter Brueggemann and Hans W. Wolff, 83—100. Atlanta: John Knox Press, 1975.

Worton, Michael and Judith Still. "Introduction." In *Intertextuality: Theories and Practices*, edited by Michael Worton and Judith Still, 1—44. Manchester: Manchester University Press, 1990.

Würthwein, Ernst. *The Text of the Old Testament: an Introduction to the Biblia Hebraica*, 2nd edition. Grand Rapids: W. B. Eerdmans, 1995.

——, *Studien zum deuteronomistischen Geschichtswerk.* Berlin: de Gruyter, 1994.

Yadin, Azzan. "Goliath's Armour and Israelite Collective Memory." *VT* 54 (2004): 373–95.

Zehnder, Marcus. "Exegetische Beobachtungen zu den David-Jonathan Geschichten." *Bib* (79), 1998: 153–179.

Zobel, Hans-Jürgen. "גָּלָה." In *TDOT,* II, 476–488.

——, "צָבָאוֹת." In *TDOT,* XII, 215–232.

*The Babylonian Talmud: Sanhedrin*, vol. 2, trans. I. Epstein; edited by H. Freedman. (London: Soncino Press, 1935.

*Midrash Rabbah,* vol. 4: *Leviticus*, trans. J. Israelstam & J. J. Slotki; edited by H. Freedman and M. Simon. London: Soncino Press, 1951.

# Index of Biblical References

# Index of Names and Subjects